THE LIVING WORLD OF SCIENCE

The Living World series comprises:

THE LIVING WORLD OF NATURE
THE LIVING WORLD OF ACHIEVEMENT
THE LIVING WORLD OF KNOWLEDGE
THE LIVING WORLD OF LEARNING
THE LIVING WORLD OF SCIENCE
THE LIVING WORLD OF HISTORY

The Living World
OF
SCIENCE

Glasgow COLLINS *London*

First printed in this edition 1962

This Impression 1972

 Printed in Great Britain by William Collins Sons & Co. Ltd., Glasgow and London.

ISBN 100105 1

CONTENTS

CONTENTS

CONTENTS

CONQUEST OF THE AIR

Daedalus made wings which were attached to the shoulders by wax; he hoped that these would enable man to fly.

We do not know when men first thought of flying, but it must have been a long time ago. In the remote past, a savage, peering from the cave in which he sought protection from his enemies on the ground, must have envied the birds wheeling gracefully and effortlessly in the sky outside.

And so, when man had learned to talk and fashion things with his hands, it is not surprising that when he dreamed of flying he should imagine doing so as a bird.

Legends, passed from father to son, tell of men who learned to fly in this manner. Most famous is the Greek story of Dædalus and his son Icarus, who made wings to escape from Minos, King of Crete. Dædalus, we are told, reached home safely; but Icarus, being young and adventurous, flew too near the Sun and the wax on his wings melted so that he fell into the sea and was drowned.

EARLY BRITISH ATTEMPTS

Less well known is the legend of the British king who tried his luck. The story, appearing in a family tree prepared for James I and now in the British Museum, tells how King Bladud, father of Shakespeare's King Lear, made a pair of wings in 843 B.C. With these he jumped off a high building in Trinavantum, which we now call London, and crash-landed on the Temple of Apollo.

A more recent story is that of John Damian who declared his intention of flying to France, starting from the top of Stirling Castle in the presence of King James IV of Scotland. He landed with a thump beneath the battlements amid a flurry of feathers. Lucky to be alive, he blamed his failure on the fact that he had used the feathers of chickens, which are " ground birds ", instead of eagle's feathers!

DA VINCI'S MODELS

Most famous exponent of flapping wings, though, is undoubtedly the great artist-scientist Leonardo da Vinci, who lived from 1452 to 1519. In his wonderful note-books da Vinci sketched scores of ornithopters, ranging from simple " shoulder harness " wings to elaborate machines containing entrance doors, and retractable, shock-absorbing, landing legs.

Da Vinci, and the other people who put their faith in wings, made the basic mistake of assuming that man had the necessary muscle power and skill to emulate the birds. He has not. Also, a second fundamental mistake was the idea that birds sustained and propelled themselves through the air by beating their wings downwards and backwards. This is not so. A bird does not—indeed cannot—beat its wings backwards on the down stroke.

What actually happens is this: most birds have four or five special feathers at the ends of their wings. When the wing is moving downwards, these feathers twist into miniature propeller blades and *pull* the wing tip—and the bird—forwards. Pictures taken by high-speed cameras show that the wing bends *forwards* as it beats downwards.

No, in his attempt to conquer the air, man had to look at things other than feathered wings.

THE AGE OF BALLOONS

The first glimmer of scientific thought came in the thirteenth century when a British monk, named Roger Bacon, suggested that the air was an invisible fluid and that if a vessel were made lighter than air, it would float on air, just as a ship floats on water.

This idea was followed up by the seventeenth-century Italian scientist de Lana, who, in 1670, proposed a boat lifted aloft by four 20-foot-diameter copper globes. The idea was to lighten the globes by creating a vacuum inside them.

Incidentally, it is recorded that de Lana was not too keen on trying to make his boat work because: ". . . no city would be proof against surprise . . . ships could be set on fire by fireballs and bombs . . . fortresses could thus be destroyed. . . ." A remarkable prediction.

Khensu, the winged Egyptian god, who incarnated the desire of the ancient inhabitants of the Nile valley to fly.

Evacuated copper balloons for "lift" in de Lana's airship.

Although de Lana's boat was very near to a practical suggestion, over a hundred years were to pass before the first " boat " of the air arrived. Two brothers, Joseph and Étienne Montgolfier, of Annonay, near Paris, are thought to have discovered the idea while sitting at home. Paper-makers by trade, one of them is supposed to have thrown an empty bag on the fire. As the flames crept up the sides, the bag went into the air. They threw on another bag with the same result. Excitedly they made a bigger bag of fine silk and found that this, too, rose when paper was burned under its open end. They made bigger and better balloons and soon were confident enough to announce a public demonstration on 5th June, 1783.

THE MONTGOLFIERS' SUCCESS

A large crowd collected on the appointed day, probably as much for the fun of a " day out " as in the hope of seeing history made. But when a fire was lit under the balloon, creating so much lift that soon eight men were needed to hold it down, it was apparent that something exciting was about to happen. Suddenly, up it shot, rising to about 6,000 feet and drifting over a mile before it cooled and landed safely. The air had been conquered for the first time.

To see whether their invention would be safe for human flight, the Montgolfiers carried out another trial in which a sheep, a cock, and a duck were carried in a wicker basket slung under the balloon. The animals suffered no ill effects, so the two brothers made preparations for what must have been the most incredible event of the time—the first human flight.

It was first proposed that a convict should be used, in case something did go wrong, but a young scientist named Pilâtre de Rozier decided that this would not be a very happy start for the new science of flight, and volunteered himself. So, on 21st November, 1783, he made the first aerial voyage in history by flying 5½ miles over Paris with the Marquis d'Arlandes.

There is little doubt of the courage of these two men, for they were able to keep airborne only by stoking the fire under their balloon; a task which had to be interrupted frequently, while they put out other fires which had broken out on the highly inflammable fabric of the balloon itself.

HYDROGEN BALLOON

But safer balloons were coming along, and on 1st December, 1783, Professor Charles, another Frenchman, made a flight in a hydrogen-filled balloon built by two brothers, named Robert.

News of these French balloon flights spread rapidly, and soon *Montgolfières* and *Charlières* were flying all over Europe. The craze spread to Britain where, on 25th August, 1784, the first brief ascent was made at Edinburgh by James Tytler.

Five months later, on 7th January, 1785, the French balloonist, Blanchard, made the first aerial crossing of the Channel, accompanied by a rich American, Dr. John Jeffries.

The full story of this flight is one of the most exciting in the history of flying. By overcontrolling they released too much gas and at one stage lost height rapidly. To lighten themselves they threw overboard everything they could—ballast, leaflets, life-jackets, anchors—even the clothes they were wearing! Even then they would have met with disaster but for a sudden gust of wind which carried them up, over the coast of France.

On 21st November, 1783, Pilâtre de Rozier and the Marquis d'Arlandes made the first aerial journey, lasting 25 minutes.

Amundsen's airship, the Norge, *which circled the North Pole on* 11*th May*, 1926, *two days after Byrd had reached it.*

Despite this and other exciting journeys, the limitations of the free balloon as a means of air travel were obvious. What was needed was a method of steering and propelling it, so that it did not always have to travel precisely down-wind. It was no use fitting sails or oars on a balloon, as there is no " wind " to act on them; a flag flown from a balloon hangs down limply.

It was not until 1850 that any real headway was made. In that year Pierre Jullien flew his clockwork-powered, streamlined, model airship *Le Précurseur*. Two years later, Henri Giffard flew from Paris to Trappes at the reckless speed of 6 m.p.h. in a partly controllable full-size airship on similar lines.

But the first completely successful airship was the electrically driven *La France*, built in 1884, by Renardo and Krebs. Providing the wind was not too strong, this could be steered in flight back to its starting point.

SANTOS-DUMONT

In 1898, the great Brazilian pioneer, Alberto Santos-Dumont, made front-page news by flying round the Eiffel Tower in an airship powered by a petrol engine. The airship had arrived.

Airships were made bigger and better, particularly by Count Ferdinand von Zeppelin, of Germany. Zeppelin's airships were not sausage-shaped balloons filled by the gas inside them, but had an outer covering stretched over a rigid framework, with the lifting gas contained in smaller bags inside the structure.

FIRST AIRLINE SERVICE

Zeppelins opened the very first airline service between Lake Constance and Berlin in 1910, and by the outbreak of the Great War in 1914, six of these slender monsters had carried 35,000 passengers. After the war the prospects of airship travel seemed even brighter when, in 1919, the British R34 made the first two-way crossing of the North Atlantic.

But Germany soon regained her lead and, in 1928, completed the *Graf Zeppelin*, one of the most wonderful aircraft ever built. Nearly 800 feet long, she had a maximum diameter of 100 feet. Five engines developed a total of 2,650 h.p. and gave her a range of over 12,000 miles. Her capacious passenger cupola contained lounges, with room to dance, a dining saloon, smoking-room, promenade decks, an orchestra—all the luxuries of an ocean-going liner. The biggest and fastest jet airliner to-day has not the spacious graciousness of these old airships. The *Graf Zeppelin* pioneered Transatlantic air travel, making more than 100 crossings and carrying 10,500 passengers in eight years of service.

FINAL DISASTER

In 1936, she was joined by the even more splendid *Hindenberg*. Then, on 6th May, 1937, while being moored at Lakehurst, New Jersey, the *Hindenberg* suddenly burst into flames and was totally destroyed, and with this tragedy the age of balloons and great airships came almost to an end.

To-day, only a few, small, non-rigid airships used by the U.S. Navy for anti-submarine patrol and radar warning duties, remain. Balloons, however, are used in large numbers for research work. Every day, meteorological balloons are

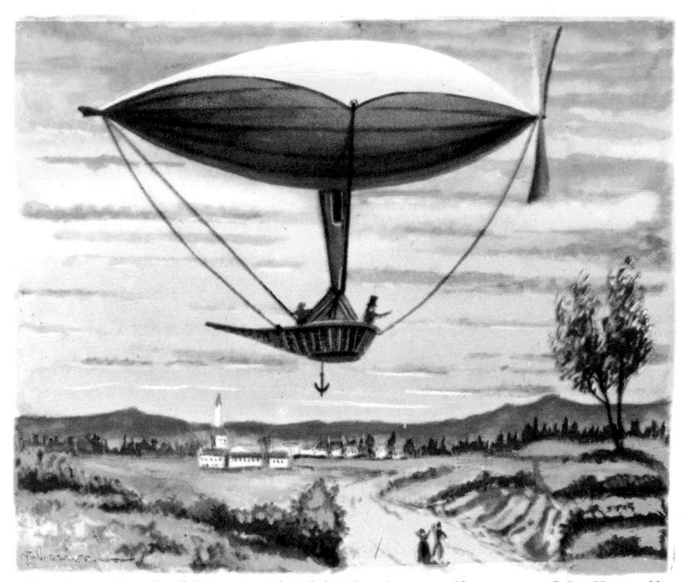

Cordenon's airship, a typical 19*th century* "*powered balloon.*"

The Graf Zeppelin, *commissioned in* 1929, *made more than* 140 *Atlantic crossings, carrying more than* 13,000 *passengers.*

released all over the world, to radio back information on the different layers of atmosphere.

Also, strange as it may seem, balloons, the earliest form of aircraft, have helped man in his latest venture—space travel. Officers and men of the U.S. Air Force and Navy were carried up to heights of around 100,000 feet by huge plastic balloons the size of a skyscraper, as part of the programme to discover how man would fare in space where there is no atmosphere to protect him from deadly radiation.

TOWARDS POWERED FLIGHT

Although the kites flown by the Chinese 3,000 years ago were a primitive form of aeroplane, Britain is the country generally credited with pioneering heavier-than-air flight. The man who pointed the way was a Yorkshireman named Sir George Cayley. We remember him as the man who discovered the basic principles of aeronautics leading to the aeroplane.

In 1804, Cayley built the first practical glider. This was little more than a kite with a cruciform tail, but it had the same general appearance as a modern aeroplane, and it flew.

Another faltering step came in 1842, when a young inventor named Samuel Henson designed a remarkable aeroplane, based on Cayley's theories and his own experience with gliders. Called the *Aerial Steam Carriage*, it looks funny to us now, but its design is more like that of modern aeroplanes than many aircraft oddities which later flew successfully. Unfortunately, Henson let his imagination run away with him and issued pictures of his *Aerial Carriage* in flight over London, France and the Pyramids, and even tried to get Parliament to authorise the setting up of the Aerial Steam Transit Company—before finding out if it would fly!

Otto Lilienthal made over 2,000 *successful glides.*

The following year he enlisted the help of another enthusiast, John Stringfellow, to build a 20-foot model of the aircraft. We know quite a bit about this, because the actual model is now a prized exhibit in the National Aeronautical Collection, London. Of course, it failed to fly and, losing heart, Henson emigrated to America.

IMPORTANCE OF A LIGHT ENGINE

Stringfellow remained and continued experimenting. He realised that the secret to success lay in providing a light, powerful engine and concentrated upon developing a tiny steam engine of his own design. He fitted this in a 10-foot model of Henson's aircraft which many books record as having flown in 1848. If this was so, it was the first heavier-than-air powered flight in history but, unfortunately, there seems to be little evidence to support this claim.

Around 1852, Cayley, now nearing eighty, built a full-size glider based on his earlier experiments, in which his reluctant coachman made a flight of 500 yards across a valley. After coming down " with a smash ", the poor man tendered his resignation on the spot. Details of this historically-important and interesting glider—the first man-carrying aeroplane in the world—have only just come to light, and provide further evidence of Cayley's great contribution to the conquest of the air.

FIRST POWERED AEROPLANE

After this came Felix du Temple, a captain in the French Navy who, in about 1857, designed and built a little $1\frac{1}{2}$-lb. clockwork-powered aeroplane which really seems to have taken off the ground, flown and then landed safely, and was thus the world's first powered aeroplane. Du Temple followed up this success with a full-size machine on the same lines.

About the year 1874, this fragile contraption, piloted by

a young sailor, ran down a short ramp and made a brief hop, but was by no means airborne long enough for this to be called a real flight. Nor was the aircraft controlled—a basic requirement for true flight.

Another early aviator deserving a mention here is I. N. Golubev, even if only because some Russian writers still consider he was the first man in the world to fly. The claim is that he flew a remarkably modern-looking, steam-driven aeroplane, designed by A. F. Mozhaisky, in July, 1884. Possibly like du Temple, he made a brief " hop " after gaining speed down a ramp, but Western experts agree that this could not possibly be called a true flight.

Similarly it has often been claimed that Clement Ader, of France, was first, since he made a hop of over 100 feet in his bat-wing shaped *Eole* in October, 1890. One glance at the aircraft, however, is sufficient to show that this could hardly have been a controlled hop, although it was more successful than Ader's later attempt to fly in his twin-engined *Avion III*, in 1897.

Two British pioneers of note were Sir Hiram Maxim and Horatio Phillips. Maxim, inventor of the Maxim machine-gun, built a 4-ton " test " aircraft in 1894, bigger than a Viscount airliner. Powered by two enormous 180-h.p. steam engines, this broke free of its guard rail during one trial and made a short, uncontrolled " flight " before crashing.

Phillips, as a result of wind-tunnel tests, discovered that a curved wing section gave more lift than any other, and accordingly built a fantastic contraption with dozens of tiny wings mounted one above the other in Venetian blind fashion. Unpiloted and aided by the restraining force imposed by a cable, this tethered craft flew around a circular track at Harrow in 1893.

But all these early pioneers lacked two things essential to flight; a suitable engine, and the realisation that to fly successfully their aircraft would have to be *controllable* in flight.

EARLY POWER UNITS

Developments in power plants were under way, and at last came the invention for which every would-be aviator was waiting—the internal combustion engine. The man chiefly responsible was Dr. N. A. Otto of Germany, who produced his famous four-stroke " silent gas engine " in 1876. To start with, these engines were still not suitable for aircraft because they weighed as much as 1,100 lb. per h.p. and ran at only 200 revolutions a minute. Then another German, Gottlieb Daimler, came on the scene and adapted the Otto type of engine to run on petrol. The speed went up to 800 revolutions a minute, and this brought the power-to-weight ratio down to 88 lb. per h.p. The power for flight was finally available.

The man we honour for demonstrating the importance of control is Otto Lilienthal who, in 1891, made a commendably simple, bird-like glider of willow-wands covered with waxed cotton cloth. This flew so well that he built an artificial hill near Berlin as a jumping-off place and from this he made over 2,000 glides in five years. Lilienthal controlled his glider by swinging his entire body in the direction he wished to go, and could cover one-quarter of a mile at heights of 75 feet. This method, however, was highly tricky and on 9th August, 1896, at the age of forty-eight, he lost control, crashed, and was killed.

The glittering prize of the first flight now lay open to the person who could marry a petrol engine with a flyable airframe and a method of control. Octave Chanute tried, and built a powered version of his successful glider, the *Hawk*, but died before he could test it.

DR. LANGLEY'S " AERODROME "

More successful was Dr. Samuel Pierpont Langley, Secretary of the famous American Smithsonian Museum. In 1896, Langley flew a flimsy, 16-foot span, tandem-wing, steam-powered model over half a mile at 25 m.p.h. Encouraged, he constructed a full-size machine on similar lines. Called the *Aerodrome*, this was powered by a remarkable five-cylinder radial engine developing 52 h.p. for a weight of only 125 lb. The machine was designed to be catapulted into the air and during the first attempt from a house-boat on the Potamac River on 7th October, 1903, it appeared to hit a post on the launching track and plunged into the water.

A second attempt, on 8th December, met a similar fate,

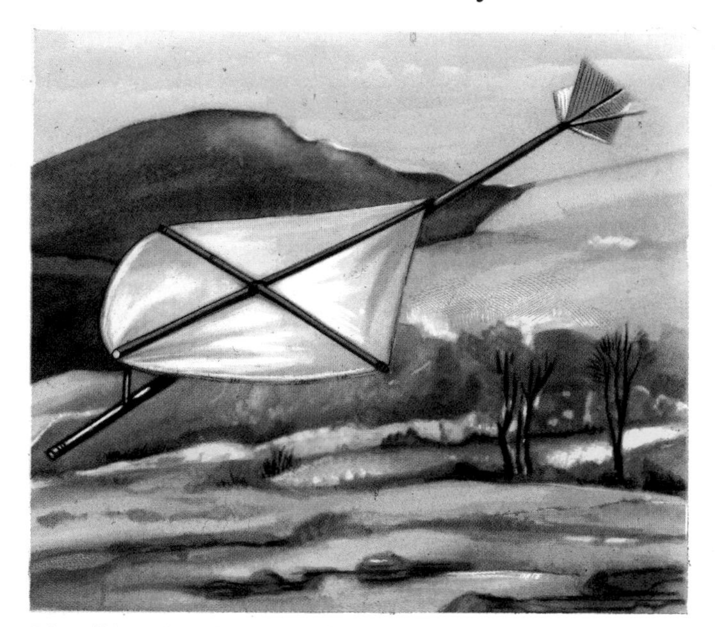

First "aeroplane" to fly; Sir George Cayley's model glider (1804).

Aeole made the first powered take-off on 9th October, 1890.

Orville Wright, watched by his brother Wilbur and nine other spectators, made the first sustained and controlled flight in a powered aeroplane at Kitty Hawk, North Carolina, on 17th December, 1903. He flew for twelve seconds at a speed of about 30 miles per hour, in a ramshackle plane powered by a home-made engine developing twelve horse-power.

the wings and tail of the *Aerodrome* being so damaged before it left the catapult that it collapsed and crashed.

Dispirited, and with no money for further experiments, Langley gave up. But it was obvious that the realisation of man's great dream would not be long delayed.

THE FIRST AEROPLANE FLIGHT

The experiments of Chanute and the successful glides of Otto Lilienthal aroused the interest of two young bicycle-makers, named Orville and Wilbur Wright, in Dayton, Ohio. So much so, that they decided that they just had to fly. This, of course, was the feeling held by all other pioneers, but the difference with the Wright brothers was that they set out to do so in a scientific manner.

First they read and learnt all about the successes and failures of other would-be airmen. Early on, they considered that the real key to success was to achieve balance (or stability) and control in flight. They also noted that although Lilienthal had made over 2,000 flights, his total flying time was only about *five* hours, and concluded that to gain the necessary experience it would be essential to try and practise by the hour instead of by the second.

GLIDING AT KITTY HAWK

They prepared to do this by building a glider which would fly at about 18 m.p.h. and then finding a place where winds of this speed were common. Setting to work, the glider was ready by the summer of 1900. For the windy site for the flights they chose Kitty Hawk, a settlement in North Carolina, bordering the Atlantic Ocean. Here the brothers very ingeniously " flew " the glider as a kite and were thus able to " practise by the hour and without any serious danger." They controlled the glider by means of an elevator at the front and by warping (twisting) the wing tips, a movement which had the same effect as moving a modern aileron. Although the glider needed a wind of 30 m.p.h. to sustain it instead of the 21 m.p.h. calculated, it flew quite well and the brothers returned home well satisfied.

During the winter they built a new, bigger, glider for the following year, with almost twice the wing area and an improved elevator. But when they flew it, they found its performance disappointing. For one thing, the lift was only about a third of what Lilienthal's figures indicated.

WIND-TUNNEL TESTS

Undaunted, they returned home, built a primitive wind-tunnel from an old starch box and tested over 200 tiny model wings in it. They soon realised that most of the information which had been published about wings was inaccurate. So they built a new glider with wings based on the best of their models, and with a rudder at the rear.

This was taken to Kitty Hawk in 1902 where they made about 1,000 flights in it, nearly 400 being made in the last six days, the longest covering 622 feet and lasting 26 seconds.

Confident, they returned home, now ready to try adding power to an aircraft. Unfortunately, when they tried to obtain an engine, nobody could give them one with the desired power-to-weight ratio. So they set to work to design and build their own engine, which they did in *six* weeks.

Construction of the aircraft started in June and by mid-September it was finished. In appearance it was similar to the 1902 glider, but slightly bigger and with twin rudders.

On the 17th December, 1903, the *Flyer*, as it was called, stood ready at Kitty Hawk. Orville lay on the lower wing, off centre to compensate for the weight of the engine on the other side. Carefully he slipped on the shoulder harness which controlled the wing warping. The 12-h.p. engine was started and just after 10.35 a.m. the biplane began moving forward along its wooden launching track; Wilbur ran alongside steadying the wings.

SUCCESS AT LAST

Reaching the end of the track the biplane suddenly lifted itself into the air. It climbed quickly—too quickly—and Orville struggled to level out. With a gentle lurch the *Flyer* plonked down in the sand just 120 feet from its take-off point.

" This flight only lasted twelve seconds " wrote Orville later, " but it was, nevertheless, the first in the history of the world in which a machine carrying a man had raised itself by its own power into the air in full flight, had sailed forward without reduction of speed, and had finally landed at a point as high as that from which it started."

SEAWEED

Millions of tons of seaweed are cast up on to the seashores of the world every year. It is one of the most prolific of all crops, and it is presented to us free. In the past, seaweed has been used as a food and as a fertiliser. Its real future, however, lies in its potential value as an industrial raw material.

Seaweeds are primitive plants called algae, and inside their simple body structures they carry a concentration of minerals and organic substances just as common land-plants do. Many of these substances are of great value, and are the raw material for all sorts of modern industries.

SEAWEED IN INDUSTRY

Seaweeds absorb minerals which are dissolved in sea-water, and will often concentrate them in their tissues. During the eighteenth- and nineteenth-centuries, seaweed was a most important source of the alkali salts which were needed by the soap and glass industries. The weed was gathered in large quantities around the coasts of Britain, Ireland, France and other countries. It was burned to form the ash called kelp, and in this kelp were the alkali and other mineral salts that the seaweed had absorbed from the sea.

INTRODUCTION OF SYNTHETICS

During the early part of the nineteenth-century, chemists devised synthetic processes for making soda, and seaweed was no longer needed as a source of alkali. By 1840, the demand for seaweed-soda had almost died away. In the meantime, iodine had been discovered in seaweed, and kelp-burning was given a new lease of life. A century ago, there were twenty iodine factories in Glasgow alone.

In 1880, iodine was obtained as a by-product from Chile saltpetre, and seaweed iodine was soon ousted from its most important markets. Since then, the production of iodine from seaweed has steadily declined although it is still extracted in some parts of the world.

RAW MATERIAL

The future of seaweed as a raw material now lies, very largely, in the organic material it contains. The carbon-based chemicals of seaweed are built up from carbon dioxide which is absorbed from the seawater in which it is dissolved. Inside the cells of the seaweed, this carbon dioxide is used for making the living matter of the plant by the process of photosynthesis, just as the land plant uses carbon dioxide taken by its leaves from the air. So, inside the seaweed we find carbohydrates, fats, proteins and other substances, which take part in the living processes of the plant.

There is a general similarity between the chemical processes in the living matter of seaweeds and those in land plants. The substances involved are similar, but not the same.

ALGINIC ACID

The structural material of the brown seaweeds, for example, is a substance called alginic acid. This is a carbohydrate which does a job similar to that of cellulose in the land plant; it is the strength provider.

Alginic acid is insoluble in water, but it is converted easily into a soluble sodium salt; alginic acid can be extracted from seaweed by boiling it with soda. When the solution is acidified, the alginic acid is precipitated.

Sodium alginate, or "algin," is a gelantine-like material. It has extraordinary thickening powers; a 2 per cent. solution of algin is so viscous that it will only just flow from a bottle. The dried material is colourless, odourless and tasteless.

Nowadays, algin has found many industrial uses and seaweed is being used in large quantities as a source of the material.

Algin can be vulcanised to a rubbery substance, which has been used in the manufacture of typewriter rollers. It can also be made into a cheap wrapping film. Algin will fireproof wood, and waterproof concrete. It is used for preventing the formation of scale in ships' boilers.

Algin has an amazing power of binding powders which do not easily stick together. Three parts of algin mixed with 97 parts of soot will form a cement that sets to a hard mass with excellent heat-insulating properties. This material is used for lagging steam pipes and boilers.

PLASTICS AND ARTIFICIAL FIBRES

Seaweed algin is also providing us with plastics and with slimming agents. It is used for preventing bleeding during operations, and for making special surgical gauzes that can be left in the body to be absorbed after they have done their work. Alginates are making machine-belts and sausage skins, toothbrushes and dusting powders.

Algin goes into all sorts of foods as a thickener and emulsifier, and into medicines and cosmetics.

Like its chemical relative cellulose, from the world of land plants, alginic acid from seaweed can be spun into artificial fibres. A solution of algin is forced through fine holes into an acid bath, and as the filaments emerge they are converted into insoluble alginic acid, or alginates, which can be stretched and processed to provide fibres for use in textiles.

Alginate fibres are widely used for achieving many special effects in spinning and weaving. The alginate fibres can be dissolved from the yarn or fabrics after they have served their purpose. Light and fluffy woollens, for example, can be made from loose-spun yarns in which alginate fibres provide the strength that is needed for processing.

OTHER PRODUCTS

Now that a seaweed-based industry has become established, other constituents of seaweeds are being put to good use. The sugar mannitol is obtained from brown seaweed; it is used in chemical and pharmaceutical manufacture, and in the production of paint. Laminarin is another material which is related to starch. It is used in medicine as an anti-clotting agent.

In temperate waters, there are also red seaweeds growing, usually at a greater depth than the brown seaweeds. For hundreds of years in the Orient, agar, a jelly-like substance, has been extracted from red seaweeds. It has become almost the standard medium for growing cultures of bacteria, providing a firm jelly that withstands normal incubation temperatures.

Agar is also used in the food industry, doing duty for pectin in jams, and gelatine in meat pies. Another red seaweed, Irish Moss, provides us with a material called Carragheenin which is used as a stabiliser and emulsifier in foods and medicines.

ARCHIMEDES

Archimedes calculated the diameters of the sun and moon.

After successfully besieging Syracuse, Marcellus the Consul returned to Rome in 212 B.C. He had been fighting in Sicily for three years and was overjoyed to be back in his capital and to hear the streets and squares ring with the cries of its citizens welcoming him home. But his joy was marred by one sad event. . . .

As commander of the republican army, Marcellus had given strict orders that the man who had turned Syracuse into a veritable stronghold by erecting new fortifications and inventing new weapons should not be killed. But a soldier had found this man—an old man of seventy-five—working at a difficult mathematical problem without a thought for what was going on around him. The soldier had no idea who the old man was and, mistaking indifference for impertinence, killed him at a single blow.

This man, although an enemy, was admired greatly by Marcellus and his Roman colleagues; he was none other than Archimedes, one of the greatest scientists of the time. Cicero tells us that Archimedes was born in Syracuse of a poor family in about 287 B.C. According to Plutarch he was related to Gerone, who was then ruling over Sicily.

In those days, the schools of Syracuse taught two main subjects: mathematics and philosophy. Having learned all he could from the teachers and professors of the town, the young Archimedes sailed for Egypt to continue his studies at Alexandria, then the most important centre of learning in the classical world. In due course he returned to Sicily with a deeper knowledge of the sciences of that age than any of his fellow-countrymen.

As a young man, Archimedes's interest in geometry and astronomy inspired him to work out a number of theorems relating to spheres and cylinders. He found a way of calculating the area of a circle, and made a fairly accurate estimate of the diameters of the sun and moon and of their distance from the Earth. His explanation of the solar system was the first rational one. But Archimedes was not a mere theorist; he was also an inventor of genius, with a highly practical mind. This soon became apparent to Gerone, who entrusted Archimedes with the task of finding solutions to numerous technical problems.

One of the first commissions given to Archimedes by Gerone was to design a ship larger than any that had ever been built. This was to be a gift to the Egyptian ruler Ptolemy Evergete. With the help of an army of workmen Archimedes set to work. He constructed a vessel so big that as much timber went into it as would have been needed to build sixty galleys. He furnished it with stables, gardens, baths and recreation rooms and equipped it with all the weapons necessary for its defence.

Archimedes then devised a system of weights and pulleys called a " trochlea " which enabled him to launch the ship. The " trochlea ", since perfected, is used to this day.

Archimedes' device, a "trochlea," was used to launch his ship.

Weapons designed by Archimedes were used to defend Syracuse.

The "cochlea," a deeply-grooved wooden screw, was devised by Archimedes for lifting water into irrigation channels.

There soon followed another invention which was to prove of immense benefit to Egypt. Every year the summer rains in Abyssinia swelled the waters of the Nile, causing floods along the lower reaches of the valley. The Ptolemies, who had long sought to check these annual disasters, invited Archimedes to study the problem. The result was a series of dykes and bridges such as even the Pharaohs had not known how to build. Archimedes also devised a primitive pump called a " cochlea " with which to irrigate fields lying at some distance from the river and to dry those that remained submerged beneath its muddy waters.

Back in Syracuse, Archimedes gave further proof of his genius by the discovery of one of the fundamental laws of hydrostatics. The story goes that Gerone, who had lately ordered a new crown, suspected his jeweller of mixing a certain amount of silver with the gold. So he asked Archimedes if he could find a way of detecting the fraud without actually harming the crown. The great scientist pondered the matter for a long time without finding any solution. Then one day while taking a bath he noticed that as he got into the water his body appeared to lose weight. He also observed that the more he went under, the higher the water rose up the sides of the bath.

The answer to Gerone's problem came to him in a flash. With brilliant intuition he summed up his observations in the following words: *When a solid is immersed in water it loses weight in proportion to the weight of the liquid displaced.* So important did he consider this principle—it is known to all who study physics as *The Principle of Archimedes*—that he jumped out of the bath and rushed naked into the street crying, " *Eureka! Eureka!* "—" I have found it! I have found it! " What he had found was a method of determining the relative density of solids, including gold, by submerging them in water. Thus he was able to examine and report on Gerone's crown without doing it any damage.

This discovery was in itself sufficient to ensure Archimedes's fame for all time. He had established a principle on which the design of ships has since been based. But his active mind did not rest there. Other inventions and discoveries followed: the sundial, which is believed to have been first devised by him; a musical organ worked by running water; various mechanical aids to assist in surgical operations; and finally what is known as Archimedes's *loculus*, a puzzle game requiring great patience, which enjoyed wide popularity among the ancients.

Surprisingly enough, some of Archimedes's actual writings are still in existence. Although fragmentary and often illegible, due to the wear and tear of two thousand years, they are expressed in a clear and precise style suggesting that as a young man Archimedes did not neglect his studies of literature. These writings include his *Principles of Mathematics*, *Concerning the Sphere and the Cylinder*, and *The Measurement of the Circle*. In them he discusses algebraical and geometrical problems, and propounds theories which are taught in schools to-day.

But the fame of Archimedes rests for ever on that great moment when the thrill of discovery brought the word " *Eureka* " to his lips. The importance of his findings are contained in his work *On Floating Bodies*, in which he treats the fundamental principles of hydrostatics, or the study of liquids. Finally, in a treatise called *L'Arenario* he set down everything that was known about astronomy at that time.

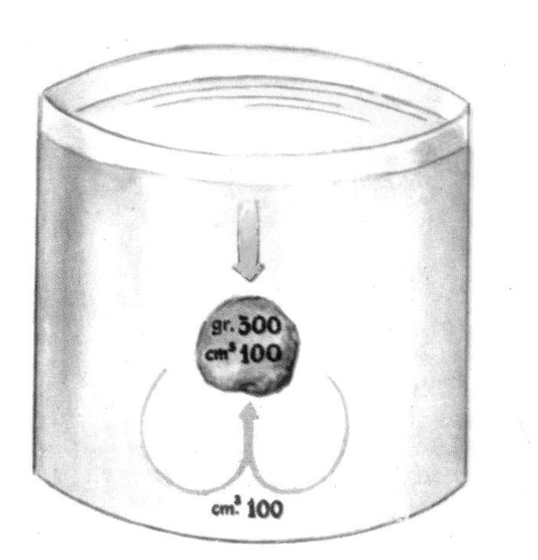

Archimedes' Principle: a body immersed in liquid suffers a loss in weight equal to that of the liquid displaced.

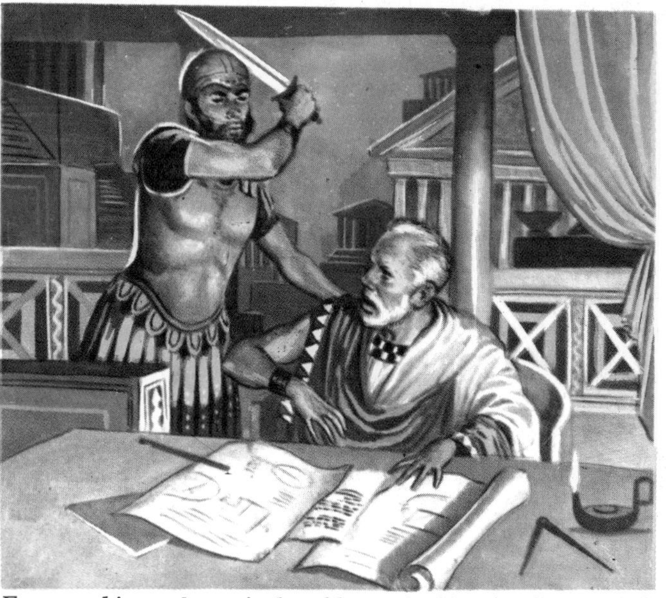

Engrossed in mathematical problems, Archimedes disregarded a Roman soldier, who killed the old man with his sword.

FIRST STEPS IN CHEMISTRY

From the very earliest times, man has wondered about the nature of material things. The world contains so many substances; such an infinite variety of forms of matter. And one form of matter may be turned into another quite different material with the greatest of ease. Wood, for example, will change from a solid mass into a powdery ash and a gas when it is burned; iron will change into red powder as it rusts in air.

The study of these changes in matter formed the very beginnings of science. The philosophers of ancient Egypt and of the early Chinese civilisations were deeply interested in science. But for many centuries, the experiments carried out by scientists resulted merely in a haphazard collection of facts and mumbo jumbo which did little to advance genuine understanding of the nature of matter.

During the Middle Ages, science became identified with the strange mixture of fact and fancy which was known as alchemy. The alchemists were obsessed with a search for methods of making gold, and for elixirs and potions that held the secret of eternal life.

Yet from this medieval alchemy has come the chemistry of modern times. Gradually, experimental facts were sifted and confirmed, and theories devised which provided a reasonable explanation of the facts which had been established. Order began to emerge out of chaos, and scientific research became identified with the logical investigations that we carry out to-day.

CHEMICAL TERMS

Every object is made of matter, and two kinds of changes may occur which influence the nature of matter: physical change and chemical change. In a physical change the actual substance of the object stays the same; a chemical change, on the other hand, brings about changes in the substance and properties of the object.

For example, if you heat a piece of iron wire until it is red hot, and then remove it from the flame, after it has cooled it will be just the same as before. In this case no substantial change has taken place in the object, and the change it underwent on heating was, therefore, only a physical one. On the other hand, if you hold a magnesium wire over the flame, you will see a white dust formed which is quite different from magnesium: this change is a chemical one.

MIXTURES

Here is another experiment. If you take a quantity of iron filings and sulphur and mix them, the result is a gritty yellowish-grey powder, technically called a " mixture ". The two ingredients can be easily separated again by using a magnet. This attracts the iron filings away from the sulphur. Or, you can throw the mixture into a glass of water and watch the iron filings sink to the bottom whilst the sulphur will rise to the surface. We can make this definition of a mixture: " The different substances in a mixture do not alter their properties, and can be separated by physical methods."

COMPOUNDS

Supposing you heat the sulphur and iron filings, mixed in a proportion of 4 parts of sulphur to 7 of iron, then through the action of heat it will turn into a " compound " called iron sulphide. You will find you cannot separate this compound by physical methods. Moreover, iron sulphide has very different properties from either sulphur or iron. You can say: " A compound consists of two or more elements associated in constant proportions, so united that they have lost their individual properties and cannot be separated by physical means."

THE ELEMENTS

In chemistry, substances which cannot be broken down

Physical changes, such as heating and cooling a metal wire, do not permanently alter the nature of the substance.

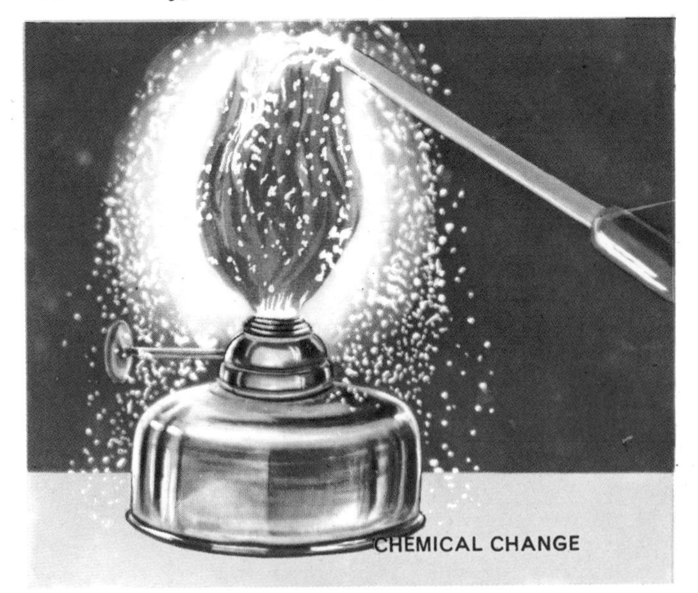

Chemical changes, such as the burning of magnesium to a white powder, produce new materials with different characteristics.

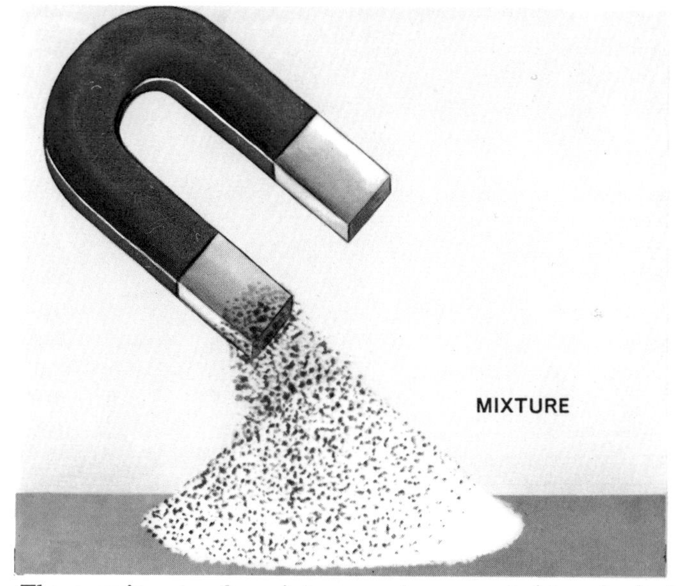

The constituents of a mixture can be separated by physical means: a magnet will separate iron filings from sulphur.

Substances which unite chemically to form a compound can no longer be separated by physical means.

into other substances are called " elements ". There are some 92 naturally-occurring elements altogether and they can be classified as metals or non-metallic elements. Among the metals, mercury is the only one to be found naturally in a liquid state. All the others, provided they are at their normal temperature, are solids. They are lustrous, ductile (can be drawn out into wires), malleable (can be beaten into sheets), and are good conductors of heat and electricity (for instance: copper, gold, iron, zinc, potassium, sodium).

The non-metallic elements are all elements that behave in the opposite way to metals. They are bad conductors of heat and electricity (e.g. oxygen, nitrogen and sulphur). They are all solids or gases with the exception of bromine, which is a liquid.

TYPE OF COMPOUNDS

Chemical substances can be either simple or compound. You have already seen that by burning magnesium you obtain a white powder. This happens because the magnesium (which is an element) joined with the oxygen in the air to form a compound, magnesium oxide. When two simple substances unite to form a compound, chemists say they have " combined ". Compound substances can be divided into oxides, hydroxides or bases, anhydrides, acids and salts.

An oxide is formed by combining a metal with oxygen, e.g. iron oxide, zinc oxide, etc. If you combine an oxide with water you get a base called a hydroxide.

A non-metallic element combined with oxygen forms an anhydride. If you then combine the anhydride with water, you obtain an acid. For instance, sulphur trioxide (SO_3) is the anhydride which, when combined with water, produces sulphuric acid (H_2SO_4).

Make a solution of slaked lime in water and dip a piece of litmus paper into it. The litmus turns blue, showing that the slaked lime is a base, proper name calcium hydroxide.

If you burn sulphur under a bell glass, it will combine with the oxygen in the air to form a compound. Sulphur is a non-metallic element so that the compound is an anhydride —in this case sulphur dioxide.

All acids contain hydrogen. Where the hydrogen in an acid is replaced entirely, or even only in part, by a metal, the resulting compound is called a salt.

Sulphur burns in oxygen to form sulphur dioxide.

Hydrochloric acid and ammonia combine to a salt.

The Rainmakers

Science these days can do all sorts of weird and wonderful things, like making atom bombs and building electronic brains, yet there are still plenty of simple, everyday problems that science cannot solve. For example, we still cannot stop it raining but, at least, we are trying.

During the last few years, physicists have established a new branch of their science, called Cloud Physics. Research has been pushed ahead rapidly, and we are beginning to understand the processes that are involved in turning clouds into rain or snow. So much so that our cloud physicists now claim to be able to produce rain from suitable clouds, and in some cases to prevent clouds turning into rain.

Since 1946, American scientists have led the way in cloud physics. On 13th November of that year, a young American scientist, Dr. Vincent Schaefer, made the first artificial snowstorm in history. It was the culmination of experiments carried out during the war by Schaefer and Irving Langmuir, a Nobel prize winner of 1932.

These scientists were studying ice-formation on aircraft and their investigations, during the war, took them to the summit of Mount Washington in New Hampshire, where they could find the sort of conditions that built up the ice on an aircraft's wings.

During their stay on Mount Washington, the scientists were surprised to find that many of the clouds surrounding them were super-cooled. That is to say, the billions of tiny water droplets that formed the cloud were actually colder than the temperature at which water normally turns to ice, yet the droplets remained as liquid water instead of turning into ice.

These super-cooled water droplets were in a very sensitive state. Given the slightest encouragement, they would start freezing suddenly and collect together as snowflakes big enough to fall to the ground.

When he returned to his laboratory, Schaefer began experimenting to find out more about these super-cooled clouds. He made miniature clouds by breathing into a refrigerator, and he found that there was a certain temperature (−39°C.) below which the water droplets had to turn to ice. Above this temperature, they could stay as liquid even though below their normal freezing point, and form a super-cooled cloud.

Schaefer then found that in a super-cooled cloud, it was only necessary to persuade a few droplets to freeze in order to start the whole cloud freezing. A metal rod, for example, chilled to below −39°C. would transform a laboratory cloud to snow if it was waved in it. The rod was cold enough to force a few droplets to freeze. And once this happened, the rest of the droplets froze too.

What Schaefer had discovered, therefore, was a way of turning super-cooled clouds into snowflakes heavy enough to fall. He had done it in the laboratory, but could he do the same thing with a full-sized cloud ?

SUCCESS

On 13th November, 1946, Schaefer put his discovery to the test. He went up in a plane near Schenectady and found a super-cooled cloud at 14,000 feet. If he could cool a few of the droplets in the cloud sufficiently to turn them to ice, Schaefer believed that he would turn the entire cloud into snowflakes. To provide the sudden chilling of the droplets, Schaefer had brought with him some solid carbon dioxide, or "dry ice" which has a temperature of −78.5°C. He scattered six pounds of his dry ice into the cloud and, lo and behold, the four-mile-long cloud turned into a snowstorm that fell 2,000 feet before evaporating.

PRACTICAL USE

The success of the early cloud physics work in America has stimulated the imagination of scientists all over the world. It appeared probable that much of our rain might be coming from super-cooled clouds triggered by some natural mechanism. The snowflakes formed in the cloud would melt to raindrops if they passed through a belt of warm air as they fell.

In 1949, during an unusually severe drought, scientists carried out the first British experiments on cloud-seeding with dry ice. On 3rd August, "Operation Witchdoctor" began, when scientists co-operated with the R.A.F. to try and break the drought over Teesside. As soon as suitable clouds had been reported by the Air Ministry, supplies of "dry-ice" were rushed to the R.A.F. aerodrome at Middleton-St. George.

A suitable cloud was sighted at 10,000 feet west of the Pennines. A plane flew over it and dropped its pellets of "dry ice." Then it flew beneath the cloud in time to meet a heavy shower of rain heading down towards the Tees Valley Water Board Catchment area.

Five days later, a second attempt was made. A larger "dry ice" container had been built, holding 300 lbs. The enemy this time was a cumulus cloud heading in over Penrith. It was 10,000 feet up, and nicely sited to drop its rain in the catchment area.

At three minutes past five in the evening, the cloud was bombed. Eight minutes later the top of the cloud had grown some 500 feet. At 5.23 p.m. a rainbow appeared underneath the cloud, and a heavy shower of rain had begun to fall. It reached the ground in the Lune Forest area, and it was estimated that half the rain from the cloud was collected by the Tees Valley Water Board.

TO BEAT THE FOG

One interesting aspect of this new technique is its application to fog. Many fogs are simply super-cooled clouds at ground level. They should therefore react in the same way to dry ice treatment. And they have in fact been cleared on a small scale by chilling with dry ice pellets.

As in most scientific experiments, the work of the rainmakers has led to completely unexpected results. One thing the scientists have found, for example, is that by overdoing the seeding of a super-cooled cloud—by using too much dry ice—they can actually *prevent* it turning into snow. Too many ice nuclei are formed, and there is not enough water in the cloud to build them into flakes large enough to fall.

This discovery opens up an entirely new research field in Cloud Physics. If overseeding could be carried out in practice, it would mean that we could persuade our clouds to float away without being able to turn to rain.

With all these exciting things happening in weather control, it is not surprising that cloud physics has become of military significance. Control of the weather over somebody else's country could be a weapon more effective than any atom bomb.

THE EARTH

If you give the sky no more than just a casual glance, you get the impression that the Earth is flat and at the centre of everything. At any rate the sun, moon, and planets all travel across the sky in a general east-to-west direction, as also do most of the stars. From this fact alone you might conclude that all these bodies move round the Earth—that the Earth is shaped like a great plate, fixed rigidly in the middle of the Universe.

Yet the true state of things is very different. The Earth is certainly solid enough, but it is neither flat nor fixed in space. Instead, it is a great spinning ball, spinning continuously and making one complete spin or rotation in about 24 hours. As it spins, we on its surface are carried round at great speed. If we live at the equator, for example, our speed is about 1,000 miles an hour, but since everything around us travels at the same speed we are unaware of any movement. Unaware, at least, unless we look at very distant objects like the sun, moon and stars. Their movement across the sky from east to west is due simply to our being carried round on the rotating Earth from west to east. The succession of day and night, the wheeling motion of the stars and the rising and setting of the moon are therefore apparent effects all brought about by our position on the rotating Earth.

The earth rotates from west to east, the time of rotation being a unit of time we call a day; this is divided into twenty-four equal parts, the hours.

THE ROUND EARTH

In the first half of the sixteenth-century the Portuguese navigator Magellan sailed right round the Earth, travelling outwards to South America and coming back via the Indian Ocean. People then knew for sure that the Earth was round. That it was certainly not flat was known long before, for as travellers journeyed far south they saw different stars. People living in London, for example, never see the stars of the Southern Cross and other " southern " stars. Similarly, people living in Sydney, Australia, never see the Pole Star and the stars of the Plough. In brief, from any one place on the Earth and at any one time we can see only one-half of the sky. The other half is hidden from view by the Earth.

By everyday standards the Earth is of immense size. Its diameter at the equator is 7,927 miles—a distance so great that if you could travel right through the Earth at a speed of 60 miles an hour, the journey from one side to the other would take about 5½ days. Its diameter measured from North Pole to South Pole, however, is 27 miles shorter, which means that the Earth is not perfectly round. Nor is it

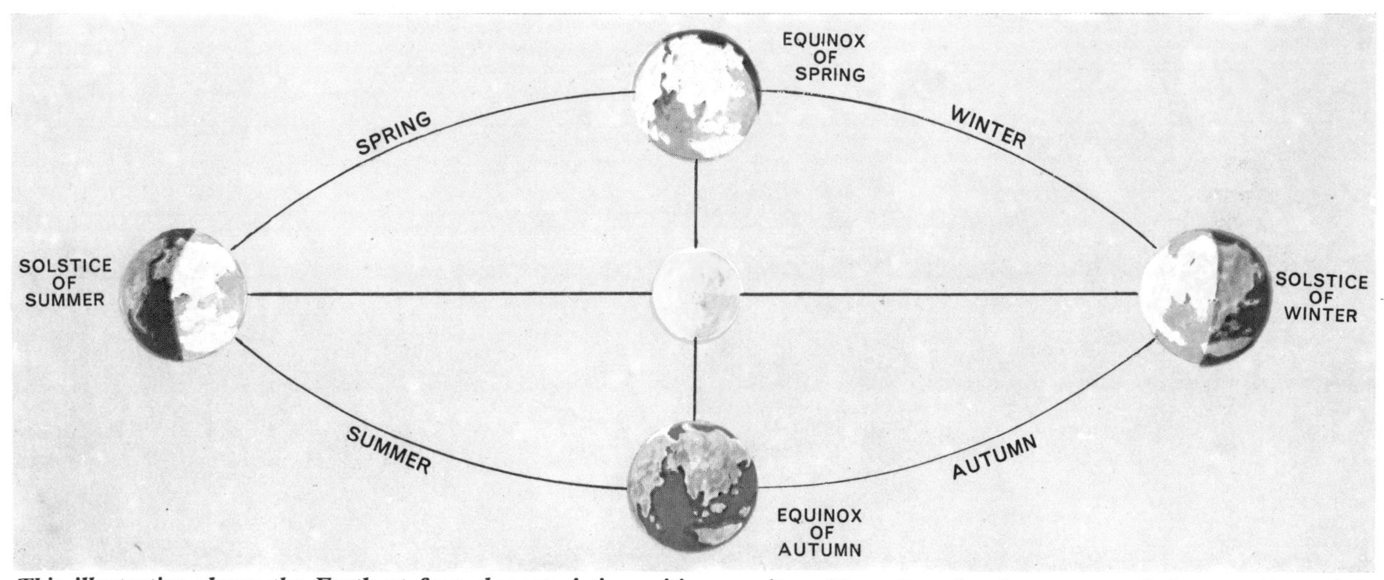

This illustration shows the Earth at four characteristic positions on its orbit as it makes its way round the sun. Two of the positions are equinoxes and two are solstices. The Earth rotates on its own axis as it travels round the sun; in passing from one of the four positions to the next, the Earth undergoes its seasonal changes.

perfectly smooth, but great mountain ranges like the Rockies and Himalayas are just the tiniest of wrinkles in its surface.

GRAVITATION

The invisible bond which keeps us tied to the Earth and prevents us from being flung from its surface is called the force of gravity. This is the force which, as the great scientist Sir Isaac Newton found, causes not only apples to drop to the ground but extends to the moon and objects far out in interplanetary space. Because of the Earth's pull, or gravity, objects thrown into the air always come down again. Even so, it is possible to overcome the Earth's gravity and escape completely from its surface. To do this, however, an object at its surface must be given an initial speed of at least 7 miles a second—a speed attainable only with the great space rockets of modern times.

Besides rotating on its axis, the Earth also travels round the sun. It travels at a speed of about 66,000 miles an hour, but so great is its distance from the sun (92,900,000 miles), that one complete journey takes a year. This means that the sun, as seen from the Earth, has different stars for its background at different times of the year. Hence there is a *seasonal* change as distinct from a *nightly* change in the night sky. In the northern summer, for example, the sun lies near the stars of Orion: these stars shine in the daytime sky but cannot be seen against the bright light of day. In winter, on the other hand, the sun lies in a part of the sky opposite to the stars of Orion which are then a striking feature of the night sky.

THE SEASONS

As the Earth travels round the sun, it keeps its axis of rotation always in the same direction. For this reason we have the seasons. In the northern winter, the north pole of the Earth is turned away from the sun, being turned away most on 22nd December. This is the time of the *winter solstice*. At this time the sun is over the Tropic of Capricorn, that is, it passes vertically overhead at midday for people living in latitude 23½° South. As seen from London, the sun spends only a short time above the horizon and its midday height is only 15°. Six months later, on 21st June, the time of the *summer solstice*, the Earth's north pole is turned to its greatest extent towards the sun. The sun is then over the Tropic of Cancer, passing vertically overhead at midday for people living in latitude 23½° North. At London the day is then much longer than the night, and the sun at midday attains a height of 62°. Between winter and summer comes the time of the spring equinox (21st March), and between summer and winter comes the autumnal equinox (23rd September). At these times the sun shines to an equal extent on both poles of the Earth and is vertically overhead at midday for people living on the equator. The day is then equal in length to the night and the sun, as seen from London, rises due east, attains a height of 38½° at midday, and sets due west.

EARTH'S BLANKET OF AIR

Fortunately for us, the Earth is covered by a layer of air called the atmosphere. This layer is most compact, or dense, at the surface and thins out gradually with increasing distance from the surface. At a height of about 5 miles, for example, the air is so thin that breathing is difficult. Climbers and fliers who ascend to greater heights have to take their own supply of air with them. Recent studies with artificial earth satellites show that there are traces of air several hundreds of miles above the Earth's surface. Even so, the full extent of the atmosphere is quite small compared with the great size of the Earth.

Because we live at the bottom of Earth's ocean of air, the clear sky appears blue. As the Sun's light travels through the atmosphere the blue rays are scattered more than those of other colours and the sky therefore appears blue. If we travel higher and higher, however, the blue colour deepens to dark blue and eventually becomes black. To a space traveller, completely free from the Earth's atmosphere, the sky would appear black all the time, whether by day or by night, and the stars would shine out like diamonds in their thousands.

To understand the reason for the different colours which can be seen in the sky it is necessary to know something about light itself. About three hundred years ago Sir Isaac

The amount of heat received by any region of the Earth varies with the length of day and the inclination of the sun's rays, depending upon the position of the Earth with respect to the sun. The globe can be divided into five zones: 1. *Arctic,* 2. *Northern Temperate,* 3. *Tropical,* 4. *Southern Temperate,* 5. *Antarctic. Above, typical Arctic, Southern Temperate and Tropical landscapes.*

Sir Isaac Newton (1642-1727) *showed that light from the sun and stars consists of a number of forms of light, each causing a different colour sensation in the eye. Combined, they produce the sensation of "white" light. Newton passed a ray of sunshine through a prism, splitting it into coloured rays of red, orange, yellow, green, blue, indigo and violet.*

Newton showed that sunlight is composed of differently-coloured lights. He placed a glass prism in a beam of sunlight and saw that it formed a *spectrum* or band of rainbow colours. He was the first to suggest that white light, or sunlight, is split up or *dispersed* into various colours when it is bent or *refracted* by a glass prism. The colours forming white light range from violet at one end of the visible spectrum through indigo, blue, green, yellow and orange to red at the other.

RED SKY AT NIGHT . . .

Remembering this, we can now explain the red sun and sky sometimes seen at sunrise and sunset. When the sun is near the horizon, or very low in the sky, its rays have to pass through a much greater thickness of air than when it is high in the sky. Now the air, as we have already mentioned, scatters the sun's light, the violet and blue rays being scattered more than any of the others. But when the sun is near the horizon and the air contains a good deal of dust, not only are the violet and blue rays scattered, but also some of the green and yellow. The sun is, as it were, robbed of these colours, and only the orange and red rays reach the observer's eye. The sun, therefore, appears reddish or orange-red in colour, as also do any low-lying clouds or mist patches which reflect this light.

Sometimes nature reproduces a spectrum in the sky—the rainbow. This great coloured arch is formed by the dispersion of sunlight, but in this case the dispersion is done not by a prism but by an immense number of raindrops. When sunlight meets these drops it is reflected inside each drop and also refracted and dispersed. The bow itself is part of a circle whose centre lies in a direction opposite to the sun. The angular distance from this centre of the red part of the bow is about 51 degrees: that for the blue part is about 54 degrees. When the sun is above the horizon we can, therefore, see only an arc of the rainbow: it appears as a semi-circle only when the sun is on the horizon. Sometimes sunlight is reflected twice instead of once inside each raindrop. This produces a secondary and larger bow outside the primary one. In the primary bow the red colour is on the outside and the violet on the inside, but in the secondary the colours are reversed.

LIFE-GIVING ENERGY

Actually sunlight is just a small part of all the energy which the sun pours out into space. The total energy is called the sun's *radiation.* Sunlight is only the visible part, or rather, the part which gives rise to the sensation of light when it enters the eye. A far larger invisible part, beyond the range of the eye, contains the infra-red (a heating radiation) and the ultra-violet (a radiation which can affect photographic plates and also start the process of producing a " sun-tan "). In addition, there are X-rays (able to penetrate into the human body) and radio waves like those used in broadcasting and television. All this radiation, light included, can be regarded as a wave motion, but the lengths of light waves are very much shorter than those of radio waves. It also travels through space at one and the same speed—186,282 miles a second—but even at this speed, and because of the immense distance of the sun, it takes over 8 minutes to reach the Earth.

Only a small part of all the sun's radiation ever reaches the surface of the Earth. The Earth's atmosphere acts as a barrier for the X-rays and much of the ultra-violet and infra-red, while layers of electrified particles high up in the atmosphere keep out a large range of the radio waves. Even the radiation which, like light, does reach the ground is screened or filtered by the atmosphere. It is as if nature had fixed two invisible windows in the sky—one to let in energy in and around the light range, and the other to let in a certain range of radio waves.

Without these windows and the filtering effect of the atmosphere, life would be impossible on the Earth's surface. If the Earth lost its atmosphere, living things in daytime would shrivel up in the fierce light and heat of the sun, and the temperature at ground level would be about that of boiling water. At night this heat would be quickly sent out or radiated into space to bring about over 200 degrees of frost. In quite a short time, therefore, the Earth would become a waterless wilderness—dead, silent and barren.

The sense of hearing is one of the most delightful gifts that nature has bestowed upon us. It enables us to talk to one another, and to listen to music; it brings us the singing of the birds and the drowsy buzzing of the insects on a summer's day. All this is made possible by the ears, which enable us to detect and decipher the messages that are carried to us by the sound vibrations in the air.

Sound is nothing more than vibrations of the molecules forming the gases of the air. These tiny particles are disturbed by the movement of whatever is producing the sound —for example the vibration of a violin string or the parchment on a drum. The particles pass on the movement from one to another, forming a wave of alternate compression and rarefaction which travels through the air.

ANALYSING SOUNDS

The ear is given the job of detecting and analysing these sound waves, and it does this with great efficiency. The sounds of everyday life are incredible mixtures of vibrations coming from all sorts of sources. The noise of a passing car is mixed with music from the radio; the dog is barking and the vacuum cleaner is going next door. All these and many other things are making the air vibrate in an infinite variety of ways, producing all manner of sounds of different pitch and intensity. Yet the ear is able to detect and assess the sounds and pass on an intelligent appraisal of them to the brain. How is it done?

The human ear consists of three parts; the outer ear, the middle ear and the inner ear. The outer ear, which is the obvious part attached to the side of the head, is the least important of the three. The others, which are very delicate, are deeply embedded in and protected by the bones of the skull.

MIDDLE EAR

Leading from the outer ear into the skull is a tube which ends at the eardrum, marking the boundary between the outer and middle parts of the ear. The wall of this tube produces wax so as to trap dust and prevent it from settling on the eardrum. Sounds reaching the ear are funnelled down the tube until they reach the eardrum, which vibrates in response to the vibrations of the sound.

On the other side of the eardrum is the middle ear, an air-filled cavity whose walls are made almost entirely of bone. A tube leads from the middle ear to the back of the throat, ensuring that the pressure of air is the same on each side of the eardrum. If the pressure were not the same, the eardrum would be pressed firmly in or out and deafness would be the result. Sometimes, during a bad cold for instance, the tube does become blocked and a vigorous swallowing action is necessary to clear it and restore normal hearing. A powerful explosion, however, may be too much for this safety device and then the eardrum may be broken.

INNER EAR

The vibrations of the eardrum are carried across to the other side of the middle ear by a chain of three little bones, or ossicles. The first of these is attached to the eardrum; the second forms a link leading to the third bone, which is attached to a thin membrane in the wall of the middle ear opposite to the eardrum. This membrane marks the boundary between the middle and inner ear.

The inner ear, which is filled with liquid, contains sensitive

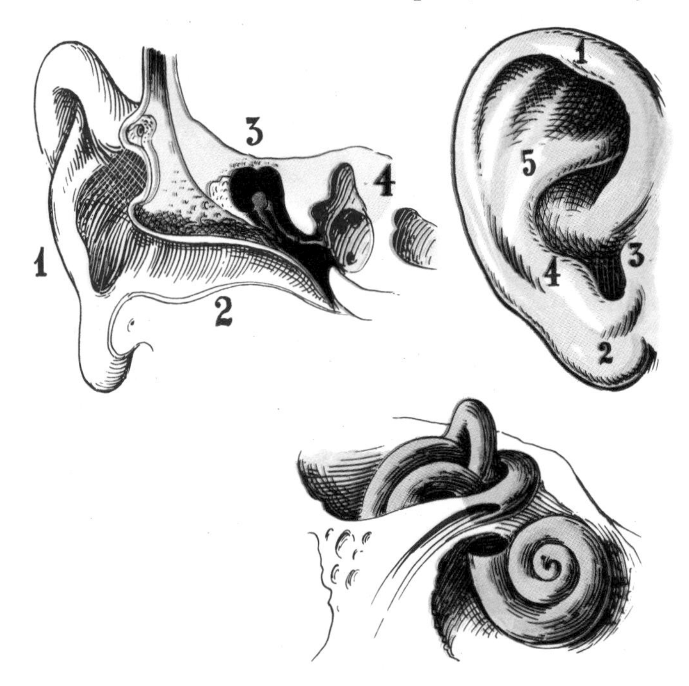

These illustrations show the construction of the human ear. Top left: *the main internal parts of the ear;* 1. *auricle;* 2. *auditory meatus;* 3. *middle-ear cavity;* 4. *inner ear.* Top right: *the main external parts of the ear;* 1. *helix;* 2. *lobule;* 3. *tragus;* 4. *antitragus;* 5. *antihelix.* Below: *cochlea, the organ in the inner ear which controls the sense of hearing.*

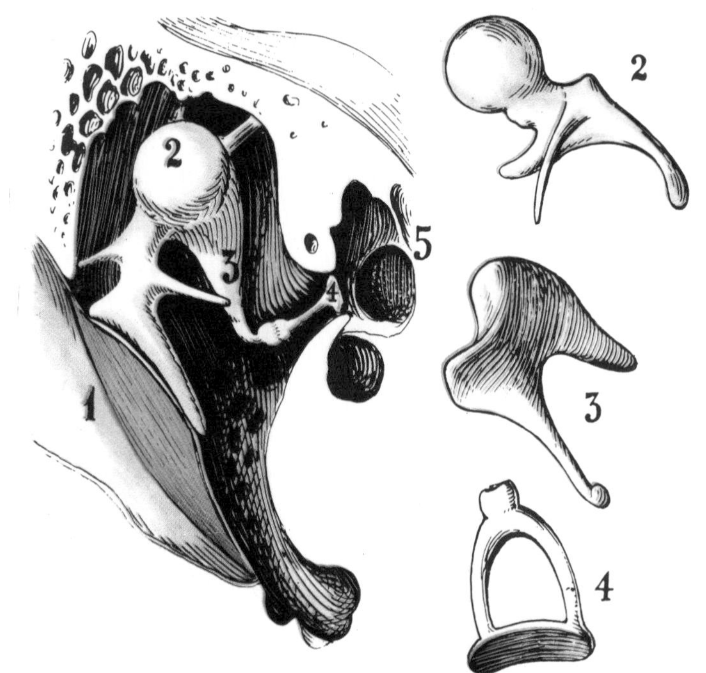

The structure of the inner ear. Left: *the ear with the middle-ear cavity.* 1. *the ear-drum;* 2. *the malleus;* 3. *the incus or anvil;* 4. *the stapes. The stapes rests upon the opening of* 5. *the labyrinth. The Eustachian tube opens out beneath the four parts detailed above.* Right: *the three ossicles are shown in detail.*

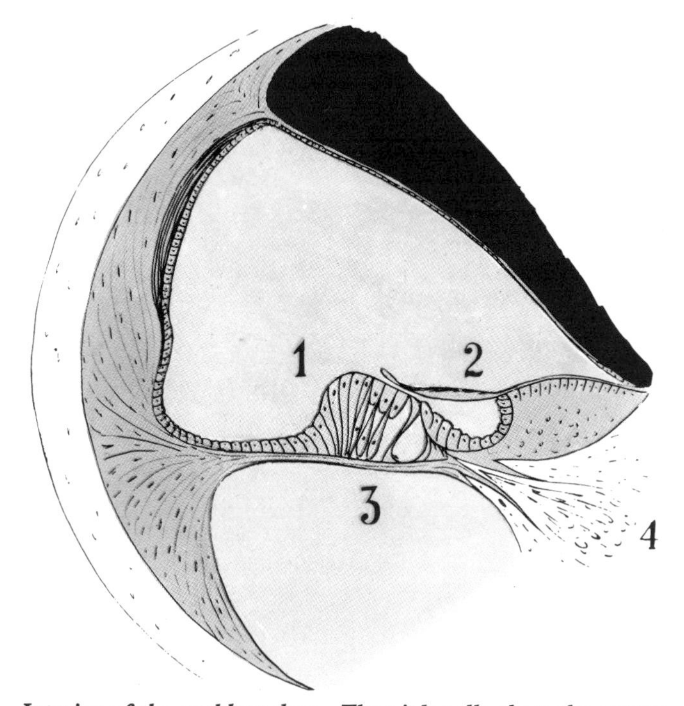

Interior of the cochlear duct. The pink cells show the cortex, the real organ of hearing. 1. auditory cells; 2. membrana tectoria; 3. basilar membrane; 4. auditory nerve. The entire organ is immersed in a liquid, the endolymph, shown in blue.

The ear-drum, struck by sound waves, vibrates like a gong, transmitting the vibrations to the very small bones of the ear and to the labyrinth. The cortex acts like a piano in which every string is an auditory cell.

cells linked by nerves to the brain. When the eardrum is vibrated by sounds in the air, these vibrations are carried over to the inner ear by the ossicles. In this way vibrations are set up in the liquid in the inner ear and as a result the sensitive cells send impulses to the brain. It is possible to distinguish between different sounds because the cells respond to particular vibrations.

BALANCE MECHANISM

Another part of the inner ear consists of the organs of balance. Certain sections of these contain hair-like sensitive cells which have tiny pieces of chalk at their tips. These cells are bent over by the action of gravity which pulls down their heavy tips, so that when you are standing up the cells are pulled in one direction, but when you are lying down they are pulled in another. Your brain is, therefore, kept informed of the position of your head and body.

The rest of the organs of balance are in the form of three semi-circular tubes. These are arranged at right-angles to one another and at the end of each is a small swelling which contains more hair-like cells. When you move your head, the tubes move but the liquid inside them does not. In much the same way you can see that water in a tumbler does not move when the glass is rotated. Thus when your head is turned, the hair-like cells are bent as they push their way through the stationary liquid. The cells send impulses to the brain when they are bent in this way; even when blindfolded you can detect movement.

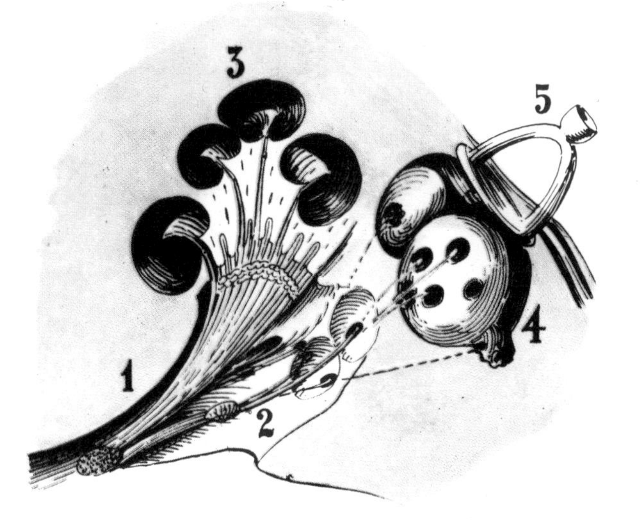

A section of the labyrinth. Left: 3. *the cochlea from which the auditory nerve* (1) *issues.* Right: *the interior of the semi-circular canals* (4) *and of the vestibule from which comes the vestibular nerve* (2) *governing balance.* 5. *the stapes.*

These two boys are creating ripples on the surface of a pond; the ripples spread out over the surface, carrying in their vibration pattern the characteristics of the movement that created them. Sound waves travel similarly through the air.

THE ELECTRIC LIGHT BULB

In 1810, more than a century and a half ago, the English scientist Sir Humphry Davy showed how electricity could jump across the gap between two carbon rods; the continuous spark, or " arc ", which was formed emitted light. This experiment, performed before members of the Royal Institution in London, was the first step towards the practical application of electricity for lighting purposes; it was to lead eventually to the development of the electric light bulb as we know it to-day.

Davy used two charcoal electrodes connected to a primitive type of electric battery. The device was not suitable for practical use, providing only a dim and flickering light.

About thirty years after Davy's experiment, a new type of battery was invented by Daniell and Bunsen; it gave a more intense and even light. This was followed by improvements in the electrodes which were introduced by Foucault, a Frenchman. Instead of using charcoal, Foucault made two carbon electrodes, and with the aid of these carbon sticks he created a primitive form of electric lighting. This invention enabled the men who were erecting the Palace of Industry for the Paris Exhibition of 1855 to work on night shifts. It was not, however, until 1878, that a first successful attempt at street lighting was made in the Place de l'Opéra, in Paris.

EDISON'S LIGHT BULB

Throughout the nineteenth-century, gas lighting came into widespread use. But the world was waiting for someone to adapt the newly discovered power of electricity for lighting purposes. Interest was especially keen in the United States where Edison, the " Wizard of Menlo Park ", who had invented the " talking machine ", or gramophone, was turning his attention to electric lighting. A group of American financiers and industrialists asked Edison if he could make a real effort to develop a practical form of electric light.

After giving much thought to the matter Edison decided to use electricity to heat a carbon filament to incandescence in order to produce light. The filament would have to be inside an evacuated glass bulb. He started work on the idea in 1878, achieving success only after two long years of tedious experiment. His inventive genius won him world-wide acclaim when, in 1882, he had some of the gas lamps removed from the centre of New York and replaced with electric light bulbs. Actually, Edison's bulb was first shown to the public at the 1881 Paris Exhibition, where visitors learned that the light was produced from carbonised filaments of Japanese bamboo. This bulb maintained a constant glow for several hundred hours.

Much had still to be done to perfect the new form of illumination, particularly when it was realised that *the strength of a light emanating from an incandescent body increases with the rise of temperature.* In other words, *the higher the temperature of the filament and the lower the loss of heat the more brilliant is the luminous effect achieved.*

THE INVENTION OF METAL FILAMENTS

In the 1890's, filaments were made of very fine metal wire with a high melting point. Osmium and tantalum were used, and in 1906, the valuable properties of tungsten were demonstrated. This metal is an excellent conductor of electricity, and it is still considered the best material for use in light bulbs. At that time the finest filaments were made by powdering tungsten and mixing it with adhesive substances. Then, in 1911, a wire-drawing process was devised and a

Simple electric lamps were made more than a century ago. Typical experimental lamps, such as that shown on the left, contained fine metal filaments which glowed when electricity passed through them. Right: *the first commercially-useful lamps had carbon filaments.*

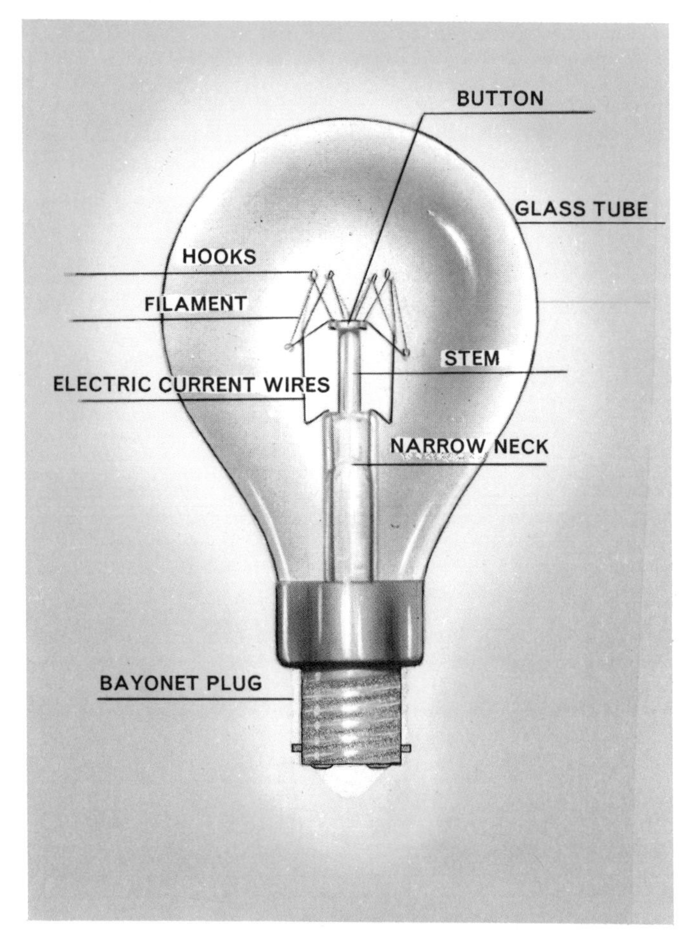

Modern electric light bulbs, manufactured in vast quantities for household use, consist of the main parts shown above.

more durable form of tungsten filament was obtained. By a new arrangement of the filament wire, consumption of electricity was reduced to *one watt* per candle power and the *monowatt* type of light bulb went into production.

THE HALF-WATT BULB

A new procedure, discovered in 1913, brought a further improvement. It had been suggested that if the bulb were filled with an inert gas incapable of chemical change the filament temperature could be increased and loss of heat checked. Greater incandescence was thus obtained, but it was still difficult to limit the heat loss.

At this stage, Langmuir found that the heat problem depended partly on the shape of the filament. He showed that heat dispersion could be reduced to a minimum by twisting the wire into the shape of a spiral. The result was a lamp bulb with a spiral filament consuming only *half a watt* of current per candle power. Another advantage was that the new method gave longer life to the filament. The wire burned out more slowly and the familiar complaint " the bulb's gone " was heard less frequently.

HOW TUNGSTEN FILAMENTS ARE MADE

While glassmakers had been able to produce suitable light bulbs without difficulty the manufacture of the new tungsten filament wires was a much more delicate matter. This metal, which is obtained from the mineral wolfram, has to be extracted by a complicated chemical process. Oxide of tungsten is mixed with small quantities of other substances and then treated in special furnaces. The air above the material in the furnace is replaced by hydrogen gas, which prevents the metal re-combining with oxygen. A fine grey powder is produced, which is pressed into ingots in moulds. These ingots are consolidated by heating in ovens, hydrogen again replacing the air to avoid oxidation of the metal. The tungsten is heated electrically to a temperature just below melting point, after which the blocks are beaten into thin wires.

The wires are drawn out at a high temperature and thoroughly cleaned. They are now ready to be twisted into a spiral shape. A high-speed machine wraps them round a cylinder of steel or molybdenum. As it is impossible to remove the filament without breaking it, the metal support has to be dissolved in acid which does not attack tungsten.

MAKING THE BULB STEM

The stem of a light bulb consists of (*a*) a wide glass tube which is welded to the neck of the bulb; (*b*) a narrow glass tube through which the air is eventually extracted from the bulb and replaced by gas; (*c*) a glass stem for supporting the filament; (*d*) the wires which carry the electric current to the filament.

A solid piece of glass is made by flattening down the top of the wide glass tube, and the narrow glass tube is sealed into the flattened end. The glass is softened during this process by heating it in a gas flame, a jet of air being forced down the narrow tube to prevent it becoming sealed and closed. The lead-in wires are held firmly at the base where they are electrically welded.

The stem is now assembled by a machine which shapes its tip into the form of a button. Several tiny hooks are attached to this button; they will carry the filament, which is threaded on by another machine. The ends of the filament are first connected to the lead-in wires which conduct the current, the rest being looped over the hooks.

The glass stem is welded to the bulb under a gas flame. At the same time a strong blast of cold air snaps off any superfluous glass that remains on the outside of the joint. A moving belt then carries the bulb to a machine which creates a vacuum by removing the air, and then refills the

Thomas Edison played an important part in the development of the electric lamp. He devoted years of study to the problem before achieving success in 1880, *with a lamp in which the filament glowed inside an evacuated glass bulb.*

Searchlights, cinema and television lamps, and fluorescent strip-lighting are a few of the many types of lamp in use to-day.

bulb with a mixture of nitrogen, argon, and krypton. The gas is introduced through the narrow tube inside the stem, after which the tube is sealed up. A metal fitment is added to the base of the bulb, being held in place with the aid of special resins, and the bulb is ready for use.

MODERN BULBS AND ELECTRIC LIGHTS

Electric bulbs are now made in a great variety of shapes and sizes, ranging from the tiny bulbs used in electric torches to the mammoth bulbs needed for street lighting. There are high-power lamps used in photography and television, and thermal lamps used in medicine. All these are direct descendants of the incandescent bulbs that were devised by Edison almost a century ago, in which electricity produced light by heating a wire to incandescence.

Nowadays, another type of electric light has come into widespread use. This is the " fluorescent " lamp in which electricity produces light by stimulating luminescent materials.

In a fluorescent light, electricity flows through a gas at low pressure. It emits ultraviolet radiations, and these radiations stimulate the luminescent materials which form a coating on the tube. The coating produces light as a result of this stimulation. The light made in this way can be modified and controlled by using different types of luminescent materials. Modern tubes, for example, can be made to emit light which is very similar to daylight.

Fluorescent lamps are more efficient than incandescent bulbs in that they return more of the electricity used as light.

Top: *a neon strip light.* Centre: *a tubular lamp with double socket for shop-window lighting.* Bottom: *a tubular lamp.*

Some fluorescent lamps use only one-third of the electricity used by a filament bulb giving the same amount of light. The fluorescent lamp does not waste electricity in producing heat; the tube remains quite cool when the lamp is switched on.

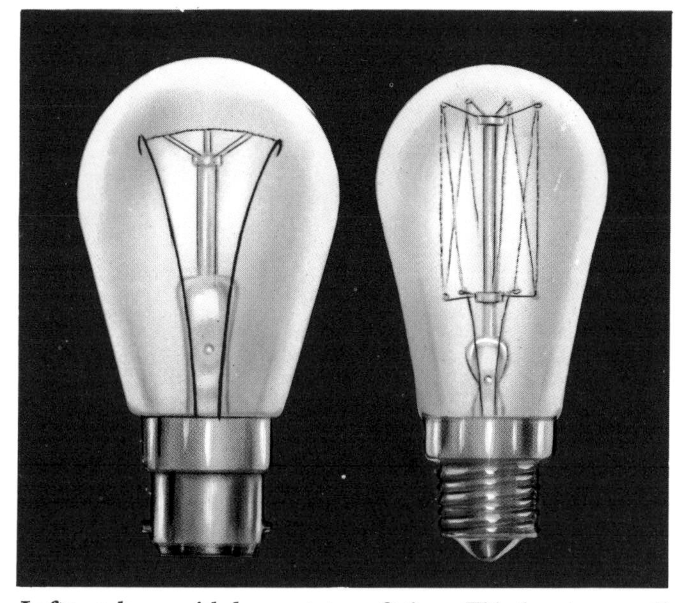

Left: *a lamp with bayonet type fitting. This has two small plates on the base which make contact with the electrical supply.* Right: *the Edison screw fitting acts as one terminal, and a single contact on the base as the other terminal.*

QUESTIONS AND ANSWERS

What are Diatoms?

Diatoms are tiny one-celled plants which form a large part of the layer of living matter, or plankton, that floats on the surface of the sea. This layer provides food for all the creatures of the sea, the diatoms and other simple plants manufacturing it from carbon dioxide, water and other chemicals just as plants do on land.

The diatoms are so small that the largest of them is just visible to the naked eye. But they multiply so rapidly when there is plenty of food for them that they form a mass of matter that colours the surface of the sea. Each diatom is enclosed in a translucent "shell" of silica that is in two halves, which fit over one another like a lid fitting over a chocolate box.

HYDROGEN

NOTE: Hydrogen is a highly inflammable gas, and will explode violently when mixed with air and ignited. All experiments with hydrogen should be carried out under expert supervision.

Hydrogen was discovered in the sixteenth-century by Paracelsus (1493-1541), a Swiss naturalist and alchemist who was also a doctor. Paracelsus made hydrogen by treating iron with dilute sulphuric acid (sulphuric acid was in those days called " oil of vitriol "). He discovered that hydrogen would burn when set alight, and he called it " inflammable air ".

In 1766, Cavendish found that water was produced when he burned this inflammable air. In the late eighteenth-century, Lavoisier, whom we think of as the founder of modern chemistry, proved that this gas is present in water (H_2O), and he called it hydrogen. This name is derived from Greek words and means " producer of water ". Hydrogen occurs very widely on Earth, and forms a fundamental constituent of the universe. It is present on other planets, on the sun, and in all the galaxies in space.

Paracelsus lived from 1493-1541. He was a Swiss doctor, naturalist and alchemist. Paracelsus introduced many substances into medical practice, including mercury, opium, sulphur, lead and arsenic. His scientific studies included the beginnings of what we now call chemistry.

WHERE DO YOU FIND HYDROGEN?

Hydrogen is a gas which is present in the air, forming part of the water vapour which brings our rain. It is present in all vegetables and animals, and takes part in the processes of decay. We find hydrogen in petrol and coal, and in many inorganic substances, including acids and hydroxides.

Hydrogen is the lightest of all the elements we know. It is fourteen times lighter than air, and was at one time used to fill balloons and airships. It was replaced by helium for this purpose because helium does not burn.

WHAT ARE ITS PROPERTIES?

Hydrogen is a colourless gas, without smell or taste. It is not poisonous, but it will cause suffocation if present in too high a concentration. Hydrogen will not dissolve in

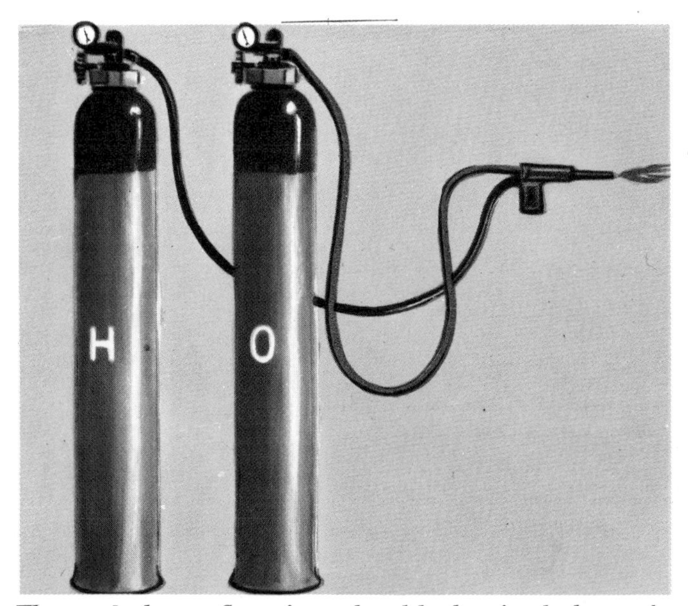

The oxy-hydrogen flame is produced by burning hydrogen in oxygen and reaches a temperature of 2800° C. This flame is used in the engineering industry for cutting and welding metals. It burns under water, and is used by divers for cutting up the steel hulls of sunken ships. Hydrogen has many industrial applications, being used, for example, in making synthetic ammonia, and for innumerable other chemical products. It is used in the treatment of fats, for example in the production of margarine, and for the hydrogenation of heavy oils to provide synthetic petrol.

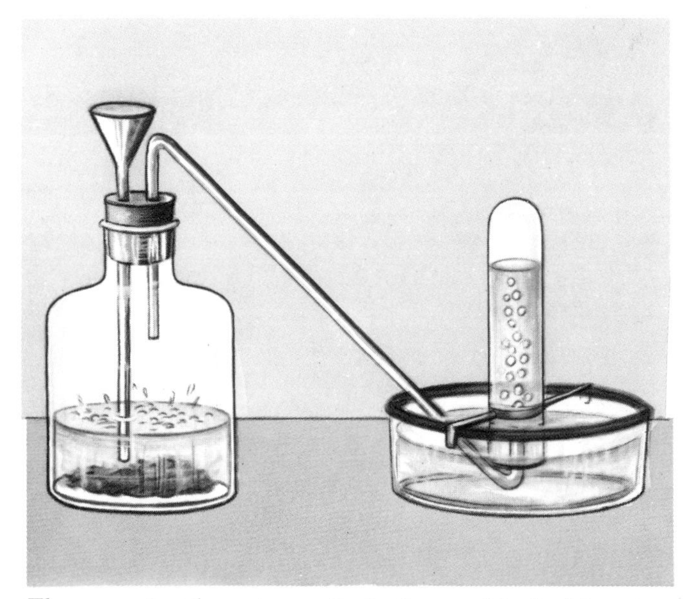

The apparatus shown is a method often used in the laboratory to make hydrogen. A bottle containing water is connected to a bowl of water by a Z-tube. One end of the tube is fixed firmly in the bottle; the other is in an upturned test-tube, also full of water. There are zinc filings at the bottom of the bottle. Dilute sulphuric acid is poured down the funnel. It combines with the metal to form zinc sulphate, and the hydrogen in the acid is released. You can see the bubbles of hydrogen escaping through the water in the test-tube and collecting at the top of the upturned tube.

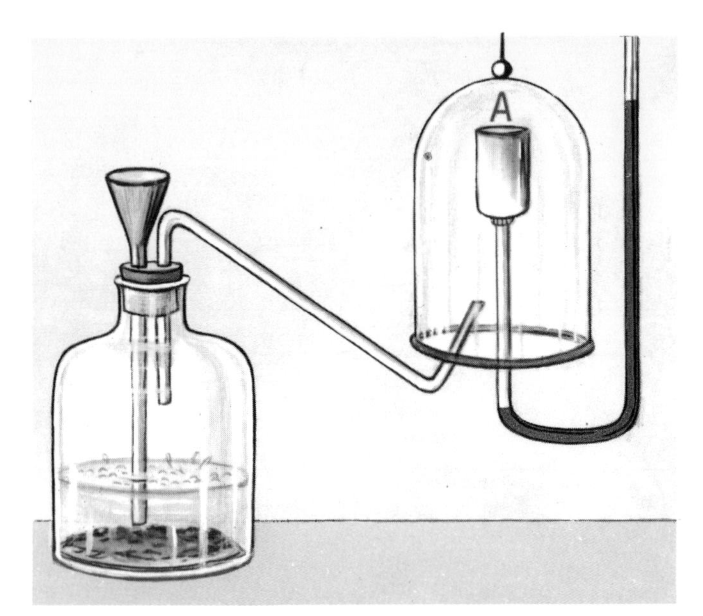

This experiment shows the speed with which hydrogen can diffuse through a porous vessel. The gas is made in the bottle, set up as before, and passes through the Z-tube into the bell glass. It is absorbed through the porous pot on the end of the U-tube, forcing the air that was in the pot downwards, so that the coloured liquid is pushed up the arm of the U-tube.

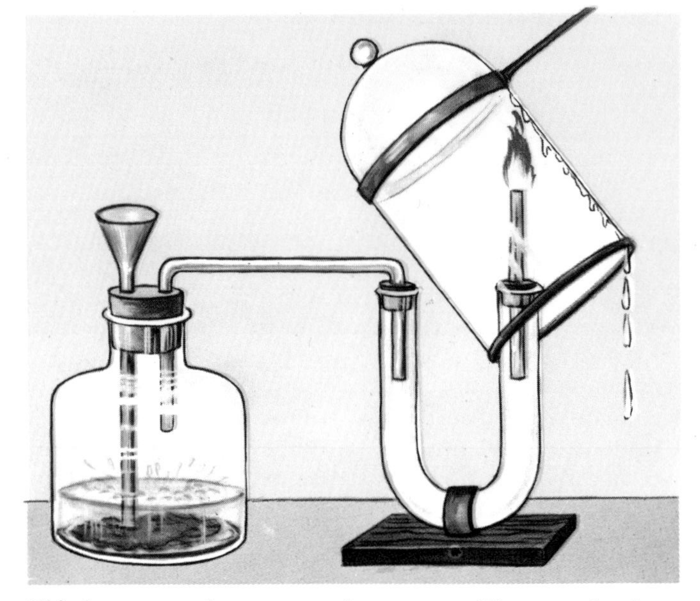

This is an experiment to produce water. The same bottle as before is connected this time to a U-tube filled with cotton-wool. The outlet from this is a very narrow glass tube. The hydrogen is forced out of this tube and it is set alight. If you place a glass hood over the flame, you will see pure water form and drip down the inner surface.

water. It will burn, and when it does so it produces a very hot flame.

If hydrogen and oxygen are mixed in the same proportion as you find in water, that is two parts to one, they will explode with a loud bang when ignited.

Industry uses a lot of hydrogen which is made in very large quantities by the chemical industry. Water is split into the two gases, oxygen and hydrogen, by passing an electric current through it.

HOW TO MAKE HYDROGEN

This is a common method of preparing hydrogen, but note that this should ONLY be done under expert supervision. The apparatus you need is shown in Fig. 1. The dilute sulphuric acid reacts on the metal which forms a sulphate and releases hydrogen.

Choose a bottle with a wide neck and make two holes in the bung. These are for two glass tubes to pass through. One tube is attached to a glass funnel, and the other is Z-shaped and runs from the bottle to a glass bowl of water. Held upside-down by clamps over the end of the Z-tube is a test-tube filled with water. This collects the gas as it is made and stores it. There must be some zinc filings in the bottle and it should be one-third full of water. Pour dilute sulphuric acid through the funnel until the mixture starts to effervesce, showing that hydrogen is being produced. The reaction, which generates heat, is as follows:

$$Zn + H_2SO_4 = ZnSO_4 + H_2$$

(Zinc + Sulphuric Acid = Zinc Sulphate + Hydrogen)

STORING HYDROGEN

The hydrogen released from the sulphuric acid appears as bubbles which collect in the test-tube; the water is forced out of the tube to make room for the gas which collects at the top. When you remove the test-tube from the clamps, you must remember to hold it upside down, otherwise the hydrogen, which is much lighter than air, will escape. If you repeat this experiment with other test-tubes, you will be able to set up a little store of hydrogen by standing all the test-tubes upside down on a pane of glass. There they will always be ready for use.

HOW TO USE A PRESSURE GAUGE

Set up half the apparatus as above, but instead of using the bowl and test-tube, put the end of the Z-tube under a bell glass. Now you must make a pressure-gauge. This consists of a U-tube containing a coloured liquid, which will reach the same height in each arm of the " U ". On one end place a porous pot (*A*). As soon as this is put under the bell glass you will see the pressure gauge working. The hydrogen will leave the Z-tube and enter the pores of the little pot placed high up in the bell glass. There it forces down the air in the U-tube and the coloured liquid is pushed along so that it rises much higher in the outside arm (Fig. 2).

MAKING PURE WATER

(*Note:* Do not attempt this experiment on your own.)

If you hold a lighted match to a test-tube full of hydrogen, you will hear the gas make a small bang as it catches fire and burns with a pale blue flame. Hydrogen burns by combining with the oxygen in the air to form water. In Fig. 3 you can see how to catch the water by holding a bell glass over the flame.

You can also release hydrogen from water. The easiest way of doing this is to use a metal that combines with oxygen. Sodium and potassium are good examples. Either of these thrown on to water will start to react violently, and great care is needed in handling them. The hydrogen is freed from the water and burns with a yellow flame in the presence of sodium and with a violet flame when potassium is used.

NOTE: Hydrogen is a highly inflammable gas, and will explode violently when mixed with air and ignited. All experiments with hydrogen should be carried out under expert supervision.

THE AEROPLANE GROWS UP

EARLY PIONEERS

On that historic day in 1903 when the first sustained, controlled flight in a heavier-than-air powered machine was made by the Wright brothers, two further flights were made by them, the last one covering 852 feet and lasting 59 seconds.

One would have thought that news of this great event would soon have flashed around the world. But this was not so. Some news got through, but even this was disbelieved. The Wrights built a second aircraft in 1904, and a further improved machine in 1905. Flying from a small field alongside a main road, they made many successful flights, including one lasting 38 minutes which covered 24 miles. No one else had flown for even a minute, but still the world at large knew nothing.

European pioneers built aeroplanes in a bewildering variety of shapes and sizes. This one by G. Vanden had tunnel-like wings. It did not fly.

FIRST FLIGHT IN EUROPE

One result of the delay of proper news of the Wright biplanes was that European pioneers continued to work on original, if sometimes fanciful, lines. All sorts of oddities began to appear, few of which could hop—fortunately for their would-be pilots. Typical of these early freaks was the aeroplane illustrated on this page. Unusual, too, was the gawky, tail-first, powered box-kite called the 14 *bis*, made by our old friend the airship-maker, Santos-Dumont. Yet, dead-end design that it was, it flew 197 feet on 23rd October, 1906, to make what is officially recognised as the first genuine flight in Europe.

In Britain, one of the first powered hops was made by "Venetian blind" Horatio Phillips, in what can best be described as a flying-runner-bean frame based on his multiple wing theory.

Developed along much sounder lines was a remarkable glider by Preston Watson incorporating a unique tilting top wing to provide lateral control. Powered developments of this flew successfully about 1910.

CODY'S "BOX KITE"

The first officially-recognised flight in a piloted aeroplane in Britain was made by American-born "Colonel" Cody in a powered "box kite", which on 16th October, 1908, flew 496 feet over Laffan's Plain, Farnborough.

The Voisin-Delagrange biplane of 1907 *was the ancestor of all succeeding biplanes. An aircraft of this type made the first European flight of a mile on* 13*th January*, 1908, *marking the start of practical flying in Europe.*

On 25*th July*, 1909, *Louis Blériot, aviator and inventor, made the first successful aeroplane crossing of the English Channel. He set off from Calais and landed at Northfall Meadow, near Dover, taking* 31 *minutes.*

Aircraft had barely begun to fly when they were being used for war. Here a monoplane is used in skirmishes with Libyan tribesmen in 1911.

On the Continent, the foremost experimenters at this period were the Voisin brothers, Esnault-Pelterie and Louis Blériot. Henry Farman, flying a Voisin biplane, won the Deutsch-Archdeacon prize of £2,000 for the first circular flight in Europe of more than a kilometer, on 13th January, 1908, thus introducing the start of practical flying in Europe.

In Britain, names now world-famous, began to emerge. Alliot Verdon-Roe started, in 1907, by winning first prize at a competition for model aeroplanes at Alexandra Palace. He then set about building a full-size version in the hope of winning £2,500, offered by the management of Brooklands to the first airman to fly round their motor-racing track before the end of 1907. To be able to afford parts for his aeroplane Roe lived on five shillings worth of food a week. Although too late to win the Brooklands prize, compensation came on 8th June, 1908, when, after taxying his biplane for a short distance, he suddenly felt the wheels leave the ground and realised that he was flying.

The flight, however, was too short to be officially recognised and the honour of being the first Englishman to fly in Britain was accorded to J. T. C. Moore-Brabazon (the late Lord Brabazon of Tara) who flew 500 yards in the French Voisin *Bird of Passage* at the Isle of Sheppey in May, 1909.

FIRST ALL-BRITISH FLIGHT

Roe, however, will always be remembered as the first Englishman to fly in an all-British aeroplane. This he did on 13th July, 1909, in a little triplane covered with brown paper and powered by an engine of only 9 horse power. Incredible as it may now seem, instead of being congratulated on his achievement, Roe was about to be prosecuted as a danger to the public when Louis Blériot crossed the Channel and was acclaimed a national hero. The case against Roe was dropped.

Along with Roe, there appeared Robert Blackburn, who had flown his own aeroplane, T. O. M. Sopwith, who had taught himself to fly, the Short Brothers of Eastchurch, the British and Colonial Company of Bristol, and Handley Page Limited of Barking.

As more aircraft were built, more experience was gained, and with this experience aeroplanes gradually ceased to be " toys " and became practical vehicles.

Official mail was carried by air and so was cargo. Flimsy prototypes of to-day's big airliners linked the capitals of England and France.

And, rather sinisterly, the aeroplane began to be adopted as a weapon of war.

WINGS AT WAR

In America, Eugene Ely flew a Curtiss biplane off a warship, and thus foreshadowed the reconnaissance " eyes " of the aircraft carriers of the future. Guns were fitted to aeroplanes and bombs dropped experimentally. In France, Antionette built an armoured aeroplane, but so overdid the protection that it was too heavy to fly properly.

Britain established the Royal Flying Corps as early as 1912, with Military and Naval Wings; but when the Great War started on 4th August, 1914, it had only 63 aeroplanes, all of which were unarmed. By contrast, Germany had 260 military aircraft, and France 156. But Britain had already shown that she could produce first-class aeroplanes, and the Government " Factory " at Farnborough, then busy designing and producing aeroplanes, was slowly developing into the vast research organisation which, now called the Royal Aircraft Establishment, has done much to help Britain to keep in the forefront of aviation development.

RECONNAISSANCE

When war started, the military aeroplane was something of a novelty; the Army thought it might be useful for reconnaissance; the Navy had considered it for over-water patrols. When war ended four years later the fragile pre-war aircraft had developed into speedy, highly manœuvrable, heavily-armed fighters, and slower, but larger, bombers carrying heavy loads of incendiaries and high explosives.

A major development in military aircraft occurred when Antony Fokker invented his interrupter gear which enabled bullets to be fired between the propeller blades. Equipped with this, the deadly little Fokker monoplanes began driving British and French aircraft from the sky.

This Fokker monoplane of 1915 *was the scourge of the Allied Air Forces. It was the first to be fitted with the revolutionary interrupter-gear, enabling the gun to be fired through the propeller disc. Attacks could thus be made from any angle.*

Alcock and Brown crossing the Atlantic Ocean, in 1919, *in a Vickers-Vimy biplane. Setting off from Newfoundland, and taking* 16 *hours, they reached Clifden in Ireland after surviving storms and mechanical mishaps.*

Britain fought back, and in quick succession produced a wonderful series of fighters, including the DH2, FE2B, Gunbus, Camel and S.E.5, and with these gradually regained superiority over the Western Front. At the same time she began to hit Germany hard with the DH4 day bomber and big Handley Page 0/400s which pioneered heavy bombing at night.

BIRTH OF R.A.F.

Before the war ended in 1918, air power had become so important that the R.F.C. and R.N.A.S. were removed from the control of the Army and Navy and were united to form the Royal Air Force, under the control of the newly-formed Air Ministry.

The aircraft industry in Britain had grown from a few small scattered factories into a complex industry employing 350,000 people, producing aeroplanes at the rate of 30,000 a year.

Following the Armistice of November, 1918, the size of the R.A.F. and the industry decreased rapidly, as might be expected, but it was obvious that the aeroplane was destined to play an increasingly important part in our everyday lives.

In 1927, *Charles Lindbergh made the first solo Atlantic flight.*

THE AGE OF GREAT FLIGHTS

Evidence of this soon came, for in 1919 the mighty Atlantic was flown by an aeroplane. First across was a big four-engined Curtiss NC-4 flying-boat of the U.S. Navy, which made the trip via the Azores and took eleven days. A month later this achievement was completely overshadowed by the first non-stop flight, from Newfoundland to Ireland, by Captain John Alcock and Lieutenant A. Whitten Brown, in a Vickers Vimy bomber. This journey was one of the most exciting ever made. First the small propeller driving the electric dynamo for the radio fell off, so that they were unable to report their position. Then there was a sudden clatter from the starboard engine and the exhaust pipe broke away, from which moment the two men were almost deafened by the stream of unsilenced exhaust gases. Just after dawn, the Vimy ran into a mountainous storm cloud, and was thrown bodily about like a leaf in a gale. Losing height rapidly, the Vimy emerged from the cloud only a few hundred

In Paris, Lindbergh was given a tremendous welcome.

Weighing 55 *tons, the huge twelve-engined German Dornier Do-X could carry* 169 *passengers. It had a top speed of* 130 *m.p.h.*

feet above the sea almost *upside down*. Quick as a flash, Alcock righted it. Not long afterwards the engines began to lose their steady beat as the airmen's worst fears were realised—there was ice on the intakes.

This time it was Brown who saved the aircraft, by crawling out of the cockpit, along the ice-covered wing to the engine, and hacking the ice away with a knife. Then he repeated the process on the other engine. This hazardous job had to be done several times.

FLIGHTS TO AUSTRALIA

Other great flights followed. Ross and Keith Smith, two young Australians, linked Britain with her farthermost dominion for the first time by flying to Australia in another Vimy. The South Atlantic was crossed in 1922 by two Portuguese Naval officers in a Fairey seaplane, and two years later four Douglas World Cruisers of the American Air Corps completed the first round-the-world flight of 27,534 miles. Perhaps the most spectacular of these flights was the epic solo journey by Charles Lindbergh, who became a world hero overnight in May, 1927, by flying 3,600 miles non-stop from New York to Paris in his small *Spirit of St. Louis* Ryan monoplane.

WORLD PROVING FLIGHTS

Many other flights, although less spectacular, helped the development of civil aviation. In 1921, Sir Alan Cobham made a 5,000-mile flight round Europe, and then gradually gained experience until, in 1926, he flew from London to Cape Town and back, and to Australia and back in a DH50 biplane. Finally, in 1927, he made a great survey flight of 23,000 miles round Africa in a Short Singapore flying-boat.

After such " proving " flights came the scheduled airliner flights. Among the first was the air link between London and Paris. Looking back at some of the trips of those days they seem exciting although the passengers at that time probably did not think so. At first there were no cabins and pilot and passengers alike sat exposed to the biting slipstream. Even when enclosed fuselages and the comfort of wickerwork chairs arrived, the cabins were often so draughty that passengers were loaned a leather flying coat, gloves, helmet and a hot-water bottle for the trip. Reliability in those days was not too good either, and on a flight from London to Paris one aircraft made twenty-two forced landings on the way, finally arriving two days late. Nor were pilots always clear of trouble when they managed to stay in the air. Navigation in those days often consisted of following the railway lines and on one occasion when an airliner encountered strong headwinds a train overtook it, whereupon the passengers complained that it would have been quicker by rail! After this incident, pilots were instructed to fly directly over the lines, so that passengers could not see any trains below.

However, with the introduction of fine aircraft like the famous Handley Page Hannibals and, in 1936, the Short Empire flying-boats, the air services developed rapidly. The

The Ju. 87 Stuka, *was used with devastating effect in the early days of World War II.*

The Hawker Hurricane which, together with the Supermarine Spitfire, won the crucial Battle of Britain.

The Avro Lancaster. This noted strategic bomber, powered by four 1280-*horse-power Rolls-Royce Merlin engines, had a range of more than* 1,200 *miles, with a bomb-load of* 18,000 *lb.*

same year saw the appearance of another new aircraft, the low-wing, twin-engined Douglas DC3 Dakota. Few people could have foreseen that, twenty-five years later, this aircraft would still outnumber any other type in airline service.

Unfortunately, as airliners spread their peaceful wings around the world, the threat of war again darkened the horizon and, in September, 1939, World War II started.

WORLD AT WAR

The dominant role destined for air power was evident right from the beginning, and although air power by itself rarely achieved complete victory, without it, defeat was inevitable. Air fleets spear-headed the German assault, first against Poland and later against the Low Countries, Norway, and France, which fell in a matter of weeks.

By June, 1940, the world's biggest air force was ranged against Britain. The German intention was to shatter the Royal Air Force in a few swift blows, before putting Operation Sea Lion—the invasion of Britain—into operation. To do this a total of 3,500 aircraft were deployed. Against this force the Royal Air Force had about 700 serviceable aircraft, of which 620 were Hurricanes and Spitfires—plus a defiant spirit and fighting skill the like of which the Germans had not yet encountered.

BATTLE OF BRITAIN

On 12th August, there began what was destined to be one of the most vital, perhaps the most vital, battle of the war—the Battle of Britain. In a systematic attack on airfields and radar stations the Germans launched five or six major raids, involving many hundreds of aircraft. The next day the Germans directed the main weight of their attacks against aircraft factories.

This massive assault was maintained, and increased, during the hectic weeks that followed. On 16th August, the Germans threw more than 1,700 aircraft into the battle. Against these vast hordes flew the teams of Hurricanes and Spitfires, the Spitfires heading off the enemy fighters while the Hurricanes attacked the bomber formations. Such was the effectiveness of this formidable combination that the Germans had to protect each bomber with three fighters.

Although the British fighters proved more than a match for the vaunted Luftwaffe, there was every likelihood that the enemy's superior resources might tell in the end.

HEAVY LOSSES

Then, in retaliation for a British air raid on the German capital, Hitler suddenly diverted the might of the Luftwaffe against London. The pressure on the airfields, radar stations and aeroplane factories slackened. Fighter Command began to recover its strength, and the Battle of Britain had been won. On 17th September, Operation Sea Lion was postponed indefinitely.

During the period of the battle, 1,733 German aircraft were destroyed, and the R.A.F. losses totalled 915 aircraft.

Of course, the battle was not won solely by fighters. It was won, too, in the factories, repair shops, operations

Japanese Kamikaze. In a desperate, but vain, attempt to halt the American advance in the Pacific, the fanatical suicide pilots of the Japanese Air Force crashed to their deaths on the decks of American warships.

American Boeing Superfortresses over Japan. An aircraft of this type dropped the world's first atomic bomb on Hiroshima.

rooms, and a host of other places. Even in the air, bombers, reconnaissance aircraft, and aircraft of Coastal Command played their contributory, if secondary, roles.

But the fighter pilots were undoubtedly the spear-head of victory and we should never forget that fateful summer of 1940, when Civilisation was saved by 1,000 British boys.

BOMBER COMMAND

With the battle won, Britain began to build up the might of Bomber Command, and soon the big, black, four-engined Stirlings, Halifaxes, and Lancasters were striking at the important centres of German armament production. This force alone dropped 955,013 tons of bombs and, together with those of the U.S. Air Force, devastated more than 500 acres in the heart of *each* of thirty-one German cities. Berlin alone lost 6,437 acres—ten times as much as London.

In addition, the Royal Air Force sank 759 enemy surface vessels by mines laid from the air; another 716 by direct attack, and 339 submarines. In so doing, over 70,000 officers and men of the R.A.F. lost their lives.

The first jet fighter, the Messerschmitt ME 262, was armed with four 30-mm. cannon and its top speed of 538 miles per hour made it the most advanced fighter of its day.

On the other side of the world, in the Pacific, air power played an equally important role. Japan entered the war by using it to cripple the American Fleet at Pearl Harbour, overrun South-East Asia in a few weeks, and to advance her armies to the very frontiers of Australia and India. A major shock for Allied pilots was the fast, highly manœuvrable Zero fighter, which took heavy toll of early obsolete British and American aircraft.

But, Japan had over-reached her lines of communication and supply and, soon, the mighty output of American war factories began to have its effect. The Japanese advance was gradually slowed, then halted, and finally rolled slowly back to Japan. The Allies advanced across the Pacific in a series of gigantic steps, from island to island. The object of the grim island-hopping campaign was to capture bases from which U.S. Bombers could attack the Japanese homeland. From the Marianas giant B-29 Superfortresses flew day after day in their hundreds. Working to a systematic plan they burned the heart out of sixty-six major cities and played an important part in the Japanese decision to surrender without invasion.

Britain's first jet was the Gloster-Whittle E. 28/29, powered by a Whittle W-1 turbo-jet of 860 lb. thrust. A second machine, with a more powerful engine, achieved a speed of 466 miles per hour.

JET ENGINES, ROCKETS AND A-BOMBS

Towards the end of the war, three important developments took place. In Europe, the German Messerschmitt Me. 262, the world's first jet fighter, went into action. Had Hitler not delayed production for a year while it was turned into a fighter bomber, this advanced aircraft might have driven the American day bombers from the skies and possibly changed the course of the war. Then Germany, with Britain almost immune from her bombers, struck back with the V-2 rocket, thereby ushering in a new era of " push button " warfare.

But it was in the Pacific, over Japan, that the most important development of all took place. There, in an effort to save the lives of hundreds of thousands of Allied soldiers who would inevitably have been killed in any seaborne invasion, on 6th August, 1945, one bomber destroyed most of the city of Hiroshima with an atomic bomb. In a single blinding flash the force of air power was multiplied a million times, and in thirty-five years had grown into a potential destroyer of the world.

THE TELEGRAPH

It is difficult for us to imagine a world without any electrical communication system. We think nothing to-day of receiving messages instantaneously from China or Australia; we expect to be kept informed of what is happening on the other side of the world, almost as soon as events have taken place.

However, it is not so very many years ago since we had to wait days or even weeks before we knew what was going on a few hundred miles away. Messages were carried from one place to another at the speed at which a horse could gallop. And it was not until man had harnessed electricity that he was able to link the world together in a communications network that carried information almost instantaneously from place to place.

The first electrical device to be invented for carrying messages was the telegraph, which came into being in a primitive form towards the end of the eighteenth-century.

COMMUNICATION BY WIRE

Ever since people realised that electricity would travel through metal wires, they tried to make use of this phenomenon for carrying messages over long distances. In 1753, an anonymous writer in the *Scots Magazine* suggested that electric currents passing along wires could be used for sending messages from one place to another. A series of insulated wires would be used, each one representing a letter of the alphabet. Any letter could be indicated by sending an electric current through the appropriate wire, and detecting it at the other end by making it move a suspended pith ball. A succession of currents passed through different wires would spell out words and messages.

In 1774, Georges Louis Lesage built a telegraph of this type at Geneva, and similar devices were used experimentally in many parts of the world. But, at that time, electricity was still being generated by friction machines, and there was no way of producing a steady current. The electric battery was not developed until the early nineteenth-century, following Volta's experiments with the electric pile.

Once the electric battery became available, progress in telegraphy was speeded up. The battery could send an electric current along an insulated wire, using the earth to complete the electric circuit. A single copper wire and a battery thus formed the basis of a system for sending currents over distances of several miles. The current could be started and stopped by using a simple switch, which opened or closed a gap in the copper wire. When the switch was " off ", it made a break in the copper wire, when it was " on ", the gap was closed and the ends of the wire rejoined.

CODE SIGNALLING

Using a switch in this way, electric current could be made to stop or flow through the wire at will. And the pattern of flow controlled by the switch could be detected in the movement of electric current at a point in the wire many miles away from the switch. Using a prearranged code, this pattern of movement of the electric current could be used for sending messages " by wire ".

The chief practical difficulty in using this type of electrical communication system lay in deciphering the pattern of movement of the electric currents at the receiving end. In 1828, an American inventor, Harrison G. Dyar, used a strip of chemically impregnated paper which moved across the end of the wire in such a way that electric currents passed through the paper from the wire. Whenever a current flowed through the paper, it caused a discolouration, so that the pattern of currents in the wire was translated into

From the earliest times men have tried to devise methods of communicating with one another at a distance. One ancient technique was to use fire and smoke signals, as is shown in the symbolic carvings on the Antonine and Trajan Columns erected in Rome in the second century A.D.

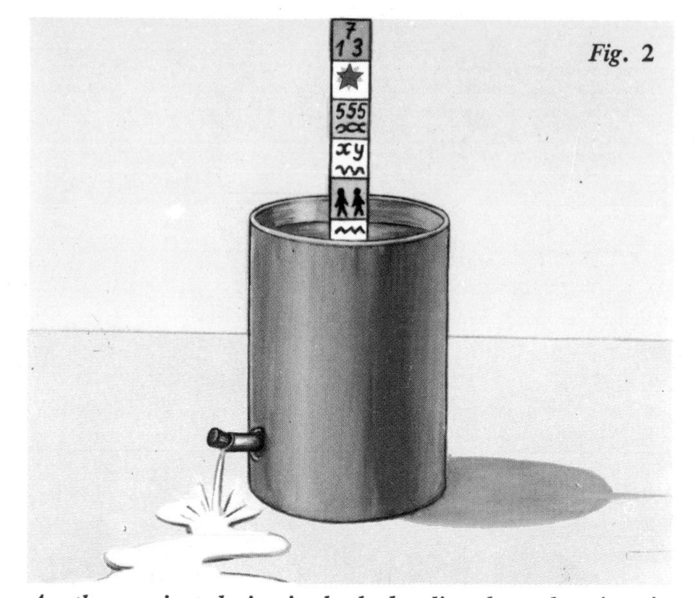

Another ancient device is the hydraulic telegraph. A series of cylindrical tanks was set up containing wooden indicators floating on cork; they were painted with identical code signs. Messages were passed by running the water out until the sign to be transmitted sank to the rim of the cylinder.

a pattern of discolouration on the paper. Using a suitable code, Dyar operated this telegraph for sending messages over a distance of eight miles on Long Island.

This method of detection was not really satisfactory for practical purposes, however, and it was not until the magnetic effects of a current were used that real progress was made. The discovery by Oersted that a current flowing through a wire could deflect a magnet was to answer the problem of detecting current movements in the telegraph wire.

MULTI-WIRE METHOD

During the first half of the nineteenth-century, many devices were invented for applying Oersted's discovery to the telegraph. The French scientist André Marie Ampère built a telegraph which used twenty-six separate lines, each one representing a letter of the alphabet. Messages were sent along the wires by sending short "bursts" of current through the appropriate wires in succession, so that the message was spelled out letter by letter. At the receiving end, magnetic needles were suspended near the wires, and the movement of a needle showed when current was flowing through any particular wire.

In 1831, the famous American scientist Joseph Henry devised a single-wire telegraph in which the current passed through an electromagnet at the receiving end. As current flowed through the coils of the electromagnet, it activated the magnet which attracted a piece of iron attached to the striker of a bell. A current of electricity in the telegraph wire was thus detected as a ring on the bell, and by using a code it was possible to pass messages from source to receiver.

The first really practical telegraph system was built in England by Sir William Fothergill Cooke and Sir Charles Wheatstone. A demonstration was given by them on 25th July, 1837, messages being sent along a line between Euston and Camden Hill. This early telegraph system was so successful that it was installed along the Great Western Railway between Paddington and Slough.

SAMUEL MORSE

Meanwhile, the famous American inventor Samuel Morse had turned his attention to telegraphy in the United States. Morse was intrigued by the magnetic effect of an electric current, and saw that this could be used effectively for sending messages over long distances by wire. In order to simplify the sending and detecting of messages, Morse devised the famous code which bears his name. Each letter of the alphabet is represented by a pattern of long and short bursts of current.

Morse constructed an experimental telegraph in which the flow of current was controlled by using a spring-loaded switch or tapping key. At the receiving end, the currents passed through an electromagnet and stimulated movement in an iron core. These movements were traced out by a pencil on to a strip of paper that moved continuously through the receiver.

In the 18th century the Scottish physicist Charles Marshall worked out a new scheme for telegraphic communication, which became known as Marshall's electrostatic telegraph. Two places were connected by twenty-six insulated wires with pith balls attached to them. An electric charge was passed first down one wire then another, so that the pith balls oscillated over corresponding letters at the receiving end, enabling words to be spelled out. The idea was further developed by a Swiss physicist, Louis Lesage.

The pattern of dots and dashes, in the form of short and long bursts of current, were thus translated into wavy lines on the paper. These waves carried the message that had been sent along the wire.

DOTS AND DASHES

Let us look at the main parts of Morse's electric telegraph.

The *transmitter* contains a switch which, on lowering the key, completes an electric circuit (see Fig. 7). The *receiver* is fitted with an electromagnet whose coils carry a current supplied by batteries. A slip of iron called the keeper is in contact with the electromagnet. On the tip of the keeper is a nib, set over a moving strip of paper, on which it inscribes the dots and dashes. The *telegraph line* is of the familiar open-wire type with poles bearing glass or porcelain insulators around which the wires must pass.

When sending his message, the operator presses the transmitter key. The current immediately passes into the receiver and activates the electromagnet which in turn attracts the keeper and brings the nib into contact with the paper ribbon. If the operator makes an instantaneous signal—about one twenty-fourth of a second—contact is just sufficient to leave a dot on the paper; if he presses his key slightly longer—one eighth of a second—a dash is registered. As everyone knows, these dots and dashes are variously arranged to make those combinations known as the Morse alphabet (see Fig. 6). A return wire is not necessary, since the earth serves as the second conductor, the terminals being attached to metal plaques and earthed in damp soil both at the transmitting and receiving ends.

Smoke signals and heliograph, both ancient methods of telegraphy, paved the way to more up-to-date signalling. In 1792, *Claude Chappe invented an optical telegraph consisting of a tall mast with three signalling arms which could be moved into different positions from below. The light cross-arms, coloured to assist visibility, were operated by ropes and pulleys.*

The electric telegraph above depended on the use of magnetic needles. The needle on the face of the instrument at the receiving end was controlled by an electric current from a battery, the direction in which it pointed corresponding to the position of a similar needle on the transmitting instrument.

FIRST EXHIBITED

Morse exhibited his telegraph at the University of New York in 1835, and three years later he demonstrated it before President Martin Van Buren and the United States Cabinet. The telegraph created tremendous interest, and in March 1843, a Bill was passed which provided Samuel Morse with 30,000 dollars to be used in constructing a telegraph line between Washington and Baltimore. The first telegraph message was sent by Morse along this forty-mile wire on 24th May, 1844. It read, " What hath God wrought."

Morse incorporated in his telegraph a relay system which enabled him to use the telegraph over great distances. One of the problems involved in the successful development of the telegraph lay in the loss of current with increasing distance. After about fifteen or twenty miles, the current became so feeble that it could not easily be detected.

SERIES OF CIRCUITS

Morse overcame this difficulty by using a succession of short-distance circuits, each operated by its own battery. The currents in the first circuit passed through an electromagnet which operated the switch of the second one; this circuit then controlled the switch of the third circuit, and so on. A pattern of current sent out by the operator into the first circuit was thus handed on from one circuit to another, each circuit being sustained by its own battery, so that strength of current in the wire was maintained no matter how far the line was extended.

Although the Washington-Baltimore telegraph was a technical success, it failed to attract much business. In 1844, the U.S. Government withdrew its financial support, as it was decided that the telegraph service was not of sufficient practical value to be a commercial proposition.

In 1845, Morse organised a private company to extend

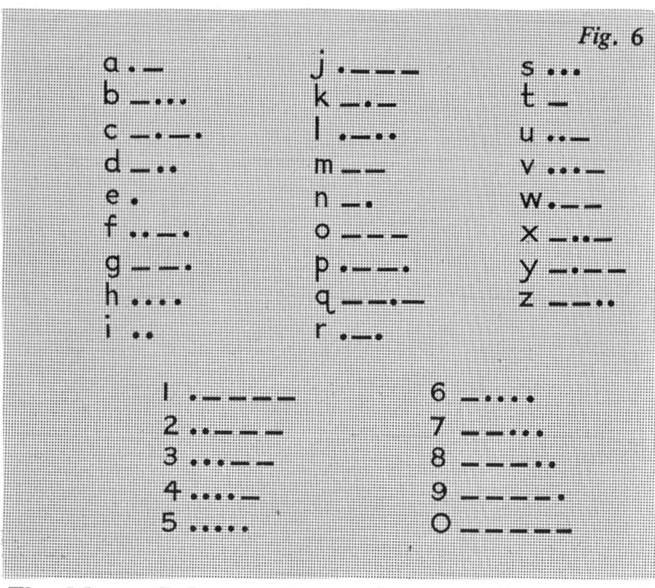

The Morse Code was first used on an Electromagnetic Telegraph, invented in 1837 by Samuel Morse. Dots and dashes, represented the letters of the alphabet and the numbers one to ten.

his telegraph to Philadelphia and New York. By 1851, the telegraph was all over the U.S., and during the next decade it established itself in Europe.

SIMPLIFIED TRANSMISSION

About ten years after the adoption of the Morse telegraph, Edward Hughes, an American physicist and engineer, found a way of using ordinary printed letters in place of dots and dashes. This meant that a message could be sent direct without translating it from Morse's code signs. Hughes's instrument, which is shown in Fig. 9, gained wide acceptance and was introduced in many European countries during the 1860's. If we look at the illustration, we can see that the table is fitted with what looks like the keyboard of a piano. These black and white keys, of which there are twenty-eight, form the transmitting manual.

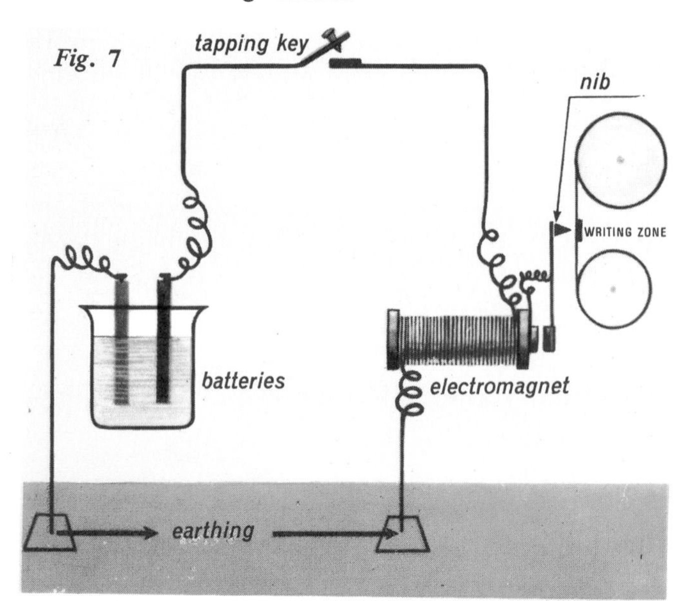

A serious objection to the early telegraph was the cost of installing wires. Steinheil suggested that existing railway lines might be used as one of the wires. Steinheil later showed how the earth itself could be used as a conductor.

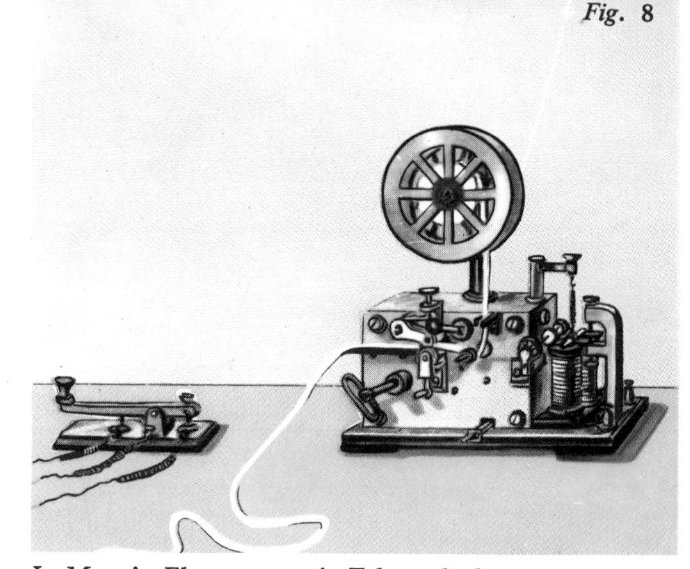

In Morse's Electromagnetic Telegraph the operator presses his tapping key, allowing an electric current to flow in the receiver circuit. As current flows through the electromagnet, a nib or marker is made to move over a ribbon.

France and England were joined by the first submarine telegraph cable in 1850. In 1857, an attempt was made to lay a cable across the Atlantic, but it broke at a depth of two and a half miles. A second attempt, in 1858, was successful, the telegraph operating for three months between Europe and America before the cable broke, and the line was abandoned.

TRANSATLANTIC CABLES

In 1866, the ship *Great Eastern* laid the first really successful cable across the Atlantic, and a second one was completed a few months later. These two cables carried all the transatlantic traffic until 1869, when a French cable was laid. Eighteen more cables were laid during the following sixty years.

The first transatlantic cable transmitted messages at the

Hughes' Telegraph was equipped with a set of twenty-eight keys, black and white. Electric current was controlled by operating the keys in such a way that the message was carried in the pattern of the current's flow.

The British vessel Agamemnon *and the United States vessel* Niagara *between them laid the first transatlantic cable from Ireland to Newfoundland in* 1857. (Right): *cross* (1) *and longitudinal* (2) *sections of the cable linking the two continents.*

rate of fifteen letters a minute. A modern cable can carry more than 2,000 letters a minute between London and New York.

Since the 1920's, the simple telegraph has been largely superseded by automatic devices. The message is typed out at the transmitting end using a keyboard similar to that of a typewriter. Each letter punches a characteristic pattern of holes into a strip of paper. This pattern of holes is converted into a pattern of electric impulses which is sent along the telegraph wire. Then, at the receiving end the teleprinter analyses the pattern and translates the succession of impulses into the letters they represent. The letters are then printed automatically on to a " ticker tape ". So a message " typed " at the transmitting end of the telegraph is reproduced almost instantaneously at the receiving end.

WORLD-WIDE USE

In spite of the changes and improvements which have taken place in the last hundred years, the simple telegraph is still in operation all over the world. The very simplicity of the telegraph makes for cheapness and reliability, and it provides a communications system which serves admirably in innumerable ways.

The development of the telegraph had an immense effect on world affairs. The movement of an electric current through a wire is transmitted over tremendous distances in a fraction of a second. Messages which previously took days or even weeks to get from one part of the world to another were now transmitted in a matter of seconds. People knew of important events almost as they happened, and the tempo of political and economic life was speeded up.

The telegraph, however, was limited in its scope. It carried messages, but could hardly support a conversation or discussion. Inevitably, inventors asked themselves whether it might not be possible to go a step further, and use these electric currents passing through wires for the transmission of human speech itself. Could not a pattern of sound waves be translated into a pattern of electric impulses, sent along a wire, and used for re-creating the pattern of sound waves again at the receiving end?

This problem was solved with the invention of the telephone.

The application of telegraphy has saved innumerable lives. Radio telegraphy, in particular, has made it possible for ships at sea to call for help when danger threatens.

LEONARDO DA VINCI

Leonardo da Vinci was born at Vinci, in the year 1452.

Among the many historic paintings hanging in the galleries of the Louvre in Paris is one of the greatest art treasures of all time. It is the " Mona Lisa ", and it was painted by a man who was probably the most versatile genius that ever lived; Leonardo da Vinci.

Leonardo da Vinci, who lived some 450 years ago, is remembered to-day very largely as the superb painter whose works of art are admired throughout the world. Every year, thousands of people gaze in wonderment at Leonardo's painting of the "Last Supper" on the wall of the refectory of Sta. Maria delle Grazie in Milan. This fabulous work of genius has survived for more than four centuries, and has been restored at least four times.

EXISTING PAINTINGS

Many of Leonardo da Vinci's paintings have been destroyed or lost. But authentic works can be seen in galleries in many countries. In Florence, Italy, there are the " Adoration of the Kings " and " Annunciation ", and parts of Verrocchio's " Baptism "; in Milan, apart from the " Last Supper ", there is the decoration of the Sala delle Asse, which was painted in 1498, and the " Portrait of a Musician "; in the Vatican, Rome, there is " St. Jerome ".

Other works by Leonardo to be seen outside Italy are " St. John the Baptist ", " Virgin of the Rocks ", " Madonna with St. Anne ", and " Portrait of Mona Lisa " in the Louvre, Paris; " Madonna Benois " in Leningrad, and " Portrait of Cecilia Gallerani " in Cracow; a later version of " Virgin of the Rocks " in the National Gallery, and " Madonna with St. Anne " at Burlington House, London; in Vienna, there is "Portrait of Ginevra de' Benci".

Apart from these authentic works there are other paintings which may have been done by Leonardo, but about which there is some doubt. A great number of Leonardo's drawings are in Windsor Castle.

INCREDIBLE VERSATILITY

If Leonardo da Vinci had done nothing more than produce his paintings and drawings, he would have gone down in history as one of the world's great men. But art was only one of his interests and accomplishments. Leonardo was interested in almost every aspect of human activity. He was a philosopher and scientist no less than a superb craftsman; he was a sculptor and an architect, an astronomer and mathematician, a botanist and zoologist, an anatomist and physiologist, a geologist and physicist, a meteorologist and engineer. Leonardo did not merely dabble in each one of this great range of interests. His penetrating mind and original ideas have left their mark on all of them to this

Mona Lisa del Gioconda inspired Leonardo to paint the picture which everybody knows by the name of the "La Gioconda."

*LEONARDO DA VINCI—The Virgin of the Rocks—
National Museum of the Louvre (Photo Alinari).*

A pupil being introduced to Andrea del Verrocchio, an expert in all forms of art, who had a studio in Florence.

day. He was one of the thinkers who laid the foundations of many fields of modern science.

Leonardo da Vinci was born on 15th April, 1452, near the town of Vinci in Tuscany. He was the son of Piero da Vinci, a lawyer, and a peasant woman called Caterina. Leonardo showed a great interest in art even when a young man, and he was apprenticed to a painter and sculptor Andrea del Verrocchio in Florence. Leonardo was greatly influenced by Verrochio, who was a highly skilled, hard working and determined man. From Verrocchio, Leonardo acquired the habit of painstaking investigation of any new subject that came his way. Verrocchio had a lively curiosity, and was interested in a wide range of technical and scientific subjects outside his artistic environment. Encouraged by his master, Leonardo began to study geometry, and persuaded his friends to help him learn mathematics. For Leonardo had had almost no formal education and everything he tackled had to be learned from the very beginning.

During his time in Florence, Leonardo came into contact with Benedetto Aritmetico, a well-known business man and scholar. Through Aritmetico, Leonardo became interested in engineering, and began to design and build machines. He devised labour-saving tools, including machines for grinding and turning, and built them with his own hands to make sure that they would work.

This interest in engineering led, in turn, to a desire to find out more about the principles upon which instruments and machines are based. So Leonardo began to study physics. And physics led him to think about the natural laws that appeared to govern the behaviour of all material things, including the stars and other bodies in the universe.

Leonardo tried to measure the positions of the stars, and follow their apparent movements in the heavens. He was hampered in his researches by a lack of even the most primitive of instruments, so he borrowed some and made others for himself. He needed a device for measuring time, so he built a water clock and also a clock that worked with the aid of compressed air.

ENGINES OF WAR

The end of the fifteenth-century was a time of conspiracy and rebellion in the land we now know as Italy. Leonardo da Vinci, living in Florence, found himself caught up in the fighting and warfare, and became interested in the engineering aspects of the military art. To Leonardo, it was not the fighting itself which appealed, but the opportunity to explore and develop a new field in which his original thought could play a part. He designed a great variety of weapons, including multi-barrelled guns, and special carriages that would enable the soldiers to move their heavy equipment with greater ease. He planned all manner of devices that could be used in siege warfare, including an enormous wheel attached to a flail-like mechanism that would prevent ladders being placed against the walls of a beleaguered fortress.

BOMBS, GRENADES AND SHELLS

Leonardo made plans for lightweight bridges which could be carried in pieces by the army and erected quickly and easily as needed. He devised a spherical projectile that

On 6th September, 1499, the French Army entered the city of Milan. After eleven days of fighting, the French occupied the castle, which had already been abandoned by Ludovic the Moor and by the Court.

Duke Valentino was at that time busy with the campaigns in the Romagna. Leonardo designed war machines and fortifications which would facilitate Borgia's conquest of the Romagna. He also directed the work on the Cesenatico aqueduct.

would burst like a bomb, and recommended that it could be made more effective by filling it with pieces of sulphur; this, he said, would produce fumes as the bomb burst. He designed fuses which would make a projectile explode on impact, and suggested firing explosive shells from heavy guns. Shells of this sort with a metal container would produce a rain of metal pieces as they exploded.

Leonardo's enthusiasm for military engineering stemmed from the sheer interest of being able to apply his inventive brain to this new field. If fighting was to be done, then Leonardo was out to make it as efficient and as effective as possible. In the hundreds of sketches which he made, he suggested all manner of devices which were to be used with such deadly results centuries after his time. Leonardo's mortars and bombs, his shells and gas generators, his shrapnel devices and hand-grenades were the prototypes of those which came into use during the nineteenth- and twentieth-centuries. He even devised an armoured vehicle propelled by eight men turning cranks; this could have introduced the tank into warfare more than four centuries before it actually appeared.

STUDY OF LIGHT

In the course of his artistic work, Leonardo studied perspective, and in typical fashion was carried from this to an investigation of the principles that lay behind it. He wondered about the phenomenon of light itself, and carried out experiments in the science we now call optics.

In Leonardo's day, the old Greek ideas on light were still accepted. Plato had suggested that light was something which emanated from the eye and was then returned to the eye by the object that was seen. Leonardo's experiments convinced him that these ancient theories were incorrect. He allowed light to pass through a small hole in a piece of paper and fall on to a white wall. And he observed that the rays of light appeared to travel in straight lines from the source. He went a stage further, and built a box with a small hole in one wall. He found that an inverted image of the scene at which the hole was directed was thrown on to the opposite wall. He then fitted a glass lens over the hole to give a stronger light.

This device was the camera obscura, which was the forerunner of the modern camera. If Leonardo had known of a way of preserving the image thrown on the rear of the box, he would no doubt have invented photography.

INDUSTRIAL MACHINERY

At one time or another, Leonardo turned his hand to the design of machinery for all manner of trades and industries. He designed looms and other machines for the manufacture of textiles, working out in his mind devices identical with those which were to come into practical use in England during the eighteenth-century. He invented a machine for making rope, and designed rolling mills for iron and steel.

Leonardo was employed by the Venetians as a maker of guns in their struggles with the Turks. As usual, his restless mind probed far beyond the limits of the work in hand. He announced to the Venetians that he had devised an apparatus which would enable the Venetians to approach the Turkish ships under water and sink them.

Leonardo's idea was a forerunner of the modern diving

Leonardo moved to the Court of Ludovic the Moor in Milan. "I shall always be proud of being Leonardo da Vinci, a Florentine," he wrote in his notes, before leaving Florence.

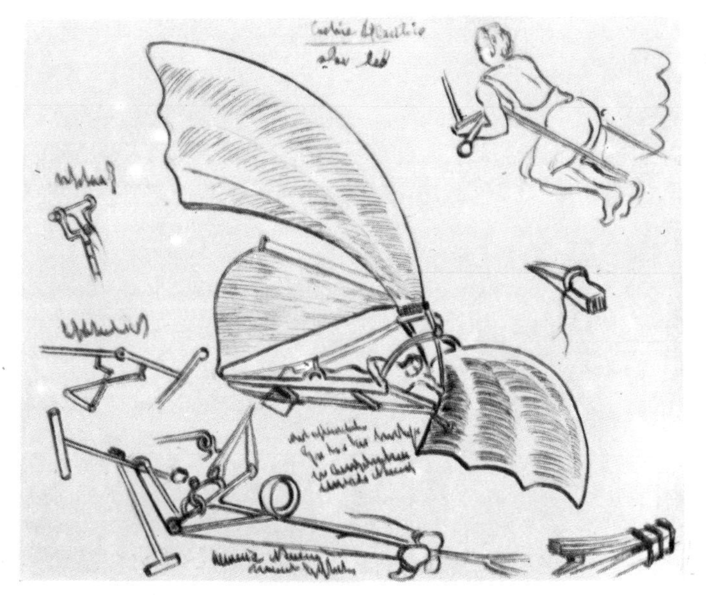

Leonardo da Vinci studied the practical possibilities of flight; here are some of his "sketches" for wings and flying machines.

dress. It consisted of a suit of plate armour, to which air would be supplied from an inflated bladder. Leonardo calculated he could supply a diver with enough air to last four hours, and worked out a plan that would enable a number of divers to destroy the Turkish fleet.

FLYING MACHINES

Perhaps the most remarkable of all Leonardo's scientific interests lay in his attempts to design a flying machine. To the people of the market place in Florence, Leonardo was a familiar figure. Regularly, he would make his way to the bird-seller's stand and purchase one of the small caged birds, only to set it free and watch it as it flew away. Leonardo had become fascinated by the manner in which birds were able to support themselves in the air. He wondered if human beings could do the same, and in his painstaking way he studied the movements and actions of the birds.

Leonardo dreamed of being able to build a machine in which a man could sit and fly by making artificial wings beat like those of a bird. He realised that there was a fundamental law which operated with respect to movement of a body through the air; an object exerts the same force against the air as the air against the object.

Leonardo carried out experiments which, he hoped, would enable him to design a machine that could lift a man into the air. He built experimental wings and tested their lifting powers. On the strength of his observations, Leonardo then designed aircraft in which a man was strapped to a framework, and operated wings by movement of his arms and legs. Then he introduced handles and cranks, and fitted rudders.

Leonardo followed up these early designs with others, in which the structure was supported on the flier's shoulders; the wings were operated by levers and stirrups. The wings themselves were designed on the basis of the wings of birds, with feathers attached to fabric which was stretched between the ribs. But Leonardo then concluded that feathers were not necessary, and decided that the wings should be modelled on those of the bat, with flexible material stretched between a supporting framework.

WINGS, PARACHUTE AND PROPELLER

A third type of flying machine then followed, in which the flier stood in a wooden harness and operated the wings by pedalling. The wings had spans of about eighty feet and the body of the machine was 40 feet wide and 10 feet high.

This flying machine, conceived by Leonardo da Vinci, was actually built. It was a forerunner of the helicopter.

Leonardo considered the danger involved in testing flying machines of this sort, and proposed that experiments should be carried out over water. But he then decided that a flier could best protect himself by letting himself fall beneath a tent roof of linen which would bring him quietly to the ground. He had invented the parachute some 200 years before the first one was put to the test.

Leonardo never reached the point of constructing a flying machine, as he realised that he needed a source of mechanical power to make it a practical proposition. He went so far as to devise a propeller that would make a machine to pull itself through the air. But four centuries were to pass before the invention of the internal combustion engine was to provide the power that would transform Leonardo's dreams into reality.

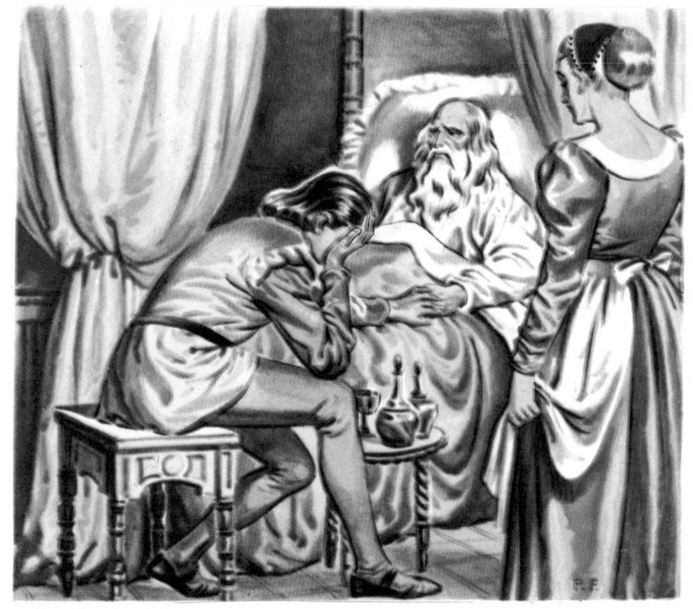

On the 2nd of May, 1519, *Leonardo da Vinci, the versatile genius who influenced many branches of science and art, died peacefully at Amboise, attended by his faithful disciple, Francesco Melzi.*

TAMING THE SCIENTIFIC SHREW

Deep down in the earth of Derbyshire and Cumberland there is a blue-green mineral called fluorspar. For years we have used it in making metals and glass, and fluorspar has been mined to meet a steady but limited demand. To-day, fluorspar has become a mineral with an exciting new future before it; for it is a source of the strange element fluorine.

During the war, a hundred thousand people took part in the most intensive research in history, and, at a cost of over five hundred million pounds, they gave us atomic energy. There were few fields of science that did not benefit from the research that made the atom bomb possible, and one indirect result of the work was to give industry an entirely unique raw material in fluorine.

To purify the uranium needed in the bomb, the metal was converted into one of its chemical compounds—the hexa-fluoride. And for this, large quantities of the element flourine were required.

ISOLATION DIFFICULTIES

But fluorine is a firebrand amongst the elements on earth —it is the most reactive element known. Before the war it had been isolated only with difficulty in the laboratory, for it would react immediately with the material of the apparatus in which it had been made. Steel, for example, will burn brilliantly in fluorine, and so will gold or glass.

Fluorine is a yellow gas that is related chemically to the chlorine that drifted over No Man's Land during World War I, but its corrosive powers are very much greater.

Using special platinum apparatus with stoppers made from fluorspar, chemists had made small quantities of fluorine before World War II. But little was known about it, and the prospect of making flourine in quantity for industrial use would not have been considered.

In wartime, nothing is impossible. Fluorine was needed for the atomic energy project, so a way of handling it had to be devised. By the end of the war, fluorine was being manufactured at the rate of several tons a day. It had become a new raw material for our post-war chemical age.

Measured against the atomic energy project as a whole, this was only a minor part of the total effort that produced the bomb. Yet it was a major industrial and scientific achievement in its own right.

Just as fluorine is anxious to unite chemically with anything that comes along, so is it reluctant to relinquish an established chemical grip. Fluorine-containing substances are extremely stable and inert. They resist all forms of decomposition and become entirely bovine in their chemical temperament.

By incorporating fluorine in the molecular structure of everyday materials, therefore, we can develop in them a tremendous resistance to the corrosion and degradation caused by heat, atmospheric and other influences.

INDUSTRIAL USES

The chemical industry has made use of this restraining influence of fluorine in many ways. One of the first commercial fluorinated materials was an entirely new class of synthetic chemicals called Freons. These are fluorine-containing liquids that are absolutely stable and inert under normal conditions. Where ordinary lubricating oils, for example, will carbonise and char under the effects of high temperature in a motor-car engine, the Freons are unaffected. Heat does not worry them.

Wherever liquids are needed to carry heat from one place to another, Freons are being used. In refrigerators and ice-plants, they act as the heat-exchange liquids that carry the heat from inside the refrigerator. They can go on doing this indefinitely without decomposing or clogging up the works, and without corroding any of the materials in which they flow. And they are entirely non-inflammable.

FLUORINE AND PLASTICS

In plastics, fluorine is also playing a most important role. Plastics are inherently susceptible to the effects of temperature; they are mostly organic materials whose chemical structure is based on the element carbon. And like other organic substances they will decompose and burn when they are strongly heated in air.

But, by including fluorine in the molecular structure of plastics, we can bring to them the inertness of substances like glass or stone. Their susceptibility to heat just disappears.

A number of these fluorine-containing plastics are now manufactured. One of the first was the plastic known as Fluon. As a plastic, Fluon was a complete breakaway from anything seen before. Chemically, it is as inert and unchanging as a brick; and yet it can be moulded into complex shapes.

Nothing has been found that will dissolve Fluon. Even aqua regia, the acid that dissolves gold and platinum has no effect on this amazing plastic. Nor does heat worry it. Gaskets made from it have kept their shape and properties after many months at temperatures as high as 315°C. Fluon is also tough and strong, and is an excellent insulator against the high-frequency currents used in modern electronic industries.

With properties like these behind them, Fluon and other fluorine-containing plastics are finding a ready market. Radio, television and radar were waiting for materials such as these; and there is a crying need for them in the chemical and engineering industries.

Fluorine plastics are finding many uses in modern developments such as jet- and rocket-propulsion. For there are few plastics that can withstand the high temperatures involved.

FURTHER DEVELOPMENT

At present, fluorine development is still in an experimental stage, and it will be many years before its industrial possibilities have been thoroughly explored.

One of the most exciting jobs for which flourine itself will be used is in the propulsion of space rockets. Fluorine can replace liquid oxygen as one of the constituents in a rocket propellant system.

Liquid fluorine is a dangerous material which must be stored at temperatures below −180°C., but techniques have now been developed which have made its use as a rocket propellant a practical proposition.

STARS AND CONSTELLATIONS

Long ago, when men first took an interest in the night sky, they imagined all sorts of pictures up among the stars. The stars in one particular part of the sky, for example, seemed to outline the front part of a charging bull, whilst those in another part roughly outlined a great bear. The fact that in many places the stars failed to outline anything at all did not worry these early star-gazers. They just filled in the vacant places with other things not minding how badly those things fitted the stars. In this way there arose the *constellation figures,* a curious collection of figures of the imagination which ranged from gods, goddesses, heroes and animals to things like a crown, harp, pair of scales . . . and so on.

For the priests and wise men of early times these figures helped to make the sky a more friendly and familiar place. To-day, astronomers do not worry at all about the actual figures themselves, but they still group the stars into constellations. This is done more for convenience than anything else, but a beginner will find a knowledge of some of the main constellation figures most helpful in finding his way among the stars. The seven brightest stars in Orion, for example, strongly suggest the figure of Orion, the Hunter, while the stars of Taurus, the Bull, do outline a bull's head and shoulders. In another part of the sky several stars fit in quite nicely to the figure Cygnus, the Swan: the five brightest form the Northern Cross, but this is just a star pattern in the constellation of Cygnus. In the same way the seven stars of the familiar Plough, or Big Dipper, really belong to the constellation of the Great Bear—the Plough itself is not a constellation.

The Zodiac is an imaginary band, divided into 12 *sections, encircling the celestial sphere.*

THE ZODIAC

Most of the present constellation figures appear to have been invented by the Greeks, but twelve of them at least are probably very much older. These are the twelve constellations of the *zodiac*; a fairly narrow band or belt in the sky in which move the sun, moon and planets. These twelve are in the order: Aries (the Ram), Taurus (the Bull), Gemini (the Twins), Cancer (the Crab), Leo (the Lion), Virgo (the Virgin), Libra (the Scales), Scorpio (the Scorpion), Sagittarius (the Archer), Capricornus (the Goat), Aquarius (the Water Carrier) and Pisces (the Fishes).

Orion, hunter of the heavens, in combat with the wild bull.

In early times wise men thought that the sun, moon and planets were gods and goddesses and they therefore worshipped them. It was important, they thought, to keep track of these deities as they wandered among the stars in the zodiac, for by so doing it might be possible to predict future events on the Earth. In brief, early star-gazers were usually astrologers, who thought that the sun, moon, planets and the twelve constellations of the zodiac had some magical influence on mankind. There are even people who think along similar lines to-day: they draw up horoscopes and pretend to foretell the future. We now know, of course, that the zodiac has no magical properties.

BRIGHT STARS

Besides being grouped into constellations the brightest stars have been given names. Most of these names are Arabic in origin, but a few are Greek. One star, at least, is very well known. This is Polaris, the North Pole Star. Throughout any one night this star seems to stay in the same place. As seen from London it indicates the direction of north, being fairly high above the northern horizon. The

Earth's axis points almost directly towards this star, and as we are carried round by the spinning Earth, the other stars appear to us to travel slowly about the Pole Star.

The actual point of pivot of northern skies is called the *North Celestial Pole.* The North Pole Star is about one degree away from this point; like the other stars it therefore appears to move during the night, but by a very small amount. The altitude or angular height above the northern horizon of the North Celestial Pole is equal to the latitude of the place of observation. It therefore follows that the altitude of the North Pole Star is roughly equal to the latitude, so that when seen from London this star is about 51½ degrees above the northern horizon. In southern skies the stars appear to move about the *South Celestial Pole* (or point towards which the southern end of the Earth's axis is directed), but there is no bright South Pole Star near this southern point.

ASTRONOMIC DISTANCES

In early times it was thought that all the stars were at the same distance from the Earth. We now know that they are at different distances, all immensely great by earthly standards. We also know that the stars are suns, and that our sun, as a star, is quite average in its size, temperature and brightness. Yet so far away are the other suns that each one appears as a tiny point of light when we look at it through even a powerful telescope. Each one shines by changing its own material into light and heat by an atomic reaction process. A star is, therefore, a vast atomic power-station in the form of a great ball of intensely hot gas. Even the sun, in order to maintain its vast output of light and heat consumes itself at the fantastic rate of four million tons a second. Yet so vast is the sun in both size and quantity of material that this process can go on for millions of years without there being any perceptible change in its appearance.

The sun is about 93 million miles away, but the next nearest star, one called *Proxima Centauri* and located in southern skies, is 26 million million miles away. These numbers are so large that they mean very little. Astronomers therefore use as the unit of distance not the mile but the *light-year.* A light-year is the distance which light travels in a year. Light travels at a speed of approximately 186,000 miles a second, and therefore in a year covers a distance of 6 million million miles. Proxima Centauri is just over 4 light-years away; we therefore see it not as it is but as it was over 4 years ago. If we could travel to the moon in 2½ hours we should be able to reach the sun in just over 5 weeks, but the journey to Proxima Centauri at this rate of travel would take about 30,000 years!

OTHER SUNS

The stars are not only at different distances from us but they also differ among themselves in size, temperature, and actual brightness. Although in volume the sun is about a million times larger than the Earth, it is a mere dwarf compared with some stars and yet a giant compared with others. Some stars could easily contain the entire path or orbit of the Earth whilst others are only a few thousand times larger than the Earth. Extremely hot stars like Rigel and Regulus shine with a bluish light. Others, like the sun and Capella with surface temperatures about 6,000° C., are yellowish, while cooler stars, like Betelgeuze and Aldebaran, are reddish in colour. The actual brightness of the sun, compared with that of some stars, is like that of a glow-worm compared with a searchlight. The star Canopus, for example, is considered by some astronomers to be 80,000 times brighter than the sun. If we replaced the sun by this star all life on the Earth would be shrivelled up and the Earth itself would disappear in a cloud of gas. On the other hand, there are stars which have only about one-thousandth of the sun's brightness, and one, called Wolf 359, is thought to be only one two-millionth as bright as the sun.

Although the telescope shows the stars as points of light, it enables us to see many more stars than with the naked eye alone. On a clear night we can see about 2,000 to 3,000 stars, but even a pair of binoculars will reveal thousands more. The Milky Way, for example, consists of millions of stars, but they are all so far away that unless we use a telescope we cannot see the individual stars. Of course, if a star appears very faint it does not follow at once that it is extremely distant—it might be a comparatively near but faint neighbour of the sun. The great majority of faint stars are, however, very distant, and the light from those in the Milky Way can take as long as thousands and tens of thousands of years to reach us.

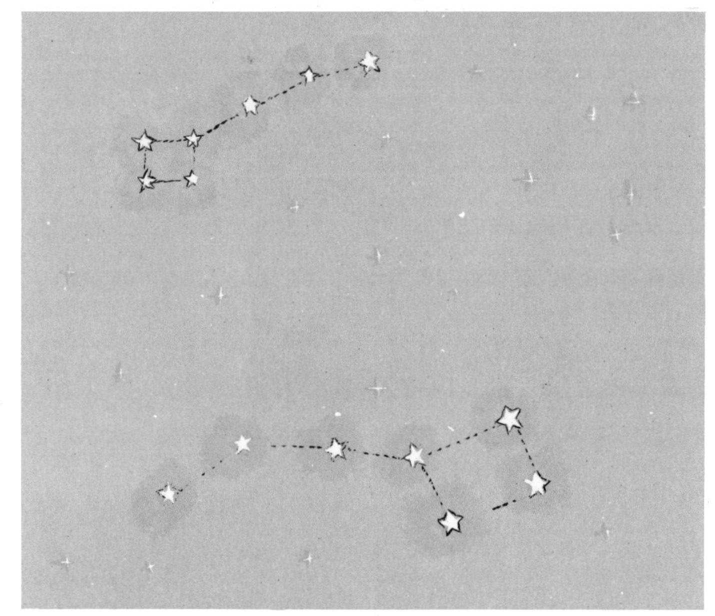

Above: *the Little Bear.* Below: *the Great Bear.*

Well known in the Northern sky is the Great Bear.

METHANE GAS

For many centuries the only form of power available to Man was his own muscular strength and that of his domestic animals. Man himself had to perform many of the heavy tasks of everyday life. But as time went on he learned to draw on the sources of power provided by nature; he used sails to harness the wind and push his boats along. Then he found that the water of fast-flowing streams could turn his mill wheels. But it was not until comparatively recent times that Man learned how to tap the power that was available to him in the form of fuels.

The discovery of new sources of power and the construction of power-driven machines have freed Man from many of his past labours. The steam engine, the internal combustion engine and the electric motor have now become indispensable to modern progress and, in the course of less than a hundred years, have changed the lives of all who live in civilised countries. But just as human beings require food and nourishment so, too, does machinery need fuel. Every type of machine must be supplied with fuel to provide the energy that operates it.

Coal and oil are two of the most important fuels. But their distribution over the world's surface is irregular, and their cost weighs most heavily on those countries that must purchase them abroad. The fear that supplies may be cut off in times of emergency, or that sources may become exhausted, spur on the search for new sources of fuel. It is for this reason that methane gas has claimed increasing attention.

WHAT IS METHANE GAS?

Methane is a hydrocarbon, related chemically to petrol. But where petroleum is a dark and oily liquid, methane is a colourless and almost invisible gas. It is very widely distributed and is found in the most unexpected places; in marshes where organic matter lies rotting; in coal mines where it mixes with air to form fire-damp, a dangerous explosive; even in the intestines of human beings and animals. More practically, it is found in oil fields from which it escapes mixed with other natural gases and rises to the surface often in great quantities.

The origin of this most useful form of natural gas is bound up with that of petroleum oil, which was formed by the decomposition of organic matter, plants and marine life deposited millions of years ago on the sea-bed. The same slow chemical processes which formed petroleum have also formed methane gas, and the two substances are usually found together deep underground. The gas often oozes to the top and bursts into flame, shooting skywards in a pillar of fire. In ancient times these fires were considered sacred, especially in the Caucasus, which was then inhabited by the Persians who built temples nearby. In this respect, methane has been known since the earliest days of recorded history, Pliny himself having written of it as an inflammable gas which springs from the bowels of the earth.

This gas was at first mistaken for hydrogen, and it is to Volta that we owe the discovery of its true nature. In the year 1776, Volta decided to investigate the gas bubbles which rose from the mud along the reedy shores of Lake Maggiore. Having collected some of this gas in a glass vessel he was able to show that it was inflammable. He then considered the possibility of igniting it in a series of small explosions with the help of electric sparks. This idea bore fruit in Volta's invention of his famous " pistol ", which was an elementary application of the principle of the internal combustion engine. His experiments with " inflammable airs ", as he called them, contributed much to our early knowledge of this principle. Some thirty years later, in 1805, the chemical composition of methane gas was established.

HIGH HEAT AND ENERGY YIELD

The properties of methane gas render it a source of energy of great value. One great advantage is that it is found abundantly in a natural state. It burns with an extremely clean flame and has a heat potential of between nine and ten thousand calories per cubic metre. A cubic metre of this gas develops as much heat as rather more than 3 lb. of ordinary coal or 2 lb. of diesel oil. It leaves no deposit or residue.

Methane gas is used for domestic as well as industrial purposes. Its cost is low and the consumers do not have to provide storage space, as they do with coal or oil. The gas is fed into a complex grid system and is available at the turn

The ancient Persians built their temples over "sacred fires" whose flames were fed by natural methane gas.

of a tap. Used as fuel in thermo-electric power stations it will produce current at a lower price per kilowatt than is possible even in large hydro-electric plants. It serves instead of electricity or coal gas for domestic heating and cooking. When distributed in cylinders it provides a convenient fuel for caravans, camping, boats and places remote from towns. The motor car industry has developed vehicles which can use methane instead of petrol or diesel oil.

The uses of methane gas are not, however, limited to its function as a producer of power; it is also used in the manufacture of many chemical derivatives of great value to all branches of industry and agriculture. Thus methane provides a raw material for the production of fertilisers used in the cultivation of the soil, and for the manufacture of synthetic rubber. In addition, a wide variety of articles in common use are made with synthetic plastics derived from methane gas.

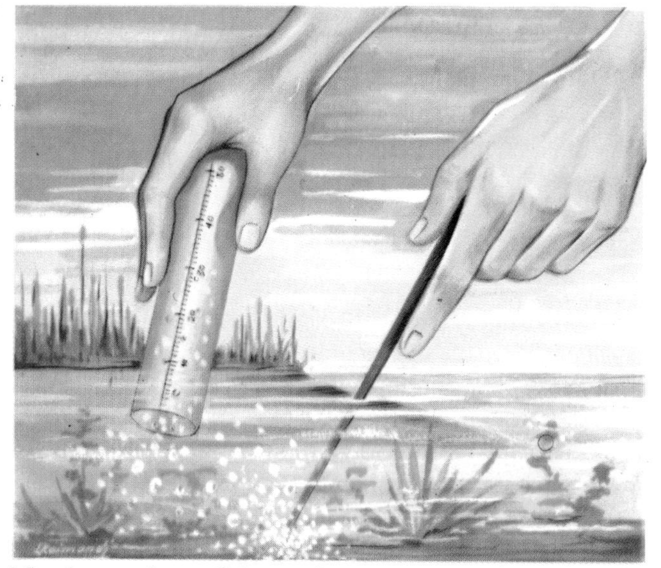

Marsh gas given off by rotting matter may be collected in this way.

PRODUCER COUNTRIES

Methane is therefore valuable both as a fuel and as a raw material. So much so that some countries, though rich in petrol and coal, have lately exploited their natural gas deposits to the utmost. In the United States, 120,000 million cubic metres are produced annually. This means that for every American citizen there are two cubic metres of this gas available every day. Over one-quarter of a million miles of piping provide for its distribution in America. The production of methane is well advanced in Canada, Mexico, Venezuela, North Africa, Russia, Borneo, Indonesia and more recently in Europe.

Although this gas is found in many parts of the world, it does not always occur in the same state of purity. Its composition varies from place to place, as, indeed, does the nature of its source. It is sometimes found in a pure state and at others mixed with water; it may also be extracted from mixtures of mud and other types of gas, or again from deposits in which it is found associated with raw petroleum.

Methane provides raw materials for the manufacture of plastics and other synthetic substances.

In some parts of Europe where coal is in short supply, great hopes have been placed in the exploitation of methane gas. First used for commercial purposes at the beginning of the century, its development was limited in the early stages to those districts where it rose naturally to the earth's surface. Methodical research did not begin until after the last war when modern techniques for surveying and boring made it possible to utilise untapped deposits. Large deposits have been found in Northern Italy, especially in the Po Valley where production is above fifteen million cubic metres per day, which is equivalent to a daily consumption of 22,000 tons of coal. The Netherlands and Great Britain are exploring the North Sea and have already found large deposits of gas which they are feeding into their distribution systems. It is estimated that by 1980 natural gas from the North Sea deposits will supply at least 20% of Britain's total energy requirements.

New techniques have been evolved for the storage and transportation of surplus production. The gas is liquefied under pressure and is transported in special tankers. The liquid can be stored in almost any sort of container and a specially ingenious type is constructed by excavating large holes and freezing the surrounding earth. Such a container, 130 ft. in diameter and 130 ft. deep, holds one day's supply for the whole of Britain.

The search for untapped deposits of methane will expand under the stimulus of the increasing demand for low cost energy as man's standards of living improve.

Rigs and drilling machinery of this type are used when boring for methane gas below the earth's surface.

THE CHEMICAL FUTURE OF COAL

All over the world atomic energy is taking over the job of producing electricity. Atoms of uranium and other fissionable elements are providing the heat that is needed for raising steam to drive the turbo-generators in the power stations.

Most of the world's electricity is produced in power stations which burn coal; and the intrusion of atomic energy into the electricity-generation industry is often regarded as a threat to the prosperity of the coal-mining industry.

In fact, nothing could be further from the truth. The coming of atomic energy, far from being a threat to coal, will give us an opportunity to use our coal to much better advantage than we have ever done before. Atomic energy, by taking over some of the power-production jobs from coal, will lift a burden from the back of the coal industry.

When we burn coal, we are releasing the sunshine energy that was absorbed by plants which grew when the world was young. This sunshine operated the living processes of the primeval plant, enabling it to turn the carbon dioxide of the air, and the water and minerals of the soil into the complex chemical substances of its tissues. The energy of the sunshine was packed away as chemical energy inside these substances. As the plants died the substances of their once-living matter formed a layer of material that became covered by rocks and sediments; the plant-residues were heated and compressed within the earth's crust, and they changed into the hard, black rock we know as coal.

RELEASING CHEMICAL ENERGY

The energy absorbed by the plants in those far-off days has remained as chemical energy in the substances forming coal. When we burn coal, we reverse the chemical process that took place inside the growing plants. The carbon of the chemicals in coal is united with the oxygen of the air to form carbon dioxide again; hydrogen in the coal chemicals unites with oxygen to form water, and in each case energy that was stored in the coal is released as heat.

Since the eighteenth-century, when the industrialisation of the western world really began, we have been using coal as our main source of heat. Thousands of millions of tons of coal have been burned, to provide heat for raising steam and providing the power we need. We have used coal because we have had no other way, until recently, of providing ourselves with the huge quantities of heat that we need. And there seemed to be no reason, in the early years of the Industrial Revolution, why we should not burn our coal in this way.

NEW PRODUCTS

But things have now changed. During the first half of our twentieth-century, we have built up a tremendous industry which is based upon the application of chemistry to the production of all sorts of products which have become familiar and essential materials in our modern world. We make synthetic fibres such as nylon and "Terylene," which have given us new fabrics and clothes; we make plastics, which are used for countless purposes, ranging from the production of vacuum cleaners and electric washers to motor-car bodies and boat hulls; we make synthetic fertilisers to feed our crops, and weedkillers and insecticides to protect them as they grow; we make drugs and medicinal chemicals to enable us to fight back against disease germs; we produce synthetic detergents and paints, rocket propellants and motor fuels. The list of these materials, all produced by the application of chemistry to industry, is virtually endless.

To make these synthetic chemical products, we need some sort of starting material which provides us with simple chemicals we can manipulate into the finished substance. And in many cases, we depend upon coal as the source of chemicals from which we start.

To release these chemicals from coal, distillation in a retort is necessary. This is what is done when coal is made into coke; the coal is heated in closed ovens or retorts, liquid and gaseous chemicals being distilled from the coal as it decomposes, and coke remaining as a residue in the retort. This gas is the familiar coal gas which is itself used as a fuel; the liquids include the viscous black coal tar which contains many different chemical raw materials.

DISTILLATION

By the distillation and chemical manipulation of these chemicals from coal, we provide ourselves with substances from which we make many of our modern chemical products. When we take an aspirin or a sulpha drug, we are consuming coal. When we buy a pair of nylons, we may be paying for chemicals that a miner has dug from the earth. When we drive a car, or watch a television set, or buy a new dress or suit made of certain yarns, we can do so because coal has provided the raw materials that made these things possible.

With so many jobs for coal to do for us in our scientific and industrial world, it is folly to waste coal as a fuel in the way we do. When we burn coal we are sending up the chimney a stream of vitamins and telephones, petrols and perfumes in return for a supply of heat.

As atomic energy takes over from coal in the world's power stations, we shall be able to use coal for the job it is best fitted to do. We shall use it as a chemical raw material instead of burning it as coal.

UNDERGROUND USE

To release these chemicals from coal, we may in the future use the earth itself as a ready-made retort by heating the coal as it lies in the seam underground, and bringing the gases and liquid chemicals to the surface through pipes.

This process of underground gasification of coal is developing rapidly in many parts of the world. In the process, air or oxygen is pumped into the coal seam, enabling a portion of the coal to burn underground. The heat from this burning coal decomposes the remaining coal and converts it to gases and liquid chemicals, which reach the surface through pipes let into the seam.

By this means, we can provide ourselves with raw materials from coal without having to go to all the trouble of digging out the coal itself, and we can make use of coal seams which are too narrow or too awkwardly situated to be worked by the usual means.

WHAT IS RADIO?

To get an idea of how radio programmes come into being, let us pay a brief visit to the broadcasting studios.

A musical programme is being broadcast at the moment. All the performers are assembled in the studios. There is a different studio for every kind of broadcast: a huge auditorium for the transmission of musical comedies, a smaller one for popular song programmes, and a third for plays. Even the announcer has his own little studio; and in each of these studios there is a small but vital instrument, the microphone. This is the starting point of the radio transmission. As well as the actual broadcasting studios, there are the staff offices and technical departments, all in the same building, which we can call Broadcasting House. A few miles outside the town is the actual transmitter with the transmitting aerial. The central Broadcasting House and the external transmitting aerial together form the transmitting station.

THE MICROPHONE

The studios are completely sealed off from one another and from the rest of the building, so as to avoid any interruption through unexpected and unwanted "noises off". To ensure this, the walls are covered with special soundproof panels. These absorb most of the sound waves and at the same time give a pleasantly mellow tone to the sounds that are transmitted. The microphone picks up these sounds and transforms the sound pattern into an electric current. This is called the *microphone current* and it contains an *electrical image* of the singer's voice and the accompanying orchestra. It consists of a continuous succession of electric current vibrations, identical in pattern with the sound waves that entered the microphone.

For a very elaborate broadcast, such as an opera, many microphones may be used.

The currents from each microphone are all drawn together to form a single current. At the point where they are blended, any one of them can be strengthened or weakened. Thus, at any moment, the technicians can give prominence to the voices or to the music, as they think necessary. That is the job of the mixer.

VALVES AND AMPLIFIERS

From the studio, the microphone current goes into the *central amplifying room.* There it is strongly reinforced by a number of electronic valves called amplifiers. The current passes through the valves in succession, gaining in strength as it passes from one to the other. The process is controlled by sound engineers who watch the needles on the many dials on the amplifying apparatus and listen to the sound reproduction from a loudspeaker or through headphones. When it leaves the central amplifying section, the microphone current, now much more powerful, travels along a special line to the transmitting station, or to the nearby transmitter.

CABLES

Sometimes the same programme is sent out by more than one station. In that case the microphone current is conveyed to the other transmitters by cables which connect the different radio stations to each other.

Before beginning a long journey along a transmission cable, the microphone current is suitably amplified. And again, after every 40 miles or so, it may be strengthened by line amplifiers. Even when the microphone current has just travelled from Broadcasting House to the transmitter, it still has to pass through more electronic amplifying valves before it is sent out into space. Again it goes from valve to valve gaining more power all the time. Finally, it emerges from the last amplifying valve and enters the aerial.

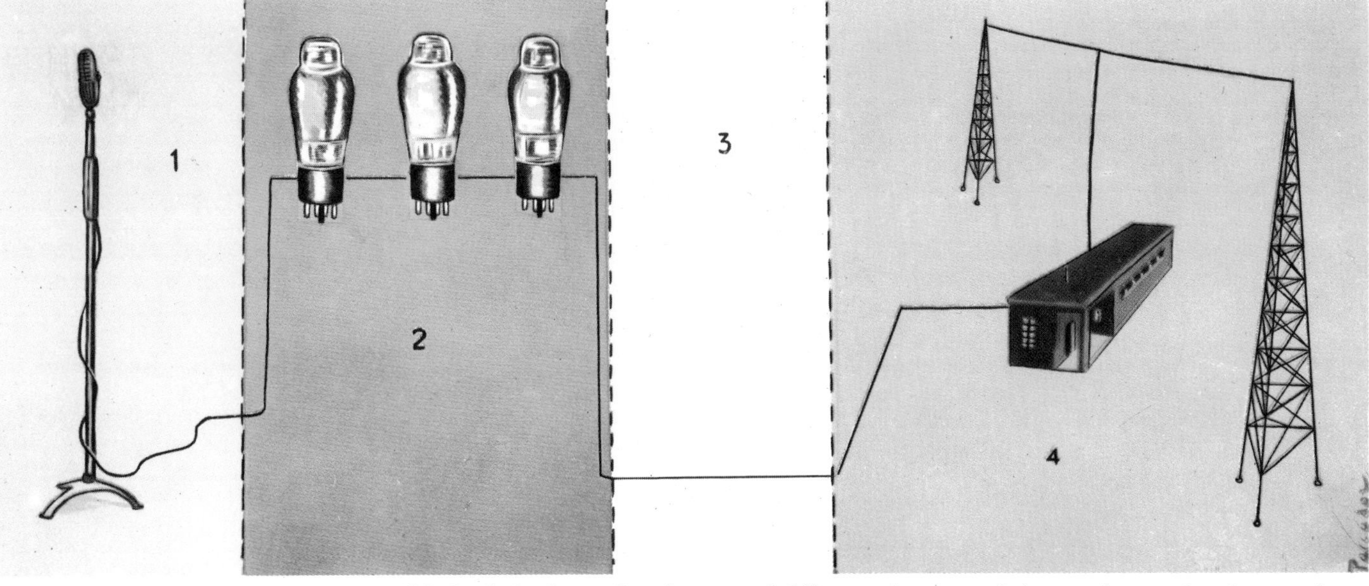

Current from the microphone is amplified. It is then taken by a special line to the transmitting station, or local transmitter. 1. the microphone; 2. the amplifying valves; 3. the line; 4. transmitting station.

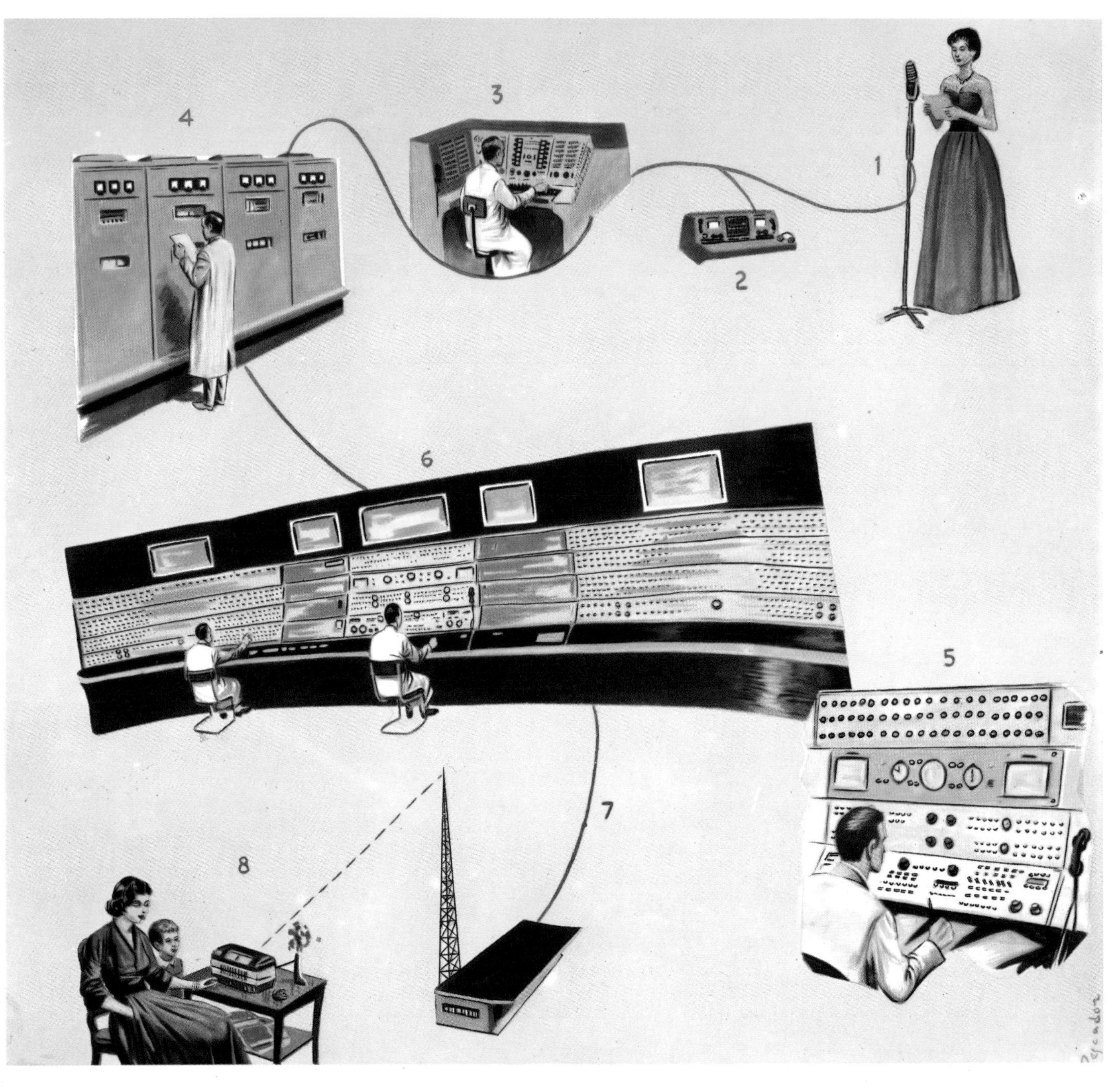

Broadcasting. This is a word meaning the dissemination of news to all men everywhere, but used to-day for the relaying of information by radio. Above is a more elaborate diagram of the stages involved in radio broadcasting. 1. *the microphone;* 2. *announcer's desk;* 3. *the mixer (voices and music);* 4. *central amplifying section where the current is amplified by a number of electronic valves;* 5. *and* 6. *sound engineers control the amplification;* 7. *line connecting Broadcasting House with the transmitting station;* 8. *the radio receiver.*

RADIO FREQUENCY CURRENT

Because the audio frequency is a relatively low frequency signal and because transmission of low frequency signals is a very inefficient process it has to be carried on a waveform transmission of a much higher frequency than itself. The carrier is termed a *radio frequency* or RF carrier, and it is produced by a device called an *oscillator* within a transmitter. The RF carrier can be of the order of thousands of Hertz per second (kilohertz) or millions of Hertz per second (megahertz). The term Hertz comes from the physicist Heinrich Hertz who propounded the theory of propagation of electromagnetic radiation.

The process of superimposing the audio signal (derived from the sound waves) on the carrier wave is known as *modulation*. The two modes of modulation in general use are *amplitude modulation* (AM) and *frequency modulation* (FM). When an RF carrier is amplitude modulated with audio information, additional frequencies are added to the existing frequency of the carrier waveform. These new frequencies are called *sideband frequencies*, and it is in these sidebands that the intelligence information is contained. An RF carrier by itself (unmodulated) does not carry information.

In frequency modulation the frequency of the carrier wave itself is caused to deviate from its constant value in proportion to the frequency of the modulating signal. This means that when an audio signal (converted from sound waves) is used to modulate a carrier through a microphone and audio amplifier, the deviations caused in the frequency of the carrier

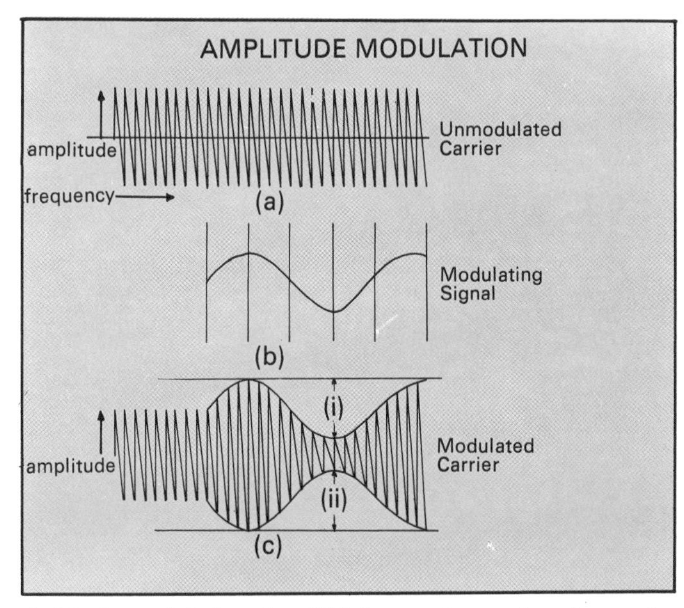

In (c) *the modulating signal* (b) *is superimposed on the carrier* (a). *Note that the amplitude of the carrier is increased due to the addition of the sidebands* (i) *and* (ii) *but its frequency remains constant.*

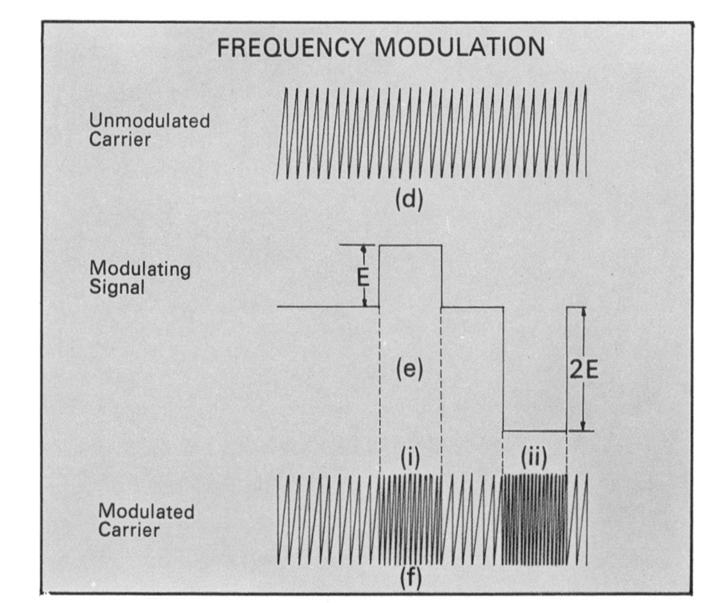

When the modulating signal (e) *is superimposed on* (d) *the amplitude of the carrier remains constant but the frequency changes. Note that the amount of frequency change increases,* (*i*) *and* (*ii*), *as the amplitude of the modulating signal increases.*

are equal to the frequencies of the sound waves entering the microphone and the degree of deviation is proportional to the loudness (volume) of the sound.

THE AERIAL

The transmitting aerial is very like the wire in an electric light bulb. One sends out rays of light and the other transmits radio waves. But light rays cannot penetrate the walls of a house nor travel farther than the horizon, whereas radio waves can travel round the world.

When these waves meet the aerial of any kind of receiving apparatus, they immediately stimulate vibrations of electric current which passes from the aerial to the radio set.

RECEIVERS

The currents generated by the incoming signals in the aerial are extremely weak. The receiver amplifies these signals and *detects* or *demodulates* them. This process consists of separating the modulated frequency from the carrier frequency in a rectifying device. The audio frequency is further amplified and applied to a loudspeaker. The loudspeaker converts the audio frequency waves into sound waves. Many transmitters are sending out signals which reach the aerial and the receiver employs tuning circuits to select the required signal. A very high degree of selectivity is achieved by a principle known as *heterodyning*. Receivers that use this principle are called *superheterodyne* receivers.

The valves in a common commercial receiver can be divided into the following groups: (1) the radio frequency amplifiers which boost the aerial current; (2) an oscillator and mixer valve which generates a local frequency signal and mixes it with the radio frequency signal to give an intermediate frequency signal; (3) amplifiers which boost the intermediate frequency signal (4) the detector or demodulator (5) the audio frequency amplifiers which boost the intelligence information prior to feeding it to the loudspeaker.

Present day radio receivers use *solid state* devices rather than thermionic valves. These are *semi-conductors* and they are normally poor conductors because they have very few free electrons to move about. *Germanium* is such a semi-conductor. If, however, other elements are infused into the Germanium, its ability to conduct is improved enormously. In semi-conductor techniques two types of material are used and these are known as N type which has a majority of *negatively charged carriers* (electrons) and P type which has a majority of *positively charged carriers*. If the two types are present in the same crystal a barrier or *junction* is formed between them.

If a battery is connected across the junction so that the negative terminal is connected to the N type and the positive terminal to the P type the junction is said to be *forward-biased* and the negative and positive charges will move towards each other and current will flow. If the terminals of the battery are reversed the positive and negative carriers are driven away from each other and no current flows across the junction. This is known as *reverse-biasing*.

The tuning knob tunes the set to the broadcasting station you want to hear by adjusting it so that it responds to the type of wave the station is transmitting.

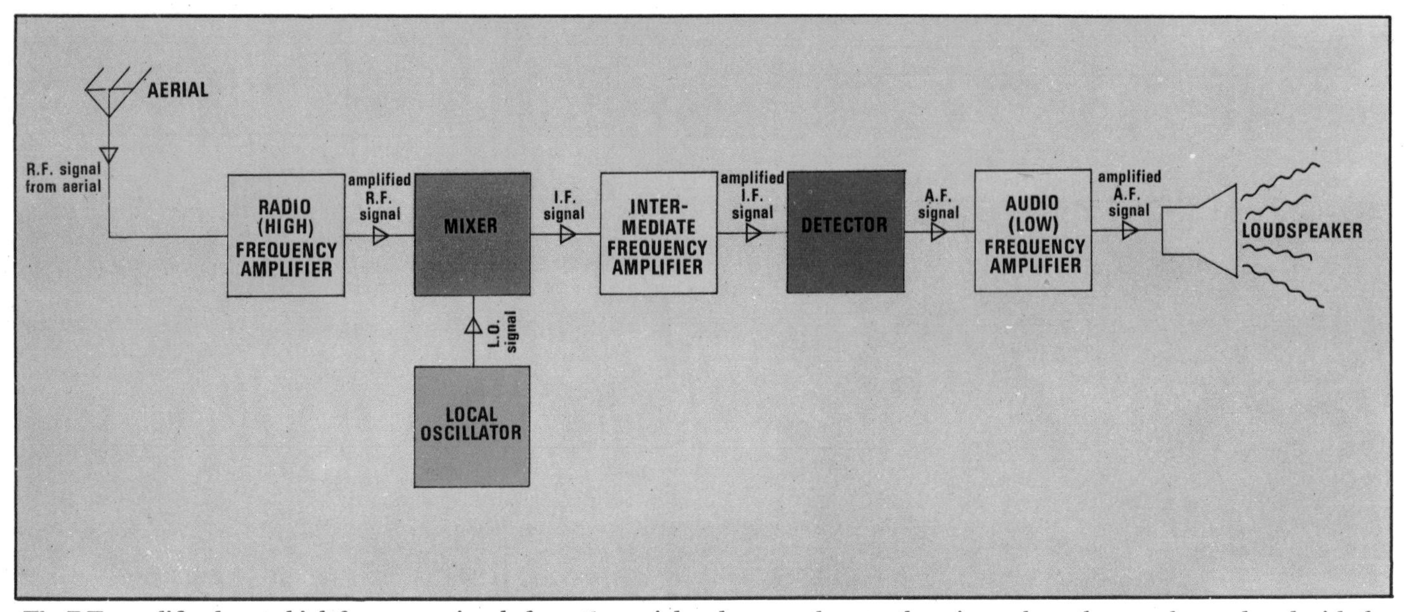

The RF *amplifier boosts high frequency signals from the aerial and passes them to the mixer where they are heterodyned with the local oscillator signal to produce an intermediate frequency signal* IF. *This is amplified by the* IF *amplifier and demodulated in the detector. The resultant low frequency* AF *signal is amplified by the* AF *amplifier and fed to the loudspeaker.*

If two PN junctions are joined at the N regions a *transistor* is formed. If now electrodes are attached to the three regions it becomes the equivalent of an amplifying valve. The three electrodes on a transistor are known as the *emitter*, the *base* and the *collector*. If batteries are connected across the emitter-base and collector-base wires in the manner previously stated, the emitter-base junction is forward-biased for current flow while the collector-base junction is biased for no-current flow. However, the base of a transistor is made extremely thin and when current flows in the emitter-base junction, the positive charges move across the base into the collector region and current flows from the emitter to the collector. The amount of current flow between emitter and collector can be controlled by varying the voltage connected to the base region.

Because the resistance to current flow is much greater between the base to collector than it is between the base and emitter, great gains in voltage or power are obtained. Semi-conductors are much more robust than valves, are more reliable, are very much smaller and need far less electrical power to operate them.

WAVE-LENGTHS

Most radio stations transmit on waves of medium wave-length. This range includes all the stations whose wave-lengths on the tuning-scale are somewhere between 200-580 metres. There are other ranges of wave-lengths; the long wave, between 1,000 and 2,000 metres, and the short wave, which ranges between about 12·5 and 25 metres.

TUNING THE SET

What happens inside a radio set when you turn the tuning knob? This knob puts the set in tune with the station you want to receive. It controls both the indicator on the tuning scale and a special selection mechanism called the variable

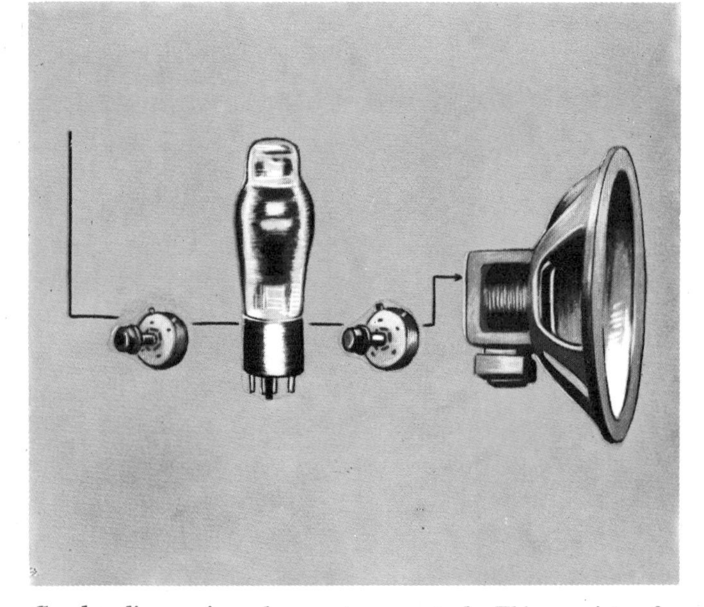

Good radio receivers have a tone-control. This consists of a rheostat, or variable resistance, worked by a knob on the front of the set.

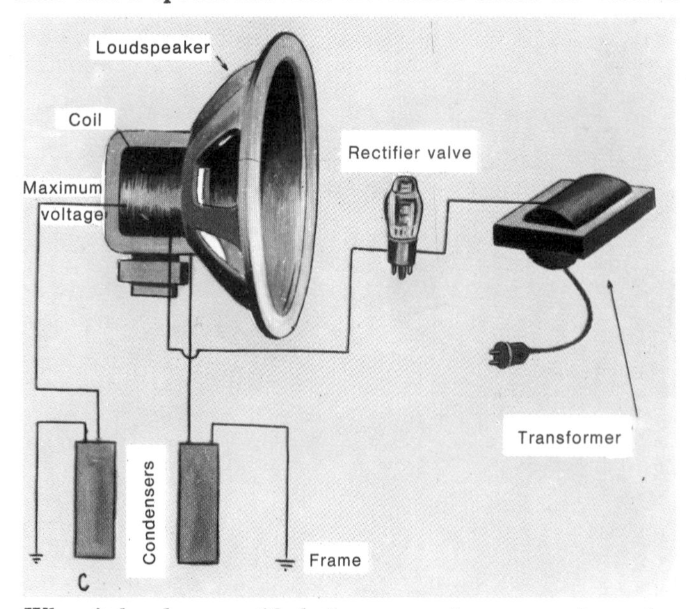

When it has been rectified, the current has to travel round a large magnet coil, which is wound round a cylindrical iron core. This coil and the two condensers at either end of it change it to direct current.

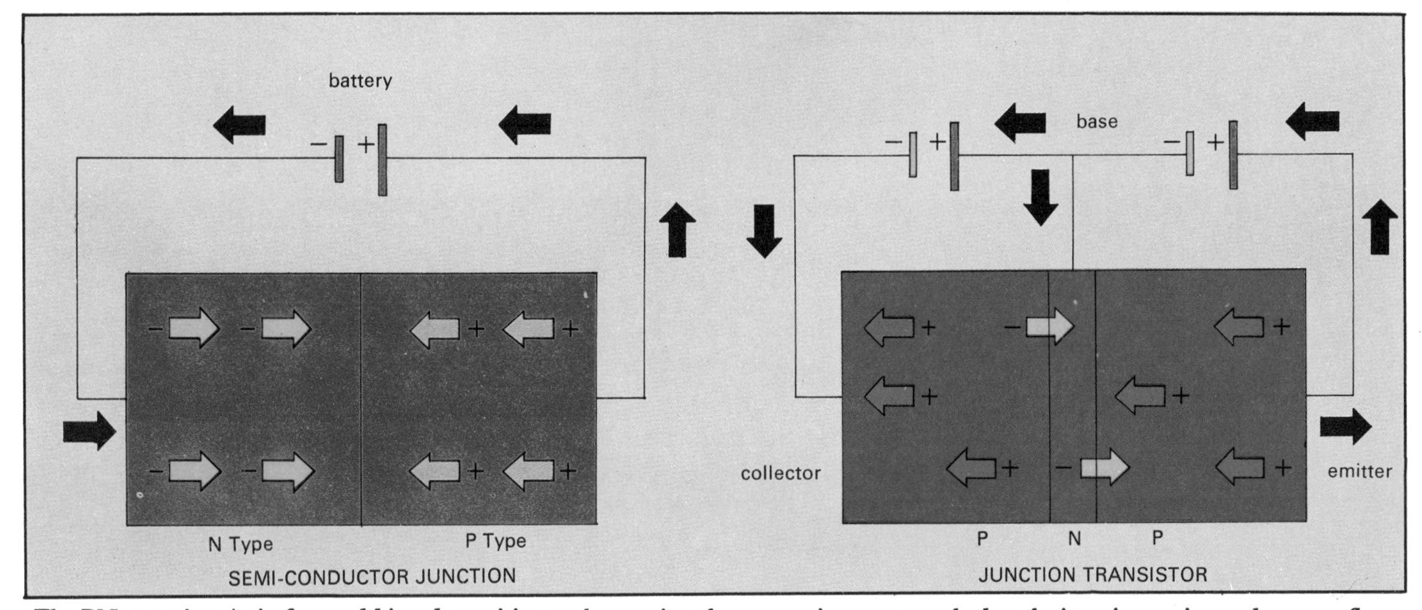

The PN *junction* A *is forward-biased; positive and negative charge carriers are attached to the junction region and current flows in the direction shown by arrows outside the semi-conductors. Although the collector-base junction in* B *is reverse-biased positive charge carriers migrate from the emitter to the collector and the electron flow is as shown in the external circuit.*

tuning condenser. If you look inside a radio set, you may see the metal plates in the condenser moving. The tuning of the set depends upon the position of these plates. Between the tuning knob and the movable plates of the variable tuning condenser is placed a device which, as well as moving the plates, also works the indicator on the tuning scale. There is a pulley on the wheel of the condenser connected by a small wire to the tuning knob and the indicator.

CONTROL KNOBS

In every radio you will find some sort of control mechanism by which the power can be regulated and the right volume of sound produced. This is connected to a knob on the front of the set and consists of a *rheostat*, or variable resistance, placed immediately before the last valves. It is called the *volume control*. Many sets also have a *tone control* which can vary the tonal quality of the sound reproduction. This too is a rheostat, controlled from outside by a knob.

THE LOUDSPEAKER

This consists of a big electromagnet and a paper cone with a little coil in the apex. Tone depends, among other things, on the amount of amplification produced by the valves and on the size of the loudspeaker. If you have a very small loudspeaker, the range of tone cannot vary much.

In order to adjust the radio receiver to one wave-length and reject other wave-lengths on the same wave-band we have the tuning indicator. It is another electronic valve, but this valve is placed on its side, so that the top of its glass bulb appears on the tuning dial. We see a glowing light behind the dial, and the smaller this light is, the more accurately the set is tuned. This little indicator is called the "magic eye".

The knob on the right is for volume control, that on the left for tone control; tuning knob is in the centre. A knob at the side controls the choice of wavelengths.

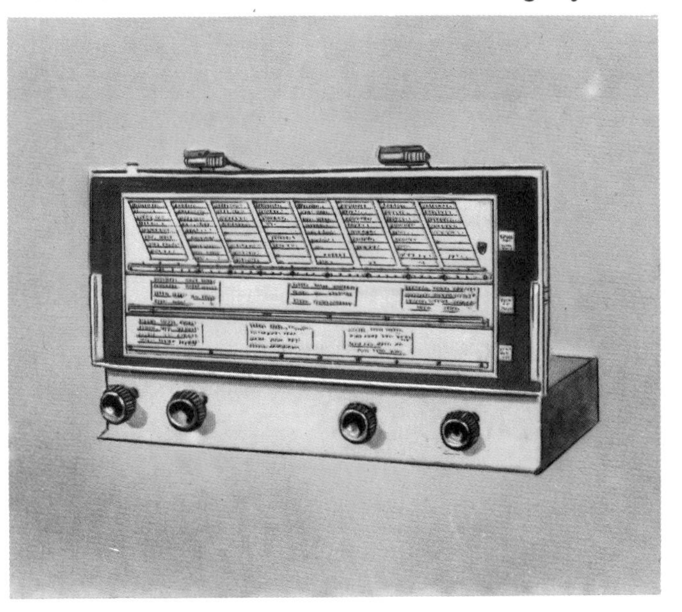

A band switch is provided for changing from one waveband to another. This switch has as many positions as there are wavebands from which to choose.

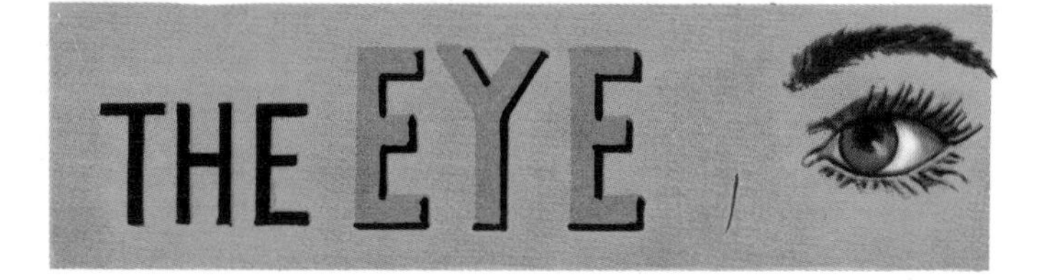

Our sense of sight depends upon the wonderful optical instrument we call the eye. Within our eyes are the most beautifully designed and delicate mechanisms which gather and control the light reaching them from the objects in the world around us. The eyes assess the information that the light has brought, and send off messages to the brain which provide a picture of the scene that lies before us.

LIKENESS TO CAMERA

In many respects, the eye is like a camera. It has a lens which focuses the light rays on to a sensitive surface on which an image is formed. The amount of light entering the lens is controlled by a device similar to the diaphragm in a camera. But the eye controls the light and registers its image by means of techniques which are all its own.

The lens of the eye is a living structure formed from many transparent cells held in a flexible case. In a camera it is the lens, and only the lens, that forms the image; but in the eye the light must pass through a transparent window at the front before it reaches the lens. This is the cornea, which plays an important part in forming the image. Between the cornea and the lens is a fluid, the aqueous humour, which is of the same optical density as the cornea. Rays of light reaching the eye are bent as they enter the cornea. As they pass from the cornea to the lens they are bent again but not so much as they were on entering the cornea. This explains why one cannot see properly when swimming under water. The image-forming power of the cornea is lost, because the optical densities of water and cornea are almost the same. The eye then becomes long-sighted and distinct vision is no longer possible.

LENS FOR FOCUSING

The importance of the lens lies in its power of focusing near or distant objects. In a camera this is done by altering the distance between the lens and the film. In the eye the process of focusing, which is known as accommodation, is brought about by changing the shape of the lens. The lens is a flexible structure which becomes thinner under tension than it is when allowed to relax.

When the eye is at rest, the lens is in a state of tension which is maintained by the suspensory ligaments attached all around its edge. In this state images of more distant objects are in focus; this avoids continuous muscular efforts, as the lens at rest meets the normal requirements of the human being. The suspensory ligaments are not muscular; they are under tension because the gap they span between the edge of the lens and the ciliary body can only be bridged when the lens is pulled out at its circumference. The ciliary body is a circular structure which is itself attached to the inside of the " white " of the eye. It contains muscle fibres

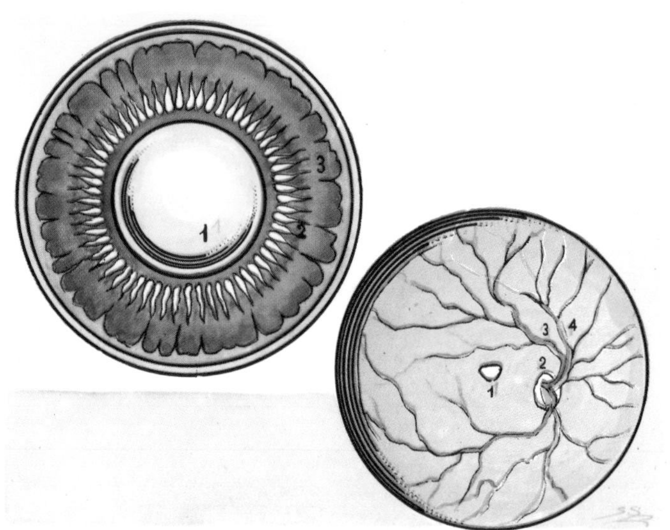

Above: *section of the eye at the back of the iris.* 1. *the crystalline lens;* 2. *the ciliary processes;* 3. *the ciliary ring.* Below: *the retina.* 1. *the central fovea and the yellow spot;* 2. *the optic disc;* 3. *the artery;* 4. *the retinal vein.*

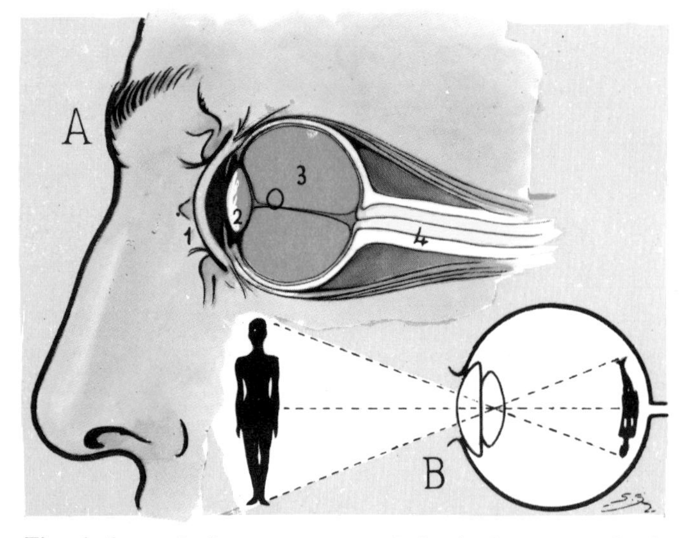

Fig. A shows the human eye as a whole. 1. *the cornea;* 2. *the crystalline lens;* 3. *the vitreous body;* 4. *the optic nerve. Fig.* B *shows how the image appears on the retina upside down, the mechanism whereby it is perceived upright is still obscure.*

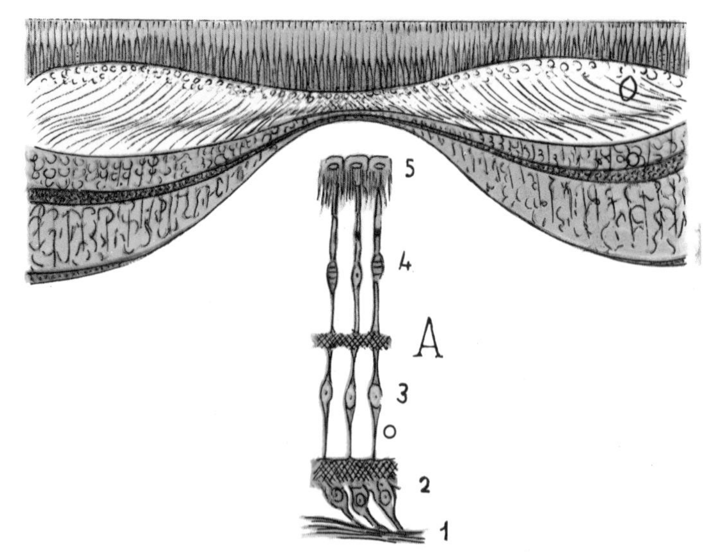

The retina is a part of the nerve tissue of the eye-ball. Here we see in (A) *a section of the retina which has been many times magnified.* 1. *layer of nerve fibres;* 2. *ganglionic layer;* 3. *outer granular layer;* 4. *layer of rods and cones;* 5. *pigmented cells.*

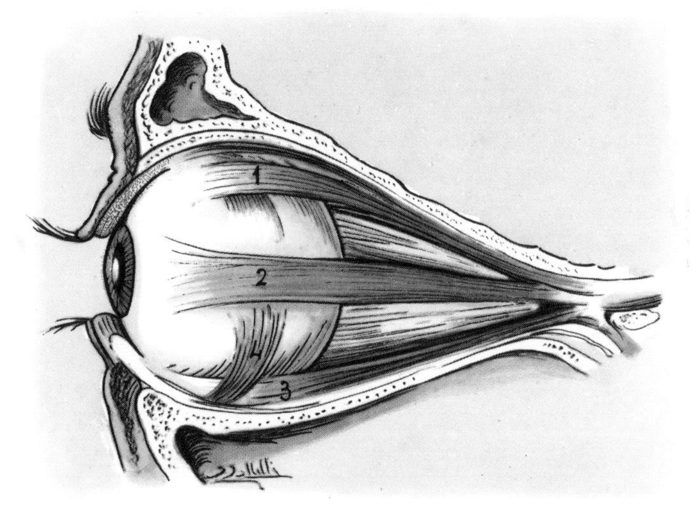

Pictured here is the ball or globe of the eye, called the eyeball, with its appropriate muscles. 1. *superior rectus muscle (which inclines the eye upwards);* 2. *lateral rectus muscle (which turns it sideways);* 3. *inferior rectus muscle (which turns it upwards to the side).*

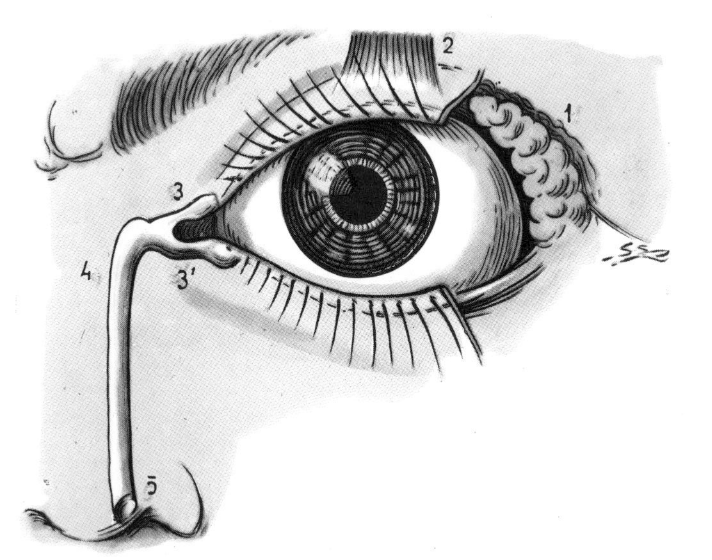

Section of the tear paths. The tears produced by the tear glands (1) *which flow inside the eyelids as far as the tear ducts* (3 *and* 3′), *and from here into the tear sac* (4) *which opens into the interior of the nasal cavity.*

which, on contraction, reduce the circumference of the circle formed by the ciliary body, and hence the gap between it and the lens is reduced. This in turn leads to loss of tension in the suspensory ligaments, so that the lens relaxes into a more swollen state. Near objects are then in focus, but this has been achieved only as a result of muscular effort. The eye therefore tends to tire with constant close work.

THE RETINA

The image produced by the cornea and lens falls on a curved sensitive surface at the back of the eye, called the retina. The retina contains two types of cells, rods and cones, so called because of their shapes. Both types are light-sensitive, but the cones can distinguish colours. The cells are linked to the brain by nerves which pass over the front of the retina and leave the eye via the optic stalk. At this point on the retina there are no light-sensitive cells, so that there is a blind spot. At the back of the retina lies a dark layer, the choroid, which prevents internal reflections inside the eye. The iris is the coloured part of the eye. It is usually blue or brown, and the hole in it is the pupil. The size of the pupil is automatically controlled by the brightness of the light falling on the retina. If the light is too bright, the pupil closes until just the right amount of light is entering the eye. It opens again in dim light.

If the body of a camera becomes bent or distorted, sharp images are not formed. Any distortion in the shape of the eye would have the same result, and it is constructed and held in such a way as to avoid any changes of this sort. In the first place the greater part of the eyeball is embedded in a specially shaped socket in the skull known as the orbit; this prevents the eyeball expanding. Contraction is prevented by the fluids, the aqueous and vitreous humours, which are incompressible. Further support is provided by the sclera, a tough fibrous coat, the visible parts of which are seen in front as the cornea, and also the " white " which continues right to the back.

A person whose eyes do not develop to the correct shape must wear spectacles in order to see properly. If the eyeball is too long, images are focused in front of the retina, causing short-sightedness. This is corrected by using a concave lens in front of the eye. On the other hand if the eyeball is too short it causes long-sightedness, a convex lens being used to allow the image to form accurately on the retina.

A set of six muscles links the sclera to the wall of the orbit and these are so arranged that the eye may be turned in any direction. The tear gland produces fluid which acts as a lubricant for the eyelids.

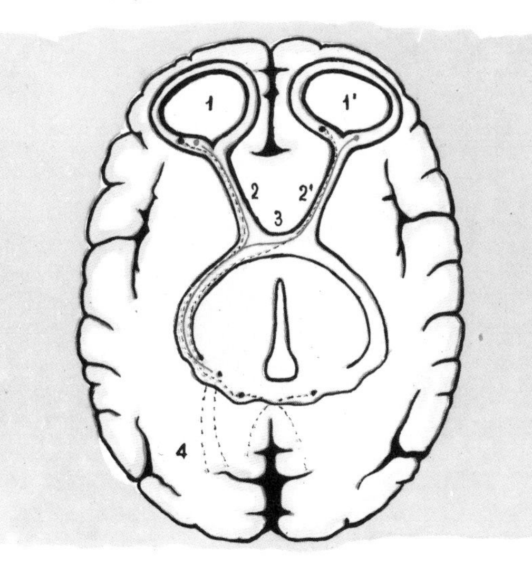

From the retinas of the two eyes (1 *and* 1′) *the image, transformed into nerve impulses, is transmitted along the optic nerves* (2 *and* 2′) *to the chiasma* (3), *where most of the fibres cross. It then proceeds towards the occipital lobe of the brain* (4).

QUESTIONS AND ANSWERS

What is a Front?

A front is a boundary between masses of air in the atmosphere. Polar fronts separate the masses of polar air from the warm westerly air streams. They cause much of the unsettled weather common to the temperate climates of the earth.

URANIUM

In 1789, a chemist named M. H. Klaproth, discovered a new element in a sample of the mineral pitchblende. The element was given the name uranium in honour of the discovery of the planet Uranus by Herschel in 1781.

Klaproth prepared what he believed to be uranium metal itself in the form of a black powder. But, in 1841, E. M. Peligot showed that the material made by Klaproth was in fact an oxide of uranium; Peligot made the pure metal by treating uranium tetrachloride with potassium.

For more than half a century, uranium was regarded as just another element. Then, in 1896, the French scientist Henri Becquerel made an astounding discovery while experimenting with uranium salts. He placed some crystals of potassium uranyl sulphate near a wrapped photographic plate, and noticed to his surprise that the plate became exposed. The uranium chemical was apparently emitting some sort of ray which was able to penetrate the paper wrapping round the photographic plate and darken the emulsion as though it had been exposed to light. The same thing happened even if the experiment was carried out in the dark, so no form of visible light was responsible.

The idea of invisible rays was very much in evidence at that time, as Professor Röntgen had discovered X-rays during the previous year. These were invisible rays emitted by the glass walls of a tube bombarded by cathode rays, and they too were able to penetrate substances which were opaque to visible light. It was inevitable, therefore, that uranium was at first believed to be emitting X-rays.

The study of these radiations emitted by uranium was undertaken by many scientists, including Pierre and Marie Curie, who were later to discover radium. It was found that uranium and a few other elements possessed this strange property of emitting radiations, no matter whether they were in the form of pure elements or in combination with other elements as compounds. The rays were not identical with X-rays, but included particles formed by the spontaneous break-up of the nucleus of the atom.

This property became known as radioactivity, and it was to lead scientists into the study of atomic structure which resulted in the release of atomic energy.

Uranium itself was to become the raw material of the atomic energy industry. In 1939, Otto Hahn and F. Strassman discovered that the nucleus of the uranium atom will undergo fission into smaller fragments forming the nuclei of other elements; in the process, atomic energy is released. Uranium, during the next few years, achieved an immense importance in world affairs, and prospectors began to seek uranium deposits just as their forebears had once sought gold.

Uranium is widely scattered throughout the rocks of the earth's crust, its average concentration being about four parts per million. Granite has a higher concentration than most other rocks. There are comparatively few minerals which can be regarded as uranium ores, of which pitchblende is the most important. This is an oxide of uranium of which the most valuable deposits are in the Congo.

Until 1942, most of the world's uranium was obtained as a by-product from the production of radium. But the development of atomic energy brought a demand for uranium that stimulated a search for other sources of uranium, and a number of uranium-containing minerals are now being worked in many parts of the world.

Uraninite, an oxide of uranium, is mined, for example, in Norway; euxenite-polycrase in Ontario, Canada; davidite in Rum Jungle, Australia; coffinite and carnotite in Colorado, U.S.A.; tyuyaminite in Turkestan; autunite in France; and torbernite in Saxony.

Many methods are used for extracting uranium metal, as the concentration and chemical nature of these ores vary greatly.

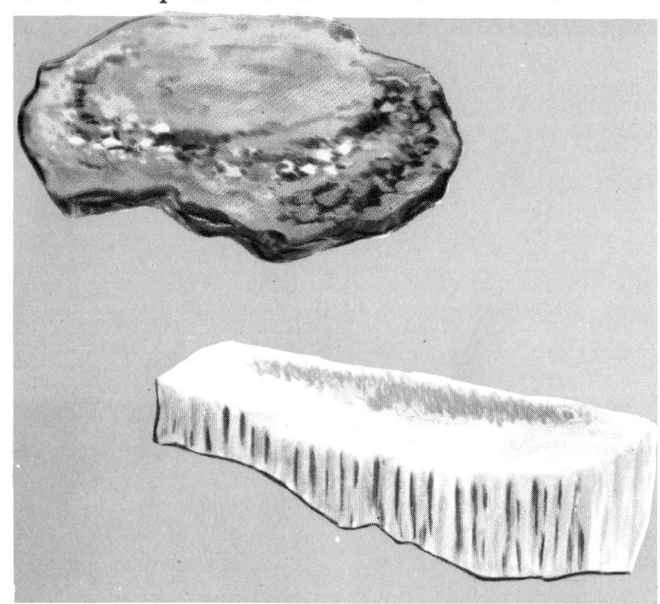

Uranium is a radioactive element of great importance. Here we see two pieces of autunite, which is a hydrated phosphate of calcium and uranium.

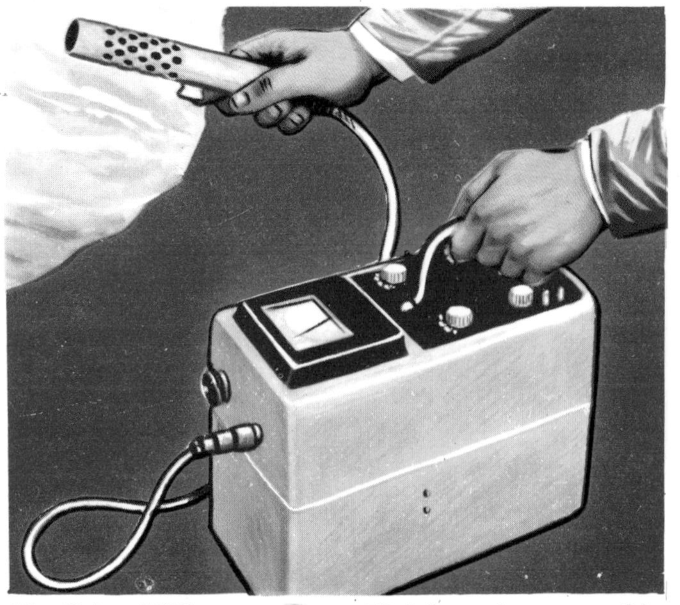

The Geiger-Müller counter, so-called from the names of its inventors, is an instrument used for detecting nuclear radiations and particles.

INDUCED CURRENTS

Little more than a century ago, the young physicist Michael Faraday carried out experiments which were to lay the foundations of our electrical industry. One of the most remarkable of his discoveries, made in 1830, was that an electric current flowing through one piece of wire would produce a current in another wire held close by.

This phenomenon is called induction, and the currents produced are induced currents. The current flowing through the first circuit is known as the primary current, and the current produced in the second circuit is called the secondary current. Faraday found that if the current in the primary circuit flowed in one direction (indicated by the arrow), the current generated in the secondary circuit flowed in the reverse direction.

FARADAY'S EXPERIMENT

If he then opened the primary circuit, leaving the key up, a new instantaneous current was generated in the secondary one, but this time in the opposite direction to the one before, and thus the same as that running through the primary circuit. The same thing happened if he placed the primary circuit farther away from (or nearer) the secondary one.

The strength of these induced currents can be increased by replacing the two simple rectilinear wires by two cylindrical coils, one of which can be fitted into the other (solenoids). The primary one (*P*), which is the smaller solenoid (inductor) carries a few turns of well-insulated thick wire; its two terminals are attached to the poles of a battery. The other one (induced), which has a number of larger turns of thinner wire, is attached to the galvanometer.

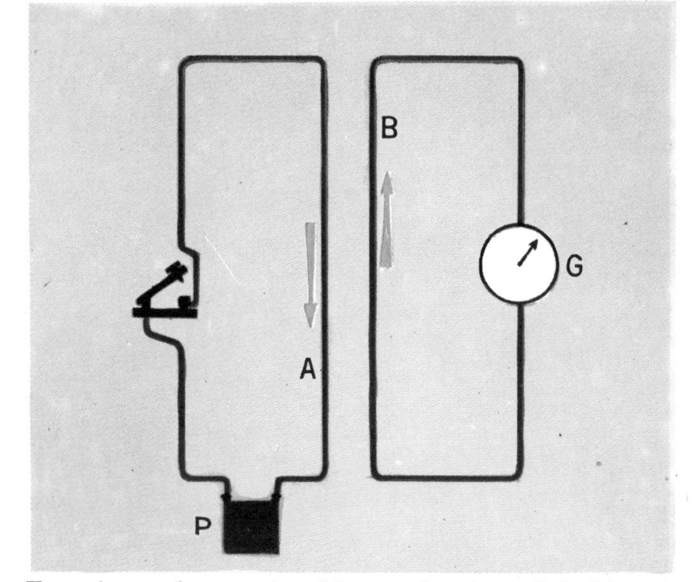

Two wire conductors, A and B, are placed parallel with each other; the first (primary) is attached to a battery, P, and a key, while the second (secondary) is attached to a galvanometer. When we push down the key and allow a current to flow through the first wire, the pointer on the galvanometer connected to the second wire moves away instantly from the normal position.

RUHMKORFF SPARK COIL

Profiting by Faraday's experiments, the German, Daniel Ruhmkorff, constructed the famous " Ruhmkorff spark coil ".

The Ruhmkorff coil consists of a core, made up of a bundle of iron wires, covered with two layers of insulated copper wire; the first, called primary or inductive, consists of comparatively few turns of thick wire; the other, secondary or induced, consists of many turns of fine wire.

A battery current is passed through the primary circuit (which is opened and closed by means of a switch con-

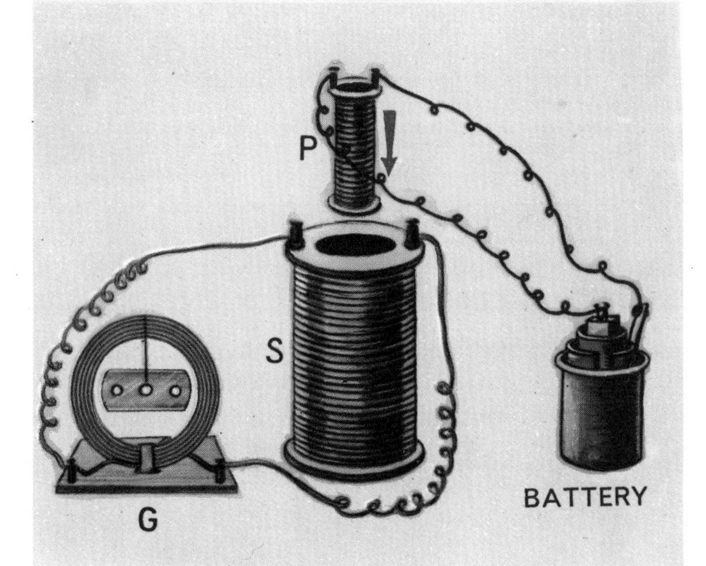

When the small coil (of short thick wire) is moved into or out of the larger coil (of long thin wire), induced currents are set up in the latter, as shown by movement of the galvanometer needle. When the small coil is moved inwards, a current is produced in one direction; when it moves outwards, the direction of the current is reversed.

The Ruhmkorff spark coil, illustrated here, was of great importance in the study of the laws of induction. It was used also in the production of electromagnetic waves, enabling such men as the inventors and physicists, Hertz, Righi and Marconi, to achieve their first great successes in the field of telecommunications.

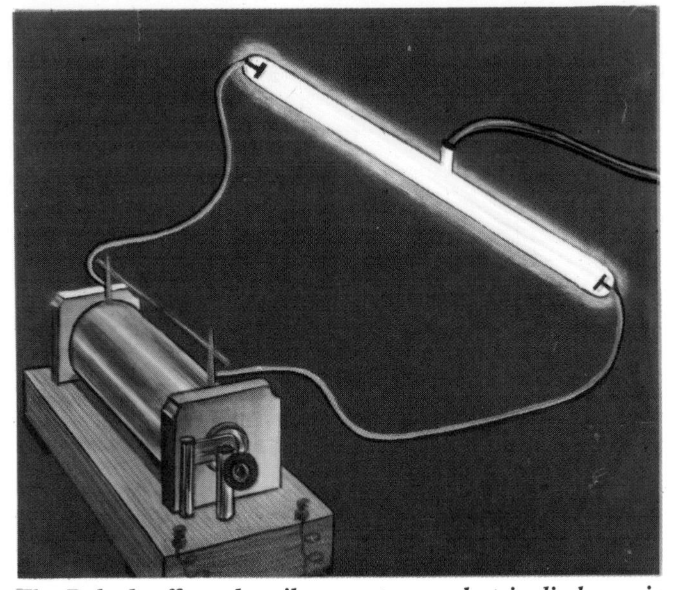

The Ruhmkorff spark coil generates an electric discharge in glass tubes filled with rarefied gas, in which cathode rays are produced. These rays are projected from the cathode at right angles to its surface; they radiate in a straight line and produce fluorescence at the place where they strike the glass of the tube.

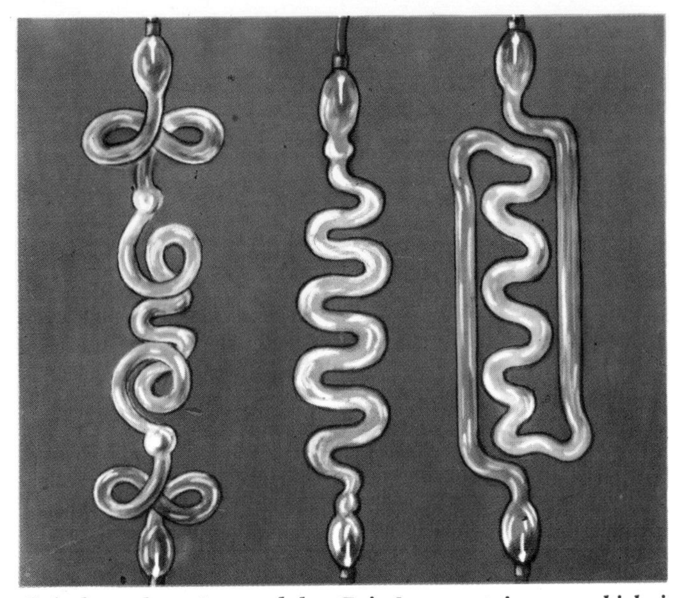

Geissler tubes, invented by Geissler, contain gas which is rarefied (at about $\frac{1}{100}$ atmosphere pressure). These tubes, of various shapes, have a terminal at each end, and are filled with gas at low pressure. On passing a current through the tube, a glow fills the tube. It may be of various colours.

sisting of a screw and a hammer). In the normal position the screw and the hammer touch.

When the primary circuit is opened, the battery current flows and magnetises the core; this attracts the hammer and so the circuit is opened. The current then ceases, the core is demagnetised and the hammer goes back to its former position, making contact again with the screw. This completes a cycle. In the secondary circuit induced and alternate currents are generated, and these change direction with every opening or closing of the primary circuit.

By passing the electric current generated by the Ruhmkorff coil through glass tubes filled with rarefied gas, other renowned scientists like Geissler, Crookes, Röntgen and Tesla were able to study the phenomena associated with the discharge of electricity through gases. The discovery of X-rays, for example, has brought a revolution in medical diagnosis and treatment, and has given us invaluable industrial techniques.

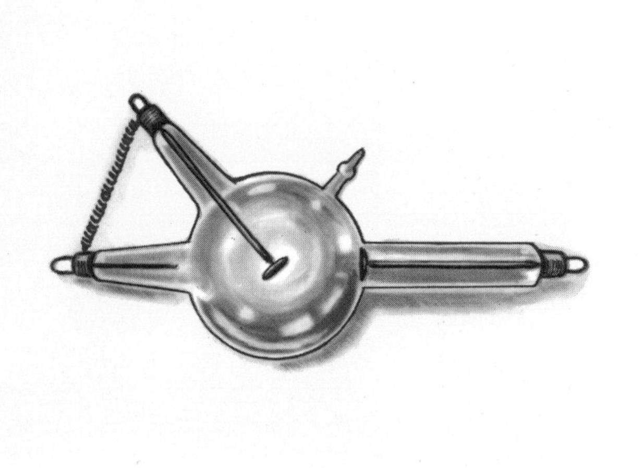

The Crookes tube produces X-rays (also called Röntgen rays, after the man who discovered them in 1895), which originate from cathode rays (i.e. those which, in the Geissler tubes, produce fluorescence) at the point at which these strike the walls of the tube. The tube illustrated above is used for the production of X-rays (which were so-called because little was known about them). Paper, wood, cloth, etc., are transparent to X-rays; glass, water and aluminium semi-transparent; metals opaque.

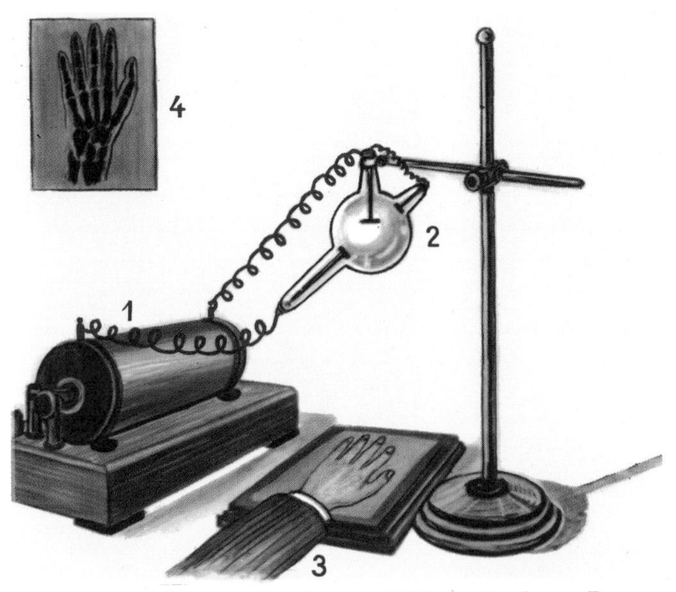

X-rays were discovered in the year 1895, by Professor Rontgen while he was experimenting with a Crookes vacuum tube. X-rays are absorbed by different substances to different degrees. They will affect a photographic plate, and will also make certain substances fluoresce. When X-rays are passed through an object consisting of materials of different density, therefore, the internal structure can be studied by allowing the rays to fall on a fluorescent screen, or on a photographic plate. Here is one of the first radiographs.

PLANTS NEED AIR

Human beings and other animals need food to provide the fuel and raw-material that sustains life. The complex chemical substances that serve as animal foods are made by plants from simple chemicals in the soil and air. Plants are the food factories that produce the food for the animal world. And they do it by means of the process called photosynthesis.

Photosynthesis means the synthesis of substances with the aid of light. It is the fundamental synthetic process of the plant world, and it is made possible by the green pigment, chlorophyll, that gives the plant world its familiar colour.

The raw materials from which a plant produces its complex organic materials are the gases of the air and the chemicals absorbed as a solution from the soil. In the cells of the leaves and other green parts of the plant, these simple substances undergo chemical changes controlled by the chlorophyll, producing materials which are the basis of all human food.

Fig. 1. Set up four bottles, all of them connected by glass tubes through which air can pass. The first bottle and the third bottle from the left contain lime water. In the second bottle there are some leaves completely covered with water. The fourth bottle works as an aspirator. Air is drawn through the system of tubes by turning on the tap at the bottom of the fourth bottle. The carbon dioxide in the air turns the lime water in the first bottle it enters milky, but is absorbed by the green leaves before it reaches the third bottle. This happens only in the presence of light.

DOES A PLANT BREATHE?

Figure 2 shows you how a plant absorbs the gases of the air. Break a single leaf from a plant and thread its stem through a hole you have made in the cork of a bottle. Fill the bottle with water so that the leaf stem dips into it. The pressure inside the bottle should be relieved by an open glass tube that also passes through the cork. If you stand the bottle in the light you will see bubbles emerging from the end of the stem, where it was broken from the plant. These bubbles consist of atmospheric gases which the plant had absorbed through the pores, or little apertures in the cell-structure of the epidermis, or outer skin.

Plants absorb carbon dioxide gas from the air which

Fig. 2. Put a fresh green leaf in one of the bottles so that its stalk is right in the water. Air is sucked out from the glass tube, and little bubbles begin to form at the end of the stalk; this is air that had lodged in the pores of the leaf's epidermis. A simple experiment for you to do at home.

Fig. 3. Put some leaves in a glass jar full of water standing in the light. Cover the leaves with a glass funnel and cap this with a test-tube full of water. Bubbles of escaping oxygen will rise in the test-tube. The action of chlorophyll in the presence of light causes the plant to give out oxygen.

Fig. 4. Starch is manufactured only in a green leaf exposed to light. The white part of the leaf shows where it has been covered by black paper or tinfoil while still on the plant. The green colour (denoting the presence of chlorophyll) was then removed from it by steeping in alcohol. Starch turns blue when treated with iodine solution; when the leaf was dipped in iodine solution, all the parts that had been left in the light turned bright blue, leaving a white strip where no starch had been produced by the leaf.

enters the pores of their leaves, but they also emit oxygen as a by-product from the process of photosynthesis.

THE IMPORTANCE OF CARBON DIOXIDE

Let us look at Figure 1. The first and third bottles from the left hold lime-water. You can make the lime-water by adding a little slaked lime to ordinary water: the lime turns the water milky. Let it stand for a moment; the lime will settle on the bottom, leaving the liquid above it quite clear. This liquid is lime-water.

Lime-water can combine with carbon dioxide in the air to form calcium carbonate, which is insoluble and forms a cloudy liquid. You can easily show that the lime-water becomes cloudy in contact with air. Just blow into it through a straw. The air that leaves your lungs is rich in carbon dioxide and will quickly affect the liquid (Fig. 5).

In the second bottle you see water and leaves. The large bottle on the right works as an aspirator. If you turn on the tap at its base a current of air will pass through the other three bottles. To watch the effect of air on the contents of these bottles you must put all the apparatus in the sunlight. After a few moments the carbon dioxide in the air will darken the lime-water in the first bottle it meets, but no change will occur in the third bottle. To reach that one, the air had to pass through the bottle containing leaves and they absorbed all the carbon dioxide leaving none to act on the lime-water.

WHAT IS CHLOROPHYLL?

Three things are necessary for the success of this experiment: sunlight, carbon dioxide and chlorophyll. If you do this experiment in the dark, or use parts of a plant that are not green (flower petals, roots, seeds, etc.) the carbon dioxide will arrive safely in the last bottle and prove its presence by clouding the lime-water there, too. This shows that chlorophyll is present in the green parts of the plant and can only do its job in the light. You can also show that plants " breathe out " oxygen, by copying the experiment in Figure 3.

TEST FOR STARCH

The action of chlorophyll produces starch. Starch turns blue when treated with a solution of tincture of iodine. This makes it easy to show that starch is made in the green parts of a plant. Choose one leaf on a growing plant and cover part of its surface with a strip of black paper or tinfoil. The next day, sever the leaf and peel off the strip of paper. You will not see any change yet. Submerge the leaf in alcohol until it turns white, showing that the chlorophyll has been removed. Dip the whitened leaf in tincture of iodine. Most of the surface area—the part that was not covered, but remained in the light—will be rich in starch. It will turn bright blue. The strip that was kept dark will remain white because it could not make any starch (Fig. 4).

Fig. 5. Lime-water is normally clear, once the slaked lime has settled at the bottom of the container. It becomes clouded and milky when combined with carbon dioxide. You can make it do this by blowing into it down a straw. The air we breathe out from our lungs is rich in carbon dioxide; bubbles of gas will escape from the straw and the lime-water will turn milky.

QUESTIONS AND ANSWERS

What is Flax?

Flax is a textile fibre from which we make the fabrics we call linen. It is obtained from the stem of plants which also provide us with linseed oil.

Flax was probably the first fibre to be used by man in the Western Hemisphere. When Tut-ankh-amen's tomb was opened in 1922, linen curtains were still hanging where they had been placed in about 1250 B.C.

THE AIR AGE

PASSENGERS BY THE MILLION

The middle of the twentieth century has been described as the Age of Transport. This is no exaggeration, the reason being that there have been rapid developments in passenger-carrying aircraft since the end of World War II in 1945.

During the war it was decided that the United States would build all the transport aircraft needed by the Allies, while Britain concentrated on fighters and bombers. This, of course, put Britain at a great disadvantage compared with America at the end of the war, because the big four-engined aircraft such as the Douglas DC-4 and Lockheed Constellation, which had been developed as military transports, required little alteration to change them into fine airliners.

As a result, B.O.A.C. and B.E.A., Britain's two National Airlines, had to make do with aircraft like the Viking and York which were developed from the Wellington and Lancaster bombers, and a number of " interim " aircraft which were not very successful.

TURBO-PROPS

Knowing that she could never hope to catch up with America's experience in conventional piston-engined airliners, Britain decided to make use of the new jet experience she had gained towards the end of the war and to go in for turbine-engined airliners.

The first result was the medium-range Vickers Viscount, powered by four Rolls-Royce Dart turbo-props and able to cruise at 300 m.p.h., which took to the air on 18th July, 1948. This was followed a year later by the much more advanced de Havilland Comet, first jet airliner in the world, with a cruising speed of nearly 500 m.p.h.

At first, some experts saw no future in these aircraft, claiming that their relatively high operating costs would make them uneconomic. But they forgot that speed is about the only advantage offered by air travel, and if achieved through skilful design, can more than offset the high fuel consumption. In addition, the jet airliners were not only faster, but, owing to the lack of vibration due to the absence of pounding piston engines, much more comfortable. They were also able to cruise far above all but the highest of bad weather, giving increased reliability.

VISCOUNTS AND COMETS

When B.E.A. released figures showing just how cheap the Viscount was to run, the result was the start of a flood of orders leading to a total of more than 400.

Light aircraft similar to the "Navion" above are suitable for business and pleasure flying.

Lockheed Super Constellation, a typical American post-war airliner which was greatly helped by wartime development and production. The smaller aircraft is the Boeing Stratocruiser airliner, based on the B-29 bomber. Now obsolete, it was flown on many luxury services.

The Vickers Viscount, of which over 400 *were sold, was one of the most successful British airliners.*

The Comet, after an initial setback through structural failure resulting from the repeated pressurisation of the cabin as it flew at 40,000 feet, was redeveloped as the Comet 4 series. With almost twice the range and passenger-carrying capacity, these fine aircraft are still in service with several airlines.

These two British aircraft set a fashion which others copied so rapidly that soon almost all major airline services were flown by jet and turbo-prop aircraft.

To meet the demand, America produced her 600-m.p.h., 150-passenger, Boeing 707s and Douglas DC-8s. Benefiting from the experience gained with tragic cost on the early Comets, these big American jets are now in service in large numbers.

Britain produced the superb VC-10, which with its four rear-mounted Rolls-Royce engines, is considered by many passengers the most comfortable airliner of its type.

ECONOMY FARES FOR EVERYMAN

As these big, fast airliners were developed, the problem arose of persuading sufficient people to use them to make them economical. It soon became apparent that there was only one sound way to attract passengers, and that was to reduce the fares until more and more ordinary people could afford to fly. So the luxuries were restricted to holders of first-class tickets, and a cheaper, tourist-class fare was introduced. The effect on traffic figures was startling. In the previous year 372,346 people flew across the Atlantic—less than half the number who went by sea. Within one year of the introduction of new low fares, air passengers had increased to 497,021. Within three years the number was 893,072, and for the first time outnumbered those carried by ship. In 1958, a still cheaper, economy-class fare was introduced, and in 1969 the number of people crossing the Atlantic by air totalled nearly six million.

This story repeated itself on most other air routes. The result is that, now, well over 300 *million* people in all parts of the world travel by air each year. To carry this staggering total, an airliner takes off from one of the world's 3,500 airports about every *two seconds* every day, every week, throughout the year.

The success of jet airliners on long-range routes led to the development of smaller jets for short and medium ranges. Among the first was the French Caravelle, which pioneered the rear-engine installation, giving a quieter ride. The Caravelle was followed by the Trident, with its three rear engines, the Boeing 727, the twin-engined BAC-111, Douglas DC-9, Boeing 737 and Fokker Fellowship. The Boeing 727 in particular proved particularly popular, both with the passengers who liked its smooth ride and the airlines for which it made money; over 800 were sold.

Behind the Iron Curtain, too, Russia produced a fine series of turbo-prop and jet airliners which introduced the benefit of air travel to millions of Russian citizens. Typical Russian jets are the long-range Ilyushin Il-62 and the medium-range Tupolev Tu-134 and Tu-154 airliners. Smallest jet of all is the diminutive Yak 40. Powered by three tiny jet engines in the tail, this carries 24 passengers.

JUMBO AND SUPERSONIC JETS

More and more people continue to fly and to help carry them bigger and faster aircraft are being developed. First of the new breed is the Boeing 747, which fully justifies its

Biggest airliner in the world is the Boeing 747, *with a range of* 7,000 *miles and a passenger-carrying capacity of* 490.

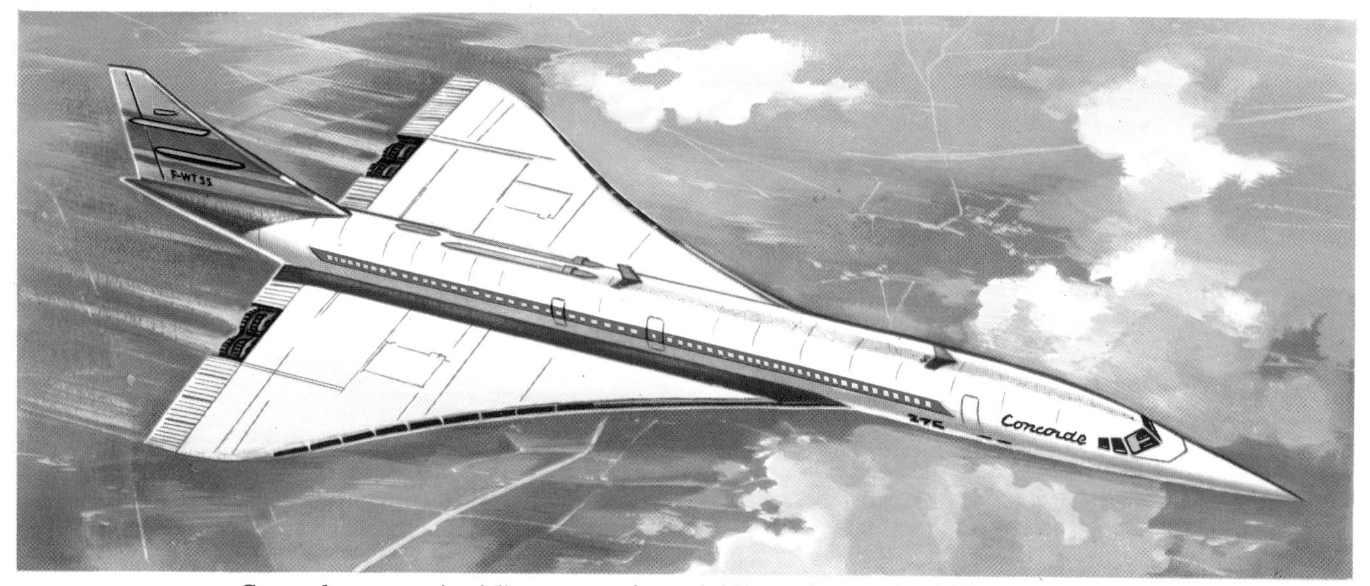

Concorde supersonic airliner can cruise at 1,450 m.p.h. carrying 144 passengers.

nickname jumbo jet. Able to carry up to 490 passengers, the Boeing 747 has a much wider-than-normal fuselage. The width of the cabin, its high ceiling and the sub-division of the long fuselage into a number of compartments has introduced a new spacious look into air travel.

Almost as big are the three-engined Lockheed TriStar and McDonnell Douglas DC-10 "airbuses". Able to carry up to 350 passengers, these are designed primarily for medium-range routes, although long-range versions are available.

The first supersonic airliner to fly was the Russian Tupolev Tu-144, designed to carry 121 passengers at speeds up to 1,550 m.p.h., but better known is the Concorde. Being developed jointly by Britain and France, this has a distinctively curved delta-wing, and is designed to carry 144 passengers, at 1,450 m.p.h. over ranges up to 4,000 miles.

Under development in the United States is the much bigger and faster Boeing 2707. Initially intended to have swing-wings, this proved too futuristic and the aircraft now has a delta-wing similar to that adopted for the Russian and Anglo-French supersonic airliners. Unlike the Tu-144 and Concorde, however, the U.S. aircraft has a conventional tailplane and elevators, so that it will not pitch up quite so much when taking off and landing. Maximum passenger capacity is 234 and the maximum speed is around 1,800 m.p.h.

MILITARY AVIATION SINCE THE WAR

Although jet aircraft were only used on a limited scale during the closing stages of the war, the air forces of the world were not slow in appreciating the new power of jet propulsion. This power was dramatically demonstrated publicly for the first time in 1945, when a Meteor of the Royal Air Force raised the world speed record by no less than 137 m.p.h. to 606 m.p.h. Since then the record has been progressively raised to the current 2,070 m.p.h., held by a Lockheed YF-12A.

Although jet propulsion greatly increased the speed and high-flying qualities of fighters, it improved the general performance of bombers even more.

DEFENCE PROBLEMS

Bombers became not only much faster and higher-flying but were able to carry atomic and the even more powerful, and deadly, thermo-nuclear bombs.

The answer to this problem seemed to be a guided rocket, fired either from the ground, or from a fighter. In view of the high speeds involved, however, it is almost impossible for a fighter to shoot down a modern bomber by using ordinary guns, and rockets are now the standard fighter armament. The latest interceptors are thus little more than mobile rocket-launching platforms, in which nearly everything happens automatically. Exact details are secret, but the general principle is as follows:

The pilot takes off normally and is guided towards the general area of the target by radio messages from the ground. When he is within a certain distance of the target he "hands over" control of the aircraft to special tracking radar in the fighter's nose. From this moment all he has to do is sit back and watch what is happening on his radar screen. The radar senses the enemy and "locks on" to it and then steers the fighter towards it by sending messages to the automatic pilot. At a certain distance the fighter's rockets are "armed" and become ready for firing. Arriving at the best position for an attack, the rockets are fired automatically, after which

The spacious and tastefully furnished Lockheed TriStar cabin gives a good impression of the " new look " air travel introduced by wide-bodied jumbo jets.

The Boeing 707 jet airliner is in service in large numbers; it carries up to 189 passengers. The B.O.A.C. 707-420 depicted above is powered by Rolls-Royce Conway engines.

With a wing specially developed for high speeds and yet retaining easy-landing characteristics, the Handley-Page Victor is one of the most effective bombers in the world.

the fighter is turned away sharply to avoid the possibility of a collision. Then the pilot takes over and lands to refuel and to re-arm.

DEFENDING THE ATTACKER

This does not seem to give the bomber much of a chance. Bomber designers, however, have retaliated by developing special decoys, which can be dropped in flight. These give off radar echoes and radio signals similar to those of the bomber, so that rockets home on the decoy instead of the bomber.

Bombers do not have to approach a target for they can carry stand-off bombs. These bombs are really small, unpiloted, aeroplanes, designed to be released when the bomber is some hundreds of miles from the target. Typical stand-off bombs are the Blue Steel, carried by Britain's Vulcans and Victors, the Hound Dog, carried by America's B-52 Stratofortress bombers, and the Kelt, carried by Russia's Tu-16 bombers.

At one time the U.S.A.F. standard bomber, the B-52, was a monster indeed. Weighing 480,000 lb. at take-off it was the heaviest aeroplane ever flown up to that time.

Today, missiles seem to have the edge over such bombers, and the duties of the B-52, Vulcan and Victor, and their Russian equivalents, have been largely undertaken by the long-range, nuclear-warheaded Inter-Continental Ballistic Missiles.

Current strike aircraft tend to be relatively small, partly because of the uncertainty of combat success and expense of big aircraft, and partly because of the awesome power that can be packed into quite a small nuclear bomb. Strike aircraft include Britain's Buccaneer which is specially designed to fly fast at tree-top height, to avoid detection by enemy radar networks.

The controversial General Dynamics F-111 fighter-bomber introduced swing-wings to military aircraft. The wings are spread for maximum lift during take-off and landing, but can be swept back for minimum drag in flight, giving a maximum

Lockheed C.130 Hercules, medium-range transport of the U.S. Air Force. Powered by four 4,000-h.p. Allison turbo-props, it can carry 92 paratroops, 74 stretchers, or 16 tons of freight. Cruising speed is 370 m.p.h. and the maximum range 3,570 miles.

The F-111 fighter-bomber's swing-wing extends for take-off and landing, and sweeps back in flight to permit high speeds.

The American X-15 rocket research aircraft, which has flown 4,000 m.p.h. and reached a height of nearly 50 miles.

speed of Mach 2.5 and a range of 4,000 miles. Other military aircraft employing swing-wings are currently under development.

Specially designed to intercept fast, low-flying raiders, possibly with "snap-down" missiles, is the formidable Russian Mig 23, code-named Foxbat. Early versions of this aircraft set up a new 1,000 km. closed-circuit speed record of 1,441 m.p.h. and a payload-to-height record of 98,349 ft.

V.T.O.L.

One new development which has attracted the attention of warplane designers is V.T.O.L.—short for Vertical Take-off and Landing. V.T.O.L. aircraft would dispense with the need for expensive concrete runways which are difficult to build but easy to locate and destroy. They would be able to operate from anywhere, even front-line areas in rough country.

Of course, a helicopter is a form of V.T.O.L. aircraft and many current projects, such as those for flying jeeps and rifle platforms, utilise rotors; but high-performance aircraft work on a different principle. Such aircraft are literally blown up into the air by downward-pointing jet engines. This can be done either by having separate "lifting" engines, or by deflecting the jet of the main propulsion engines.

The revolutionary Hawker Harrier uses the second system. On this close-support fighter, the engine jet stream exhausts through four rotating nozzles. For take-off the jet thrust is deflected downward, to provide the vertical lift. When airborne, the nozzles are rotated 90° to direct the thrust rearward, when the wings provide the lift and the aircraft performs like a conventional fighter.

Germany's Do-31 transport utilises separate lift-jet engines, mounted in batteries of four in two wing pods, as well as deflected main engine thrust, to take off and land vertically. Once airborne the lift engines are switched off and the main engine thrust deflected rearward for conventional flight. V.T.O.L. aircraft such as this are the forerunners of the city-centre-to-city-centre airliners of tomorrow.

Mig 23 Foxbat. This formidable Russian warplane is designed to intercept enemy aircraft flying fast, low down. Early versions gained speed and height records.

Playing an increasingly important part in military aviation are vertical take-off machines. Shown here is the revolutionary VTOL Harrier, in service with the Royal Air Force.

GALILEO GALILEI

One day nearly four hundred years ago a lonely young man leaned over the parapet of the Ponte Vecchio in Florence, utterly desperate and weary with life. At twenty-three he could see no future for himself, yet he was to attain immortality, the lasting fame of a name which will always stand for genius: Galileo Galilei.

Galileo was born in 1564, in Pisa, but moved with his family to Florence while still a child. He was educated at the monastery of Vallombrosa, and was then sent by his father to the University of Pisa to study medicine. The boy knew he would never do well at something he hated so much, but he found consolation in the study of mathematics. As Galileo's knowledge of mathematics developed, he longed to study physics as well. But still his father insisted that he should stick to medicine. The boy declared he would rather die than become a doctor, and after bitter arguments, he forced his father to give him a chance. They agreed that Galileo could change his course of study if he won a grant from the ruling family. But Fate was against him and his application was turned down.

Galileo's father often sat among the silks and brocades of his draper's shop, singing, with young Galileo listening to him.

PENDULUM AT PISA

In the midst of his despair, the young mathematician made one of his most famous discoveries. He happened to be passing Pisa Cathedral one day when he saw signs of bustle and activity inside. Some workmen were rehanging the great lamp in the central nave after making repairs to it. As they moved it into position it was swinging slowly and steadily. Galileo moved forward, fascinated by the arc the lamp was describing in the air. He watched the lamp and became convinced that the time taken for each swing was constant, and independent of the arc through which it moved.

Galileo checked this by timing the swinging lamp against his pulse, and suggested that the pendulum might be a useful method of making exact measurements of the passage of time. More than half a century later, Galileo used this principle of the pendulum in designing a new form of clock escapement.

For a long time Galileo could think of nothing but the mathematics of pendulums. As a consequence, he failed his examinations at the end of the year and had to go back to work in his father's shop.

THE DEPTHS OF DESPAIR

From the heights of elation, he fell into despair. All hopes of proving himself as a scientist were shattered. He used to

Galileo hated the study of medicine, which his father had chosen for him as a career. He and his father quarrelled over Galileo's preference for physics. His only pleasure at the University was in wearing the dignified academic gown.

One day Galileo watched some workmen rehanging the great chandelier in the central nave of Pisa Cathedral. He was fascinated by its swinging movement and from this chance interest came an important new principle of physics.

wander about Pisa to get away from his home, and one day he leaned over the bridge and imagined his body sinking to the bottom of the muddy waters. Idly he tore up a piece of paper he was holding and watched the shreds float away downstream.

Galileo noticed how lightly the bits of paper were floating on top of the water and wondered whether his body would float, too. He pondered on the relative weight of his body and the volume of water displaced by it, and his thoughts on this subject led him to the invention of the hydrostatic balance.

Galileo's interest in science revived, and he passed the next few years engrossed in study. At last he became a fully qualified mathematician and was rewarded with a lectureship at Pisa University. During his time at Pisa, Galileo put forward his famous theory that all bodies falling under the attraction of gravity move at the same speed, no matter whether they are large or small. He proved this to his own satisfaction by dropping objects from the Leaning Tower of Pisa.

Once again, he found himself in trouble. The authorities considered that he was too modern in his teaching and were afraid of his lively mind. He moved to Padua, where his ability had gained him the University Chair of Mathematics.

Now the young professor settled down to a period of immense activity. In 1606, he wrote " The Workings of the Geometrical and Military Compass "; " Treatise on the Sphere " which was based on the Ptolemaic system; a small work called " Mechanics ", about simple machines; and a treatise on " Accelerated Motion ".

THE COPERNICAN THEORY

Galileo was busy with the work he loved; he never tired of solving the problems that science presented. He read what

One day, while idling by the river, Galileo threw scraps of paper into the water. The paper floating downstream inspired him to work out another law of physics: an object loses weight in relation to the volume of water it displaces.

Galileo was offered the chair of Mathematics at Padua University. His father disapproved, however, and Galileo was forced to leave his home, overcome with grief at his father's attitude, which seemed to Galileo so unreasonable.

In 1609, *Galileo invented the telescope. We can imagine the wonder with which he saw distant objects "come close." The telescope was presented to the Doge of Venice, and all the important members of the Senate came to gaze through the telescope from the top of the bell tower of St. Mark's.*

Copernicus had written and agreed with his theory that the sun was the centre of the Universe and that the Earth, like all other planets, revolved round it. He became an enthusiastic astronomer. His invention of the telescope in 1609 cost him a lot of money and the hard work exhausted him.

After the public acclamation of his discovery, Galileo retired to his little observatory. He had an important project to complete. He was working on the Corpernican theory again, elaborating it from his own original researches. On the 29th January, 1610, his treatise was finished: it was called *Sidereus Nuncius* (*The Message of the Stars*).

This work was sensational: its fame spread through Europe, and the philosopher Kepler used Galileo's information and succeeded in seeing the satellites of Jupiter with his own eyes.

Galileo spent his nights gazing at the stars. He corresponded regularly with Kepler, and in his private letters, Galileo continued to insist that the Earth revolved around the sun.

FAME AND APPLAUSE

In 1623, he published a new work, called *Il Saggiatore* (*The Experimenter*). This explained the direction scientific reasoning should take. The new pope, Urban VIII, liked the treatise and invited Galileo to discuss it with him. But Galileo could win no support for the theory that the Earth revolved round the sun.

Finally, Galileo gave up trying. Instead, he obtained the Papal seal for the first edition of his masterpiece, *Dialogue on the Two Principle Systems of the World.* It was published on his sixty-eighth birthday, in 1632.

THE INQUISITION

The weary scientist felt his task complete. Now at last he could rest—but this hope was soon destroyed. Suddenly his book was banned by the Papal court, which absolutely forbade its sale, and he was summoned to Rome by the Inquisition. Galileo was tired and ill. In 1633, at the trial in the Santo Uffizio, he was forced to renounce his convictions, which were found heretical and contrary to the Catholic Church. Then he was sentenced to imprisonment—to be released at the discretion of the Inquisition.

What a reward for all his work! Pope Urban managed to soften the sentence a little. Galileo was imprisoned in Siena, in the house of the Archbishop Piccolomini, until he was allowed to retire to Arcetri. Before he died, he learned that his sentence and all his imprisonment had not been legal!

UNBEATEN TO THE END

Still the old man was not cowed. Helped by two pupils, Viviani and Torricelli, he determined to write another treatise. In 1634, though handicapped by arthritis and failing sight, he published *Discourses on Two New Sciences.* In 1637, he became blind and feeble, and on 8th January, 1642, the great scientist died.

After the trial of the Santo Uffizio, Galileo went to the Jesuit cathedral to thank God that he was not to be burned at the stake as a heretic. Coming out of the cathedral, he looked back at the Santo Uffizio and repeated his conviction that the Earth did move round the sun: Eppure si muove! (*and yet it does move*).

LIQUID AIR

A liquid that turns solid on the fire and boils on ice.

Have you ever wondered how a Thermos flask works? It is a very useful development of the Dewar flask, which works on the principle of thermal insulation. As you can see in Fig. 2, each flask is made of two glass containers with silvered walls, one inside the other. Between the two glass walls is a vacuum, and it is this that seals in the heat, forming a barrier across which heat finds difficulty in escaping.

Receptacles 1 and 2 in Fig. 2 contain liquid air. It is obvious from the picture that it is not an ordinary liquid. There is a white vapour escaping from the neck of the container that looks just like steam, but if you were to try corking this in, you can see from vessel 2 what would happen. Either the cork would be forced out immediately or the whole bottle would explode. This is because liquid air evaporates so rapidly; and it can be very dangerous.

ITS PROPERTIES

Here are a few facts about this strange liquid. It is pale blue and very volatile. Its temperature is fantastically low: -207 degrees Centigrade, and to look at it you would think it was a most inoffensive liquid, not likely to do you much harm. A chemist could pour some over the back of his hand, and as long as it ran off again immediately he would not feel anything at all. He would, in fact, just see a lot of white vapour. This is due to the process of evaporation that liquids go through when they fall on a hot surface (Fig. 1). Compared with liquid air, a human hand is very hot indeed! If a drop of water falls on to a red-hot copper plate it will evaporate very slowly. That is because it is actually surrounded by vapour that prevents the liquid from coming into contact with the hot plate. The vapour will go on protecting the water until the plate has reached a certain temperature. When this happens the water will evaporate all at once.

Fig. 2. Dewar flasks (1) *were the model for the Thermos flask* (3). *A Dewar flask has double walls made of silvered glass. Between them is a vacuum, which insulates the liquid in the jar, preventing the passage of heat. When the flask contains liquid air it must not be tightly closed.*

PLAYING WITH FIRE

This formation of a vapour barrier also explains why you can dip your finger into molten lead for an instant, without hurting yourself. But woe betide the experimenter who tries

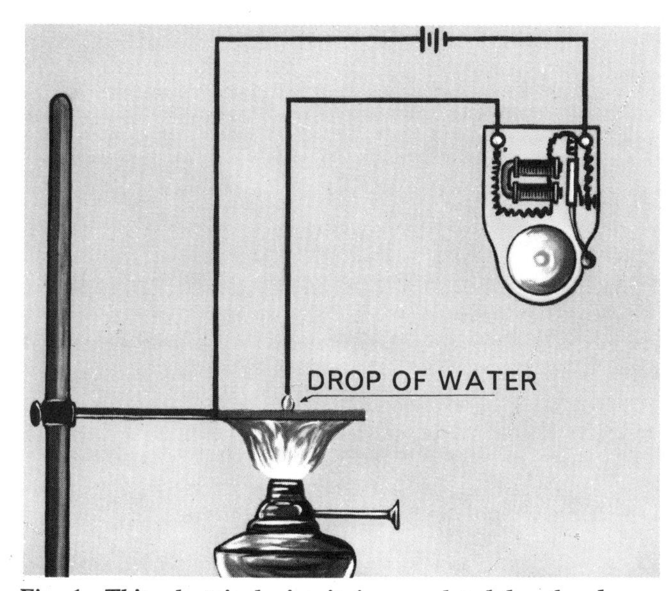

Fig. 1. This electrical circuit is completed by the drop of acidified water allowing the current to pass through it. If, however, the copper plate is heated, vapour surrounds the water; the circuit is broken and only restored when the copper plate cools and the vapour disappears.

Fig. 3. A rubber tube loses its elasticity when dipped into liquid air. It becomes very brittle and can be smashed with a hammer as though it were made of glass. The same thing happens to other organic substances exposed to the action of liquid air.

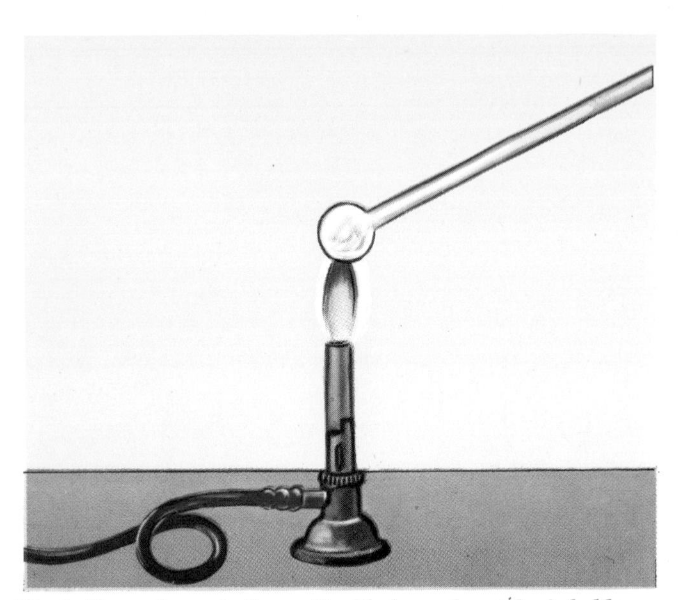

Fig. 4. For a flame to freeze liquid air, a glass tube is held over a bunsen and liquid air poured down it. When it reaches the flame the heat turns the liquid into vapour and the evaporation produces intense cold. The air freezes so that you see a globule of solid in the flame.

Fig. 6. There is liquid air in this coffee pot. As soon as it is placed on the block of ice it starts to boil. Compared with liquid air (—207 degrees centigrade), ice has a very high temperature (0 degrees centigrade). If you dip a coil of lead wire in liquid air, it becomes as elastic as a steel spring.

to hold liquid air in his hand! It would damage the tissues beyond repair and the hand would become brittle and lifeless. But it is quite possible to handle liquid air for a short time, because our skin temperature, 37 degrees C., is so high in comparison with that of liquid air, −207 degrees C. The heat of the hand immediately produces vapour which forms a protective barrier and which prevents any direct contact between the liquid and the skin.

Many substances are made hard and brittle by contact with liquid air. A rubber tube will stiffen until it can be shattered with a blow from a hammer just as though it were a clay-pipe (Fig. 3). Grapes and cherries harden until they look like glass marbles. But these changes are only temporary. When the objects return to their normal temperature, they also recover their familiar texture.

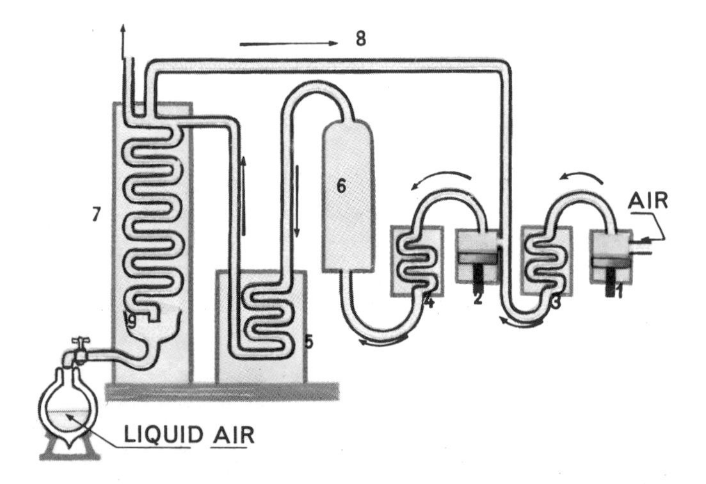

Fig. 5. Linde's machine for the liquefaction of air, consisting of a series of compressors (1 and 2) and refrigerators (3, 4 and 5), a purifier (6) and an expander (7). The air is compressed and cooled and freed of dust and impurities, and arrives at the expander already very cold. It returns through the connecting pipe (8) and repeats the circuit over and over again until it liquefies. Then it drips gradually into the receptacle (9).

BURNING ICE

To show that liquid air really does turn solid on a fire, one can conduct a simple experiment. Holding a tube of glass above the flame of a bunsen-burner, liquid air is poured carefully down it. When it arrives at the end over the flame, it will turn into a solid globule. Evaporation produces such intense cold that it solidifies the liquid (Fig. 4).

Another experiment will produce the equally strange sight of a liquid boiling on ice. If you fill a coffee-pot with liquid air and put it on a block of ice, huge puffs of white vapour will pour out of the spout, just as though the pot was standing on a gas-ring instead of a block of ice (Fig. 6). It looks very odd, but you must not forget that, compared with liquid air, ice has a very high temperature.

HOW IS LIQUID AIR MADE?

Fig. 5 is a diagram of a liquefaction machine. " Liquefaction " means changing a substance from the form of gas or vapour to a liquid state. This is done by cooling it. For example, the steam from a cooking pot will collect in little drops of water on the underside of a cold plate placed on top of the pot.

It is possible to liquefy a gas at normal pressure by cooling it sufficiently. Ammonia, for example, turns to liquid at −57 degrees C. But air liquefies at −207 degrees C. and hydrogen at −270 degrees C. How did scientists manage to achieve such temperatures?

Cailletet was the first man to attempt to liquefy air, in 1887. Eight years later a Bavarian, Linde, invented a machine that could liquefy air in quantities large enough to use industrially. It works by first compressing the gas, and then expanding it, before finally cooling it (Fig. 5).

The liquefaction of air is now an important industry. The constituents of air all boil at different temperatures, and they can be separated from one another by the distillation of liquid air. Oxygen, nitrogen, argon, helium and neon can all be produced on a commercial scale in this way.

ELECTRIC CURRENT - An Unseen Power

Our modern world runs on electricity. We are used to seeing electric bulbs light up when we press a switch, or watch an electric fire glow red as electricity provides us with heat. We accept the fact that electricity drives our trains, and provides us with our television and radio. But there is an application of electricity which we seldom encounter in everyday life; it is the electrical phenomenon we call electrolysis.

Electrolysis describes the chemical action which is caused by electric currents passing through solutions of substances in water.

Many scientists took part in the study of electrolysis. A priest, Father Beccaria, was the first to observe that a series of electrical discharges from a Leyden jar (the early condenser) produced gas bubbles when passed through water. Two Englishmen, Nicholson and Carlisle, carried out the electrolysis of water to produce its constituent gases, hydrogen and oxygen. The English physicist, Michael Faraday, explained the relationship between electricity and the chemical changes taking place in electrolytic processes.

ELECTROLYSIS OF WATER

Here is an experiment which shows what happens when an electric current passes through a conducting liquid.

Fill a glass tank with water and dissolve in it a spoonful of ordinary cooking salt (sodium chloride). To this add a few grains of phenolphthalein (you can buy it quite cheaply at any chemists). Then take two bare wires attached to a *battery* (do not on any account try to use mains electricity) and dip them into the water. The negative wire, which comes from the zinc, will turn the surrounding water red, while the positive wire from the copper has no effect at all.

A solution through which electric current is passed is called an " electrolyte ". When electricity passes through an electrolyte, a series of chemical changes may take place involving the " solvent " (e.g. water) and the " solute " (e.g. salt). The metal conducting wires that are submerged in the liquid are called " electrodes ": the positive wire is the " anode ", and the other the " cathode ".

THE VOLTAMETER

There is a special apparatus for the electrolysis of water and it is called voltameter. As you know, water is composed of oxygen and hydrogen. One of the properties of oxygen is that it supports combustion, so if you take the test-tube containing oxygen from the voltameter and put it near a smouldering taper, the taper will start to burn brightly.

Hydrogen, on the other hand, is combustible (that is to say, it will burn) but it does not support the combustion of other substances. So if you put a lighted match in the test-tube containing hydrogen, there will only be a tiny explosion.

ELECTROLYSIS OF COPPER SULPHATE

Instead of adding salt to the water, you could do another experiment by adding copper sulphate ($CuSO_4$). This is a compound made from sulphuric acid and copper. This

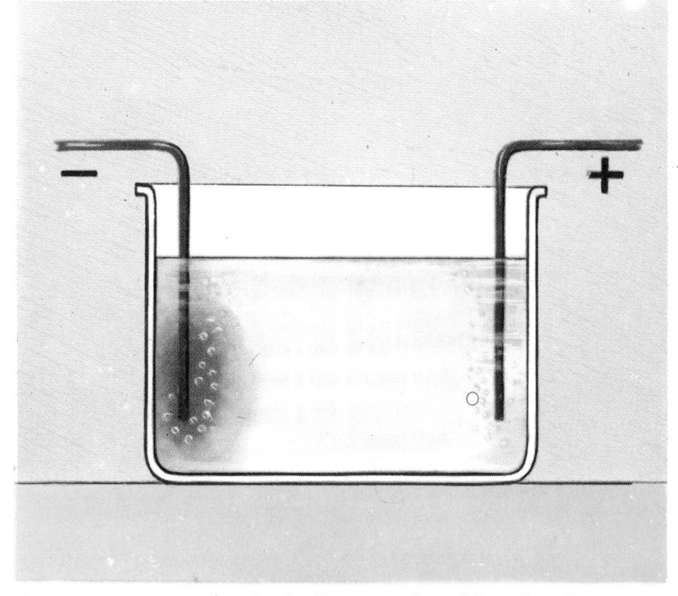

One of the many chemical effects produced by electric current can be seen in this very simple experiment. Shake some ordinary cooking salt and a few grains of phenolphthalein into a basin of water. Then connect up an electric battery to wires which are submerged in the water. You will see the liquid around the negative wire turning red, whilst the wire from the positive terminal remains the same, no colour change occurring.

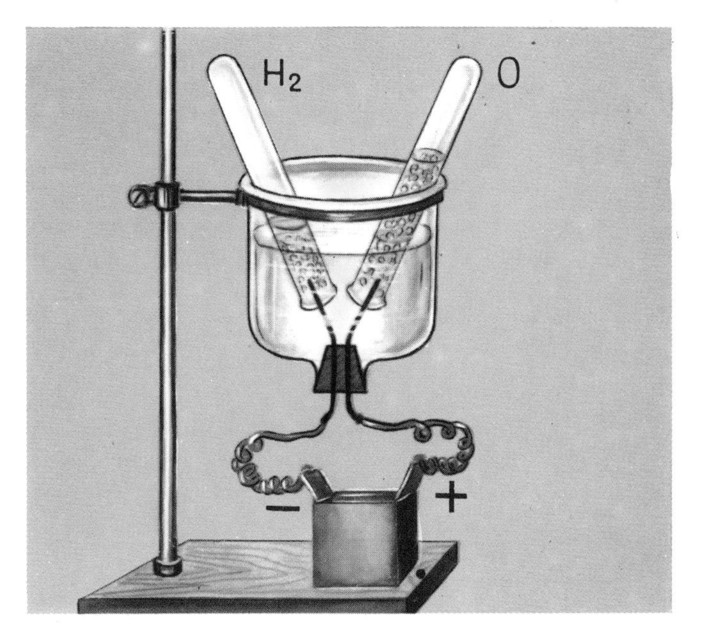

This voltameter is used in experiments with electrolysis. Two copper or nickel wires (electrodes) are attached at one end to the terminals of a battery, and the other two ends are placed in a solution of water and soda. If two test-tubes are placed over the ends of the wires, gas bubbles will form inside them. The positive electrode will release one part of oxygen (0) *for every two parts of hydrogen released by the negative electrode.*

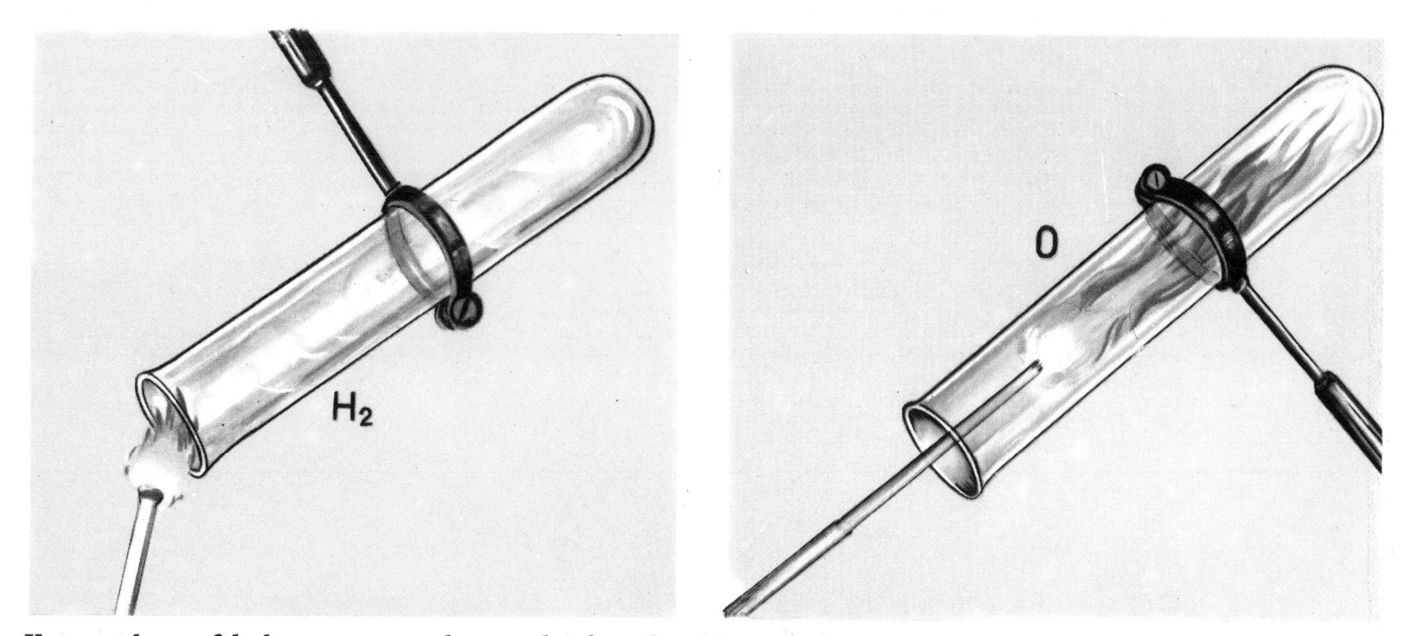

You must be careful when you remove the test-tubes from the voltameter. Oxygen is heavier than air, so it will sink down to the bottom if you keep the tube upright, with the opening at the top. Hydrogen, however, is lighter than air, and if you kept the tube upright the hydrogen would escape. It will be quite safe, however, if you hold the test-tube upside down. If you hold a match in the test-tube containing oxygen the match will burn readily; the hydrogen will produce a small explosion.

time electrolysis will have quite a different effect. The copper sulphate will separate again into two parts: copper and SO_4. The copper, thus freed, will deposit itself on the negative electrode.

If, on the other hand, you just put sulphuric acid in the water, this will be split into its two parts: H and SO_4. The H will make for the cathode (the negative electrode), and the SO_4 will join with the hydrogen atoms in the water, thus freeing the oxygen from the water. This oxygen is released at the anode (the positive electrode).

When you realise the wide variety of results that electrolysis can produce, it is easy to understand why it is considered so important in industry. Some branches of the metal industry —like electro-plating and electro-deposition—are based almost entirely on the principle of electrolysis.

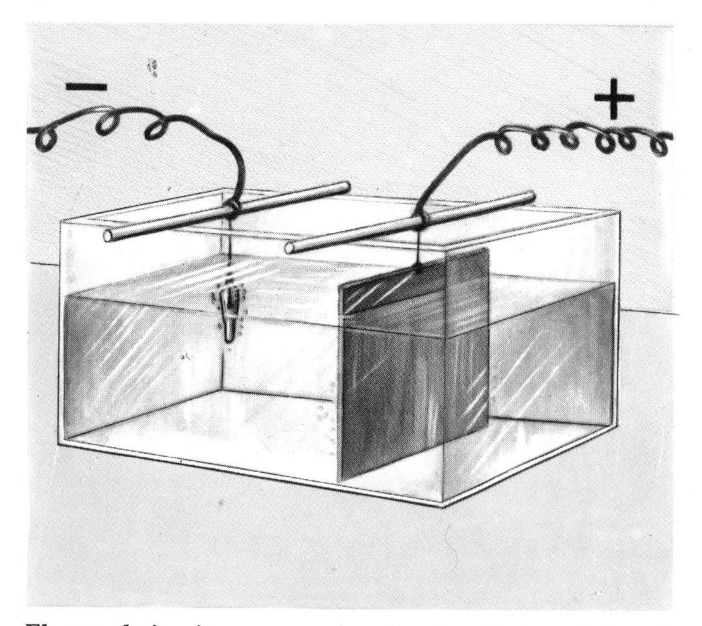

Electro-plating is a common application of electrolysis. It consists in coating one metal with another, with the help of electricity. To cover a steel pen-nib with copper, for example, you attach the nib to the negative terminal of a battery and a plate of copper to the positive terminal. Submerge both in a solution of copper salt and the nib will take on a thin coating of copper.

ELECTRO-PLATING

Electro-plating is a way of covering one metal with a thin coating of another. By this means a common metal can be made to look like a precious one.

This is how it is done: fill a glass tank with a concentrated solution of copper sulphate. Take the end of the negative wire and fix it to a steel pen nib. Fix the positive wire to a plate of copper, and submerge both in the solution. Before long the nib will be covered with a layer of red copper.

ELECTRO-DEPOSITION

Electro-deposition is a similar process, but it provides a way of covering substances other than metals with a metal coating. For instance, if you want to copy a medallion, the first thing to do is to make a wax impression of it. Coat this with a thin layer of graphite or black lead. Both of these are excellent conductors of electricity. When this has been done, fix a copper wire round the wax impression of the medallion, and suspend it from a glass rod hung on the rim of a glass tank filled with copper sulphate solution. The next step is to connect the copper wire with the negative terminal of the battery. The rest of the procedure is exactly the same as for electro-plating, and the result is also similar— the medallion is covered with a copper coating and looks for all the world just like the original.

PRECIOUS METALS

Copper-plating is by no means the only technique: nickel-plating, silver-plating and gold-plating are equally important. For these the " victim "—that is the object to be covered— must be cleaned and completely freed of grease. It is then fixed to the negative terminal of the battery.

To the other terminal a sheet of nickel, silver or gold is attached, and both objects are submerged, as usual, in a

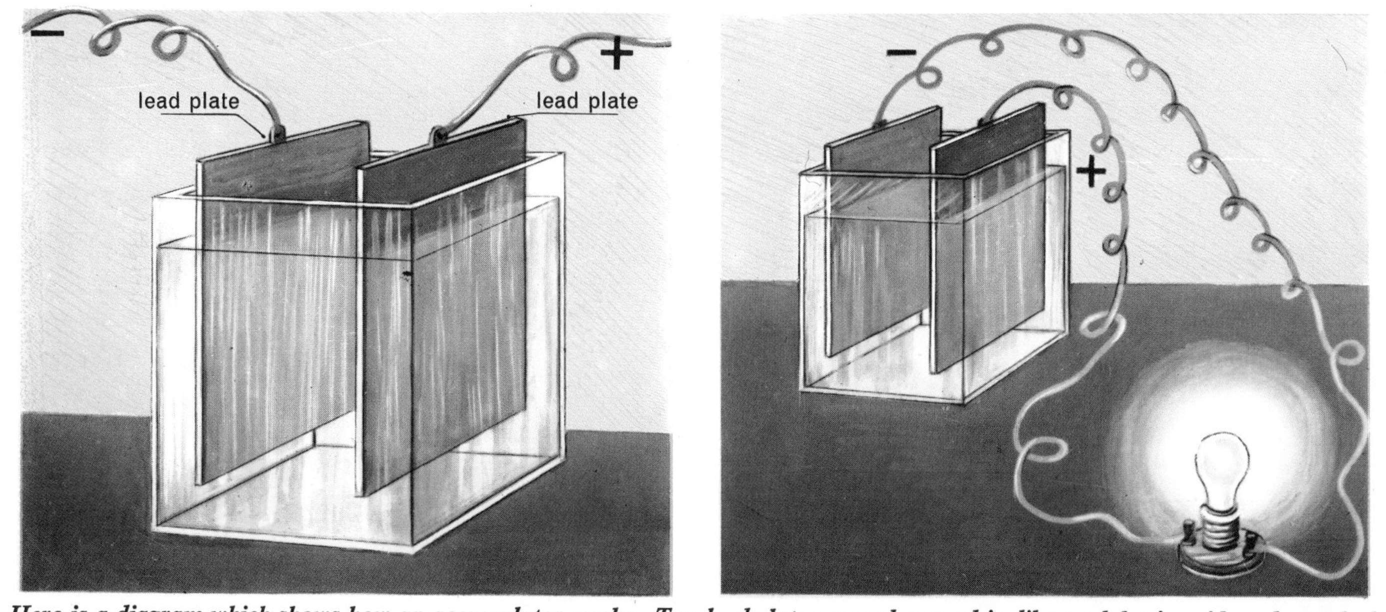

Here is a diagram which shows how an accumulator works. Two lead plates are submerged in dilute sulphuric acid, and attached to them are the two terminals of a battery. A coating of lead peroxide will form over the lead on the positive electrode, whilst the other sheet of lead will become spongy. This phenomenon is reversible. If you attach the two wires to an electric light bulb, it will light up. At the same time, the plates of lead will tend to return to their original condition, using up in the light.bulb the energy they had stored in themselves.

solution of a salt of whatever metal is fixed to the positive terminal. Gold-plating, for example, is done with a sheet of gold in a gold salt solution.

METALLURGY

Electric current can also be used for separating pure metals from their ores by means of electrochemical techniques. Electrolytic copper can be separated from copper sulphate, aluminium from bauxite, and sodium, potassium and magnesium from their respective chlorides.

ACCUMULATOR

If an ordinary battery is inadequate, an accumulator may be used. This will provide a heavier current for a longer time. An experimental accumulator can be made as follows:

The apparatus above consists of a square glass or ebonite jar containing dilute sulphuric acid in which two lead plates are half-submerged. These are connected by wire to a direct electric current. When this current flows, it takes the oxygen in the electrolyte (the acid solution) to the anode (+). There it forms a layer of lead peroxide—red brown in colour. Meanwhile the hydrogen is attracted to the cathode (−), where a layer of spongy lead is formed. When the electric current has been passed through for a while, the accumulator is disconnected, and re-connected to an electric light bulb of low voltage. This lights up, showing that the chemical energy stored in the accumulator is now being converted again into electrical energy.

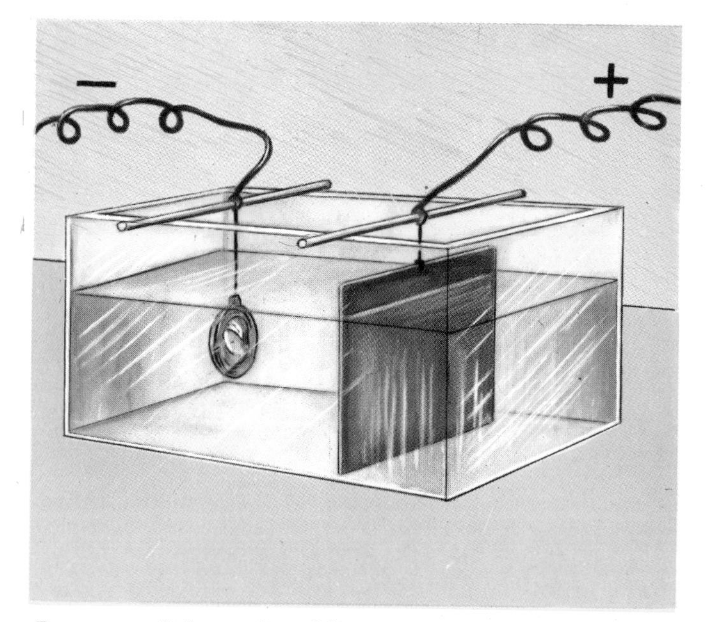

By means of electro-deposition you can cover any object with a metal coating. For example, make a wax copy of an engraving and coat it with a graphite so that it will conduct an electric current. Attach it to the negative terminal of a battery and lower it into a solution of copper salt. Attach a sheet of copper to the positive terminal, and the wax will soon be covered by a layer of copper, an exact copy of the engraving.

N.B. *Great care is needed in carrying out experiments with electricity. On no account must the mains supply of electricity be used, except under the supervision of an experienced teacher.*

QUESTIONS AND ANSWERS

What is a Booster Rocket?

This is a rocket used for providing an extra burst of power which supplements the main propulsion system of a plane or space vehicle. Modern high-speed planes, for example, use booster rockets to help them rise more quickly from the ground. The rockets provide a powerful but short-lived burst of power when it is most needed.

Booster rockets are used to lift space vehicles from the launching pad, providing power that overcomes the strong gravitational forces and air resistance at low altitudes.

HOW OUR SOLAR SYSTEM BEGAN

One of the most interesting parts of the science of astronomy is *cosmogony*, or the study of the origin of things. It tries to answer questions like: " How and when was the Earth created? ", " Was the Earth once part of the Sun? " and " How did the solar system begin? " It cannot, of course, give definite answers, but it does at least offer suggestions, using as a basis what is already known about the universe.

For example, we know that over 99·9 per cent. of the material in the solar system lies in the Sun, the remaining 0·1 per cent. being shared by nine major planets, several thousand asteroids, numerous comets, and an immense number of meteorites. We know also that all the planets (and most of the other bodies) travel round the Sun in the same direction and in almost the same plane.

By considering these and other facts of a similar kind, the French mathematician Simon Laplace suggested that the solar system was formed from a giant gas cloud or nebula. The whole cloud rotated slowly and in so doing grew smaller and took on the shape of a cartwheel. As the speed of rotation of this " wheel " or disc increased, material was flung off the edges in a number of separate rings. The material in each ring then condensed to form a planet, and the remaining central part condensed to form the Sun.

This *nebular hypothesis*, thought out by Laplace nearly two hundred years ago, sounds reasonable enough until it is studied mathematically. It is then found that if the solar system had been formed in this way, the masses and the speeds of the planets would be quite different from what they really are.

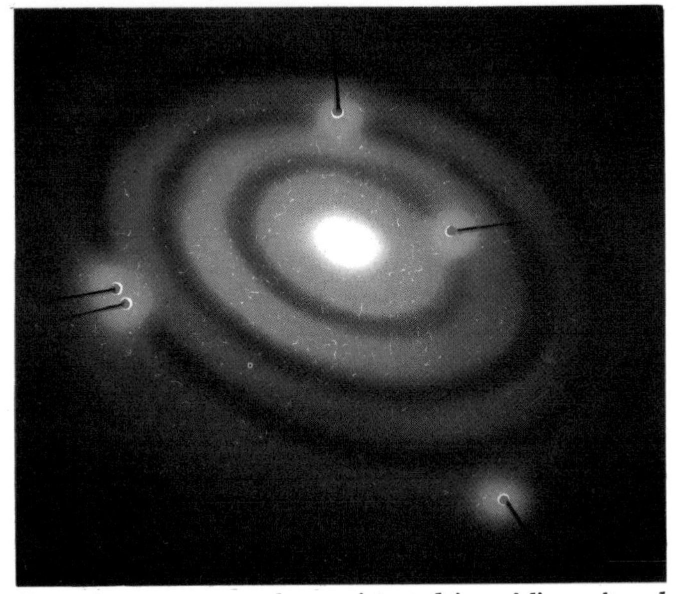

Our solar system may have originated in swirling grit and dust, brought together by gravitational forces to form spinning clusters which eventually fused into masses of matter.

NEAR COLLISION

Another idea, suggested by Jeans and Jeffreys about thirty years ago, was that the planets were formed as a result of a near approach of another star to the Sun. Although the two stars did not collide, the visiting star passed so close to the Sun as to raise great tides on its surface. As a result, intensely hot material was drawn off the Sun in the form of a huge cigar-shaped arm. The arm then broke up into a number of separate parts, each of which finally condensed to form a planet.

The sun and the worlds of the solar system, namely, planets, which circle around the sun in orbits, and which are drawn here in proportion: 1. Mercury; 2. Venus; 3. Earth; 4. Moon (satellite of the Earth); 5. Mars; 6. Jupiter; 7. Neptune; 8. Saturn; 9. Uranus.

This *tidal theory*, as it is called, appears to have one great weakness—that two stars can and do come very close to one another. Present knowledge tells us that the stars are separated one from another by immense distances—that they have as much room at their disposal as would eight tennis balls arranged evenly inside the Earth. The chances of a near collision are therefore extremely small.

TWIN STARS

Another tidal theory, developed in recent years by Lyttleton, supposes that the Sun was once associated with another star. The two stars formed a waltzing pair until a third one came along, and raised such great tides in the Sun's companion as to break it up into parts which eventually became the planets.

To-day, many astronomers favour theories which involve interstellar gas and dust. We now have plenty of evidence that the great spaces between the stars are not necessarily empty but in many parts of the sky contain great clouds of extremely thin gas and tiny dust-like particles. The Sun may have been formed by a condensation in one of these clouds, while the planets could have grown from other separate condensations. As far as the planets are concerned they need not have condensed from hot material but may have been built up by the sticking together of myriads of comparatively cold particles.

THE MEASUREMENT OF TIME

Since the beginning of time, the sun in its course has revealed to Man the rhythm of the seasons, marking for him the unending procession of day and night. But the sun is no longer adequate for marking the passage of time in our complicated modern world. We now rely upon that marvellous human invention: the clock.

Many ages passed before our ancestors felt the need to measure the length of their days and divide them into hours; for centuries, they were content to watch the sun rising and setting, tracing on the quadrant of the sky the two faces of time: day and night. Shepherds in ancient times were among the first to assess the time of day by watching the shadows shorten and lengthen as the sun passed overhead. This became the basis of the first timepiece invented by Man: the sun-dial.

The sun-dial enabled man to divide his day into smaller units; he split up the day, which was established naturally by the rotating Earth, into twenty-fourths, and began to mark out time in hours.

Erone, *a well-known physicist of* 200 B.C., *using his hour-glass for measuring time as he takes his pulse.*

THE SUN-DIAL

It is believed that the Chinese used sun-dials as long ago as 2670 B.C. and the ancient Egyptians and Assyro-Babylonians had similar instruments. But credit for the invention in 500 B.C. of a really scientific solar timepiece goes to the Greek, Anaximander. Sun-dials had appeared in Rome by 291 B.C.: the iron hand of one famous sun-dial was attached almost perpendicularly to a wall, on which radiating lines marked the hours of the day as the shadow fell upon them.

THE HOUR-GLASS

In the third-century B.C., the popularity of the sun-dial was threatened by the hour-glass, which the Greeks had brought back from the Orient. At first the hour-glass contained water which dripped through the narrow opening between an upper and a lower vessel; the device was later improved by replacing the water with very fine sand. The length of time taken for the upper glass to empty was carefully measured and when the water (or sand) had all reached the bottom, the hour-glass was reversed.

Erone, a great physicist who lived about 200 B.C. used an hour-glass-chronometer for taking his pulse. At Greek trials the time allowed the defendant for pleading his case was limited by the hour-glass.

Another method of time-telling used by the Romans was to burn candles marked to indicate the passing of the hours, and rich people could buy pocket sun-dials. Then about 130 B.C., *Ctesibius*, a mathematician, had the brilliant idea of constructing an hour-glass in which the action of the dripping water set in motion a system of wheels. These, in their turn, were connected to a little statue which slowly climbed a notched column, marking off the hours on it with a stick.

THE MECHANICAL CLOCK

In the eighth-century, a forerunner of the mechanical clock, moved by weights, was made by the Archdeacon of Verona and given by the Pope Paul I to King Pippin the Short. At the beginning of the ninth-century, Charlemagne received from the Caliph Harun-el-Rashid a timepiece which struck the hour by letting a certain number of metal balls fall on to a bronze bowl. But until 1280 even clocks as complicated and ingenious as these were still based on the principles of the hour-glass.

The first description of a truly mechanical clock is found in the early fourteenth-century in the writings of the great Italian poet, Dante. The parts of this clock seem to correspond to those of a modern clock: the *motive power* (a weight); the *driving mechanism* (composed of various wheels); the *escapement* (a transmission wheel which sets the others in motion); the *regulator* (which in this first example is actually

A gift from Harun-al-Rashid to Charlemagne: a timepiece which struck the hour by dropping metal balls on to a bronze bowl.

In 1344, the first astronomical clock was hoisted on to the tower of the Town Hall in Padua.

In 1462, Bartholomew Manfredi invented the first "portable" clock.

a rough circular balance wheel). These four parts, though improved and streamlined, are to-day still the fundamentals of the mechanics of clock making.

Towards 1300, large mechanical timepieces driven by weights began to appear on towers. In 1344, the first astronomical clock was hoisted on to the tower of the Town Hall in Padua: in addition to marking the hours, it bore the signs of the zodiac and recorded the movements of the heavens. In the following century, these public clocks were embellished with moving figures that struck bells on the hour or appeared in procession.

THE POCKET WATCH

In 1462, Bartholomew Manfredi of Mantua constructed the first clock intended for " carrying on one's person ". Half a century later, the German, Peter Henlein produced the famous " Egg of Nuremberg ", popularly thought to be the first pocket watch. The motive weight was replaced by a spring, but in place of the chain escapement adopted later, there was a piece of fine catgut which was easy to break and liable to stretch. From these beginnings the watch-making industry made rapid progress. To-day there still exists a little watch that once belonged to Mary, Queen of Scots, and it is as small and elegant as any modern lady's watch. The Emperor Charles V owned a fairly accurate watch set in a ring. In 1595, the Duke of Ferrara received a gift of a chiming clock, the first one known to history, and Catherine the Great of Russia later owned one the shape and size of an egg, which played a little melody every hour.

Galileo's discovery of the pendulum at the end of the sixteenth-century, marked another milestone in the development of the clock. The regular swing of the pendulum, applied to a timepiece, enabled it to achieve that constant, steady rhythm long sought and never before attained. The pendulum became a basis of clock design. Christian Huygens incorporated the pendulum movement into the mechanism of the clock, and also invented the spiral spring. About a century later, an Englishman, John Harrison, constructed the first chronometer, achieving a remarkable degree of precision. At about the same time George Graham, another

The first "speaking clock" introduced into the French Court, gave one of the princesses the vapours; she complained that the new instrument broke life into little pieces.

Whilst watching the huge bronze chandelier in Pisa Cathedral, Galileo realised that each of its oscillations as it swayed from side to side, took exactly the same amount of time.

From Galileo's observations and subsequent discovery of the pendulum, the grandfather clock was born. Huygens later invented the spiral spring.

A modern clockmaker's laboratory. Nowadays, clocks are guaranteed to keep time to a very high degree of accuracy. To date, the most accurate timepiece is the atom clock, recently developed at the British National Physical Laboratory.

Englishman, invented the cylinder escapement; the lever escapement, a most practical and ingenious device, was a more recent invention which has been used to great advantage by Swiss craftsmen.

In 1844, Adrien Philippe invented the *remontoir*, or winder. The pocket watch no longer required a separate key.

ELECTRIC AND ATOMIC CLOCKS

Electricity soon found its way into the clock-making industry. Its application is attributed to the physicist, Hipp, in Geneva, where clock manufacture had become established. The usual type of electric clock is built round a central regulator which is very accurate; this closes an electric circuit once a minute and makes the clock hand jump forward one minute at a time. (This circuit can connect all the clocks in a building, or even in a town). In its turn the wheel that controls the minute hand also drives the gear that regulates the hour hand.

Finally, the ultimate in chronology (timekeeping) is the newly developed atomic clock which operates with almost absolute precision. The atomic clock is accurate to one second in 230 years. The movement of its hands is controlled by the vibration of the atoms present in the molecules of ammonia gas; their rhythm remains constant and is unaffected by external influences. The accuracy of the atomic clock surpasses that of the balance wheel, the pendulum, and even the quartz crystals which have been used until now in the most accurate chronometers.

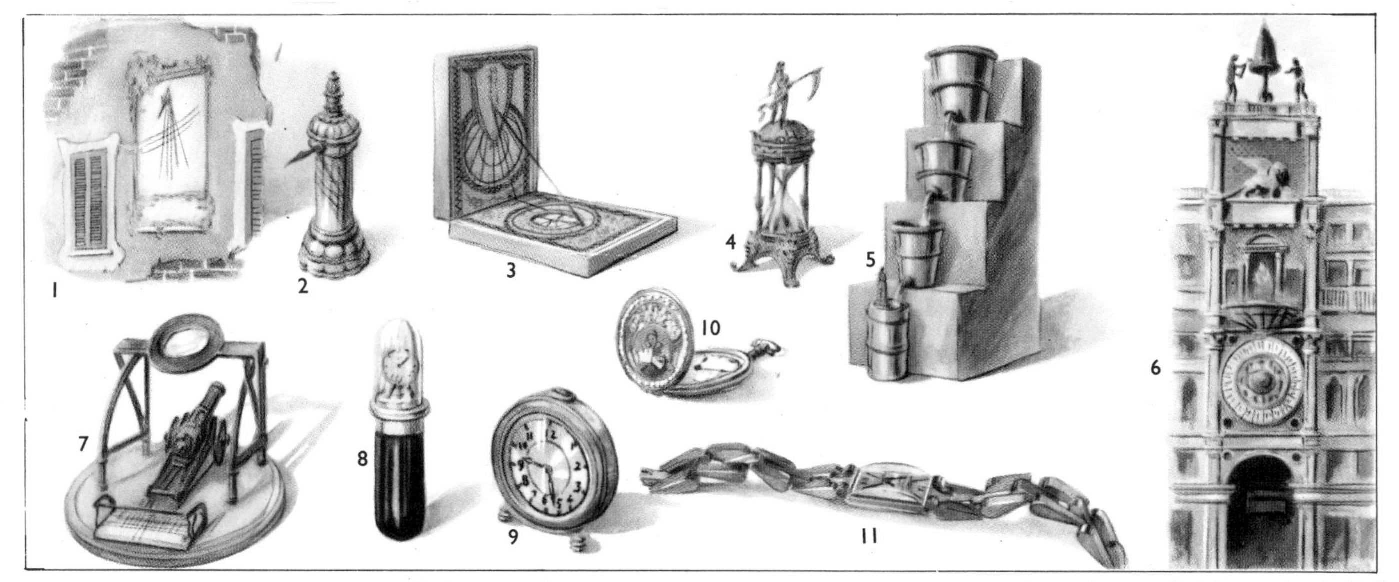

Clocks through the ages: 1. the sundial; 2. ancient table sundial in the shape of a column; 3. pocket sundial in use in the 7th century A.D. *the hour is indicated according to the latitude by the shadow of the thread which comes out of a little hole, 4. an hour-glass; 5. the famous hour-glass of Canton in China, it takes twelve hours for the water to pass from the first to the last urn, 6. the famous clock-tower at Venice; 7. midday-signal in use in the 19th century, the cannon fires when the rays of the sun, concentrated by the lens, set off the detonator, 8. modern atomic clock kept under a pressurised hood which maintains it at a constant temperature; 9. an ordinary alarm clock; 10. a pocket watch; 11. a modern wrist-watch.*

SALT

Salt is an essential constituent of human blood, and it plays a vital part in the proper functioning of our bodies. Man's instinct has always led him to search for supplies of salt, especially when the cooking of food became accepted practice, and salt had to be added to foods from which it had been removed during cooking. Nature's most abundant supply of salt is in the sea, and it was probably from this source that our ancestors first extracted it. Beds of rock salt, mostly of marine origin, may also have been known to primitive cave-dwellers.

It is impossible to say when the systematic production of salt began. But in Mediterranean countries it was already an important industry in early Roman times. It was then that a first experiment in nationalisation was made, the extraction, transport and sale of salt coming under State control. It remains so to this day in some Latin countries.

The ancient historians Livy and Pliny tell us that the salt trade was put on a commercial basis by Anco Marzio, whose salt pans at Ostia near Rome had long been known. The custom then grew up for salt concessions to be let by the State to private contractors on payment of a fixed rent. Under the Republic these contractors were forced to re-sell their salt at a price which was decreed by the Roman Censors. The salt was transported by boat up the Tiber to riverside warehouses whence it was distributed to shops with retail licences rather of the sort that modern tobacconists require. Internal transport was by mule and pack-horse, and public demand for salt, even in those distant days, is evident in the name of *Via Salaria*, one of the roads that leads to Rome.

SALT FROM SEA WATER

Sodium chloride (common salt) makes up between 70–80 per cent. of the salt content of sea water. It has been calculated that every cubic mile of sea water contains more than 100 million tons of salt. The concentration varies in different parts of the world. It is affected in some areas by heavy rainfall, in some by the geological nature of the sea-bed, in others by various secondary factors which increase or decrease the amount of salt in the water.

Salt is extracted from sea water by evaporating the water in the sun and wind. For this reason the exploitation of nature's inexhaustible reserves of sea salt is easiest along sunny, wind-blown shores. The climatic conditions of the Mediterranean are ideal and salt production around this large inland sea is a traditional and profitable activity.

The usual method is to admit the sea water to wide basins, or pans, whose shallow depth—little more than a foot—speeds up evaporation. The task of the salt worker is to arrange his basins in such a way that the water can pass freely from one to another, depositing as it goes the different grades of salt it contains.

Sea water is brought up by a small canal fitted with a kind of lock gate which regulates its flow into the basins. The first basins are the largest, each lying a little below the level of the previous one, so that when required the water can flow into it by force of gravity. As the water moves on and more and more liquid evaporates, it naturally takes up less space. The basins, therefore, grow smaller and shallower until, at length, a highly concentrated solution reaches the last pan where sodium chloride, or common salt, is deposited. This particular basin is built to a special design with a curved base and stone or wooden tiles round the sides.

The basins are linked to one another by a system of controlled channels, one set of which is used for draining off the top level of water which has already given up its salt. Near the pans an area is reserved for storing the salt in piles that look like white ricks. Behind these is a broad ditch to collect rain and flood water which, in large quantities, would dissolve

Close to the shore and linked by small channels and locks, these basins are for the extraction of salt from seawater.

The seawater is run into the basins; there it slowly evaporates, depositing a layer of salt.

the salt and undo the patient work of months in a very short time.

CLIMATIC INFLUENCES

The modern technique of salt production of course takes into consideration the long experience gained in different regions where salt workings have been established for many centuries. Due to different climatic conditions, the methods employed are not always the same. For instance, the time taken to complete a production cycle varies from place to place. " Salt cropping ", as it has been called, takes anything from a minimum of five months in the Mediterranean area to as much as twelve months in certain tropical regions.

All forms of work which require man's co-operation with nature are inclined to be slow. " Salt cropping " is no exception. Before starting production, rainwater must be removed from the basins. Where they still contain some of the previous season's residue, this has to be dried out in order to obtain a salt saturated bottom. Again, before the real work can begin, the connecting channels may have to be repaired and their banks pointed. Then, when all is ready, the first basins are filled at high tide.

SALT " CROPPING "

While the water is passing slowly down from one level to the next an important job is put in hand in the last of the salt pans. The floors of these pans have to be levelled and rolled hard after each " crop " has been lifted from them. Mud collects in them, for which reason some salt workers put down a layer of seaweed to sponge up any water and form a sort of carpet for the salt.

Meanwhile the salty water will have reached the basin before the last one, and its salt content is now high. The moment has come for the delicate operation of feeding this solution into the final pans. It is introduced little by little so that at each operation a new layer of salt-saturated water is deposited over the surface. A good salt worker is able to see immediately how much salt remains in the water at every phase of the operation, although an instrument called a salinometer may be used to read the density of the solution.

In any case, when the water is ready for final treatment in the salt pans, it has an unmistakable look. There is a sparkle about it which comes from the tiny salt crystals floating on the surface. The last of the moisture now evaporates and there remains a crust of salt which grows thicker and thicker. About four inches is the normal height of a salt layer when it is " cropped ". In the Mediterranean area about three months are needed from start to finish to obtain this result.

The salt, when quite dry, is stacked in white ricks of symmetrical shape built on rising ground along the edge of the salt pans.

TRANSPORT AND STORAGE

In places where salt is extracted in very large quantities, transport is by tip wagons, which run on narrow-gauge rails to the permanent deposits. Sometimes mechanical elevators are used to dump the salt on mounds as big as a fair-sized house. There it remains until lorries come to take it to the nearest port for shipment.

To look at them when they are new one would think that those white salt ricks would crumble to pieces and melt like snow at the first rainstorm. Tiles or tarpaulin covers are, in some places, used to protect them in wet weather. But, as a rule, the hard crust which forms in contact with the air and wind-blown dust is a sufficient covering. The amount of salt obtained from sea water differs according to the locality, but normally the yield is about one hundredweight for every seven square yards of salt pan.

When rock-salt mining is difficult, water is piped into the mine and the brine which forms is pumped back to the surface.

EXTRACTING ROCK SALT

Rock salt consists almost entirely of sodium chloride and is found in crystalline form mixed with clay and other impurities from which it takes a greyish colour. Certain substances mixed with the rock salt may give it a red or violet tint. These underground deposits of rock salt are the residue from salt-saturated water which evaporated in remote geological times.

There are three methods of extracting rock salt: digging, mining and leaching. When the deposits lie near the surface they are excavated by means of wide tunnels which require no particular form of support, due to the very solid nature of the material. In Cheshire there is a rock salt mine underground, where salt is mined in the same way as coal.

Leaching is a process by which water is percolated into the rock salt of the subsoil and then drawn off in the form of a salt-bearing brine. By evaporation, the brine is made to yield a salt of the purest quality.

SALT DEPOSITS IN BRITAIN

A considerable quantity of salt is obtained from underground brine springs like those at Droitwich, Worcestershire. These springs, which are rich in dissolved sodium chloride, in some places rise naturally to the surface. Elsewhere, the brine is tapped and released by drilling.

The purity and quality of common salt varies widely, depending on its source and the methods used in extracting it. These variations affect the uses to which different grades of salt are put. Sea water salt is well suited to the requirements of farming, refrigerating plants and industry. Selected qualities, also obtained from sea water, are used for salting fish. When intended for human consumption, whether as cooking or table salt, magnesium and other foreign substances must be removed from the salt. First-rate table salt is produced from the underground salt-water springs like those at Droitwich.

THE CELL

Until the microscope was invented, biologists had no way of studying the fine structure of plant and animal bodies. About three hundred years ago, the application of the microscope opened up a wonderful new world of exploration to science, and it was soon found that the bodies of living things were built up from tiny compartments which became known as cells.

It is now recognised that all living things consist of these little units, which can be regarded as the building blocks of the plant and animal worlds. The larger animals and plants are made up of enormous numbers of cells, but some of the smallest may consist of a single cell. The growth of living things takes place by an increase in the number of cells. A human being, for example, begins as one cell which, by

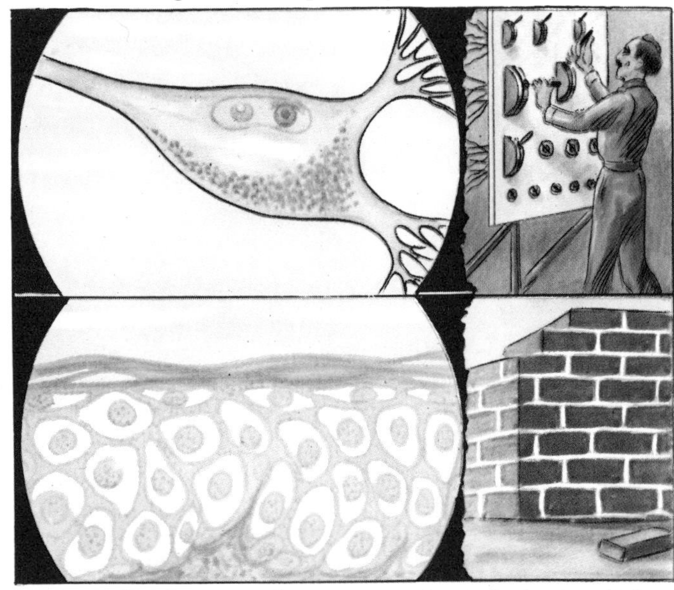

Nerve cell, above, carries messages from the brain. Below, "epithelial" cells which form the "building bricks" of the skin.

constant division, gives rise to the millions which are present in the body of the adult person.

PROTOPLASM

In a complex living organism, there may be many types of cells, but they all have certain things in common. Each is filled with a substance called protoplasm which is like a soft jelly. It is transparent and contains a large amount of water in which are dissolved salts, sugars and other materials. Substances such as oils, which are not soluble in water, are present in the protoplasm as little droplets. Still other materials, such as the proteins, are in the form of tiny particles. Living protoplasm has the ability to form a membrane at its surface, called the plasmalemma. In plants this protoplasmic membrane produces a cellulose wall all round the cell. Unlike animals, which are usually supported by some sort of skeleton, plants are supported by all the cellulose walls of the cells forming the plant body.

The protoplasm of the cell consists of the cytoplasm, which is the material occupying most of the cell, and the nucleoplasm which is contained in a rounded body called the

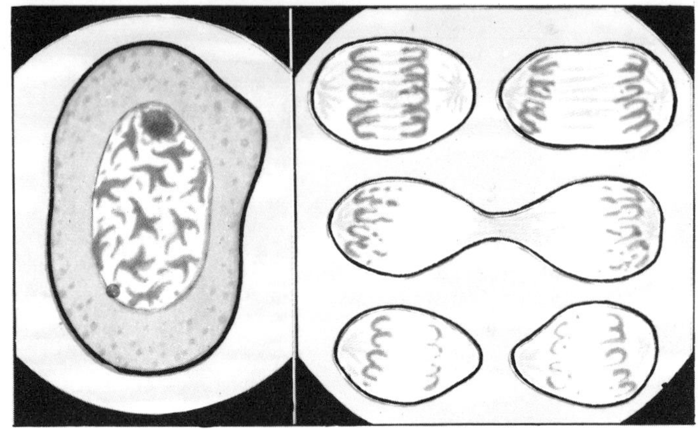

On the left we see a cell magnified, showing the central nucleus surrounded by cytoplasm and the membrane. On the right are shown the various phases of "mitosis"; the dark filaments are the "chromosomes."

nucleus. This is the control centre of the cell, and most cells die if it is removed. It contains the chromosomes which carry the characters that are handed on from one generation to the next. When the cell divides, the chromosomes split lengthwise, forming pairs, each of the new cells being provided with a set of chromosomes identical with the original ones.

SINGLE CELL

In a unicellular animal or plant the single cell of which it is composed carries out all the vital processes connected with respiration, feeding, movement, the excretion of waste material and reproduction. On the other hand, in a living thing which has many cells there is usually an arrangement in which each cell has its own special task to perform.

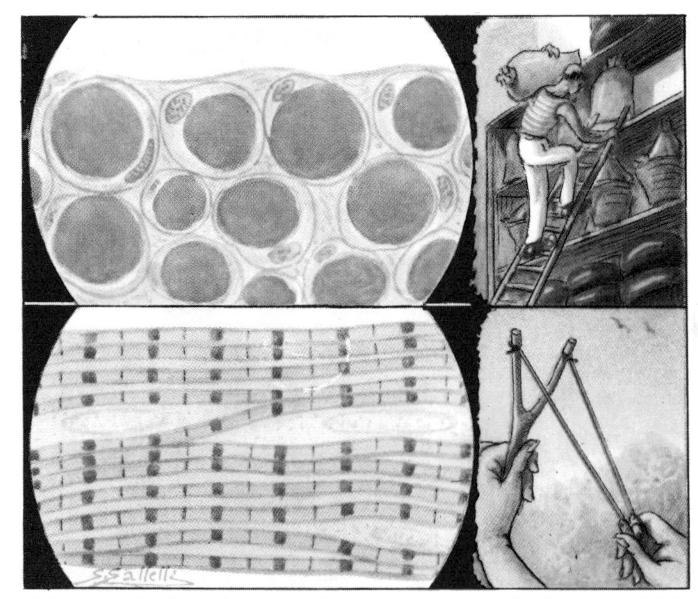

Illustrated above is some fatty tissue; the dark mass which appears in each cell is a droplet of fat. Illustrated below are muscle fibres.

THE TELEPHONE

The simple telegraph transmits messages from place to place by using electric impulses which travel along a wire. The pattern of movement of the impulses carries the message in the form of a code.

The knowledge that information could be transmitted in this way led to many attempts to transmit the patterns of vibration forming human speech itself. The problem was much more difficult than that which faced the inventors of simple telegraphy.

Human speech, in common with all sounds, is carried through the air as waves. These waves are in the form of to-and-fro movements of the molecules of gases in the air, which are stimulated by vibration of the vocal chords. As these oscillations reach the ear, they cause movement of the eardrum and the pattern of vibration of the eardrum corresponds to the pattern of vibration that produced the oscillatory movements in the air at the source of the sound. The nature of the sound itself is determined by the characteristics of the waves. The more vibrations there are per second, the higher is the pitch of the note; the greater the distance through which the molecules oscillate, the louder is the sound we hear.

TRANSMITTING SOUNDS

The problem of transmitting sounds by wire consists essentially of being able to analyse the air vibrations at the source, impress the pattern of the vibrations on to an electric current, dispatch the current along a wire, and then translate the pattern carried by the current into vibrations in the air at the receiving end.

In 1861, Philipp Reis built one of the earliest sound-carrying instruments at Friedrichsdorf in Germany. A membrane was stretched over a hole in a box. When sound waves struck the membrane, they made it vibrate in sympathy. Attached to the rear of the membrane was a little platinum plate which was adjusted to make contact with a platinum wire when the membrane moved inward. Contact was broken when the membrane moved outward.

BELL STUDIES HUMAN EAR

Fifteen years later, the famous Scots-Canadian inventor Alexander Graham Bell perfected the first successful telephone. Bell's interest in the subject came from his work as a teacher of deaf mutes, and he tried to devise an instrument which would translate vibrations of the air into something that his pupils could see and understand.

The more Bell thought about his problem, the more his interest grew in the subject of transmitting sounds from one place to another. He built an apparatus for playing musical instruments at a distance; the strings of a piano were operated by electromagnets which were activated by electric currents passed along wires.

For three years, Bell worked on his musical telegraph, helped by his assistant, Thomas Watson. One day, Watson was adjusting a faulty contact in the transmitter, and Bell heard the twang of a steel spring coming from the receiver. He realised that a spring of this sort could be made to vibrate in sympathy with the sound waves created by human speech, and the vibration pattern could be impressed on the flow of current through a wire.

Bell began to experiment, and within a year had built a workable telephone. The transmitter picked up sound waves with the help of a skin stretched over the mouthpiece. The centre of the skin carried a piece of iron, behind which was an electromagnet. As sound waves reached the skin, they made it vibrate to and fro, and the movements of the piece of iron caused corresponding fluctuations in the current of electricity flowing through the coils of the electromagnet.

These currents were carried along a wire to a receiver which was similar in construction to the transmitter. Current passing through the coils of the electromagnet attracted the iron attached to the centre of the skin diaphragm. The fluctuating current from the transmitter thus caused vibrations of the diaphragm, which produced corresponding vibrations in the molecules of the air.

The characteristics of the sound waves produced in this way were similar to those of the waves detected by the transmitter, and the device was able to reproduce the complex vibrations of human speech.

On 10th March, 1876, Graham Bell made the first telephone call to his assistant in another room; he said, " Mr. Watson, come here; I want you." On 6th October, Bell spoke to Watson over a line joining Boston and Cambridge, Massachusetts, demonstrating conclusively that his telephone was able to operate over long distances.

EDISON'S IMPROVED TRANSMITTER

In the year following Bell's discovery, a new form of transmitter was invented by Thomas Edison. This instrument made use of the effect of pressure on the ability of a mass of carbon granules to carry an electric current.

Carbon is a good conductor of electricity, and a mass of tiny granules packed together will carry a current so long

The first telephone exchange was inaugurated by Graham Bell.

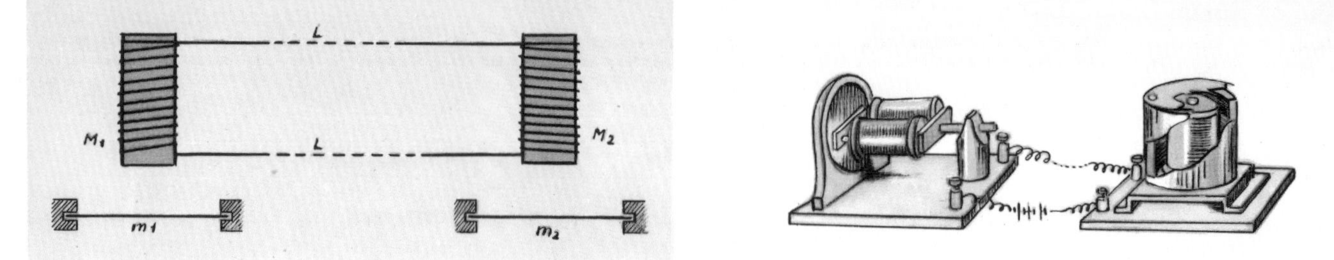

As in the case of many other inventions, several people were working at the same time on the telephone. Different claims have been made as to who was first, but it is generally acknowledged that Alexander Graham Bell patented the first telephone capable of reproducing speech. This instrument (top right) *was exhibited at the Philadelphia Exhibition in* 1876. *The figure on the left represents two permanent magnets* (*M*1 *and M*2) *whose pole pieces carry wire coils forming the circuit shown by the lines* (*L*).

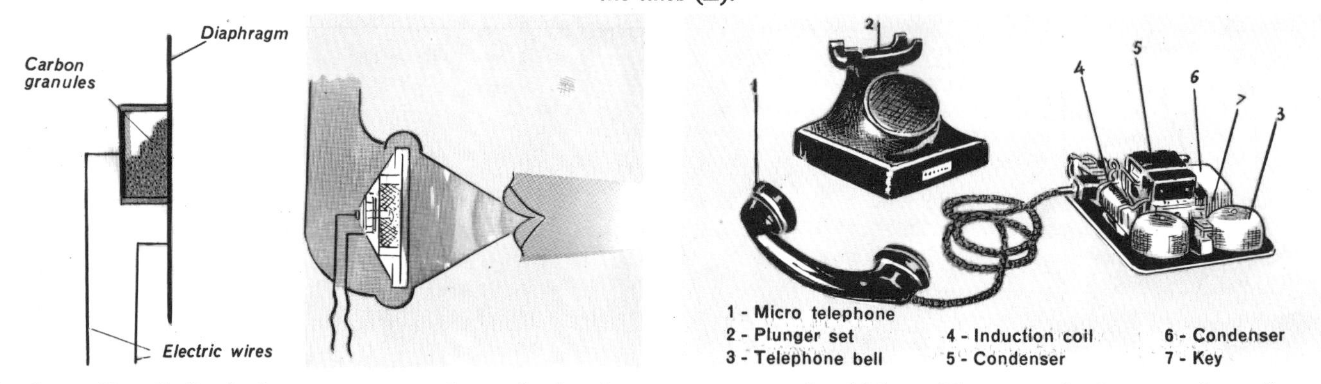

In the earliest Bell telephones an extremely weak electric current was used, which could carry only for very short distances. Further improvements to Bell's instrument were carried out by Thomas Alva Edison; the English inventor, Professor D. E. Hughes, went a stage further and adapted an idea of Edison's. He fitted the existing instrument with a microphone containing carbon granules. The effect was to modulate the current and increase the efficiency of the instrument. Left: *diagram of the microphone box, a device converting sound vibrations into electric currents.* Right: *a modern telephone set.*

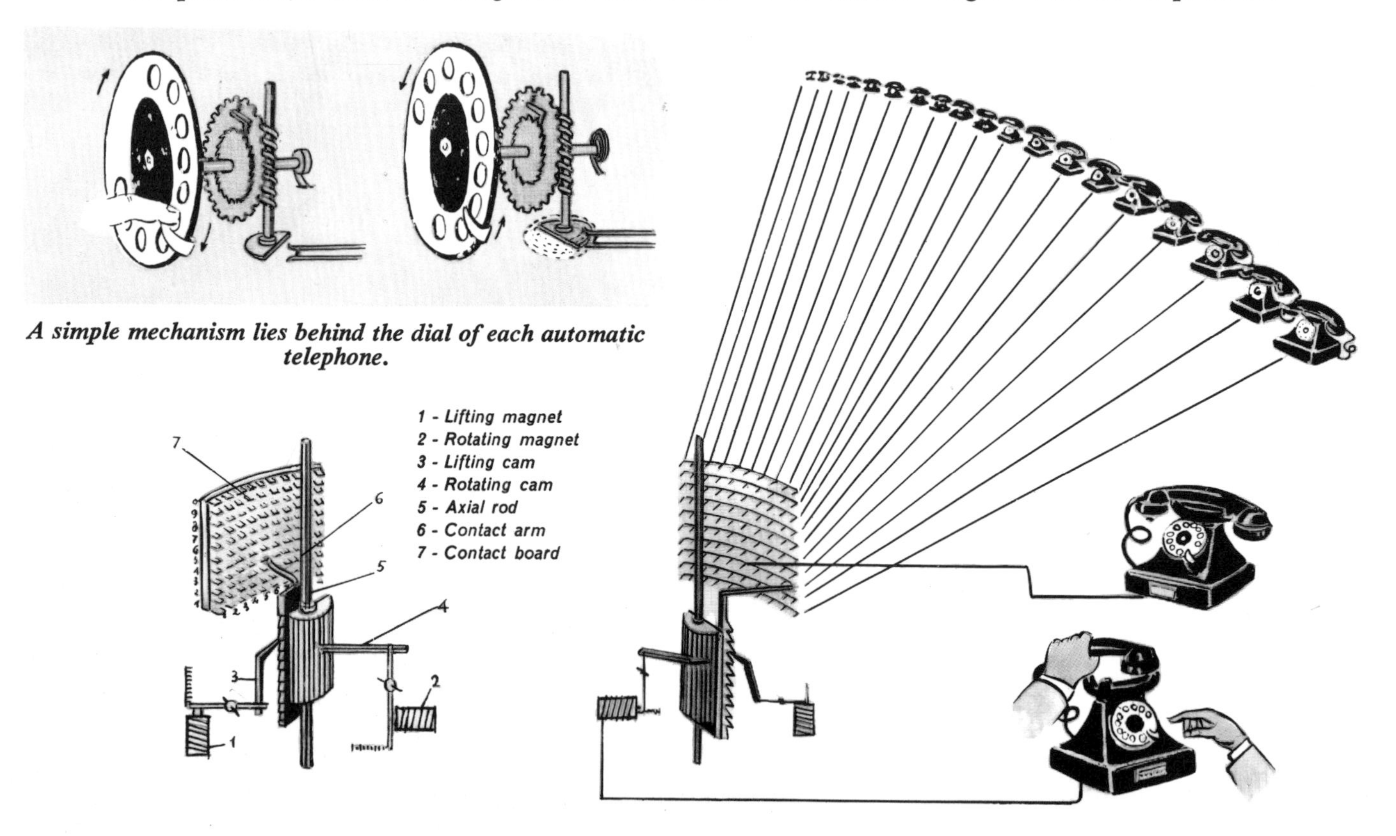

A simple mechanism lies behind the dial of each automatic telephone.

An automatically-operated call is put through in the following way. The subscriber on picking up the handset sets in motion the pre-selector which contacts one of the free selectors. Where five numbers are used the first to be dialled brings the selector into action and moves the plug pins into the area of the number required. The second and third effect the final selection, while the last two choose the tens and digits of the number the caller is dialling.

as there is a contact between the individual granules. If the mass of particles is pressed together, the contact between the particles is good, and current flows readily. If the particles are packed loosely, however, contact between them is poor and the flow of current is restricted.

In his telephone, Edison packed powdered carbon between two platinum discs, and joined one of the discs by an ivory button to a sheet of mica in the mouthpiece of the instrument. A current of electricity was passed through the carbon granules, flowing from one platinum disc to the other.

When sound waves reached the instrument, they made the mica diaphragm vibrate in sympathy with vibrations of the molecules in the air. These movements of the diaphragm were passed on to the platinum disc via the ivory button, and the movements of the disc caused alternate compression and relaxation of the particles of carbon packed between the two platinum discs.

DIAPHRAGM AND ELECTROMAGNET

The fluctuating currents which were sent out by Edison's transmitter were passed through an electromagnet in the receiver. A metal diaphragm was fixed near to the magnet, and this was attracted towards the magnet when electricity passed through the coils. Variations in the strength of the current caused corresponding variations in the pull exerted by the electromagnet; acting against the natural springiness of the metal diaphragm, the fluctuating current of electricity caused vibrations of the diaphragm that corresponded in pattern with the fluctuations in the current. The diaphragm, in turn, created sound waves in the air which were similar in their essential characteristics to the sound waves which had stimulated the diaphragm at the transmitting end.

The modern telephone has developed from this instrument invented by Thomas Edison. Inside the mouthpiece of the telephone is a microphone which contains a box of carbon granules. Vibrations of a diaphragm cause a fluctuating current to be sent off to the earpiece of the receiver. Here, an electromagnet sets up vibrations in a metal diaphragm, corresponding to the fluctuations in the current coming from the mouthpiece at the other end of the wire.

Strangely enough, the telephone was received with the same indifference that had marked the discovery of the telegraph. After Bell demonstrated his telephone in 1876,

Manually-operated switchboard connecting caller and listener.

The caller (1) *having selected and engaged his number on the control panel* (2) *is in conversation with his contact, whose picture is shown on the viewer* (3).

some of his friends attempted to establish a telephone system. It was not until January, 1878, however, that the first telephone switchboard came into operation.

Graham Bell made a trip to his native Scotland during that year. He travelled to London and presented Queen Victoria with a pair of ivory telephones. This gift did much to stimulate interest in the telephone in Britain, and in 1879 the first of London's telephone exchanges was opened.

THE VIEWPHONE

Not so very far away in the field of telephones is the introduction of the push-button or keyphone, and these developments could eventually completely displace the conventional dial telephone. The uses to which such a system could be put are wide and varied, but one which is of special interest is the viewphone. This is a telephone system which includes a control panel, a camera and a television-type viewing unit. Subscribers to this system will have a coded card which has to be inserted into the control before a call can be made. When the card is inserted a call is made by pressing push-buttons on the control panel, in sequence, to obtain the desired number. The numerals are displayed on the screen of the viewing unit allowing a check to be made before the connect button is pressed to make the call.

Once the call is established, two-way viewing facilities can be brought into action by pressing a vision button. The recipient of the call will be displayed on the caller's viewing screen and the caller will be seen on the recipient's screen.

Experiments have already been conducted in the United States of America and Britain with trial installations of the viewphone and these have indicated the possibility of multi-party or conference-linking arrangements. This would entail the linking of several viewphones, with voice switching of the viewers arranged so that it is always the speaker's face that is displayed on remote viewing screens whilst his viewer retains the image of the previous speaker.

The effect of the viewphone on community life could be very beneficial. If, for instance, the viewphone was connected with the local communications network, the subscriber could have access to a variety of services, such as library, entertainment and information services, without leaving his house.

ROCKETS FOR WAR

The big rockets upon which the present armed strength of the United States of America and Russia is largely based, are considered to be the " last word " in weapons of war. In some respects they are, but it will surprise many readers to learn that the rocket is in fact one of the *oldest* weapons of which there are records. A Russian encyclopædia suggests that in elementary form they originated in China about 5,000 years ago. There is a big gap of more than 4,000 years to the next historical record—A.D. 1232—and this is the one usually accepted as the date of their introduction. The Chinese chronicle concerned, in describing an ancient war with the Mongols, mentions dreaded " arrows of flying fire ". Almost certainly, this is a reference to crude rockets.

The first mention of rockets in European history occurs in the Chronicle of Cologne, in the year 1258, and later the Italian historian, Muratori, credits the rocket with an important victory in the battle for the Isle of Chiozzia, in 1379. One defending tower withstood all conventional assaults until a direct hit by a rocket set it on fire.

MORE RECENT USE

By the middle of the fifteenth-century the rocket had become a fully-fledged, if somewhat unreliable, weapon of war, and numerous reports refer to its use in various battles. During the Thirty Years' War, they were used on a large scale against Phillipsburg in 1645, and are claimed to have hastened the downfall of the city. Nor was the use of the rocket confined to Europe, for the following paragraph appears in a description of the battle of Paniput, India, in 1761:

> " As the Rohillas had a great number of rockets, they fired volleys of two thousand at a time, which not only terrified the horses by their awful noise, but did so much execution also, that the enemy could not advance to the charge."

Over 25,000 *rockets were fired during the siege of Copenhagen in the year* 1807.

Back in Europe, rockets played an important part in the battle of Boulogne in 1806, and also in sinking a portion of the French fleet.

NAVAL BATTERIES

For the attack on the French fleet the rockets were fired, in salvoes, from twenty-four special boats which were towed to the scene of the battle by parent vessels. Special rockets were used which contained a liquid incendiary filling inside a sharply pointed nose. The pointed nose stuck in the sides of the enemy ship, whereupon the filling, which was alight, oozed out through a number of holes in the head. It is easy to imagine the devastation these dreadful weapons inflicted upon the wooden men-o'-war of that time.

In 1807, Copenhagen was almost burned to the ground by a rocket barrage, during which 25,000 missiles were fired. These rockets, and those used against the French fleet, were designed by the British artillery expert, William Congreve. They weighed 32 lb. and carried a warhead, varying from 8 to 20 lb., about two miles.

So effective had Congreve's rockets become that, in 1812, the British Army formed a Rocket Brigade, which later saw action during the Battle of Waterloo in 1815. For a while it seemed as if the rocket might replace the cannon for battlefield use; but improvements in gun design, such as breech loading and rifling, improved the rate of fire and accuracy so much that rockets became obsolete for nearly a century.

During the Great War of 1914–18, the only application of military rockets was by the French, who fitted Le Prieur November-the-Fifth-type rockets to the wing struts of aircraft for use against captive observation balloons. A similar ground-fired weapon seems to have been used against the German Zeppelins and is credited with the destruction of Zeppelin No. LZ 77 as it made an attack on the railroad junction at Révigny, near Brabant-le-Roy.

ROCKETS THROUGH SPACE

But the day when the war rocket really grew up was 3rd October, 1942. For on that day the Germans carried out the first successful launching of their 46-foot, 12-ton, A-4 missile, thereby creating rocket history. As Major-General W. R. Dornberger, who was in charge of the German Army rocket development from 1930 to 1945, explained, supersonic speed was achieved for the first time by a liquid propellant rocket. Also, the rocket, in reaching an altitude of nearly 60 miles broke the world height record of 25 miles. The record at that time being held by the shell fired from *Big Bertha*, the almost legendary gun which shelled Paris in 1918. Space was invaded for the first time and used as a bridge between two points on the Earth.

Two years and 65,000 drawing alterations later, the first of over 1,000 A-4s fell on England, killing three people and injuring ten. Referred to as the Vergeltungswaffe zwei (V-2)—Reprisal Weapon No. 2—by Germany's Propaganda Ministry, this missile, the forerunner of those which would be used in push-button warfare, killed a total of 2,724 people

The German V-2 of 1944 re-introduced the rocket into modern warfare. Above, a battery of the missiles preparatory to firing.

and seriously injured 6,000, besides causing havoc and damaging many thousands of buildings. The rocket had indeed grown up.

ROCKETS ON PARADE

At the time V-2s were falling on England, many armchair strategists criticised the use of this weapon, comparing its relative ineffectiveness with the damage wrought by the ten-ton bomb loads of the Lancasters of the Royal Air Force. From the German viewpoint it would have been fairer to compare it with the then current performance of *their* bombers. As Dornberger inquired, " How often, after 1941, could a German bomber fly to England before being shot down? "

Today, however, a survey of the Armed Forces of the major powers would indicate quite clearly that the V-2 ushered in the era of push-button warfare. The twin development of jet propulsion and atomic bombs created the need for new defensive counter-weapons, and the rocket has now been greatly developed to help fulfil this need.

AIR-TO-AIR MISSILES

As the description " air-to-air " implies, these are rockets designed to be carried by aircraft and fired at airborne targets. Many missiles of this type are little more than highly developed unguided November-the-Fifth-type rockets. Usually fired in great salvoes of up to a 100 at a time, however, each stands a good chance of destroying the biggest bomber in the world to-day.

The latest interceptors tend to carry two, or four, bigger guided missiles with a longer range. Typical weapons are France's Matra, Britain's Firestreak and Red Top, Russia's Atoll, and the U.S. Falcon, Phoenix, Genie, Sidewinder and Sparrow.

The Sparrow is a beam rider, that is, it flies along a thin pencil-like radar beam transmitted from the launching aircraft. This beam follows the aircraft, which is being attacked, like an invisible searchlight beam; and the missile, flying along the beam, is inevitably guided towards the target. When it approaches within a lethal distance of the quarry, a proximity fuse explodes the warhead.

The Sidewinder, Falcon, Firestreak, Red Top and Atoll are designed to home on to the infra-red or heat rays emitted by the engines of an aircraft. Known as infra-red or passive homing, this method of guidance is comparatively easy to develop and has the advantage that the source becomes stronger the nearer the missile gets to its quarry, thus increasing its accuracy. The Sidewinder has the distinction of being the first such missile to see active service. In operations off Formosa, fourteen Chinese Mig. 17s were reported to be destroyed in a single day by Sidewinders, launched from Sabres of the Chinese Nationalist Air Force.

A disadvantage of this type of guidance is that an enemy aircraft might, theoretically, be able to elude a missile by flying into cloud, but the great operating height of most modern warplanes makes this unlikely. The U.S. Air Force has, however, developed evasive manoeuvres to outwit such missiles.

GROUND-TO-AIR MISSILES

Many modern interceptors are little more than manned rocket-launching platforms. It is apparent that it would be an advantage if, in some instances, an interceptor was unpiloted, and this is, in effect, what is done in the case of the ground-to-air missiles. Virtually all these types of missiles have been developed for use against aircraft. They support, and in some cases supplant, the air-launched missiles.

In 1945, at the end of the war in Europe, the Germans had several such anti-aircraft missiles, all in advanced stages of development. However, the first missile to be extensively deployed, at least outside Russia, was the U.S. Nike Ajax. Weighing 1,100 lb. this missile had a speed of around 1,500 miles per hour and a range of from 10 to 25 miles. Guidance was by radar command. With this system, one radar tracks the target, while another tracks the missile. Each radar feeds data into a computer, whereby steering impulses are transmitted to the missile to effect a collision. When the missile is just under the nose of the target, its warhead is detonated by a command signal from the ground.

From the Nike Ajax, has developed the much-improved Nike Hercules. This has a maximum speed of over 2,000 miles per hour, and a slant range of up to 75 miles. Guidance

The Hawker Siddeley "Firestreak" homes on to the "infra-red" or heat rays, emitted by its target.

The BAC "Vigilant", a simple type of anti-tank missile. Vigilant is guided by signals transmitted through a fine wire attached to the missile. This wire unravels as the rocket speeds towards its target.

is beam-riding with semi-active homing. Under this system of guidance, as the missile approaches its quarry, it picks up and homes on to reflected radiation from the target, the latter being " illuminated " by powerful signals from a ground radar. The Nike Hercules warhead embodies new principles of fragmentation. It is claimed that the Nike Hercules could destroy any of to-day's bombers *before* they were able to drop a free-falling bomb on an area defended by the missile.

Forming the United States primary high-altitude anti-aircraft weapon, over eighty batteries of Nike Hercules rockets are deployed in the United States and ten in Europe.

Other ground-to-air missiles include the U.S. Redeye and Britain's Rapier. The Redeye is a one-man, shoulder-fired, weapon of the "bazooka" type, designed to give combat troops protection against fast, low-flying aircraft.

On sighting an enemy aircraft, the Redeye gunner takes aim and tracks it, at the same time energising the missile guidance system. A buzzer indicates when the missile is ready to fire. Upon firing, a small booster propels the missile out of the launch tube, so that it is well clear of the gunner when the main rocket ignites. Britain is developing a similar weapon called Blowpipe.

The Rapier is a highly efficient mobile weapon intended for defence against aircraft and helicopters flying at heights from ground level to 10,000 ft., and yet, like the Redeye and Blowpipe, can be operated by one man.

In action the weapon system detects a target aircraft at a range of about three miles and automatically determines if it is hostile or not. If the former, the missile and tracker automatically align themselves on the aircraft. Coming within range, the aircraft is tracked visually until a red light indicates that the missile should be fired. The operator then guides the Rapier by keeping the target centred in his sight. A computer steers the missile along the line of sight to ensure a direct hit on the target.

SURFACE-TO-SURFACE

This category includes both the smallest and biggest missiles yet developed. At the lower end of the scale are the anti-tank missiles. Some of these, such as the BAC Vigilant and Swingfire, are small and light enough to be carried by infantrymen. The Vigilant, in fact, can be lifted in one hand by a soldier and was specifically designed for this purpose. It is carried in a cleverly designed fibreglass case which not only provides protection against rough usage, but also acts as the launcher.

Other anti-tank missiles in this class include the French Entac and Nord SS 11, German Cobra, U.S. Dragon, Russian Snapper and the Australian Malkara. The Malkara, in service with the British and Australian Armies, is considered capable of putting out of action the biggest tanks in the world.

All these missiles are comparatively simple, and all are wire-command controlled. In this method the missiles are guided by signals transmitted through a fine wire which unravels as the missile speeds towards its target. This gives precise and unjammable control, but can only be used over short ranges. Manoeuvrability, however, is excellent and, with practice, wire-guided missiles can be steered accurately down roads, round trees and under telephone wires, to their target.

TACTICAL MISSILES

Next up the scale in size are the relatively short range tactical missiles. Missiles in this category are designed for use in the battlefield as a supplement to conventional artillery, and include the U.S. Honest John, Lance, Sergeant and Pershing, and the Russian Frog and Shaddock. Also included in this class of missile are the ship-borne surface-to-surface naval weapons, such as the Italian Sea Killer, U.S. Asroc and the Russian Styx. The Styx proved its capabilities by sinking the Israeli destroyer Eliat in 1967.

STRATEGIC MISSILES

Much bigger and even more deadly are the IRBMs (Intermediate Range Ballistic Missiles). IRBMs have a range of between 1,000 to 2,000 miles and can carry devastating warheads of atomic and thermo-nuclear bombs.

Mightier still are the even bigger ICBMs (Inter-Continental Ballistic Missiles), such as America's Minuteman, Polaris, Poseidon and Titan, and Russia's Savage, Sawfly and Scrooge. Able to carry multi-megaton warheads over ranges

The mighty Inter-Continental Ballistic Missiles are the most awesome rockets yet built. The nuclear hydrogen warheads could destroy any city in the world.

up to 7,000 miles or so, they were once considered to be the " ultimate " weapon long dreamed of by military strategists. But, initally fired from fixed bases, they were extremely vulnerable to surprise attack. This fact resulted in later ICBMs being housed in strong concrete-lined, well-like silos, giving protection against everything except a near direct hit from an incoming nuclear missile. The fear of surprise attack also led to the development of submarine-borne ballistic missiles. With the oceans covering nearly three-quarters of the surface of the Earth, it is obviously virtually impossible for an enemy to destroy all the submarines simultaneously. The United States of America, for example, has a fleet of atomic-powered submarines, each of which can carry 16 Polaris missiles armed with nuclear warheads.

SPECIALISED MISSILES

In addition to the three broad groups of missiles described so far, air-to-air, ground-to-air and surface-to-surface, there are many produced for specialised duties.

Two such missiles are the Australian Ikara and French Malafon anti-submarine weapons. Both of these resemble small aircraft and both carry homing torpedoes. The missiles are launched and guided into the general area of the submerged submarine. When near the target the torpedo is ejected. Once in the water, it searches for and homes on to the submarine.

Another range of specialised missiles are the decoys. Dropped from bombers these act, as their name implies, as decoys for any missile launched against the bomber. The U.S. Quail is one such missile. Other air-launched missiles include the stand-off bombs, such as Britain's Blue Steel, the U.S. Hound-Dog and the French TV-guided Martel. This latter missile incorporates a TV camera which transmits a picture of the target back to the parent aircraft. In the aircraft an operator, in front of a TV screen steers the missile on to the target.

Quite different, but just as effective for its particular duty, is the " Concrete Dibber " used by Israel to put Arab airfields out of action in the June war of 1967. Consisting of a rocket-powered bomb, this is first slowed by forward-firing rockets and then, in a vertical dive, boosted into the ground by other rockets.

One of the latest, and most terrifying, specialised missiles is the FOBS (Fractional Orbital Bombardment System) being developed secretly by Russia. In simple terms the FOBS is a " space-bomb " and it works like this. The bomb is fired, like a satellite, into an orbit about 100 miles above the Earth. Then, at a given point, and before completion of the first orbit, a retro-rocket slows the bomb and causes it to drop on its target. The advantage of such a weapon is that warning times are reduced and America's defences could be penetrated from the south. Several Cosmos satellites orbited during the past few years are believed to have been trial launches of FOBS bombs.

All this array of rocket hardware has been developed to give each country the power to strike back if attacked. Even if an aggressor should launch his missiles first, the idea is to have a sufficient number of widely dispersed rocket sites to ensure the destruction of the aggressor's country, too. The big rockets thus act as deterrents to all-out war and so far they have, together with the big bomber fleets of the respective countries, succeeded in keeping an uneasy peace.

The Lockheed "Polaris" ICBM, launched from a submerged submarine, represents the "last word" in military missiles.

CRYSTALS

We think of our material world in terms of living things and of inanimate matter. The living animals and plants are creatures capable of movement; the inanimate rocks and stones—the " mineral " world—are still and dead.

Yet these lifeless lumps of mineral are, in fact, in constant movement. Their atoms and their molecules are vibrating to and fro with fantastic speed; the particles inside the atoms are, in turn, vibrating and rotating in their micro-world of incessant, feverish agitation.

Our human senses, delicate as they are, cannot probe into this invisible world of the atoms and molecules which make up inanimate matter. But this does not mean that it does not exist; minerals display a fascinating world of their own within their still exteriors.

REAL AND ARTIFICIAL CRYSTAL

Minerals as a whole do not have any characteristic shape. However, this is not to say that they are never found in the geometrically-precise, multi-sided forms called crystals. When we look into the double six-sided pyramid of a piece of quartz we find it hard to imagine that these crystals are the products of nature. We feel astonished that their shining facets and perfect angles, their limpid transparency often tinted with delicate colours, is really the work of natural forces.

These crystals are not to be confused with the material we know as crystal glass. There is a fundamental difference between natural crystals and the " crystal " hangings, for instance, of a glass chandelier. The attraction of the latter comes from the skilful shaping of its surface, but the beauty of the real crystal lies in the depths of its inner structure. The difference can be seen in the results of breakage. Glass breaks into thousands of irregularly shaped bits and pieces. But the fragments of a piece of natural rock crystal retain the shape of the double six-sided pyramid, each little piece retaining the same angles as the original between adjacent faces.

HOME-MADE CRYSTALS

How are natural crystals made? If we could watch what happens in the world of atoms and molecules, we could see these tiny particles taking up position alongside one another, jostling and pushing until they finally link up together to form the regular shapes seen in Fig. 1.

We can imitate nature and make our own crystals with such common substances as sulphur and kitchen salt. Sulphur crystals, for example, can be made by melting sulphur in a crucible, removing it from the flame and pouring the molten sulphur slowly away through a hole in the cooling crust. It will then be seen that the sides and bottom of the crucible are covered with a residue of well-formed crystals. (See Fig. 2, number 1.)

To make crystals of common salt, we dissolve a small quantity of kitchen salt in water and leave it to stand. In a short while it will be seen that crystals have formed at the bottom of the vessel. As the water evaporates the salt solution becomes more concentrated and the salt particles close in on each other to form a solid crystalline mass. To make a single specimen crystal, one should suspend a tiny crystal in the salt solution from the end of length of thread. The atoms from which the salt is composed settle on the crystal " seed ", and build up to form a large regularly shaped crystal such as you see in Fig. 2, number 3.

NATURE'S USE OF CRYSTALS

Water provides us with interesting examples of natural crystals in the form of snow, ice and frost which, on examination, are found to be made up of minute hexagons with angles of 60°. These hexagons cling together in a great variety of forms.

So, too, with the clouds. Those white fleecy clouds which we see in the sky are made up of myriads of needle-shaped ice crystals. And when a halo appears around the sun or moon, it is being formed by these tiny crystals; they are breaking up the light rays and dispersing them in different colours.

So, in the clouds above our heads, and in the stones and pebbles on which we walk, we find nature at work, shaping inanimate matter into crystalline forms of great symmetry and beauty

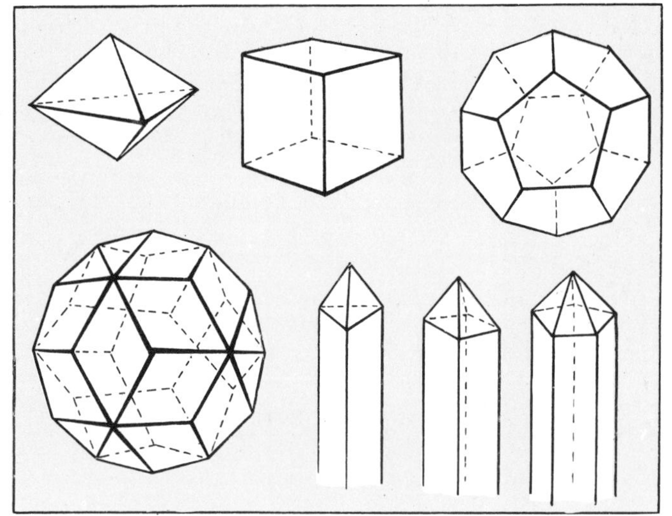

Fig. 1. A crystal is a solid body of regular shape. Shown above, typical many-sided crystals of different minerals.

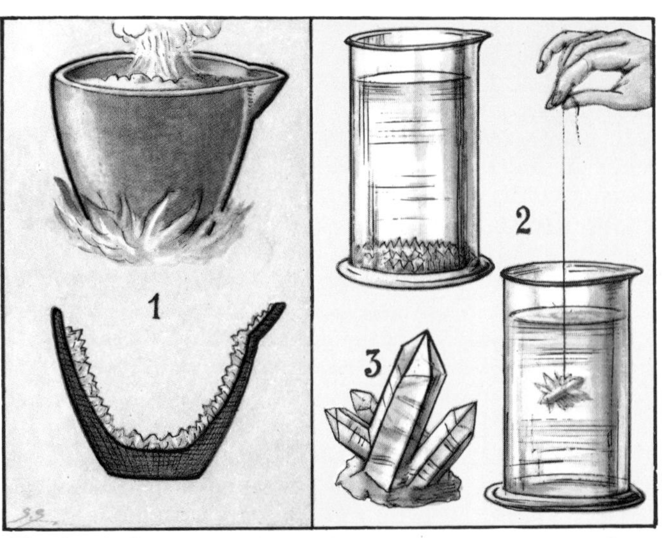

Fig. 2. A simple experiment for you to do at home, making crystals with sulphur and common salt.

BENJAMIN FRANKLIN

Franklin was a politician and a scientist, a brilliant inventor and a profound scholar; in everything he did he was a tireless worker. A single sentence of his own is the key to his whole personality: " Never waste time; it is the very essence of life."

Philadelphia was a bustling city even in 1723. The sort of place where you might dream of making your fortune. And one cold October morning there was a new face among the crowds. It belonged to a boy of seventeen, with too much sense to build fantastic castles in air, but with enough determination and skill to make a good living for himself. But that morning he walked slowly and heavily, for he had come a long way. His clothes were travel-worn and splashed with mud, and he longed for the comfort of a bed.

REST AT LAST

Suddenly he heard voices emerging from a building. He ventured through the wide doorway and found a small gathering of people listening to a public lecturer. The boy wriggled through the knot of people until he reached the back of the hall. There he saw an empty seat, and curling himself up on it, he gradually fell asleep.

That was Benjamin Franklin's first day in Philadelphia. He arrived there poor and friendless, but one day the big city would recognise him as one of her most honoured citizens.

TOO MUCH DISCIPLINE

Benjamin was born in Boston in 1706. His family were modest working people so he soon learned to fend for himself. His schooling finished at the age of ten, when his father took him to work in a candle factory. Luckily for Benjamin this job did not last long. Two years later an elder brother offered Benjamin employment as an apprentice in his newly-opened printing shop.

The business was successful and eventually became one of the best-known presses in Boston. But Benjamin found his apprenticeship too strict. His masters were severe and often unjust. He dreamed, as all boys dream sometimes, of the big city and the fortune that might await him there. One day, the temptation overcame him. He gathered up his little bundle of clothes and set out for New York. He had just enough money to pay for the journey and he knew better than to think riches would fall into his lap. However, he knew his trade, and there should be work for him. He found no work in New York, but heard there might be some in Philadelphia.

HIS FIRST JOB

So, worn out but determined, Benjamin arrived in Philadelphia. The next day he set about finding work. The proprietor of a printing works was impressed by his intelligent air and easy manner, and was given a job.

Benjamin was pleased with this first success but there were more ambitious plans in his head. He wanted to have a press of his own and spread his own political and social ideas among the people. Even in Boston his enthusiasm had been fired by politics and now he wanted to print books and journals that would reach all the outlying districts and start the people thinking about how their country was run.

WORKING IN ENGLAND

To make this dream come true, he needed money, and even more important, he must become a really expert printer. America was very much behind Europe in the art of printing, as in many other things. England was still the mother country, and Benjamin seized the opportunity, when it came his way, to go and work in London, in a famous printing

At the age of 14, Benjamin Franklin worked in his brother's printing shop. In his spare time he wrote mature and penetrating articles for the "New England Courant."

Franklin was still young when his secret dream came true: to have his own printing press and publish a periodical that would awaken people's interest in their country's politics.

One stormy day, in 1752, Benjamin Franklin launched a kite so that it soared into a thundercloud, and found that he could draw electric sparks from the end of the damp cord. Electricity and lightning were, apparently, the same.

Franklin set up a lightning conductor inside his house. The electricity raced down an iron pole on the roof and along a wire which ended outside his bedroom door.

house. When he returned to Philadelphia he put into practice all the modern developments he had learnt in London.

HIS OWN PRINTING PRESS

So, very quickly, Franklin's dream came true. He was only twenty-two when he acquired his printing press. With his own press he could at last take an active part in politics. Indeed, he started a periodical which had quite a large circulation in Pennsylvania. His aim was always to prepare his readers for the time when America would claim independence. The people living around Philadelphia were mostly rough farmers who gave little thought to politics. Franklin hoped to awaken in them an interest in the politics of their country. Then he could show them how the administration needed to be reformed.

PUBLIC SERVICE

Benjamin Franklin was never ambitious for himself and never sought high-sounding titles. But, in 1736, the citizens of Philadelphia urged him to take office and he did not disappoint them. While he was on the council he set up a body of men to form a night-watch, and a fire-fighting force (Philadelphia was one of the most advanced cities in its precautions against fire). These were just two of his innovations. Under his guidance the town became as modern and progressive as many European cities.

Meanwhile he had not forgotten his printing works. He had opened up branches in the surrounding towns that were managed by printers he had trained himself. Soon, however, his scientific studies and his public life forced him to give up his business.

THE FRANKLIN STOVE

It was in 1740, that Franklin really made his mark as an inventor. His first invention showed all his practical nature. But perhaps even more characteristic of him was its usefulness. His one aim had always been to help others and to work for a better society. His inventions were just one example of this.

The first invention was the Franklin stove. He had always worried about the menace of the frequent fires in Philadelphia, and he soon realised that a great many of them were caused by the open fire in the hearth. This seemed to him a dangerous and wasteful method of heating a house. So he set to work and constructed a special iron stove. It became popular even in Europe and was named after him.

SCIENCE AND POLITICS

Franklin was a surprisingly modest man and a great humanitarian. He had not even been afraid that such a practical invention would lessen his dignity as a politician. And he never wanted to register his many inventions. He believed that anything that was useful to society should be available to everyone without restrictive patents.

Science was a wonderful food for his practical mind. His greatest triumph in the scientific world was his invention of the lightning conductor. His fame spread all over America and Europe; he became known as the electrical "magician".

Electricity had been his major interest for a year, when, in 1747, he made tremendous discoveries about the behaviour of electric sparks. He had been conducting the famous

" Philadelphia Experiments " and was struck by the power of pointed objects to attract and repel electric flashes. This first stage started him testing his electric theories. Then, in 1753, he finally came across definite proof.

FRANKLIN'S LIGHTNING CONDUCTOR

This is Franklin's own description of that dramatic experiment. . . . " The iron pole (to attract the lightning into the house) was fixed to the chimney stack and rose about nine feet above it. From the foot of the pole a metal wire ran down the roof enclosed in a glass tube, then passed through a hole to the landing. Opposite my bedroom door the wire divided into two separate threads about six inches apart. To each one was attached a little bell. Between the bells a little copper ball hung on a silk thread. This was to act as a pendulum and strike both bells when the clouds overhead sent a charge of electricity down the wire."

This experiment showed clearly how a lightning conductor could be constructed. It was not long before all the details had been worked out and American and European houses were safe at last from the threat of lightning.

AMBASSADOR AT LARGE

But while we admire Franklin's scientific inventions, it would be unfair to him to forget his political life. In 1778, he took the fate of the American colonies in his hands. His membership of the State Assembly of Pennsylvania had given him good training in political administration and negotiation. Several times he had been invited to London to defend the interests of the American colonies. Britain was preventing America's natural growth by restricting the rate of her production.

THE AMERICAN REBELLION

Then, in 1776, the thirteen American colonies rebelled against their Mother country, and it was Franklin who made sure of the support of France. France was already nursing a grudge against Britain, and her ready alliance with America turned the scales in their favour. Britain suffered defeat at Yorktown, in 1781, and it then became obvious that she had lost her American colonies for ever.

In the moment of victory, Benjamin Franklin was already old. His active life had never allowed him a moment's leisure. Right to the end he spent all his energy in working for the benefit of the community.

ALL THE WORLD MOURNS

The great man died in 1790, in his home in Philadelphia. New America, the young country he had helped to create, honoured him with two months of national mourning. And Europe remembered him, too, with deep admiration. France was just emerging from the first bloody days of her own Revolution. Her new leaders looked upon Benjamin Franklin as a man of ideals, who stood for a free and enlightened democracy. They, too, ordered nation-wide mourning and hailed him as one of the great new political idealists.

Lightning is the flash of a discharge of electricity between two clouds, or between a cloud and the earth. If it occurred at point (A) in the clouds, it might strike the highest point (B) of the house. But a lightning conductor saves the house by providing an easier path for the electricity at (C), conducting it safely to earth.

Franklin helped to draw up the Constitution of the United States and, towards the end of his life, in 1785, he received a delegation of Philadelphian citizens who conferred on him the honorary title of "councillor of the City."

THE BLOOD SYSTEM

In an organism as complex and delicate as the human body, it is essential that there should be some arrangement for keeping the cells and tissues supplied with everything they need. The living cell needs food and water to provide the energy and raw materials, and it needs oxygen to release energy by " burning " the food. It also needs supplies of hormones produced by other organs in the body, which control its chemical processes. And it has to have some waste-disposal system which can remove the carbon dioxide and other unwanted products resulting from its synthetic activities. This job of internal transport is entrusted to the blood.

Blood, seen through the microscope, consists of innumerable tiny particles suspended in a liquid. The particles are living blood cells or corpuscles. There are enormous numbers of them and they make up about half the volume of the blood. Most of them are red, and they give the familiar

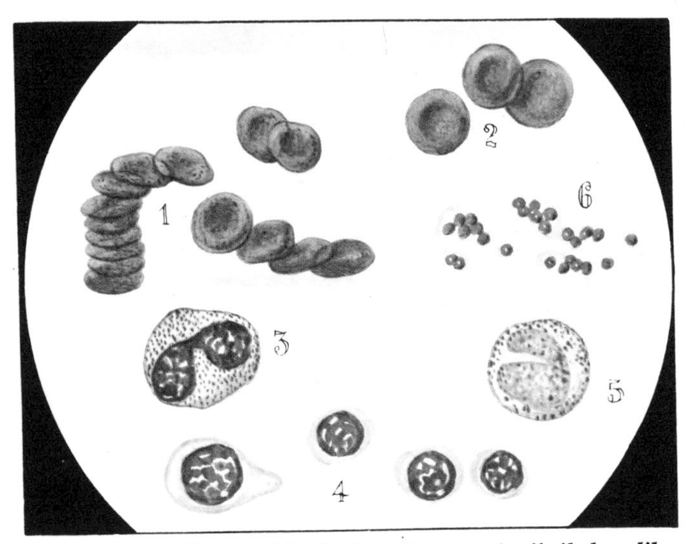

Constituents of human blood. 1. *red corpuscles "piled up like coins"* and 2. *separated;* 3. *granular neutrophils;* 4. *lymphocytes;* 5. *granular eosinophil;* 6. *platelets.*

red colour to blood. The liquid part of the blood, the plasma is a straw-coloured fluid.

RED CORPUSCLES

There are a number of types of blood corpuscles. The red corpuscles are most numerous; there are about five million of these in every cubic millimetre of blood. They are tiny discs, about eight-thousandths of a millimetre in diameter, and concave on both sides. Their red colour is due to an iron-containing pigment called hæmoglobin. This takes up oxygen when the red cells are passing through the lungs and gives it up again to living cells in other parts of the body. If the number of red cells in the blood falls below four million per cubic millimetre, the body cannot maintain its oxygen circulation. This lack of red cells is called anæmia.

The red cells are short-lived, each one only lasting about three months. An adequate supply of iron in the food is

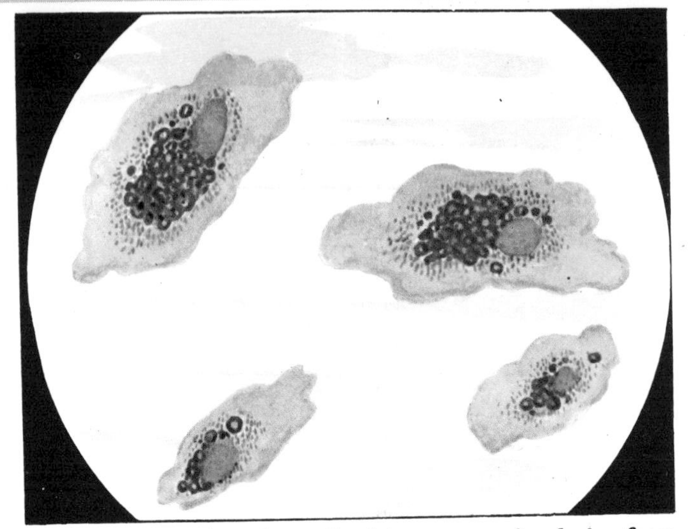

The blood of birds and reptiles (the two species derive from the same ancestors), has features differing from that of the mammals. Above are monocytes from the blood of a fowl.

necessary to produce red cells needed to replace those that die.

WHITE CORPUSCLES

The white corpuscles do not contain hæmoglobin. There are fewer of these cells than there are red cells; usually about seven thousand per cubic millimetre. There are several different types of white cell with diameters ranging from fifteen-thousandths to six-thousandths of a millimetre. The body depends on them to protect it from disease, some producing substances which counteract the poisons released by germs, and others actually " eating " and destroying germs. The numbers of white cells may increase considerably when the body is suffering from disease.

Finally there are very small cells, called platelets, which help to clot the blood in wounds. They are only two-

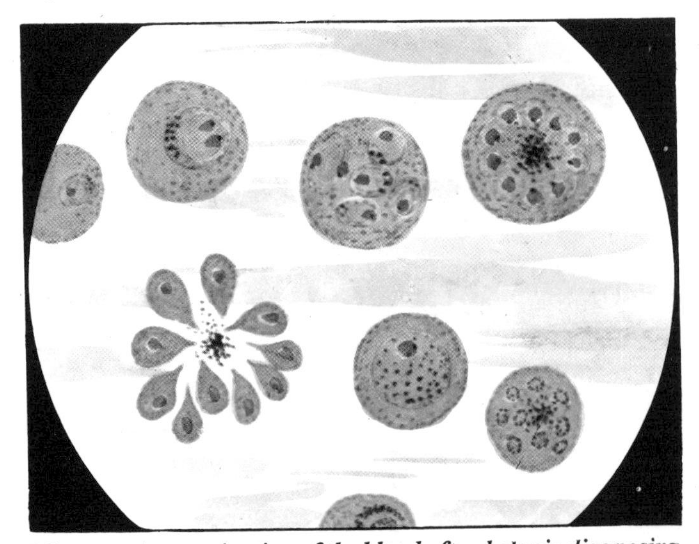

Microscopic examination of the blood often helps in diagnosing diseases. Above: *in diagramatic form, the plasmodium of malaria, a minute protozoon which develops in human blood.*

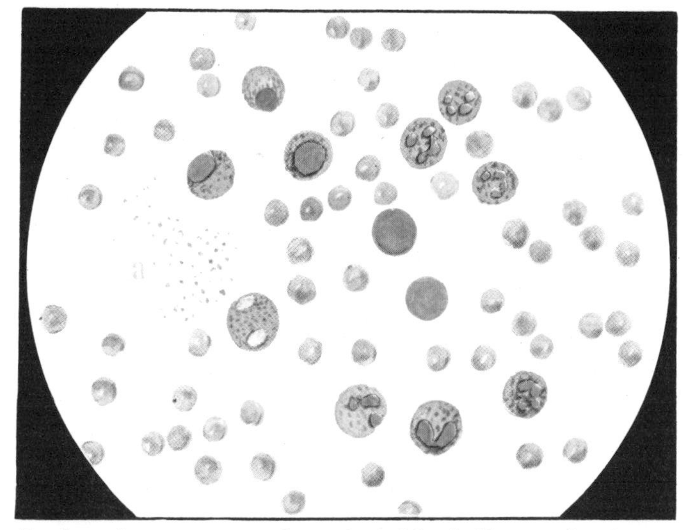

Leukaemia, an extremely serious blood disease, is characterised by the breakdown of the red cells and the subsequent abnormal increase in white cells circulating in the blood. Various types are shown in this diagram.

thousandths of a millimetre in diameter and there are normally about four hundred thousand per cubic millimetre of blood. They are usually grouped together in clumps of ten to fifteen.

PLASMA

These cells are all suspended in the liquid plasma which carries them round the body. Ninety per cent. of the weight of plasma is water, the remainder consisting of substances in solution, including common salt. Dissolved in the plasma are food materials which have entered the blood through the walls of the intestine and are being carried to parts of the body that need them. The amount of food in the blood at any time is carefully regulated by the liver. All blood from the intestines must pass through the liver before going into general circulation. This prevents a sudden rush of food materials into the blood immediately after a heavy meal. At night, on the other hand, when food is not taken, the liver releases the necessary amount from its reserve to keep up the supply in the blood.

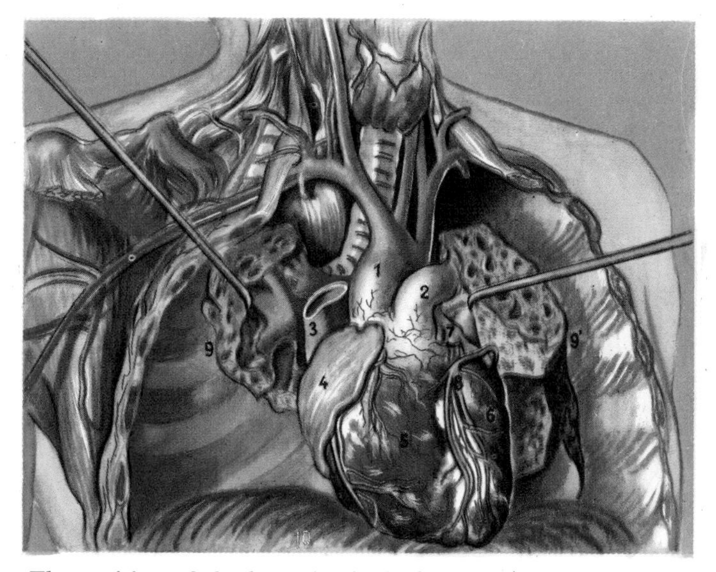

The position of the heart in the body is in the centre of the chest, slightly to the left side between the lungs. 1. *aortic arch;* 2. *pulmonary artery;* 3. *descending vena cava;* 4. *right auricle (below which is the right atrium);* 5. *right ventricle;* 6. *left ventricle;* 7. *left auricle;* 8. *coronary arteries (vessels which feed the heart);* 9. *and* 9′. *sectioned lungs.*

Substances which are going to be passed out of the body are also carried in the plasma. Urea, for example, is taken from the cells to the kidneys which remove it and release it to the bladder as urine. All cells produce carbon dioxide, which is carried by the plasma to the lungs for discharge into the air.

HORMONES

Substances formed by special glands in the body are carried by the blood to the other regions of the body. These are the hormones, or " chemical messengers ", which play a vital role in controlling the activities of the body. Adrenalin, for example, is made in the adrenal glands near the kidneys; it speeds up the rate of breathing and increases the heart beat, and is released when the body is " keyed up " for some vigorous activity.

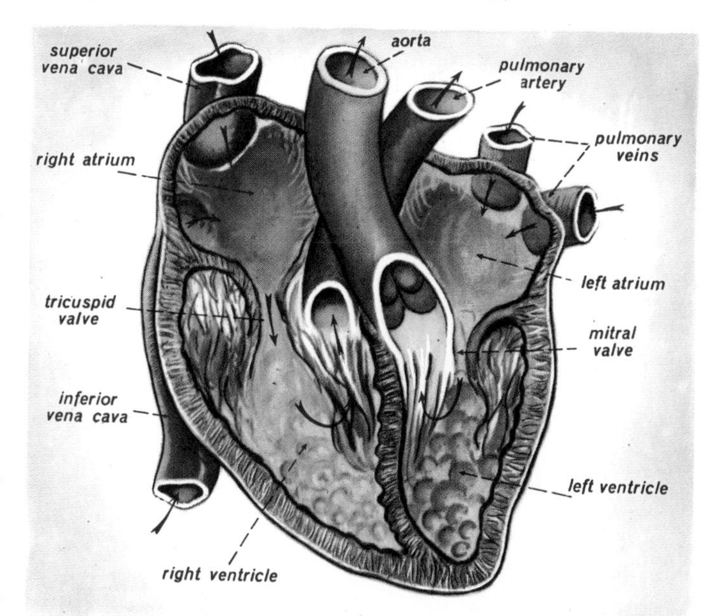

Section of the heart. The area shown in blue is occupied by venous blood; the area shown in red by arterial blood. Note the valves between the auricles and ventricles. The two pockets at the mouth of the aorta are aortic valves, which prevent the blood flowing back into the left ventricle.

BLOOD GROUPS

Although it is possible to take blood from one person and give it to another by a transfusion, care has to be taken to see that it is of the correct blood group. Both the cells and the plasma contain chemicals that react with the cells and plasma in blood from a different group. Before a transfusion takes place, therefore, the patient's blood must be tested to find which group it belongs to. Then the doctor can choose the proper blood to use in the transfusion.

DISTRIBUTION SYSTEM

Blood is circulated to all parts of the body by the heart, which is a pump connected to a system of tubes: the arteries, veins and capillaries. The heart has four chambers; the lower two are called the ventricles, and the upper two are the auricles. The ventricles have much thicker muscular

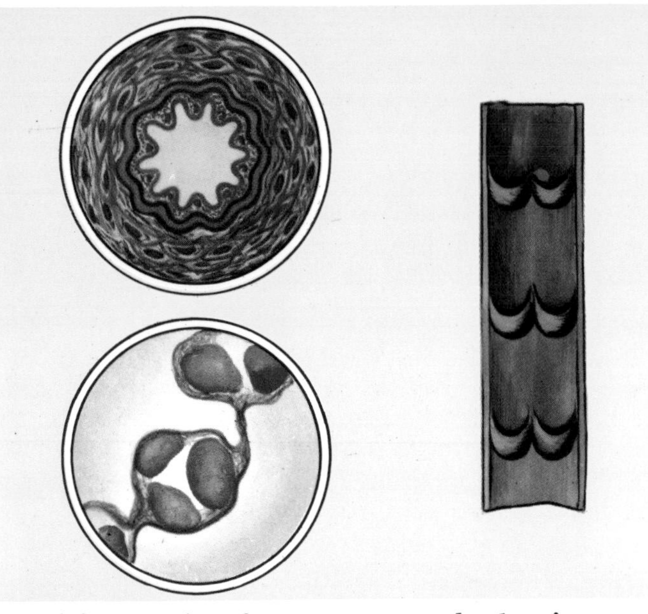

Top left: *a section of an artery, seen under the microscope, with the elastic fibres shown in blue.* Bottom left: *pulmonary capillaries containing red corpuscles. Note the thinness of the wall (in this illustration magnified about* 20,000 *times).* Right: *a longitudinal section of a vein, showing the "swallow's nest" valves.*

walls than the auricles. When the left ventricle contracts, blood is forced out into the aorta. This is the largest of the arteries, which are thick-walled to resist the pressure which results when the heart forces blood into them. The arteries carry the blood, still under pressure, to all parts of the body, the vessels becoming smaller and smaller as they branch continually to form a fine network.

CAPILLARIES

At the ends of the small arteries are the capillaries, which may be so narrow that the blood cells pass along them in single file. Here the blood comes into the closest contact with the cells of the body, to which it supplies oxygen and food; it also removes the carbon dioxide and other waste materials that they have produced.

The blood flows back along the veins to the heart, entering the right auricle. As this contracts it forces blood into the right ventricle, which in turn sends it to the lungs so that it may release its carbon dioxide and absorb oxygen. Returning from the lungs to the left auricle, the blood is pumped out from the left ventricle to the rest of the body once again. Valves in the various parts of the system prevent the blood from flowing in the wrong direction.

TOTAL QUANTITY

There are usually about eleven pints of blood in the body. It is circulated very rapidly; for instance, in twenty-eight seconds blood is taken from the left foot back to the heart and lungs and then to the right foot.

THERMOSTATIC CONTROL

Human beings are warm-blooded, and it is very important that the blood should be able to remove heat from parts that are too hot or warm up places that are too cold. During exercise, much heat is given out by the muscles, and the whole body is in danger of being over-heated. To prevent this, capillaries in the skin are opened up so that more blood flows near to the surface of the body. Here it is cooled partly by direct heat loss to the atmosphere and partly by the loss of heat used in the evaporation of perspiration. It is for this reason that people become " red in the face " as a result of exercise. When the body is too cold, the capillaries are closed and the skin becomes very pale or faintly blue in colour as there is very little blood near the surface.

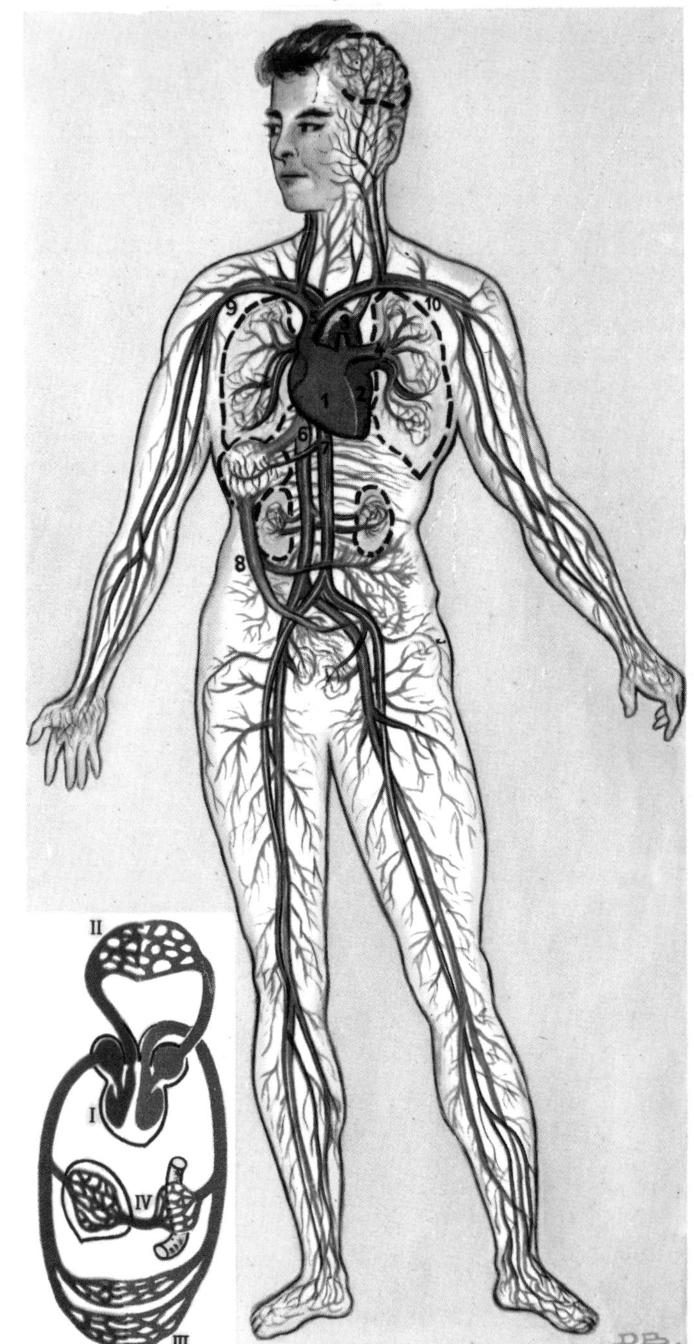

The circulatory system, the flow of blood from heart to arteries, arteries to capillaries, capillaries to veins and veins back to the heart, was first discovered by Harvey in 1628, *diagram above.* 1. *right ventricle;* 2. *left ventricle;* 3. *aortic arch;* 4. *pulmonary artery;* 5. *superior vena cava;* 6. *inferior vena cava;* 7. *aorta;* 8. *portal vein;* 9. 10. *subclavian veins and arteries. The arteries are shown in red, the veins in blue.* Below left: *a simplified diagram. I. heart; II. pulmonary circulation; III. main circulation; IV. portal circulation. Note how the arteries are linked with the veins, through the capillary network.*

THE STORY OF GLASS

The history of glass-making goes back to ancient times, when glass was regarded almost as a precious gem. Glass manufacture has now become a highly technical modern industry, providing us with a material with innumerable applications.

Glass plays its part in modern life in many different ways. We have glass windows in our houses, and glass mirrors on our walls. We drink from glass tumblers and peer through the glass lenses of our spectacles. Glass gives us milk bottles and light bulbs, microscopes and TV tubes. It takes our photographs and shows us the stars; it protects our medicines and preserves our food.

Glass has become so common-place a material that we tend to forget it is not provided ready-made by nature. Every scrap of glass we use is manufactured by one of the world's oldest and most important industries.

The story of glass dates back to ancient times. The arts and technical skills that give us our glass to-day have developed over many centuries. Without this background of generations of experience and technical knowledge, glass could not have become the wonderful material that serves us so well in our modern world.

FROM THE SANDS OF THE DESERT

The claim to have invented glass has been made on behalf of both the ancient Egyptians and the Phœnicians. Tradition has it that on returning to their native land from Egypt a party of Phœnicians stopped at Sidon. Beside the River Belus they unloaded some sacks containing *natron*, or carbonate of soda, which was used at that time in the dyeing of wool. After lighting a wood fire they arranged some lumps of *natron* around it as a support for their cooking pots. Then they ate their meal and went to sleep, leaving the fires burning. When they awoke they found that the lumps of *natron* had vanished, and in their place were blocks of glistening material which looked like enormous gems.

The Phœnicians knelt around the ashes of the fire, thinking that some unknown spirit must have performed a miracle. Then their leader, a wise man named Zelu, noticed that the sand beneath the *natron* blocks had also disappeared. He ordered his men to re-light the fire and in a short time a stream of steaming, red-hot liquid began to pour from the ashes. While it was still soft Zelu took a knife and modelled some of this strange substance into the shape of a beautiful vessel. Cries of amazement rose from the Phœnician merchants who watched this historic event—the discovery of glass.

This story, told by Pliny, is probably an elaborated version of what really happened. In fact, excavations made in old tombs show that the manufacture of glass was practised as early as 4,000 B.C. It was the custom of the Egyptians to bury treasures of great value alongside the mummies of the Pharaohs and their high priests. Among these were coloured balls of glass exquisitely worked in the manner of precious stones. It is thought that the Egyptians, by about 1,400 B.C., had begun to blow glass, devoting themselves in particular to the production of small artistic and decorative objects. Little by little they perfected the technique of colour work, as may be seen from specimens excavated from the tombs at Tel-el-Amarna. In time, the Egyptians and Phœnicians became masters in the craft of glass-making. Competing with each other in its manufacture and sale, they sent their glass wares to all the markets of the known world. Potentates and princesses wore glass beads and necklets whose radiant lustre was comparable with that of precious stones.

THE GLASS TRADE OF THE ANCIENTS

When the power of Imperial Rome spread to the southern shores of the Mediterranean, Egypt became a province of

Beneath the cooking fires lit by Phoenicians, silica in the sand fused with soda to form a pool of molten glass.

Egyptian and Phoenician craftsmen discovered the art of glass blowing, nearly 3,500 years ago.

the Cæsars. As was customary in those days, the vanquished nation paid tribute to its conqueror. Not only were the Egyptians ordered to send large quantities of their glass wares to Rome, but many of their best craftsmen were transferred to the capital as well.

Tastes were changing and the simple ways of the early Romans became more sophisticated. Patrician families sought greater beauty and refinement. They vied with one another in adorning the walls of their houses with glass mirrors. Strangely enough, they made little use of glass in the windows of their homes. Even in the most luxurious Roman houses the windows consisted of small apertures closed by single panes. The larger openings were protected, when necessary, by wooden boards.

The triumphant success of glass as a luxury article spread with the Roman conquest of new lands. Gaul, Spain, Britain, the Rhineland and Portugal were occupied, and this new industry was established far and wide. But with the fall of the western Roman Empire in the fourth-century A.D. the manufacture of glass became more and more an Eastern speciality. Byzantium, now known as Istanbul, dominated the trade until well into the Middle Ages. This prospering industry soon engaged the attention of the Syrians and the Venetians, who probably learnt the secret of glass-making from the people of the Levant.

VENETIAN CRAFTSMEN

The first glass factory in Venice was opened in the tenth-century. Later, the Council of Ten, who governed Venice, ordered that all glass factories should be transferred to the Island of Murano in order to preserve secret processes from foreign investigators.

We know that in 1317 the Venetians had already discovered how to make mirrors. At this time the title of master glass-maker was much respected; it was an honour which passed from father to son. Meanwhile the countries of northern Europe had not remained indifferent to this new and thriving industry. After heavily bribing one of the leading Venetian glassmakers, an agent of the King of France succeeded in finding out how glass was made. The secret spread from France to Bohemia and other parts of Germany, and it was not long before a number of new factories were in compe-

Glass blowing, which is still practised in modern foundries, requires great skill and exceptional lung power.

The first apparatus for making lenses was constructed to the designs of Leonardo da Vinci.

tition with Murano, whose decline started at the beginning of the Modern Age.

Glass was not, however, to remain a prerogative of the rich. In 1876, an American inventor named Weber devised a bottle-making machine. Glass vessels for domestic use were now within the reach of every family.

THE RAW MATERIALS OF GLASS

Silica, the essential raw material of glass, is found usually in river beds and quarries in the form of sand, shingle or quartz. This mineral is common in many parts of Europe, especially in the Fontainebleau-Chantilly region of France, in Germany and Tuscany, and to a lesser extent in other countries.

After the sand or quartz has been excavated and crushed, it is thoroughly washed in order to remove clay and other foreign matter. It is then mixed with the other materials and melted down in heat-resisting crucibles. The vitreous mixture obtained in this way liquefies at a temperature of about 1,300° C., and during the melting process insoluble impurities come to the top and are skimmed off. When the refining stage is complete, the mixture is cooled to a temperature of 800° C., at which it is more easily workable.

HOW GLASS IS MADE

Visiting a glass factory is rather like plunging into an inferno. Tall flames shoot from dome-shaped furnaces and the air is almost unbearably hot. Inside these furnaces are large crucibles which contain the liquid glass. The glass worker, who is a true craftsman, takes an iron tube, dips it into the boiling glass and picks up a blob of white-hot molten glass with the tip of his tube.

The utmost speed is necessary to transform this glowing substance into the shape of, say, a small phial or flask. The craftsman gives his tube a few deft twists and turns, then blows down the tube into the molten glass. The blob swells up into an elongated bubble and, with skilful handling, takes on the required shape. The vessel is then baked, after which it is ready for use.

Work of this kind is exhausting and even dangerous, and long practice combined with an artistic sense are necessary for success. Glass blowing is far from being a pleasant job,

About 1600, *the son of a Dutch optician accidentally hit upon the principle of the telescope.*

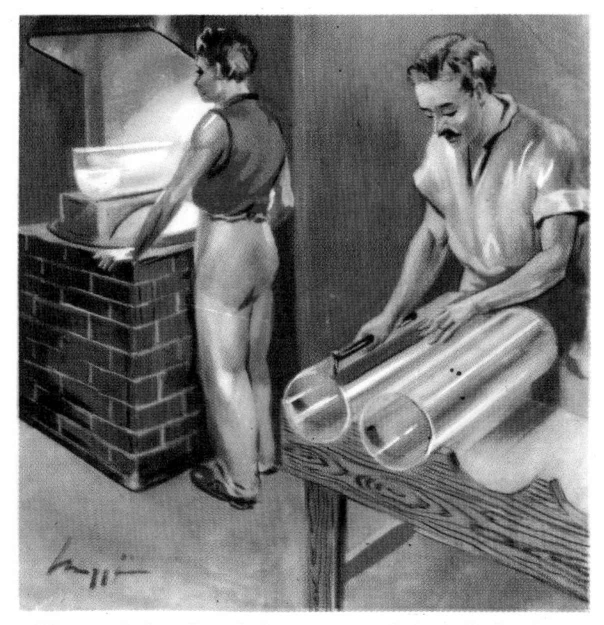

Sheets of glass for windows are made in cylinder form.

for the atmosphere in which the man must work is extremely hot and its effect is harmful both to the eyes and the lungs.

WINDOW AND PLATE GLASS

Molten glass for making window-panes is prepared in another department. Here again the semi-liquid material is whisked up with the aid of a long tube, but in this case the craftsman throws it on to a marble slab where it is shaped into a cylindrical form. The cylinder must then be cut, an operation carried out by a second workman with a red-hot knife. The glass sheet is softened again in a furnace and spread on a smooth table. It is then flattened out with a wooden rolling-pin just as if it were a piece of pastry. Another roller, this time of iron coated with fine, damp sand, is used to polish and clean the glass, after which it is ready to be cut to the required size.

Recently, a British firm has perfected a " flow " technique for the manufacture of plate and window glass. The molten glass is poured across molten metal, and emerges, polished, in a continuous ribbon.

Wherever one goes in a glass factory there is some new surprise in store. In the art department, for example, the engravers sit at long tables inscribing fragile tankards and decanters with finely drawn lettering and figures. This detailed work calls for the same patience and devotion that our forebears showed in the making of lace and embroidery. The article which is being engraved is covered with a film of wax and turpentine on which the designer works with steady hand. Hydrofluoric acid is used to burn the glass along the lines of the inscription. Bottles, glasses and decorative objects skilfully treated in this way become objects of very great beauty.

No less extraordinary is the skill of those glass-blowers who make thermometers. One man blows a vitreous blob into the shape of a pear, while a second sticks his rod into the bubble and walks backwards until the pear has been drawn out into a thin tube perhaps over a hundred feet long. Inside the tube is an almost invisible channel for the rise and fall of the mercury. After being cut to measure they are engraved with the temperature scale.

We owe the discovery of the telescope to the curiosity of the young son of Hans Lippershey, a Dutch spectacle-maker. About the year 1608, while playing about with his father's lenses, the boy noticed that when placed one in front of another the lenses sometimes produced the strangest effects. Looking across the road through both a concave and a convex lens the house opposite appeared to be much closer. The boy's father set the two lenses in a darkened tube and handed the world's first telescope to his small son. In 1610, Galileo Galilei perfected this primitive instrument and used it for his astronomical studies.

It is much more expensive to make glass for optical purposes than for ordinary use. The best quality material is chosen

The secret of unbreakable glass is attributed to a craftsman whom Emperor Tiberius had executed in order to preserve the secret.

and put into a special furnace where it is melted at an extremely high temperature. It is then cooled slowly in the same crucible. Next the solidified glass is pulverised to disperse any possible flaws. The crushed glass is then heated slowly until it melts again, and poured into moulds of various shapes and sizes according to the type of lens that the optician needs. Leonardo da Vinci was the first to develop this process for making lenses, and the original drawings demonstrating his method still exist.

UNBREAKABLE GLASS

Surprisingly enough, the production of unbreakable glass goes back to Roman times. Under the reign of Tiberius, a certain glass-maker presented himself before the emperor with a vessel made of this material. The man hoped that this discovery would earn him a reprieve from the sentence of exile to which he had been condemned. To prove its qualities he threw the vessel on to the ground at the emperor's feet.

" Are you the only person who knows this secret? " asked the emperor.

" The only one," replied the glass-maker, who thought that he would thus gain the emperor's favour.

" If that is so, you had better die, because if glass were to become unbreakable, it would lose its value and our great industry would be ruined."

Such matters are no longer left to tyrants like Tiberius to decide, and splinter-proof glass is now in everyday use. It is made from two sheets of ordinary glass between which a film of transparent plastic is inserted under high pressure. This type of glass is used in the windows of trains, motor-cars, aeroplanes, in fact in all kinds of vehicles as well as for motorists' and flyers' goggles. To-day it is being used more and more for the manufacture of domestic articles, thus reducing the danger of cuts and injuries.

LOOKING-GLASSES

There was a time when looking-glasses were made from highly polished sheets of bronze or silver. Eventually, glass came into use for this purpose, and the mirror is now a feature of every hall, bedroom and bathroom in the country.

Glass for making mirrors is melted down in a crucible with two long handles. It is poured on to a bronze slab over which runs a metal roller. The sheets are then taken to a special room where they are left to cool for three or four days. Next, the glass is polished with a wooden block sprinkled with fine, wet sand. A second polishing imparts a really shiny surface. But no amount of polishing will turn a sheet of glass into a mirror. For that, it must be backed with tin, a thin layer of which is spread over one side of the glass sheet. Even so, this is not sufficient to provide a perfect reflection. For the final touch a thin coating of mercury is added to the tin, which reflects the light waves so that they bounce back and form the image in the mirror.

One of the most interesting applications of the glass-maker's art is in the production of stained-glass windows. Those magnificent windows, which we have all admired in our churches and cathedrals, are made from a jig-saw of pieces of coloured glass joined together by strips of lead. In this way religious scenes, often of high artistic merit, are brought to life in a great variety of beautiful colours.

In the manufacture of stained-glass, pigments are mixed with the molten glass, thoroughly blended and stabilised by the addition of special fluxes. One of the main difficulties in this type of work lies, however, in transferring a complicated design on to so many small pieces before they are joined together. One has only to think of the thousands of fragments that go into the making of these mosaic pictures to understand what difficult and laborious work this is.

BUILDING MATERIAL

Another more recent development in the use of glass has been its adaptation to building purposes. Glass blocks are now used in the construction of modern buildings, their advantage being that they admit more light. This is of great benefit to workers in factories and offices.

Most interesting of all the latest applications of glass is in the production of glass fibre. This is made by allowing molten glass to drip steadily on to a revolving cylinder which spins it into fine filaments. The result is a mass of silky fibre which appears to have little in common with the shapeless mass of sand and quartz from which it came. It is a poor conductor of heat, and serves as an extremely valuable insulating material. Other uses to which glass fibre is put is in the manufacture of suitcases and dress and household fabrics.

How astonished the ancient Phœnicians would be to see how their glass serves us in so many ways to-day.

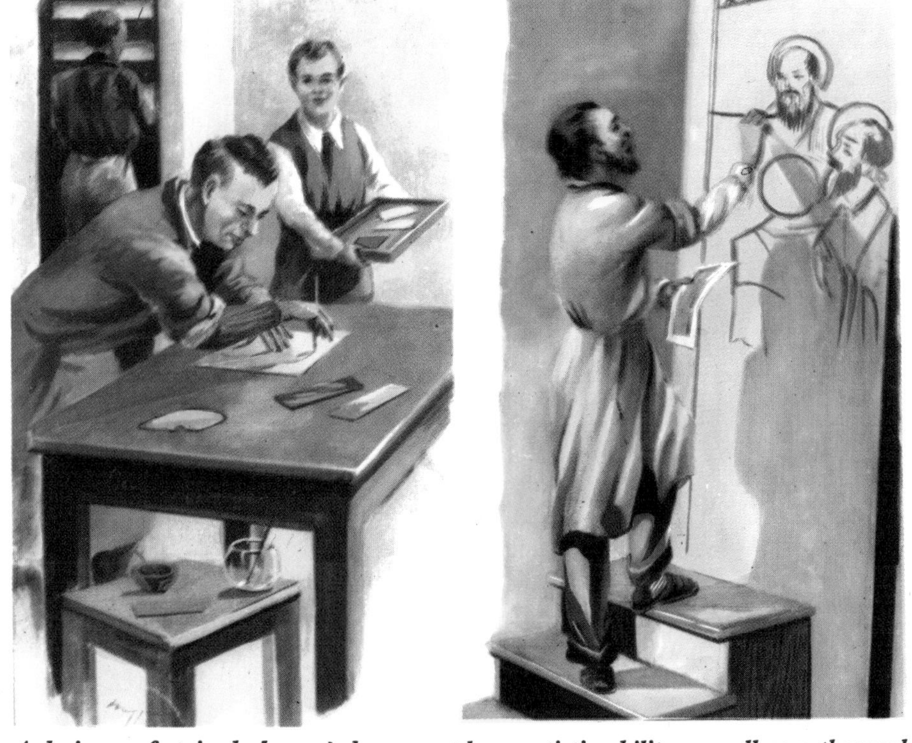

A designer of stained-glass windows must have artistic ability as well as a thorough knowledge of glass. Biblical scenes are brought to life in many of our churches by the light and colour effects achieved in stained-glass windows.

People are fond of proclaiming that the weather nowadays is not what it was when they were young. But we have to take this sort of pronouncement with a pinch of salt. Human judgment is apt to be uncertain when it comes to comparing present conditions with those of a generation ago.

In order to find out if there *is* any change in the weather we experience, we have to make a study of the general weather trends over long periods of time. That is to say, we have to study climate, taking into account the rainfall, warmth, humidity, sunshine, wind, air pressure and other factors that are involved in the behaviour of the atmosphere which gives us our weather.

Taken over the years, the weather conditions over any region of the world form a recognisable pattern representing the climate of that region. But if we study the weather over very long periods of time, we can follow the changes that have taken place in the climate of the world as a whole and of the various regions on its surface.

Accurate measurements of rainfall, temperatures and other factors in the weather have been made only for a comparatively short time. We cannot use these for following climatic changes taking place over hundreds or even thousands of years. But scientists have discovered various methods of studying the sort of climate that the world has had in the far distant past. They have found that there have been continual changes in the climate of the world, with a succession of ice-ages as the climate has become colder, followed by periods of warming-up as the temperature has begun to rise again.

There are indications that this climatic pendulum is swinging still, and the climate of the world is now becoming warmer as we recover from the most recent ice-age.

One of the methods of following changes of this sort, which take place gradually over many years, is by studying the movements of the timber line. This is the boundary, fixed by nature, beyond which the climate is too cold for trees to flourish. In northern Europe, there is a timber line which surrounds the Polar region; north of this imaginary line, the climate is too harsh to support tree growth. On mountain ranges, there are timber lines which mark the point above which it is too cold for trees to grow.

There is evidence that these timber lines are moving farther north and farther up the mountain-sides. Trees are growing in areas of northern Europe, and at higher altitudes than they ever grew before.

LESS ICE

The huge raft of ice that lies over the North Pole is also shrinking gradually. The rivers of ice forming glaciers in the world's mountain ranges are melting faster than they are being replaced. During the past century, glaciers in the Alps and elsewhere have become perceptibly smaller, and some have disappeared entirely. In Iceland, the melting of glaciers has uncovered land that has been hidden from view for hundreds, or even thousands, of years.

FEWER SEVERE WINTERS

There is no doubt that the climate of the Northern Hemisphere is warming up generally in this way, but nobody can yet be certain of the time-scale which is involved. We may be experiencing a minor fluctuation taking place over a few centuries, or we may be involved in one of the great climatic changes that extends over periods of thousands or even millions of years. If accurate records of the world's weather conditions had been kept for these long periods, it would be possible to trace the pattern of the climatic swing. Weather records do not go back more than a century or two, so scientists must obtain their evidence of past climatic changes in other ways.

SIGNS IN TREES

The growth of trees, as shown by the annular rings in the trunk, provide useful information of weather conditions in bygone years. Every year, trees add a layer to their trunks as they grow. The number of rings in the trunk when the tree is cut down tells the age of the tree. And the thickness of the rings gives an indication of the climate during the year when the ring was added.

There are also geological methods of assessing climate in prehistoric times. When glaciers covered the land, water from the melting ice flowed away from the glacier, carrying along particles of solid matter with it. The coarser material settled out quickly from the water, but the fine silt remained suspended and settled slowly in the lakes that the water formed.

The sediment from these lakes now provides a record of the changing weather conditions from year to year. The thickness of the layer of sediment from any year is a guide to the amount of ice that melted during the year. And this in turn depends upon the climate during that year.

ICE-AGES

Using methods like this, scientists have been able to assess climatic changes that have taken place over long periods of the Earth's history. It is now established that the Earth has passed through a succession of ice-ages separated by intervals of many thousands of years.

The ice now covering the Antarctic is a legacy from the most recent ice-age. Underneath the layer of ice there are coal seams and the remains of huge trees, showing that Antarctica once supported a luxuriant vegetation.

CONSEQUENCES

As the warm-up continues, the ice covering the poles will go on melting, and the extra water will cause a rise in the level of the oceans. Much of the world's low-lying land will be inundated. The Polar ice-cap is often more than a mile thick, and it covers millions of square miles. If the ice melted completely it could raise the level of the sea by as much as 150 feet. Much of Britain and Europe would be submerged.

What is causing these fluctuations in the world's climate? Nobody knows. The Earth's supply of heat comes from the sun, and it may be that the radiations from the sun are changing as a result of disturbances in the sun itself. If this is so, there is very little we can do about it here on Earth.

THE ATOM

Throughout the ages, philosophers have wondered about the nature of matter. What would happen, they have asked, if you were to take a piece of solid matter and cut it into smaller and smaller pieces? Could you go on indefinitely, with no limit to the smallness of the pieces of matter you produced? Or would you reach a point where you had the smallest possible particle, an ultimate particle, of matter?

Democritus and Leucippus, great philosophers of ancient Greece, believed that matter was not infinitely divisible, and suggested that the ultimate, the last tiny particle which could not be subdivided, should be called the " atom " (in Greek this means " that which cannot be divided ").

EARLY RESEARCHES

Many centuries were to pass before this idea was to be accepted into scientific thought. At the beginning of the nineteenth-century, John Dalton, an English elementary school-master who had dedicated himself to the study of physics and chemistry, established the atomic theory which was to become the foundation on which science grew to its present stature. Dalton said that the atoms of any given element (for example iron, aluminium or sulphur) were all identical; they were the same weight, the same size and the same shape.

From 1800 until to-day, scientific research has made phenomenal progress, and the atomic-molecular theory constitutes the basis of modern physics and chemistry. In recent times it became apparent that atoms were themselves constructed from smaller units, and the atom has become a world in itself, infinitely small, but complex and marvellous.

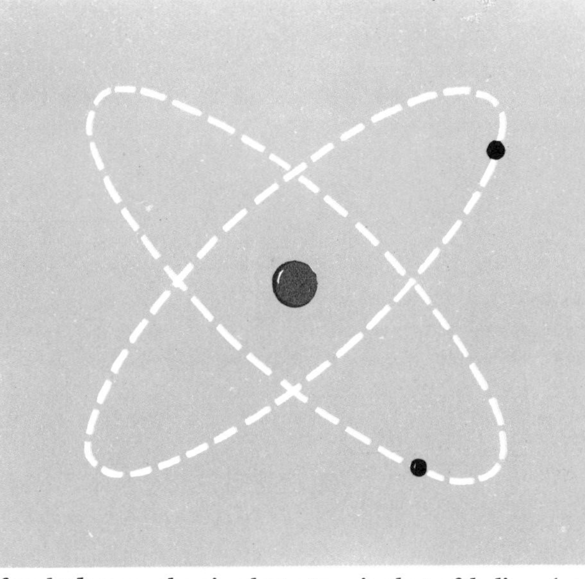

After hydrogen, the simplest atom is that of helium (atomic symbol He). Two planetary electrons, each in its own orbit, revolve around the nucleus.

WHAT IS THE ATOM?

Everything existing in the world is made up of elementary forms of matter, of " elements " — metallic and non-metallic—which combine among themselves to form all the substances that are found in nature. For example, water is made up of the elements hydrogen and oxygen which combine, atom with atom, in the proportion of 2 to 1. A molecule of water consists of two hydrogen atoms and one oxygen atom. Thus, in the case of water, atoms of different types unite to form a compound which has characteristic properties of its own.

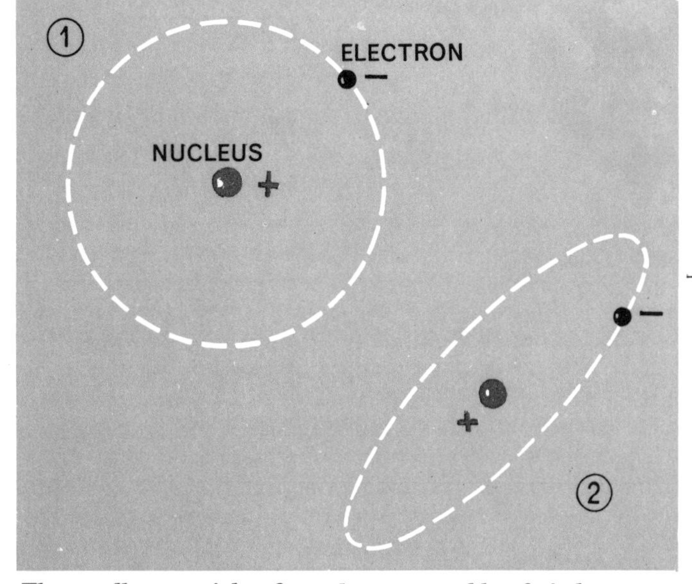

The smallest particle of an element capable of independent existence is called an atom. The simplest one is the hydrogen atom, shown in the diagram front view and in profile. As can be seen, it consists of one electron which circulates round the nucleus.

This illustration shows in detail the structure of the atom; the nucleus is made up of protons, shown in red (positively charged), and neutrons, shown in purple (neutral). Negatively-charged electrons, shown in blue, circulate in orbits round the nucleus.

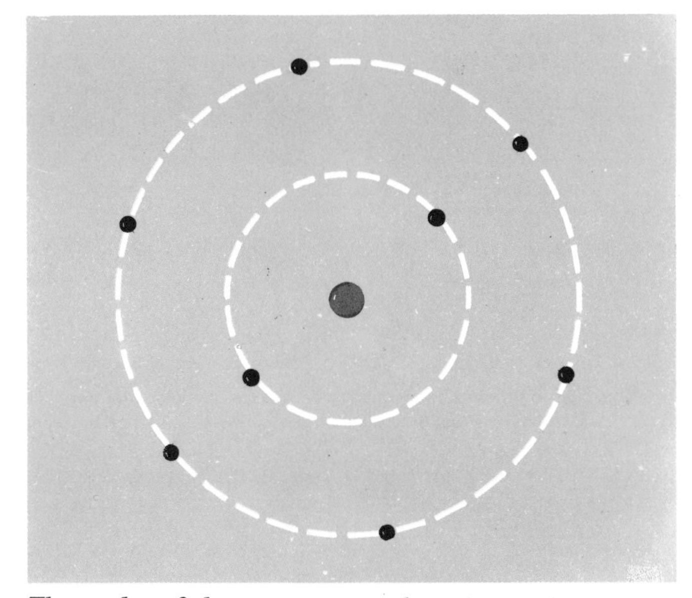

The number of electrons corresponds to the atomic number of the element. Here we see the oxygen atom (atomic number 8) *with its eight electrons.*

SPLITTING THE ATOM

During the last half-century, physicists have probed into the internal structure of the atom itself. And they have found that all atoms are made up from the same types of basic particles arranged in a familiar way. Any atom consists of a central mass, called the " nucleus " around which other particles, called electrons, revolve like planets round the sun. The nucleus has a positive electrical charge, while the electrons are negatively charged, and the two cancel each other out. The negative charges attract the positive ones, and vice versa, and there are different numbers of electrons in the atoms of different elements.

THE SATELLITES

The hydrogen atom, for example, has only one electron, while the uranium atom has ninety-two, a sort of atomic solar system with ninety-two satellites which revolve around the sun (the nucleus).

We now know that the nucleus, in turn, is made up of particles of two different types—neutrons and protons. Protons have a positive charge and serve to balance the negative charge of the electrons, whilst the neutrons, as the name indicates, are neutral, having no charge.

In some elements the electrons circulating round the nucleus are easily detached, and they can roam about the material quite freely. This movement of the electrons in certain elements like copper, can result in a stream of electrons, and this is what we recognise as an " electric current ".

Within the nucleus of the atom there are immense resources of energy. We have now learned how to harness this energy and atomic energy (or nuclear energy) is now producing electricity for mankind to use.

The nucleus of the atom, from which this energy is obtained, is so small that we cannot imagine it. The nucleus of the hydrogen atom, for example, is about one-tenth of a millionth part of a millimetre in diameter.

This "Atom smasher" built in Massachusetts, U.S.A., has a potential of about 10,000,000 *volts.*

QUESTIONS AND ANSWERS

What is a Virus?

A virus is a tiny particle of matter that behaves like a living thing in that it can multiply inside a living cell.

Viruses cause many human diseases, including poliomyelitis, smallpox, influenza and the common cold. Animals and plants suffer from a variety of virus diseases, such as distemper in dogs, and mosaic disease of tomatoes.

Virus diseases are highly infectious, and in this respect they resemble diseases caused by the tiny living organisms which we call rather vaguely "germs." An animal or plant suffering from a virus disease will pass it on, as though some "infective agent" was being passed from one to the other.

For a long time, scientists were baffled by this infectiousness of virus diseases. It was apparent that something was being passed from one individual to another, but by using even the most powerful optical microscope it was not possible to detect any visible organism. In bacterial diseases, the germs could be seen, but in virus diseases, there was nothing to be seen.

Eventually, the mystery was solved with the invention of the electron microscope. This wonderful instrument allows us to see things so small that they are invisible through even the most powerful optical microscope. And it showed us the tiny virus particles that were responsible for passing on virus diseases from one individual to another.

In recent years, scientists have found out much about the nature of viruses, and the more they discover the more mysterious viruses become. Unlike ordinary bacteria and other living micro-organisms, viruses cannot be grown on special food-materials in the laboratory. They will multiply only inside an appropriate living cell, where they produce new virus particles which emerge to invade other cells. In this respect, the virus behaves like a living thing. Yet outside the cell, it is virtually a particle of inanimate chemical. It shows none of the characteristics we associate with life. Inside the living cell these strange chemical particles are able to "come to life" and produce others of their kind.

FORECASTING THE WEATHER

When you plan a day's outing in the country or at the seaside do you first study a weather map or wait for a weather forecast? Those who have done so often complain that the meteorologist or " weather man ", who made the map and gave the forecast, was wrong; that if he had forecast a warm and bright day it had turned out to be cool and dull or *vice versa*. Yet if we consider how fickle the weather can be, especially for a place in the British Isles, the wonder is that anyone can even begin to draw up a forecast of any value.

To understand how forecasts are made is to appreciate that what we call the weather is no simple or straightforward thing. It seems simple enough at first sight, but this is because we are usually concerned with broad effects, such as whether it is wet or dry, hot or cold, bright or dull, still or windy. A meteorologist, however, must have the measure of these things, and he sees them all as parts of elements of a greater and much more complex thing—the general state of the atmosphere. He cannot define the weather for a particular place and time unless he knows the temperature, air pressure, rainfall, wind strength and direction, humidity, visibility and amount of cloud for that region at that time. Before he can begin to make a weather forecast he must know the values of these elements for several places in the region, and these values should, ideally, be taken at the same time. Only then can he think in terms of the changes and trends of each element, of the way the temperature and air pressure will change, whether the speed of the wind will increase or decrease, whether the sky will clear or grow more cloudy, and so on. If the weather was a simple thing, reliable forecasting would be a correspondingly easy task.

CAREFUL RECORDS

For successful forecasting the weather-expert, or meteorologist, must also know about the normal or average weather

Clouds are caused by the ascent of moist air, the type depending on the way the air ascends and the height at which condensation occurs. Whatever their formation (cirrus, cumulus, stratus or nimbus), clouds are merely masses of water droplets suspended in the air. Under suitable conditions, the droplets may come together and fall to the ground as rain or snow.

This illustration shows how the cycle of circulation of water in the air takes place. The sun causes evaporation of water from the sea; if this moisture-laden air is cooled, the water may condense to form clouds. Under suitable circumstances, the water may fall as rain, which runs off the high ground back to the sea.

conditions of the region. The weather it has had, and will continue to have, depends to a great extent on its geographical position, on ocean currents, on the type of surrounding country and, of course, on the time of year. Weather observations taken over many years are a great help in this connection; they provide the forecaster with useful guides regarding the type of weather to be expected in the region during a particular season of the year. In addition, the forecaster knows that the weather is not so fickle as we might at first suppose. For example, after a run of several rainy days the chances that the next day will also be wet are greater than the chances of a fine day. Similarly, after a run of several fine days the chances that the next day will also be fine are greater than the chances that it will rain. In other words, wet weather and fine weather show a decided tendency to persist.

COUNTRY WEATHER LORE

Yet, with all our present-day scientific knowledge of the weather and its elements, we often find that a countryman can make a good forecast of local weather merely by looking up at the sky. He might say that the sky is " weak " and that the sun shining through cloud has a " watery " look. He will know that when in winter walls and stones become wet after a spell of clear, cold weather, rain is almost sure to follow. He will associate different types of cloud with different types of weather: low, dark and ragged clouds denote a troubled sky, but high, wispy clouds indicate a settled sky. The behaviour of birds and insects also provide guides to changes in the weather, and there are a great many other things of this kind which make up a countryman's " weather lore ". Many items in this weather-lore are, however, quite unsound. It is a very common belief that the moon influences the weather. Many people think that a full moon drives away the clouds and that when the crescent moon lies " on its back " it holds a lot of water which will spill over as rain. Although this is nonsense, a halo seen close to the moon is often a sign of rain, for it is produced by comparatively large raindrops held in the clouds. The sky colours at sunrise and sunset also depend to a large extent on the presence of raindrops. If the morning or evening sky has a red and angry look, stormy weather is likely to follow. A common belief is that a " low " barometer is a sign of good weather. The words " low " and

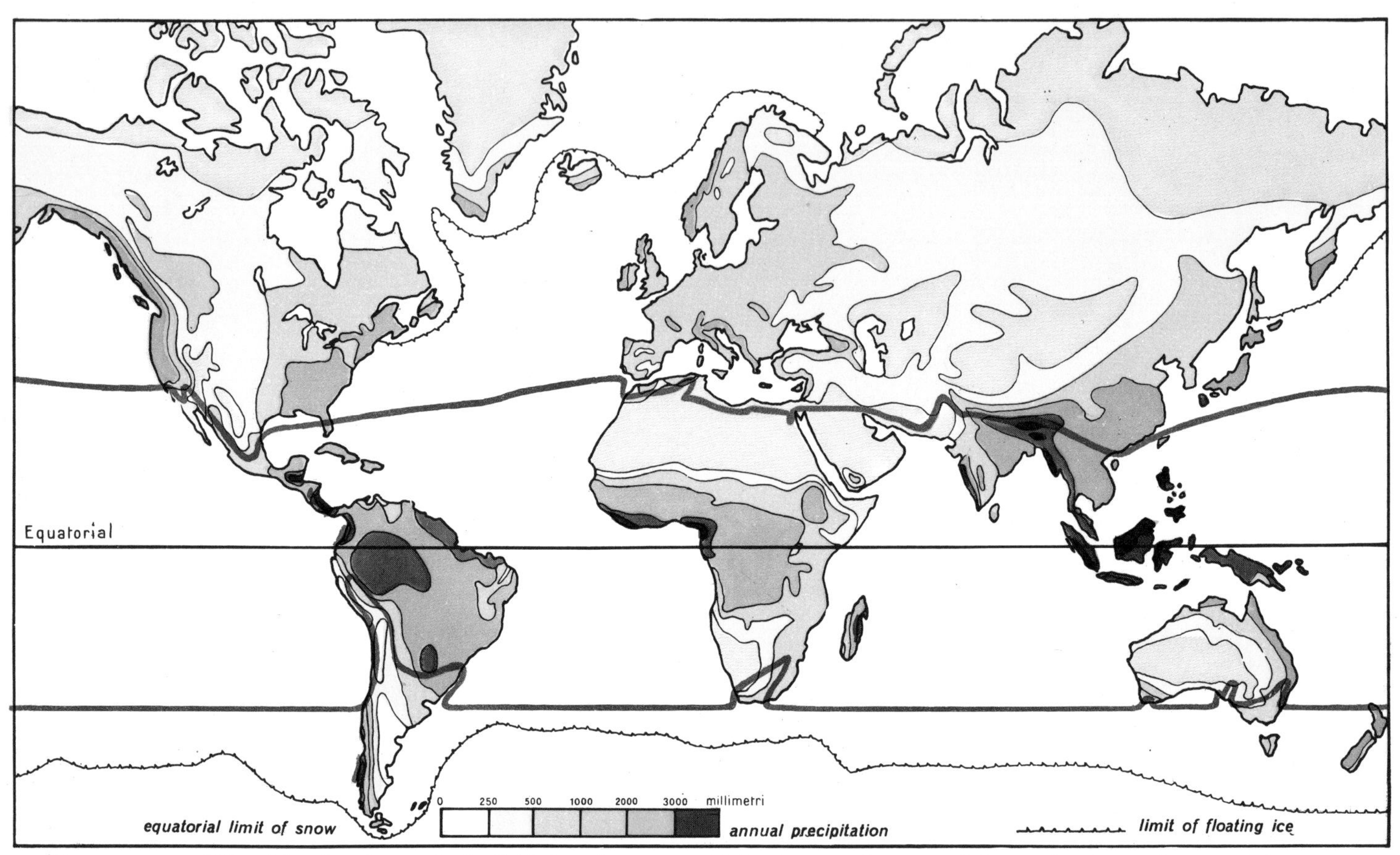

For purposes of identification the world is divided up into terrestrial zones; each terrestrial zone having a characteristic pattern of rainfall. The illustrated map above shows the distribution of the Earth's annual rainfall.

" high " refer to the pressure of the air which a barometer measures, but it is quite misleading to interpret the readings in this way. Sometimes a barometer carries the words " fine, changeable, rainy " but these have no real value. What is important is not the actual reading of the barometer but the changes in its readings, and these most people ignore.

MEASURING TEMPERATURE

An important element used when describing or forecasting the state of the weather is *temperature.* To measure this, meteorologists use a mercury thermometer which has either a *Centigrade* or a *Fahrenheit* scale. Both scales are based on two fixed points, the melting point of ice and the boiling point of water under standard conditions, that is, under standard air pressure at sea-level in latitude 45°. In the Centigrade scale the melting point of ice is 0° and the boiling point of water is 100°. The interval between the two is divided into 100 equal divisions, or *degrees Centrigrade.* In the Fahrenheit scale the melting point of ice is 32° and the boiling point of water is 212°. The interval between the two is divided into 180 equal divisions, or *degrees Fahrenheit.* In use, the thermometer is usually mounted in a special box with partly open or louvred sides. This box, called a *Stevenson screen,* is painted white and mounted in the open above ground level and away from the shelter of trees and houses. The air can then circulate freely around the thermometer, which then records the temperature of free air.

MERCURY BAROMETER

Air pressure, another element, is measured by a mercury barometer. In its simplest form this consists of a glass tube about 36 inches long, closed at one end, filled with mercury, and then inverted over a basin of mercury. The mercury stays up the tube to a height of about 30 inches, being supported by the outside air pressure. The standard value of this pressure is 760 mm. or 29·925 inches, and by studying the variations from this value meteorologists can learn a great deal about the circulation of the air in the atmosphere. By setting up barometers at weather stations over a large area it is possible to plot the positions and movement of whole regions or " systems " of high and low pressure. This is of great importance in forecasting, for fine weather is usually associated with an *anticyclone* (system of high pressure) and bad weather with a *cyclone* (system of low pressure).

AERIAL WATER RESERVOIR

Two closely-linked elements are rainfall and humidity. The Earth's atmosphere acts as a vast overhead water reservoir, but most of the water is in the invisible form of water vapour. Warm air can hold much more water vapour than can cold air. Because of this, and if warm moist air is suddenly cooled, some of the water vapour is condensed into liquid water in the form of tiny drops. These tiny drops form clouds, but if the drops are larger and therefore heavier than usual, they fall to the ground as rain. The amount of rain can be measured by collecting it in a *rain-gauge.* This consists of a funnel, 5 inches in diameter at the top, which collects the falling drops and passes them into a measuring glass scaled in either inches or centimetres.

Humidity is a measure of the amount of water vapour present in the air. That the air is sometimes more humid

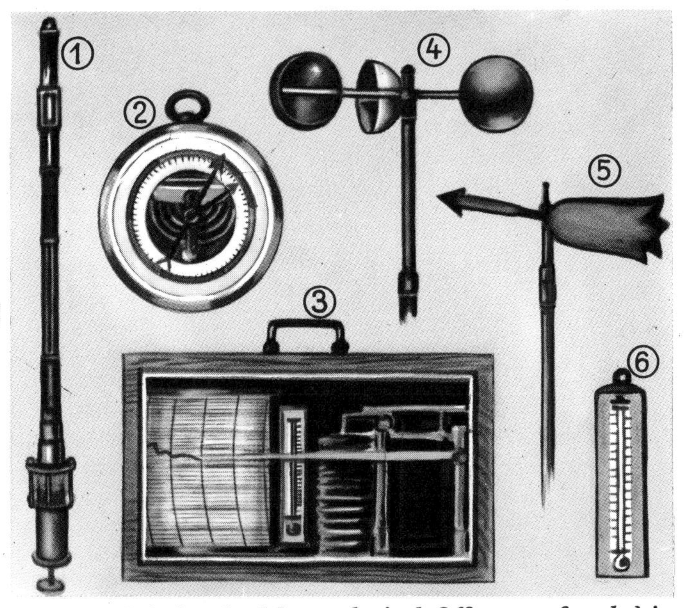

In Great Britain, the Meteorological Office was founded in 1854. *Examples of meteorological instruments are:* 1. *mercury barometer;* 2. *aneroid barometer;* 3. *barograph;* 4. *anemometer;* 5. *wind-indicating weathercock;* 6. *thermometer.*

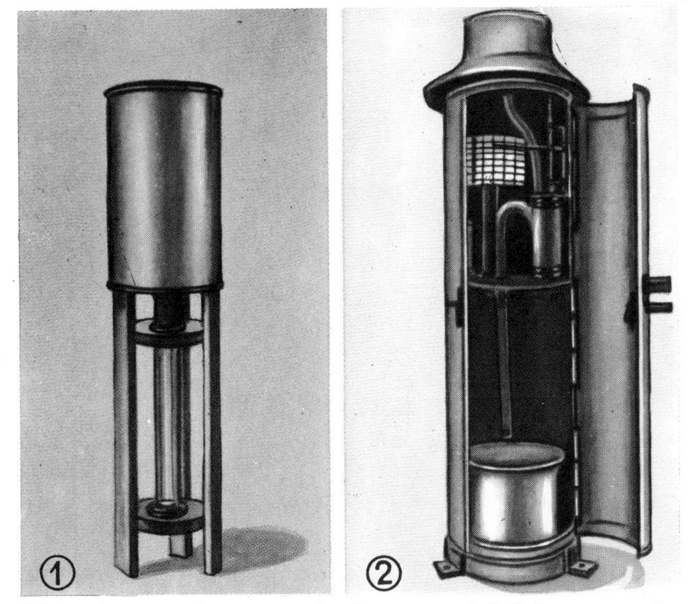

The rain gauge has a mouth of exact and definite area. An indicator shows the rain or snowfall. If the indicator is attached to a pen, variations in precipitation over a period may be recorded (2).

and therefore more moist than at other times can be seen by hanging a broad band of seaweed in an open place. In dry air the seaweed is stiff and brittle, but moist air makes it soft and limp. To get a more exact measure of humidity, weather experts use a *hygrometer.* Usually this takes the form of two thermometers mounted side by side, one with its bulb free to the air, the other with its bulb kept moistened by a damp rag. The " wet " thermometer gives a lower reading than the " dry " thermometer, and the less the moisture present in the air the bigger the difference between the two readings.

WIND AND SUN

The direction of the wind is, of course, indicated by a weather-vane, but to measure its speed meteorologists use an *anemometer.* This consists of two arms at right angles, to the ends of which are attached hollow cups. As the wind blows into the hollows of the cups it pushes them forwards, and in even a light breeze the anemometer arms spin round at great speed. This speed is a measure of wind-speed, and the instrument can be designed so that it gives its readings directly as wind-speed in miles per hour.

The only sure way of recording the amount of cloud is to make a direct estimate with the unaided eye, but since this is not always possible, weather-experts use a *sunshine recorder.* In this a glass ball focuses sunlight on a curved strip of paper thereby causing it to burn a small hole in the paper. The length of the burned line formed during a sunny day gives a direct measure of the number of hours of sunshine, the missing parts indicating the times when the sun was hidden by cloud.

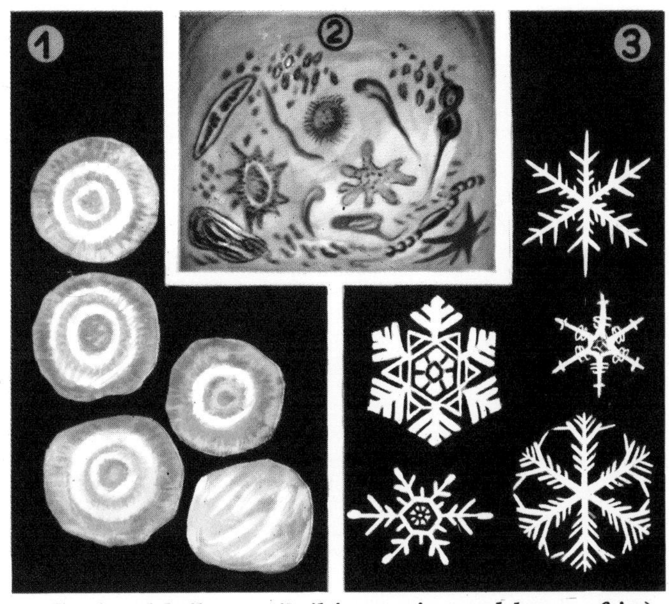

1. *Sectioned hailstones* (*hail is superimposed layers of ice*); 2. *drop of water seen through the microscope, revealing a world of micro-organisms;* 3. *snow crystals under the microscope.*

QUESTIONS AND ANSWERS

What is a Geyser?

A geyser is a jet of water and steam that spouts into the air from a natural hot spring. The action of a geyser is usually intermittent, the jet lasting for a short time and then dying away for a period. Many geysers "perform" with great regularity. The famous "Old Faithful" geyser at Yellowstone National Park, U.S.A., throws out its column of water at intervals of about an hour. The jet has a duration of about five minutes and reaches a height of about 150 feet.

Geysers are formed by the volcanic heating of water far underground, which suddenly boils. Steam is generated, and some of the water lying above the steam is blown out at the earth's surface. This lowers the pressure on the underground "boiler" and allows more water to boil. More water is ejected, and so the geyser continues until all the available water has been thrown out.

CHEMICALS THAT "LIVE"

Many of the diseases we suffer from to-day are caused by "germs" so small that we cannot see them even through an optical microscope. These invisible micro-organisms, which we know as viruses, have become the centre of some of the most exciting and important research going on to-day.

We human beings have an impressive account to settle with the virus. Poliomyelitis, for example, is a virus disease, as are influenza and the common cold—both of which cost us millions of pounds in lost working time every year. Viruses cause any number of other ailments, from serious diseases such as smallpox and yellow fever to minor infections such as warts and cold-sores.

NON-HUMAN DISEASES

But human beings are not alone in being attacked by viruses. Foot-and-mouth disease in cattle, fowl pest, and distemper in dogs are examples of animal virus diseases. Viruses attack our crops, causing immense losses in potatoes, tomatoes and other food plants every year. They will attack insects such as the honey bee and the silkworm, and even infect their fellow-germs, the bacteria.

These viruses appear to attack all living things. Until quite recently we knew little about them, and their existence had to be taken very much on trust.

CRYSTALS

In 1935, an American scientist, W. M. Stanley, made a strange discovery. He isolated a crystalline substance from the juice of tobacco plants suffering from mosaic disease—a disease that had been recognised as a virus disease. These crystals were able to pass on the infection from one plant to another. Rubbed into the leaf of a healthy tobacco plant, they would infect it with tobacco mosaic disease.

The crystals appeared to be inanimate, like salt or sugar crystals. They showed none of the characteristics we associate with normal living things. Incubated on broth, the crystals did not grow or multiply as normal bacteria would.

Yet, once inside a tobacco plant, the crystals appeared to come alive and infect the plant with mosaic disease. Evidence accumulated to show that they were, in fact, formed by aggregation of billions of virus particles which had assumed a crystalline form such as we associate with inanimate chemicals. Other viruses have since been isolated in crystalline form.

ELECTRON MICROSCOPE

Moreover, individual virus particles can now be seen with the aid of that wonderful instrument, the electron microscope, which can magnify 100,000 times and more. We no longer need to take the existence of the viruses on trust; we can see them and take their photographs.

The more we learn about these viruses, the more intriguing do they become. Outside their natural living environment, they behave as inanimate materials and are often crystalline. They do not move, nor do they breathe or reproduce. They are "mineral" rather than "animal" or "vegetable." Yet, once inside a suitable living cell, the virus can come alive. It will disappear inside the cell and in due course many new virus particles will appear. In its ability to multiply, the virus particle is exhibiting an essential characteristic of a living thing.

" MISSING-LINK "

This double existence of the virus has given it a "missing-link" status that bridges the inanimate world and the world of living things. We can no longer regard the virus simply as an unusually small type of bacterium; it differs fundamentally from bacteria, which will thrive and multiply outside the living cell.

Viruses are, in general, unaffected by the antibiotic and synthetic drugs that have been so useful for treating bacterial diseases. To defend ourselves against virus diseases we must still rely very largely on the natural defences of the body itself.

PROTECTION AGAINST VIRUSES

When a disease-producing virus finds its way into the body, there is an immediate call-to-arms, and the bloodstream produces antibodies which attack the invading virus. Providing that the antibodies are generated in sufficient strength, they will deal with the virus before it can establish itself and get the upper hand. We can help the body in its task by injecting vaccines into the bloodstream. These vaccines contain inactivated, or relatively harmless, viruses similar to those causing the disease. Antibodies are generated by the blood, just as though the viruses in the vaccine were dangerous ones. These antibodies remain in the blood, sometimes for only a short time, but often for life; they are ready and waiting to deal with subsequent infection by dangerous relatives of the virus from which the vaccine was made.

BREEDING VIRUSES

In 1940, Professor F. M. Burnet, an Australian, discovered a method of cultivating influenza virus inside living hens' eggs. Injected into cells surrounding the embryo, the virus multiplies as it does inside a human being. After incubation, the concentrated virus is removed and after inactivation to make it harmless is used for making vaccine. Injected into the bloodstream it brings the antibodies into action, ready to cope with subsequent invasions by similar influenza viruses.

As viruses reproduce, they can undergo mutation and form variants. Influenza virus, for example, is known to exist in a number of different strains. They are all basically influenza viruses, but differ one from another, for example, in the virulence of the disease they cause.

The existence of viruses in different strains is of the very greatest interest in more fundamental virus research. Here we have viruses which can be isolated and purified as chemical entities, and which can at the same time reproduce and live inside a suitable cell. As chemicals these viruses are capable of chemical examination and analysis. We therefore have the prospect of being able to determine chemical differences between strains and relate these differences to varying characteristics of the living virus. Research is now being carried out along these lines.

HOW GAS IS MADE

Ever since man discovered fire, he has been burning wood, coal and other materials of vegetable origin. These solid fuels served admirably as a source of heat, but they were of limited use as a source of light. They could not conveniently be used as a fuel for lamps.

During the late eighteenth-century, it was discovered that coal, wood and other combustible materials of this type provided an inflammable gas when they were heated in closed retorts. And this gas could be burned in air to provide a novel form of artificial light. This was the beginning of the great coal-gas industry, which is so important to-day.

One of the earliest experimenters with inflammable gas was a Frenchman, Philippe Lebon, who was born at Brachay in the Upper Marne Province of France on 29th May, 1769. From earliest youth, Lebon was interested in everything around him. His curiosity was never satisfied and he had that ingenious turn of mind which readily takes to all kinds of new activities.

GAS FROM SAWDUST

One day while testing the reaction to heat of various substances, Lebon put a handful of sawdust into a flask and set it over a burner. Dense pungent-smelling fumes were soon pouring out of the tube. Then Lebon applied a light to the tip of the tube and found that the gas would burn. From similar experiments he learned that other substances of organic origin, such as coal, gave off gases which could be used for lighting and heating.

Lebon's next step was to purify the gases he was burning by removing the bituminous and acid impurities. This he did by passing the gases through water. He was then able to collect the pure gas in a simple type of gasometer. The apparatus used by the inventor for this purpose was constructed on much the same lines as our modern gas plants, though of course in miniature. First the distilling plant, then the purifier and, finally the storage container—a model of that same huge cylinder by which we all recognise a modern gas works.

INSIDE A MODERN GAS WORKS

Gas is no longer used to any great extent for ordinary lighting. But it is still produced in very large quantities as a fuel for stoves and cookers, refrigerators and heaters. On visiting a modern gas works we would see the coal, from which gas is now obtained, being fed into huge containers made either of iron or fire-clay. Here it is heated up to a high temperature. Dense fumes are given off, consisting of coal gas mixed with impurities, including ammonia and tar. The gas passes along a tube to the purifiers, leaving behind a residue of degassed coal which we know as coke. Another by-product, graphite, is left clinging to the walls of the container; this is used in making electric batteries.

The effect of the purifiers is to cool and wash the coal gas, removing a sticky, shiny black substance which we know as coal tar. The gas is now passed through two filters, one of crushed coke and the other of lime. At this stage the gas gives up its ammonia, which is a valuable by-product used in industry and agriculture. The purified gas then flows on into huge metal gas-holders where it is stored under pressure.

THE USES OF COAL TAR

During the early years of coal-gas production, the coal-tar removed during purification was an embarrassing and useless by-product. But the nineteenth-century was a time of intense activity in scientific research, and chemists discovered in coal-tar a store of chemicals which were to become the raw materials of many important industries. These chemicals are all organic substances; they are chemicals based on the element carbon, a legacy from the synthetic activities of the plants from which the coal itself was made.

At first, the uses of coal tar were limited to such things as the caulking of wooden boats, or the tarring of timber and rope as a protection against damp. It was used for making roads, being superseded eventually for this purpose by asphalt, the tarry material obtained from petroleum.

The discovery of coal-tar as a source of chemicals, however, has created an immense demand from industry for the products of coal-tar distillation. Chemicals such as naphthalene and benzene, aniline and phenol are the raw materials from which we make synthetic dyes and drugs, antiseptics and insecticides, plastics and synthetic fibres, perfumes and medicinal products.

GASLIGHT COMES TO TOWN

This great modern industry, based on the distillation of coal, has developed largely from the experiments carried out by Philippe Lebon in France, and by the famous British engineers, William Murdock and James Watt in England.

Lebon became convinced that his inflammable gas could be produced on a commercial scale. He withdrew to the

Philippe Lebon, discoverer of fuel gas, heated sawdust in a corked flask to which was attached a glass tube. A flame put near the mouth of the tube ignited the sawdust gases.

Coal gas, developed shortly after wood gas, was soon put to use. It gave our great-grandfathers an efficient form of street lighting; this created the job of lamp-lighter.

country to work quietly and develop his plans for the construction of the first real gas works. This he did at great personal sacrifice, spending his own money on the scheme. Work progressed well, until at length he felt that the time had come to ask for recognition and financial support from high authorities. But he did so in vain. Everyone thought his project a crazy one.

In desperation Lebon spent what was left of his money in renting the Hôtel Seignelay in Paris. He installed his ovens and tubes in the cellar and fitted the whole building, including the facade, with tubes and jets. Then one evening he turned the gas on and lit it. The hotel sprang to life in a blaze of lights burning brightly in every room and from every outside wall. In the year 1800 such a sight had never before been known. Lebon became the talk of Paris.

Napoleon Bonaparte heard about Lebon's work, and gave Lebon a piece of land in the Forest of Rouvray " to develop an industry for the distillation of wood and the manufacture of luminous gas." Napoleon also ordered him to send all the tar and acetic acid he could make to Le Havre for the use of the French fleet. Lebon's luck had turned. But his good fortune was to be short-lived. His factory was destroyed by a furious storm; and on 2nd December, 1804, Lebon was stabbed to death by an unknown assailant in the Champs-Élysées.

WILLIAM MURDOCK

In England, the development of coal-gas lighting had been making rapid progress. Early experiments had been carried out by William Murdock, an engineer employed by the famous Birmingham firm of Boulton and Watt.

Towards the end of the eighteenth-century, Murdock was working at Redruth in Cornwall, where he was supervising the installation of a pumping engine. He began experimenting with coal-gas, and by 1792 had installed gas lighting in his cottage.

In 1799, Murdock returned to Birmingham and continued work on the purification and production of coal gas. By 1802, he had made such progress that coal-gas lighting had been installed on the outside of the Boulton and Watt factory in Soho, Birmingham.

A year later, the inside of the factory was illuminated by coal-gas, and this was followed by installation of the new lighting in the Lyceum Theatre in London. By 1809, gas lamps were shining in Pall Mall, and within a few years gas lighting had spread throughout Britain.

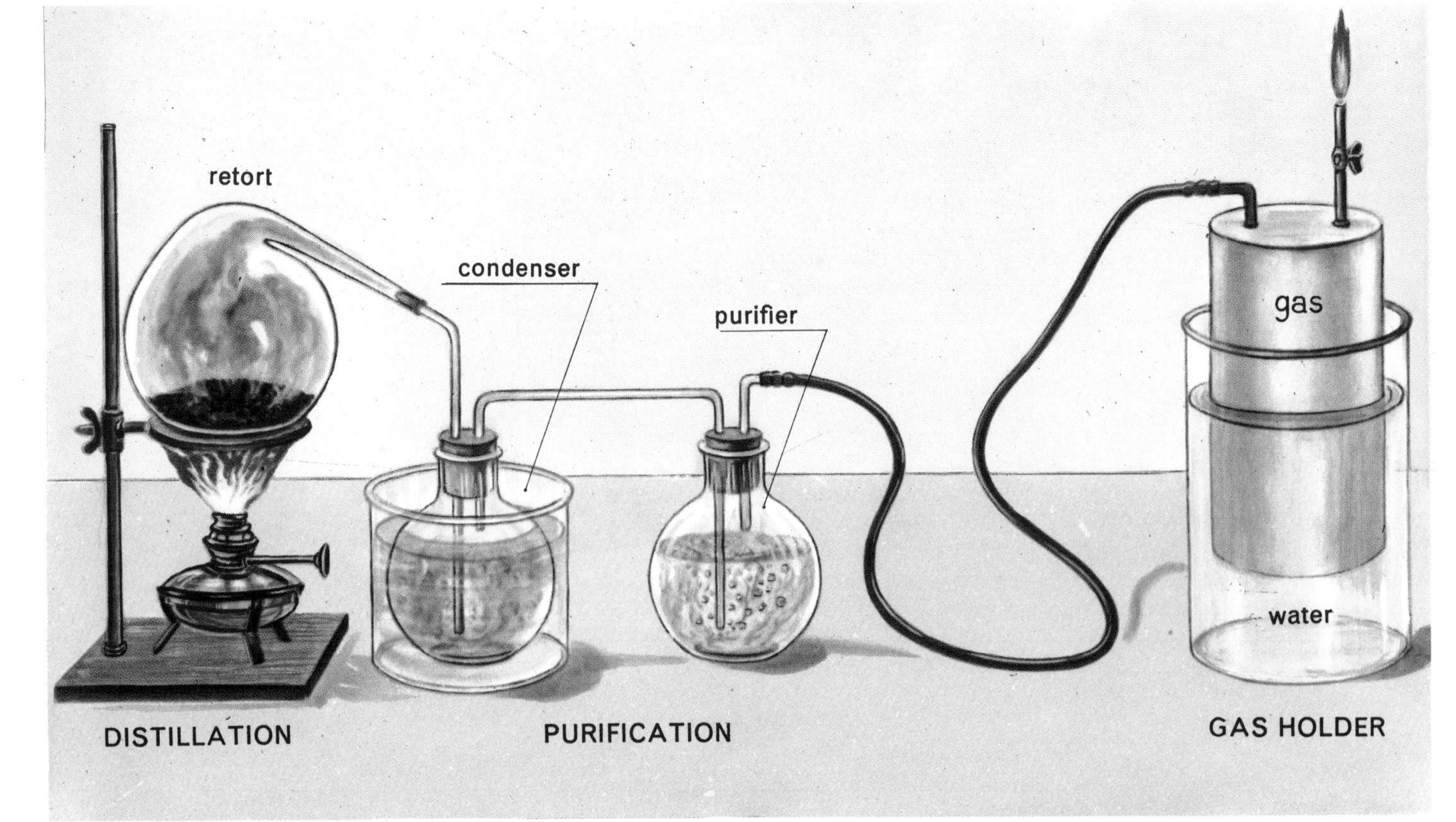

Fumes from coal pass through water; coal tar and acid remain, the purified gas passes through to a small gasometer.

The Bunsen burner provides great heat but little light, due to the gas mixing with air drawn through an intake in the vertical tube, before burning at the top of the tube.

In an age of electricity, gas still plays an important role in our daily lives. Many housewives prefer gas for cooking and heating.

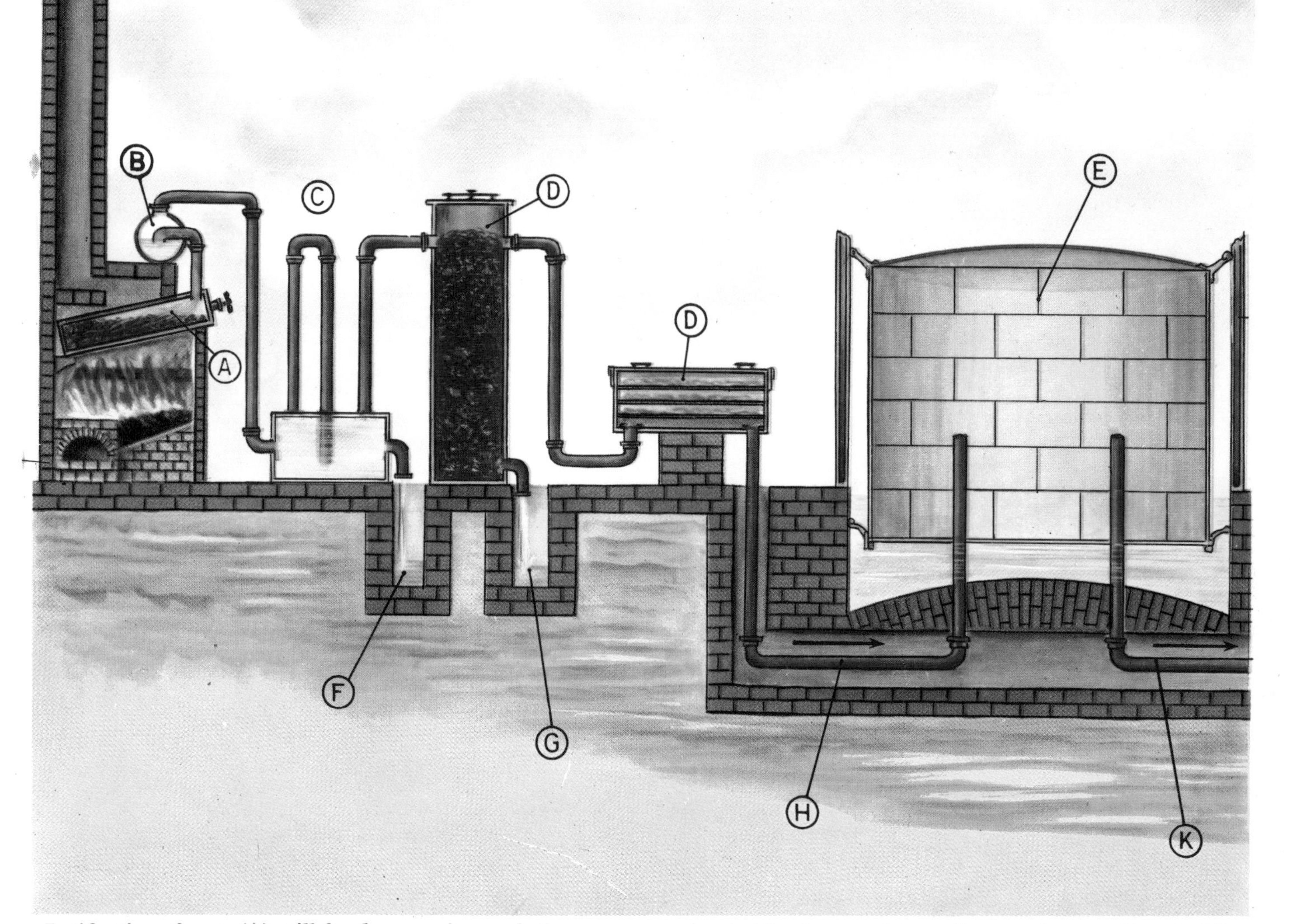

Purification of gas: (A) *still for decomposing coal, the vapours passing to* (B) *where coal tar and ammonia are collected. The gases are cooled and washed in tubes* (C). *As small quantities of tar and ammonia still remain, these are removed by filtering the gas through vessels containing coal and lime* (D). *Tar and ammonia by-products from* (B) *are collected at* (F), *and those from* (D) *at* (G). *Pure gas is piped* (H) *into the gasholder, where pipe* (K) *carries it to the consumer.*

ALESSANDRO VOLTA

Alessandro Volta was a backward child who showed no inclination to speak during his early years. Yet, in a way, this handicap was to prove a blessing in disguise. For Alessandro learned to observe and reflect on everything that happened around him.

At last, when he had reached the age at which most children are going to school, Alessandro Volta began to talk. And his friends were soon astonished when they saw how quickly he learned to read and how eager he was to absorb knowledge. He was not satisfied with superficial facts, but probed deeply into his subject in the manner of a research scientist.

In addition, Volta was gifted with a lively imagination which sometimes carried him away into those realms of fancy that lie between the world of reality and the world of dreams. This capacity is essential to those who are to develop the deep insight of genius. At the age of twelve, for example, the man who gave his name to the word *volt* became intrigued by a story that gold was to be found at the bottom of a pool near his home; and he was very nearly drowned looking for it. The thought of hidden treasure had stirred his imagination, and his practical nature urged him to seek the gold even at the risk of his life.

As a young child, Alessandro Volta found great difficulty in speaking. This worried his mother who spent many hours giving him word exercises and simple lessons.

HIS TRUE VOCATION

After losing his father at an early age, Alessandro and his family went to live with an uncle who was a priest. His greatest interest still lay in science, but literature and philosophy also attracted him. He developed a faculty for writing verse in Latin, French and Italian.

Young Volta knew, however, that his future did not lie in the legal or ecclesiastical professions. His true vocation was to delve into the scientific basis of things. This was his main preoccupation at an age when most boys are interested in finding out more about the world in general and its pleasures.

ELECTRICITY: A NEW MYSTERY

In the mid-eighteenth century (Alessandro was born in 1745), physics was at an interesting stage of development. Electricity and magnetism had claimed the attention of only a few scientists since the days of Pliny the Elder. Their mysteries were now being probed in earnest, and recent

Volta, in his own laboratory, constructed a machine for generating static electricity. His work gained him recognition and membership of scientific institutions all over Italy.

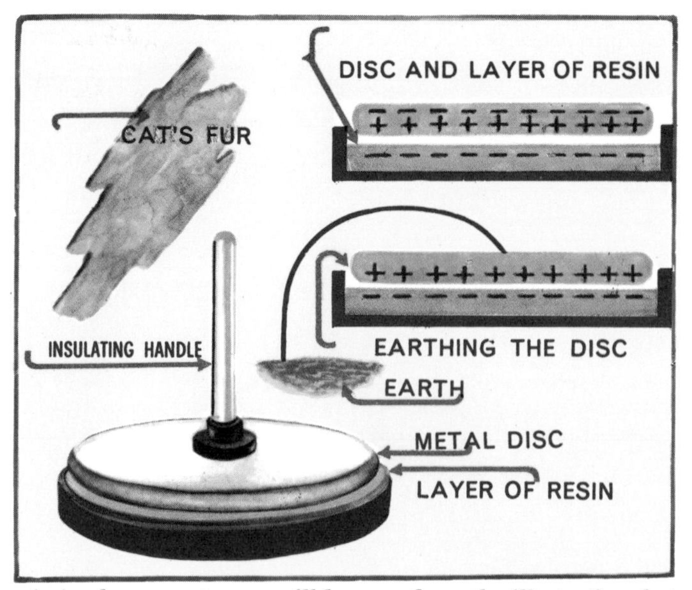

A simple apparatus, as will be seen from the illustration, but one which proved most effective for producing electric sparks. Volta called it his electrophorus.

While walking round the cane plantations at Angera, near Lake Maggiore, Alessandro noticed gas bubbles rising to the top of the water. These bubbles were the natural gases released by the decaying of vegetable matter. Volta tested them to see if they were inflammable, and after further experiments established the properties and uses of marsh gas, now called methane.

researches had led to the discovery of electrical condensers, as demonstrated by the Leyden jar. Bose had ignited gunpowder with the aid of electricity and Winkler had constructed a primitive frictional electric machine.

FIRST ACHIEVEMENTS

In his uncle, Alessandro had a good friend and patron who gave him encouragement and financial help to carry on his researches. This he did to the exclusion of other studies and so never obtained a university degree. After attempting to make sense out of some of the current theories of physics, he began to work on electricity and its practical applications. His reports on his experiments gained him his first recognition, and set him on the path which was to lead to success. By now he was twenty-four years old, and the years that followed were most fruitful in the formulation of scientific principles and laws which paved the way for later discoveries.

This work enabled Volta to perfect—at least by contemporary standards—a number of inventions which even without his discovery of the electric battery would have given him a place of eminence in the history of physics. Among these were his *electrophore*, a machine for generating static electricity; the *eudiometer*, an instrument used for measuring the quantity of oxygen in the air; and the *condenser*, devised in 1782, for storing electricity.

Another of Volta's early achievements was to demonstrate the properties of marsh gas. While wandering round some swampy cane fields near Lake Maggiore in northern Italy, Alessandro noticed that gas bubbles kept rising to the surface. Having made a long study of the chemical reaction of acids and metals and of the inflammable gases they produce, the young scientist jumped to the conclusion that these gas bubbles were also inflammable. He collected some of the gas and tested it, with the expected results. At that time, in

Volta retired to his native town, but Napoleon on hearing of the invention of the Voltaic pile, invited Volta to Paris and made him a Senator of France. The French Academy awarded him their Gold Medal.

the year 1776, he was teaching at Como: this was the town where he spent most of his life, and which has since honoured him with monuments and statues well known to summer visitors.

A SCIENTIFIC DISPUTE

Volta's work on marsh gas and its applications was more readily understood at that time than were his theories about electricity. He was awarded the chair of experimental physics at the university of Pavia, an appointment which brought him into contact with Luigi Galvani, who was then teaching anatomy at the University of Bologna. Galvani, who was interested in Volta's work, had been testing the reactions of certain animals to electricity. Why, he asked himself, did the muscles of freshly killed frogs contract when touched by certain metals?

Volta made a detailed investigation of the phenomenon. He showed that what he called the *electromotive force*, which caused these contractions, did not originate in the frog but

Volta's invention of the pile brought him many awards and high honours from all parts of the world.

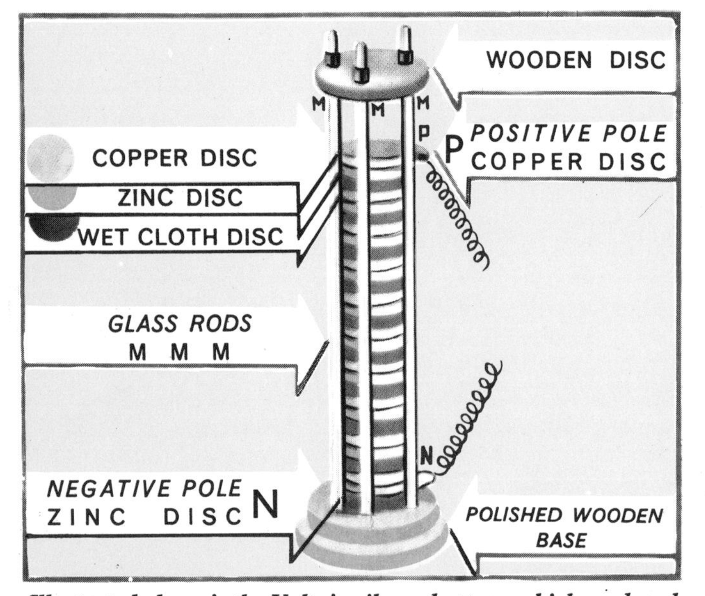

Illustrated above is the Voltaic pile, or battery, which produced the first electric current to be obtained by chemical action. The copper and zinc discs are arranged in couples with a disc of damp cloth between each pair. If a copper wire is attached to the copper disc at the top and another to the zinc one at the bottom, a current of electricity will flow when the wires are joined.

from the contact of two different metals. There followed a heated controversy from which emerged two discoveries of immense importance. The greatest of these was the Voltaic pile or battery; the other concerned the laws of electro-physiology, the study of electricity of living creatures.

VOLTA WINS WORLD HONOURS

It took Volta many years to bring to a successful conclusion the research work stimulated by this controversy. Finally, detailed tests made on metals and all kinds of liquids enabled him to establish that the electromotive forces of certain substances are accumulated when combined in couples set in the same order. It was on this basis that he created the famous Voltaic pile shown in our illustration.

The word pile comes from the Latin *pila* meaning a column, and Volta's pile was, in fact, a column. He announced his discovery on 20th March, 1800, calling it an " electromotive column ". Then he sent it to the President of the Royal Society in London whom he felt was the best person to pass on the news. The world of science was astonished. On 6th November, 1801, Napoleon received Alessandro Volta at the Tuileries in Paris and made him a senator of France. The French Academy also awarded him its Gold Medal.

AT HOME ON LAKE COMO

Invitations to lecture and to demonstrate his experiments now arrived from all sides. But Volta took his success modestly. His work, his family and the lakes beneath the Alps were dear to him, and he worked on in the peaceful surroundings of his home on Lake Como. The death of a son came as a shock from which he never fully recovered. He died on 5th March, 1827, when he was a venerable old man of eighty-two.

Success and world recognition did not change Volta's liking for the peace and quiet of his home on Lake Como. He died there in 1827, at the age of eighty-two.

THE CONQUEST OF SPACE

As with most great technical developments, men dreamed of travelling through space long before the means were available for them to do so. One of the earliest " dreams " is recorded in a book written nearly 2,000 years ago by a gentleman called Lucian of Samos. Entitled rather mischievously *True History*, this describes how a group of sailors were sailing in the Mediterranean near the famous Pillars of Hercules, when a great storm arose. A large water spout formed, trapped the ship, lifted it up and, a week later, dropped it, unharmed, on the moon. There the sailors found the inhabitants riding about on big, three-headed birds. These birds were very clean and tidy, and when they died vanished in a puff of smoke, leaving nothing to bury! But the inhabitants were like humans in one way, they were aggressive and were on the point of declaring war—on the sun!

Apart from this early exception, however, such stories were neglected for many hundreds of years. One reason for this was the religious belief that there could be no other world except Earth, which was thought to be the centre of the universe. Then, after fifteen hundred years, the Italian scientist Galileo developed the telescope. It is difficult for us to realise just what this great invention meant to people living at that time. Galileo, as he focused his crude instrument at the moon, planets, and stars, learned secrets which until then had remained hidden. He saw clearly the mountains and plains on the moon, proving that it was indeed a solid world.

LIMITS OF ATMOSPHERE

The existence of other worlds could be denied no longer and within a few years space-travel stories began to appear. An example was the first English story of a trip to the moon —Bishop Godwin's *Man in the Moone*, published in 1628. Godwin's hero made the journey on a flimsy raft towed by trained swans. The visit was, in fact, accidental, because all the gentleman intended was a short journey on Earth. What he did not know was his swans' habit of migrating to the moon, and so off to the moon they flew, taking the intrepid hero with them. Twelve days later he arrived safely, no breathing troubles apparently being experienced on the way. However, the hero's reduction in weight as he drew away from the Earth was mentioned, as was the lower gravity on the moon—two quite remarkable predictions.

All such early stories contained the grand fallacy that the air extended all the way to the moon; so that, once the art of flying had been mastered, a journey to the moon presented no great difficulties.

Then, in 1656, a book appeared, *Voyage to the Moon and Sun* by Cyrano de Bergerac, which for the first time contained a description of a flying machine which did not need witchcraft or magic to make it work. The craft was very simple, just a wooden box with a number of rockets attached to it. Thus, to Bergerac must go the credit for first suggesting rocket propulsion, for the air does *not* extend all the way to the moon and the only practical means of propelling a machine through the vacuum of space is by means of rockets.

SERIOUS RESEARCH

However, Bergerac's book was just a novel, and it was not until the turn of the present century that the first serious technical studies began to appear. In 1895, the Russian Konstantin Tziolkovski suggested rockets as a method of propulsion able to function in the vacuum of space, and he prepared a remarkably advanced detailed study of a liquid-fuelled spaceship in 1898. This had a fine, streamlined shape divided up into a long conical combustion chamber, propellants tanks, and a living compartment. Its major con-

Some 2,000 years ago, Lucian of Samos described an exciting voyage to the moon on top of a waterspout.

With his telescope, Galileo saw that the moon and planets appeared small only because of their distance from the Earth.

The first liquid-fuel rocket. From this crude device have developed the powerful motors which to-day are launching satellites and taking man to the moon.

tribution to astronautics was the use of liquid fuels. All previous rockets had burnt "solid" powder fuel, but Tziolkovski realised that liquid fuels were more powerful. Another advantage of liquid-propellant engines is that their power can be controlled in the manner of an ordinary car engine. A simple powder rocket cannot be "throttled back" once it has been ignited. Also of interest is the fact that the propellants suggested by Tziolkovski, liquid hydrogen and liquid oxygen, are those being used to-day in the latest satellite launching vehicles being developed in the United States!

SUITABLE PROPELLANTS

In 1907, another early pioneer, the French engineer Robert Esnault-Pelterie, began a mathematical investigation into the possibilities of space flight.

In the same year an American, Robert H. Goddard, prepared a paper suggesting that heat from radioactive materials could be used to provide sufficient power to permit navigation in interplanetary space. This idea, however, was some forty years ahead of its time, and the article was rejected outright by several influential U.S. scientific journals.

Goddard's interest in rockets started even before this, for one of his note-books, written in 1899 when he was only seventeen, contains a comment about the possibility of using rockets as a means of carrying instruments.

Goddard's theories, like Tziolkovski's, indicated that the power of liquid propellants would be needed for interplanetary flight, and he started practical research. At first he made powder rockets, but soon turned to the more advanced liquid-propellant motors. By 1923, he had made a small rocket working on this principle, in which liquid oxygen and petrol were fed by pumps to the motor. This was fired several times on a test stand, but was not launched in free flight.

FIRST PRACTICABLE ROCKET

A second, improved, motor was made in 1925. In this the propellants were forced into the combustion chamber by pressurised nitrogen.

This was followed in 1926 by a similar rocket, but employing oxygen pressure feed. It was a spidery contraption hardly recognisable as a rocket, with the exhaust chamber

HOW A ROCKET WORKS

IMAGINE A FIREWORK BANGER INSIDE AN OPEN ENDED TIN.

THE FIREWORK IS LIT, AND EXPLODES.

PIECE 'A' FLIES OUT OF THE OPEN END AND HAS NO EFFECT.
PIECE 'B' HITS THE END OF THE TIN — AND MOVES IT ALONG.

Rockets obtain thrust by forces acting against the inner end opposite the nozzle, not by exhaust gases pushing against air.

mounted *in front of* the propellant tanks, which consequently had to be protected from the hot gases by a conical shield.

On the 16th March of that year, the rocket was launched from a site at Auburn, Massachusetts. It flew for only 2½ seconds and covered a distance of 184 feet at an average speed of 64 m.p.h. From this crude beginning however, the huge Saturn V booster rocket with five engines each producing a thrust of 1,500,000 lbs. has been developed and used to launch Apollo 11 which successfully put a man on the Moon.

HOW A ROCKET WORKS

Even to-day, with rockets quite commonplace, many people are puzzled as to exactly how a rocket works. It should be obvious—but it often is not—that a rocket does *not* work through the exhaust gases " pushing " against the air behind it. If this were so, a rocket would not work in space, and tests have shown that a rocket actually works *better* in a vacuum.

A rocket depends not on the resistance of the atmosphere, but on *internal* reaction—the pressure of the gases acting on the *inside* of the front end.

Imagine a cocoa tin on the ground, with a firework " banger " inside it. The firework is lit, and explodes. What happens? The force of the explosion will push against the sides of the tin, but it will not move sideways because these forces balance and cancel each other out. One end of the firework will be blown out of the tin and clearly has no effect on it. The other end will shoot up the inside of the tin and hit the end hard; as it does so the tin will move forwards under the impact.

This is just what happens inside a rocket, except that the explosion is continuous. In the previous example the piece of firework flying out of the end of the tin represents the exhaust gases, and the piece of firework hitting the end of the tin represents the internal pressure on the inside face of the rocket moving it forward.

ADVANTAGES OF A VACUUM

Now you can understand why a rocket works better in a vacuum. Not only can the gas escape more freely and thus develop more thrust, but a rocket in the atmosphere is actually slowed down by the resistance of the air in front of it—in space no such resistance exists.

Since the historic flight of Goddard's rocket engine in 1926, many other engineers have helped to " give us space flight ". With the exception of Dr. Wernher von Braun, designer of the German war-time V-2 (the first successful large rocket) and now playing a leading part in the U.S. space exploration programme, they are too numerous to mention here. However, the exciting results of their ingenuity and inventiveness could eventually lead mankind to probe the very depths of outer space.

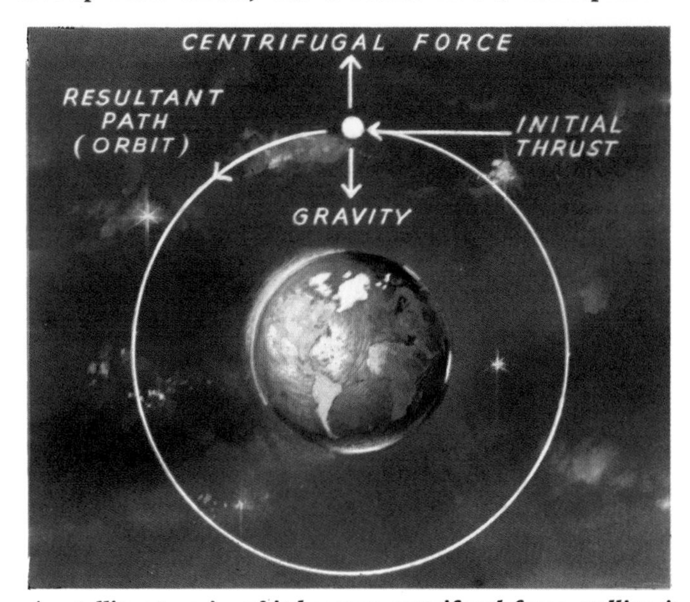

A satellite stays in orbit because centrifugal force, pulling it into space, is balanced by gravity, pulling it inwards.

HOW A SATELLITE STAYS UP

You probably wonder how a satellite stays up—and why some of them come down. The explanation is quite simple. Satellites stay up because their speed is such that the centrifugal force, trying to make them fly off into space, is exactly balanced by gravity, trying to tug them inwards.

As gravity decreases with increase of distance from the Earth it follows that for any particular height a certain speed, known as orbital velocity, is required. If the satellite is moving faster than this speed, the increased centrifugal force will make it move away from the Earth; if it is moving too slowly, gravity will be able to tug it inwards.

Satellites, of course, must first be lifted above any effective atmospheric resistance, turned parallel to the surface of the Earth and then accelerated to orbital velocity so that the centrifugal force exactly balances gravity.

IRREGULAR ORBITS

In this example, the satellite path would be circular, but it need not be; in fact, most satellites, artificial and natural, have elliptical orbits. In such orbits the " balance of power " is constantly shifting from gravity to the centrifugal force, and the speed of the satellite consequently varies.

The key points in an elliptical orbit are the apogee, the point farthest from the Earth, and perigee, the point closest to the Earth. As the satellite " climbs " to apogee it gradually loses velocity because it is actually travelling away from the Earth, against gravity. At apogee its velocity, and therefore its centrifugal force, has reached a minimum, and gravity starts drawing the body earthward.

WHY SOME SATELLITES COME DOWN

If a satellite is sufficiently high, it will continue to orbit the Earth virtually indefinitely. Many satellites, however, although in space for most practical purposes, are in constant collision with minute particles of the upper atmosphere. Eventually this atmospheric friction slows the satellite down a little. This reduction in speed results in a corresponding drop in centrifugal force, and the path of the satellite curves downwards under the force of gravity.

The satellite then accelerates to more than its original speed, and centrifugal force tends to move it outward again. But increased speed in the denser atmosphere multiplies drag, and the satellite starts slowing down before regaining its original course. It again loses altitude.

The process continues, the satellite dropping ever closer to the Earth. Eventually orbital movement ceases and the satellite begins diving to Earth. The intense heat due to atmospheric friction then literally " melts " the satellite and complete disintegration occurs. Special techniques are required to permit the safe recovery of those satellites and capsules designed to be brought back from orbit.

THE WORLD OF SOUND

The blanket of air which covers the Earth provides us with the oxygen we need to breathe. It also serves as a medium through which we can communicate with the help of sound.

Our world is full of sounds. We hear the chatter of voices and the drone of insects, the chirping of birds and the whistle of the wind in the trees. These sounds are all carried to our ears through the air, and if there were no air we should live in a silent world.

You can illustrate this fact by doing a simple experiment. Place a small electric bell worked off a pocket battery beneath the hood of a *vacuum machine* and pump out the air from inside the hood. As the air is removed from the hood, the ringing of the bell will become fainter and fainter until it is completely inaudible, although through the glass you can plainly see that the bell is still working.

WHAT IS SOUND?

When you knock or brush against an object, it will tend to vibrate, and its vibrations are passed on to the molecules of gas forming the air. The vibrations travel through the air until eventually they reach our ears. (Fig. 1).

If you drop a pebble into a pool of still water, you will see a series of circular ripples leaving the point where the pebble hit the water. Sound waves travel in a similar way through the air, spreading out in every direction from the central source of sound, forming " ripples " by successive thinning and compression of the air as they move through it.

Sound travels out from its source in all directions. As the distance increases the sound becomes fainter, and it has been calculated that the volume of sound decreases in direct proportion to the square of the distance travelled (Fig. 2).

THE SPEED OF SOUND

In the air, under normal conditions, sound travels at a constant speed of 340 *metres* per second (about 760 miles per hour). Our ears are only capable of hearing sounds whose vibrations are at least 16 per second and not more than about 20,000 per second. There are sounds with a higher number of vibrations per second, but we are not equipped to hear them; they are called *ultra-sonic* waves. Some animals, for example bats, have hearing sensitive enough to pick them up.

Physicists have established that the speed of sound in water is 1,437 *metres* per second (about 3,200 m.p.h.), and through solid matter it is 5,000 *metres* per second (about 11,200 m.p.h.).

It is easy to appreciate that light moves much faster than sound. We all know that during a storm the lightning is seen first, followed by the sound of thunder, perhaps seconds later, even though the two phenomena occur at the same instant.

EXPERIMENTS WITH SOUND

By measuring the distance between the place where the sound is made, and where it is heard, dividing it by the number of seconds that elapse from the time when the sound was created to when the sound is heard, the speed of sound can be calculated. Fig. 4 gives an idea of how we can measure the speed of sound in water.

If you knock two stones together under water, the sound

Fig. 1. The German physicist, Kladne, succeeded in making the vibrations of a metal plate visible. He covered it with a sprinkling of sand and then drew a note from it with a violin bow. The sand could be seen gathering in certain parts of the plate, forming definite patterns in accordance with the vibratory movements of the plate.

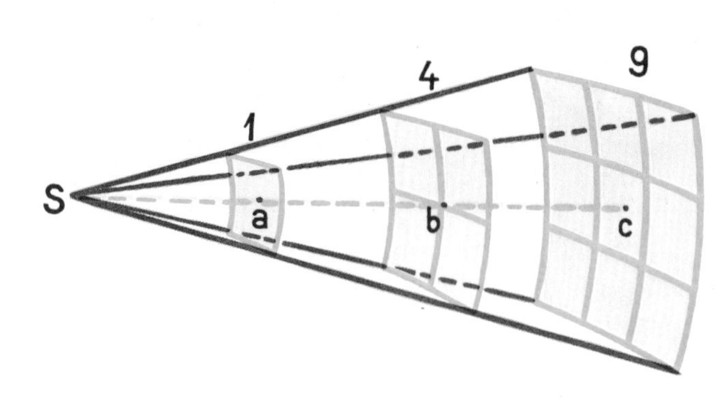

Fig. 2. The loudness of sound as it travels through the air is inversely proportional to the square of the distance it has travelled. The sound will be four times less distinct at (b) *than at* (a), *and nine times fainter at* (c). *The use of a loudspeaker, or megaphone, however, increases the carrying-power of a voice.*

of the blow will reach your ears far more quickly than it would through air, simply because the speed at which the sound travels underwater is so much greater.

Sound carries even better through solid matter. Red Indians use to throw themselves flat and press their ears to the ground to detect the approach of their enemies. They could even tell the direction, and how many people to expect.

An experiment can be done to prove that sound waves do not involve the actual movement of matter from the source to the detector. Take any ordinary tube, open at both ends, and fill it with smoke: place a lighted candle at one end and at the other end clap together two wooden blocks. The smoke will remain in the tube, but the candle flame will flicker. This shows that it was vibrational *energy* that was transmitted through the tube.

ECHOES

The ripples caused by a pebble hitting the water travel outwards in ever-widening circles, until they meet an obstacle. Then they rebound, or more precisely, are reflected from it. This also happens to sound waves. When they meet an obstacle, they are reflected from its surface and travel back as if they had come from a point the same distance behind the obstacle causing an echo.

This reflection of sound, or echo, is a familiar feature of underground caves (Fig. 3). In Syracuse there was an ill-famed cave called the " Ear of Dionysius ". This cave had been hollowed out of the rock above the cells where the tyrant kept his prisoners. Any sound made in the prison cells could be heard there, so that Dionysius was able to overhear every word his victims uttered.

PITCH AND DISTANCE

As we know, sound waves travel outwards in a straight line from the source when the air is still and of uniform temperature. But when they move in layers of air where the temperature varies (as often happens) then the sound waves undergo refraction, altering the direction in which they are moving. That is why voices can be heard at enormous distances in the mountains: and in a boat in the early

Fig. 4. Experiment to measure speed of sound through water.

morning, when the water is still cold, singing or talking carries much farther than it would under normal conditions.

Sounds can be classified by their volume, pitch and tone. The volume depends on the extent of the vibrations which reach our ears; the pitch is governed by the number of vibrations per second, and the tone depends on the form of the sound wave. This is shown when the same note is struck by different musical instruments.

The pitch of a sound can be recognised with the help of a tuning-fork (Fig. 5). This is a steel fork mounted on a metal base: when one of its prongs is struck it gives out a musical note, such as *A* (435 vibrations per second). It is used by musicians for tuning their instruments, and by choirs, to give them their note. If two tuning-forks are placed a little distance apart and one is tapped lightly, the second one will start vibrating with the same note, even if the first one has already been stopped. This is because the vibrations of the first produced sound waves which set off the vibrations of the second fork. This phenomenon is called resonance.

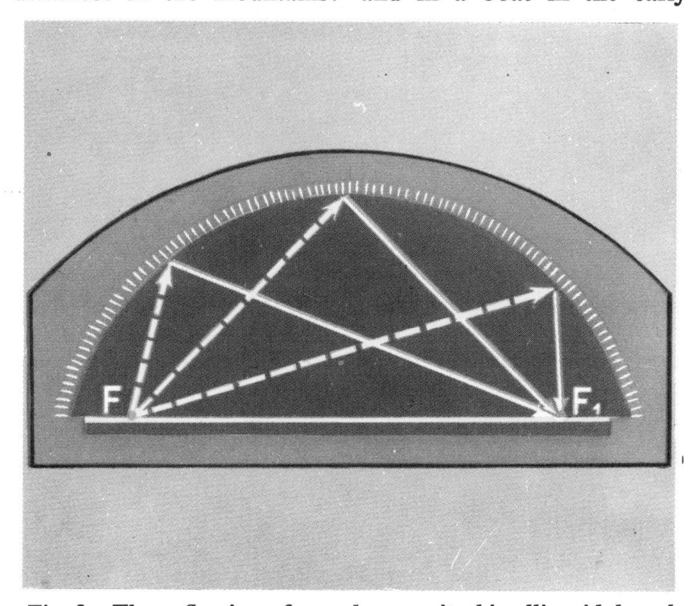

Fig. 3. The reflection of sound waves in this ellipsoidal vault has this result. Someone whispering at (F) *will be heard at* (F′), *which is the focal point of the ellipses, but nowhere else.*

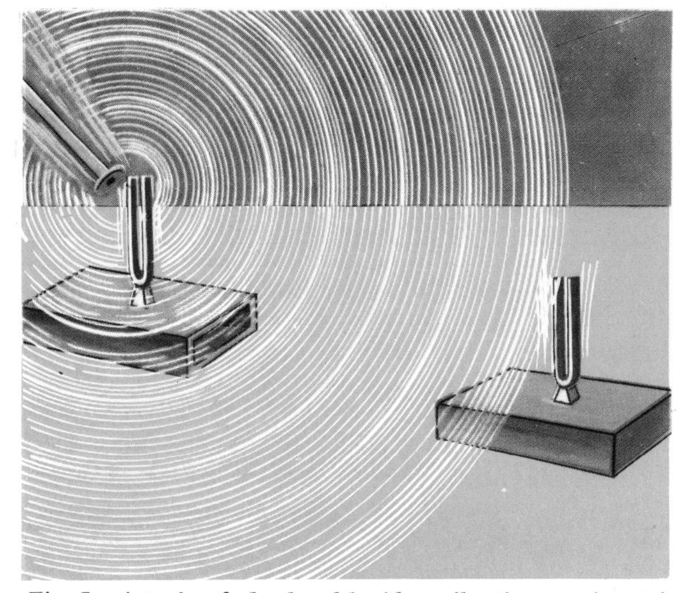

Fig. 5. A tuning fork placed beside a vibrating one is set in motion by the sound waves from the first fork. This is called "resonance."

High up in the atmosphere, five or six miles above the Earth, a great river of air rushes on a non-stop journey round the globe. Meandering along between the Arctic Circle and the Tropic of Cancer, moving always from west to east, this air-river, which we call the jet stream, carries with it our hopes for a spell of decent weather.

Since the end of the war, scientists have been making an intensive study of the jet stream, and its strange characteristics are now fairly well understood. But we are still as far as ever from knowing how it is caused; and we still cannot predict with accuracy the route that it will follow from day to day.

WEST TO EAST

For forty years and more, British meteorologists have known that balloons sent up into the air are often whipped away to the east by winds blowing at a height of several miles. But it was only during the war that these high-level winds were recognised as part of a sort of atmospheric Gulf Stream that flowed unceasingly round and round the world.

As planes began to fly ever higher in a search for speed and storm-free air, the phenomenon of the jet stream became more and more important. When the U.S. Air Force started the high-level bombing of Japan in 1943, pilots found that their planes were often "standing still" during bombing runs at 30,000 feet. The air was moving at 300 miles an hour in a direction opposite to that in which they were flying. And when the planes flew home, they were carried along at twice their normal speed.

STREAMS DIVERGE

Research has shown that the jet stream blows fastest just below the stratosphere, usually about six miles high. It moves as narrow jets that converge to form the main stream, like tributaries running into a river. High mountains, like the Himalayas, can split it up again into separate streams that follow divergent courses, perhaps to merge again after hundreds of miles.

In winter, the stream flows round the Earth near the Tropic of Cancer; in summer it contracts and moves north towards the Arctic Circle.

During winter, the jet stream blows faster than in summer. Its peak speeds are reached as it leaves the coast of Asia and sets out across the Pacific; one pilot reported a jet-stream speed of 450 m.p.h. over Japan.

If the jet stream followed a simple circular course on its journey round the Earth, it would be easy enough to check its position at any time, but it behaves in many ways like an ocean current, meandering like a huge snake over vast areas of the earth. Its path will undulate as it sweeps south towards the equator for two or three thousand miles, only to swing back in a huge loop towards the pole. Up and down it goes, tracing a wave-like pattern round the world.

As it meanders up and down, the jet stream drags huge lobes of cold polar air into lower latitudes. Then, after following its undulating course perhaps for weeks, the stream cuts across the base of a lobe, leaving a great pool of cold air above thousands of square miles of land. Far to the north, upward-reaching lobes of warm air are left by way of compensation.

This switching of huge pools of air between the poles and the tropics is nature's way of mixing the air that covers the Earth. Heat from the tropics is carried into the colder regions.

UNCHARTED SOUTH

In the Southern Hemisphere, meteorological information is sparse. But we know that a jet stream speeds round the south polar regions, travelling in a westerly direction like its twin in the north.

If we could follow and predict the behaviour of the jet stream that girdles and contains the polar air, we should be able to make more reliable forecasts of the weather. Until then, our meteorologists can lay the blame for forecasts that go wrong on the unpredictable meanderings of the jet stream as it snakes around the globe.

If the position of the jet stream could be followed accurately from day to day, it would be possible for pilots to use the stream in routine flying. By keeping in the stream a pilot could double the speed of his plane by relation with the ground. And by keeping out of the stream on the return journey, he could be sure that he was not "standing still" in the air.

NARROW AND TURBULENT

Using the jet stream in this way is not so foolproof as it sounds. The stream itself is narrow and often difficult to find. Even the main stream formed from several tributaries of air will sometimes be as little as 200 miles wide.

Also, pilots flying in the jet stream have flown into areas of severe turbulence. Suddenly, and without warning, their planes are bumped and battered as though by a giant hammer. These areas of turbulence are often 100 miles wide and nearly a mile thick.

Even so, experienced pilots are now flying the stream where they can find it, almost as a matter of course. Planes flying the Pacific from Japan to the U.S. can save six hours flying time and more than 2000 gallons of fuel by thumbing a lift from the jet stream.

ORIGIN UNCERTAIN

Though meteorologists have done a lot of speculating about the cause of the jet stream, nobody yet knows what it is that concentrates the high-level air into this narrow, fast-moving stream. It has been suggested that hot air rising from equatorial regions pushes up against the cold air flowing from the poles. Unable to move up or down under the terrific pressure, a layer of air squeezes along the edge of the two opposing masses to form the jet stream.

This theory is as plausible as any, but an immense amount of research will be needed before we can assess the value of one theory against another. In spite of all that has been done since the war, we know almost nothing of the course followed by the jet stream over vast regions of China and Siberia, or over the Atlantic and Pacific Oceans.

We know even less about the twin jet stream that flows unheeded in the Southern Hemisphere.

LOUIS PASTEUR

Louis Pasteur was born in Dôle, France, in 1822. His father was a tanner and was poor, but he did his best to give Louis a good education even though he showed no special talent at school or college. He was twenty-six, in fact, when he first gave evidence of his later brilliance by making an important discovery in chemistry.

It was by chance that his interest was later switched from chemistry to quite a different subject. A manufacturer of beetroot alcohol was worried because the beet juice in his vat was turning sour, Pasteur was called in to advise, and he discovered that it was living cells which were causing the trouble. It was a turning point in his life, for the idea occurred to him that perhaps similar " microbes ", living organisms too small to be seen by the human eye, invaded the human body and caused infectious diseases.

MICROBIOLOGY

After this, he became involved in the famous dispute about " spontaneous generation ". Some scientists believed that microbes sprang into being of their own accord, from nothing. Pasteur, however, showed that they were born from parents of their own kind. He maintained that they were carried in the dust of the air, and that if this dust could be shut out, milk or any other substance which normally goes bad, would remain in good condition indefinitely, not merely for weeks, but for years. He showed this to be true by a brilliant series of experiments. It was this work which led the Scottish surgeon, Lister, to suspect that germs might be responsible for infection in wounds, and to attempt to exclude them.

Pasteur had no contact with work on disease until he was forty-three, and then his first patients were silkworms. Disease was killing off the silkworms of Europe; great hardship and financial ruin faced the provinces of the south of France where silkworms were grown. When all the growers and all the silkworm experts had failed to find any way of dealing with the disaster, Pasteur was asked to take charge. He was rather alarmed by this request, for he knew nothing whatsoever of silkworms and their diseases, but he was a man of courage as well as a great scientist, and he accepted the challenge. In a very short time, he knew as much about silkworms as any of the local growers and could recognise a sick worm more quickly than they could. He then found out the cause of the disease and was able to show the growers a way of selecting eggs for breeding which would be sure to produce uninfected offspring.

Louis Pasteur peers into his microscope, watching the movements of strange micro-organisms. Modern bacteriology is based on the findings of this great man.

PROTECTIVE INOCULATION

Pasteur's great work, however, lay in discovering the principle of " protective inoculation ". He discovered how to protect people from a serious attack of an infectious disease by giving them a small, safe attack. He stumbled on this discovery almost by chance. Pasteur, however, said that " chance only favours the prepared mind." He had also begun to study chicken cholera, a very serious disease which attacks and kills probably nine out of ten hens in the farmyard. The germ which caused the disease had already been discovered, but Pasteur was the first man to find a way of growing it in the laboratory. He grew the germs in broth made from chicken gristle and found that a few drops of the broth in which these microbes were growing was sufficient to kill a chicken.

During the summer holidays, the laboratory was closed for a few weeks, and when Pasteur and his assistant returned they had only an old culture of germs with which to infect hens with chicken cholera. The injections were given, but the hens, instead of becoming seriously ill, merely drooped a little, were slightly ill, and then became as well as ever. A fresh batch of germs was prepared and a fresh batch of hens was inoculated. Almost as an afterthought, the hens which had received a dose of the stale germs were inoculated, too.

DISCOVERY OF IMMUNISATION

The result was completely unexpected. The new hens fell sick and very quickly died; but the other hens did not. The germs in the stale culture had lost their power to kill, but they had retained the power, it seemed, to give protection against a second attack. Pasteur had discovered " immunisation ". From this day he devoted himself to finding out ways of weakening germs. " Attenuating " them, he called it, so that, like the stale culture of chicken cholera germs, they should give protection and yet be safe.

About this time, a very serious outbreak of anthrax was killing sheep and cows and causing great loss to the farmers. Pasteur made experiments and found a way of weakening the germs of anthrax by growing them at a high temperature. From these weak germs he made a vaccine with which he injected fourteen sheep. The sheep suffered no ill effects even when later he gave them an injection of deadly anthrax germs. Carried away by enthusiasm, as he often was, he accepted a challenge to a sort of scientific duel. Before a large audience, he was to inject twenty-five sheep with his vaccine; then, after a suitable interval, these sheep, plus a further twenty-five which had *not* been given the vaccine, were to be inoculated with fully active anthrax germs. His assistants were horrified by his recklessness, but Pasteur remained confident and the test turned out a triumphant success. The twenty-five protected sheep lived, and all the others died. He became a public hero, and in the very next year 613,740 sheep and 83,946 oxen were vaccinated.

WORK ON DREADED RABIES

Pasteur was nearly sixty when he determined to investigate one of the most dreadful diseases a man could have; hydrophobia. This is caused by the bite of a mad dog, so Pasteur arranged for mad dogs to be brought to his laboratory. He tried to find in the saliva and in the brains of the dogs, the germ which caused hydrophobia but he found nothing. He then decided, even though he could not find them, that the germs *must* be somewhere in the nervous system since it is the brain and nervous system which are chiefly affected by the disease. Accordingly he made the experiment of hanging up, for fourteen days, a small piece of spinal cord taken from a rabbit which had died of rabies, and then injecting a preparation made from it into a dog. The dog did not fall ill or become mad, so Pasteur decided that the germs, which must be present in the dog, had been weakened by the drying process. The next day, Pasteur injected a preparation of spinal cord which had been dried for thirteen days, and so on until the dog received an injection from an animal newly dead of rabies. This would have meant certain death to an unprotected animal, but the dog was apparently unharmed.

The method was tried over and over again and was always successful, but Pasteur was frightened to take the next step and try it on a human being for it was just possible that his treatment might be fatal to humans. Then, on 6th July, 1885, a little boy of nine, badly bitten by a mad dog, was brought to Pasteur's laboratory. He was Joseph Meister of Meissengott. The doctors told Pasteur that the boy was quite certain to die, so Pasteur gave way to the mother's entreaties and treatment was begun. It was a time of dreadful anxiety for Pasteur, which ended in triumph; the boy lived, and his health was unaffected by his experience.

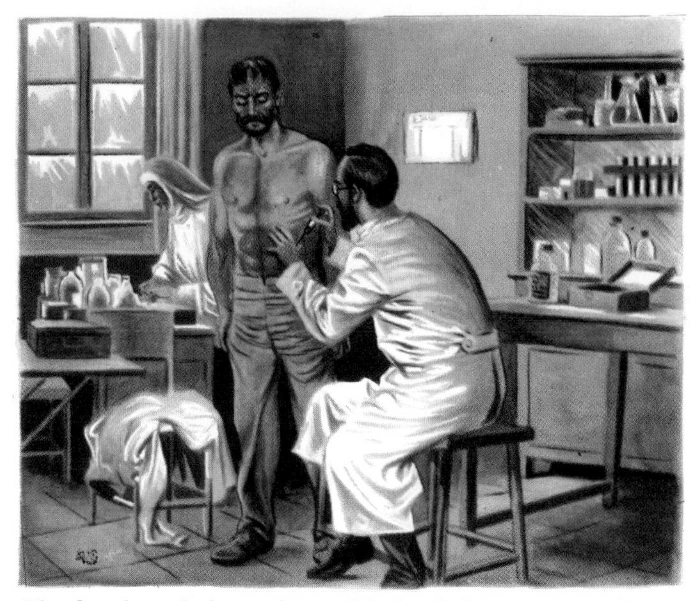

The first inoculations with anti-hydrophobia vaccine. Nowadays, the Fermi vaccine is found to be more effective.

THE PASTEUR INSTITUTE

Pasteur became famous, and men, women and children came from all over the world for treatment. Sometimes it was too late to save those who came, but on the whole the treatment was a success. In 1888, the Pasteur Institute, which has since become world-famous as a centre of medical research, was built in his honour.

It was a great thing to have discovered a treatment to prevent hydrophobia, but far more important was the fact that for the first time an artificially prepared vaccine had been used on man with success. The same principle was quickly applied to other diseases; the principle of preparing a vaccine from a weakened form of the germ which causes the disease, and vaccines against cholera, plague and other infectious diseases soon followed.

Pasteur had suffered a stroke in middle life and had been left partly paralysed as a result. In his late sixties he became ill again and he died in November, 1895.

QUESTIONS AND ANSWERS

Who was Piltdown Man?

This was the name given to a supposed ancestor of man who was believed to have lived between 500,000 and 1,000,000 years ago. The existence of this primitive form of man was deduced from the examination of fragments of fossil bones and teeth found in a gravel pit at Piltdown, Sussex in 1911-1913.

The first piece of bone was found by C. Dawson in 1911; a jaw bone was discovered in 1912 and a tooth in 1913. These were reconstructed to form a skull, which scientists regarded as representing the skull of a primitive man. He was given the name *Eoanthropus dawsoni* in honour of his discoverer, and became known popularly as Piltdown Man.

From the age of the gravel deposit in which he had been found, and from other evidence, Piltdown man was regarded as having lived between 500,000 and 1,000,000 years ago. The shape of the reconstructed skull suggested that Piltdown Man was of a very primitive type, with ape-like features. Crude flint implements found near the fossils suggested that he had reached a stage of using simple tools.

Many scientists studied the Piltdown remains, and were convinced that he represented a genuine stage in man's evolution from the ape. But some scientists, especially anatomists, felt that the bones did not fit together as they ought to, and were sceptical about the fossil man.

In 1949, British scientists re-examined the Piltdown remains, using modern techniques for assessing age. And they found that the jaw bone and tooth had come from a modern ape. They had been filed and stained to give them the appearance of great age, and to make them resemble a human jaw bone. Piltdown Man, accepted by the scientific world for 40 years, was the result of a carefully planned hoax.

OXYGEN

Two eighteenth-century chemists, K. W. Scheele in 1772, and J. Priestley in 1774, discovered oxygen independently of each other. Scheele called the gas " fire air " and Priestley " dephlogisticated air ". But the credit for showing us what oxygen really is goes to A. L. Lavoisier, a French scientist who studied oxygen thoroughly and proved that it is present both in water and in air. Lavoisier named the gas "oxygen" from the Greek words meaning " generator of acids "

ELEMENT OF LIFE

We human beings live at the bottom of a sea of gas which covers the entire surface of the Earth. This gas is our atmosphere, and its most important constituent, so far as living things are concerned, is the colourless gas oxygen.

Oxygen, which forms about one-fifth of the atmosphere, is an active chemical. Atoms of oxygen will unite with atoms of almost every other element to form " compound atoms " (molecules) of new substances. Most familiar of all the compounds of oxygen is water; this is the result of union between one atom of oxygen and two atoms of hydrogen.

Eight-ninths of the weight of all the water on Earth consists of oxygen. Half the weight of all the rocks in the Earth's crust is oxygen; almost every rock and mineral is a compound in which oxygen atoms have combined with atoms of other elements. There is oxygen in sand and silica, in limestone and chalk, in clay and granite. It is the most abundant element of all.

The oxygen in the atmosphere is in a free state. Its atoms are not united with atoms of other elements. They are simply mixed with the atoms and molecules of nitrogen and the other gases of the air.

This store of free oxygen in our atmosphere is a reservoir from which oxygen reaches the innumerable processes involved in life and living. For oxygen, by its eagerness to take part in chemical changes, is in a state of constant movement between the atmosphere and the living and inanimate things on Earth.

COMBUSTION

When anything burns in air, some or all of its constituent elements are combining with the oxygen of the air. A flame is a region in which this union involving oxygen atoms is taking place. The heat of a flame is energy liberated as a result of the chemical change.

Most of the fuels we burn as a source of light or heat are substances containing the element carbon. This element forms a constituent of almost every substance involved in the structure of living things. Animals and plants are constructed from carbon in association with hydrogen, nitrogen and other elements. Most substances which have come from living things—such as wood or coal—will burn in air as the carbon they contain combines with oxygen in the air to form carbon dioxide gas.

The stored fuels such as oil or coal, which we use so lavishly to-day, are stores of carbon chemicals which release heat energy as their carbon and other constituents combine with oxygen in the air.

SPONTANEOUS COMBUSTION

In the case of a fuel, the combination with oxygen takes place rapidly and often violently. But many substances combine with oxygen more slowly, without producing a flame. For example, many metals will corrode in air, the oxygen taking part in combination with the metal to form a new compound. Oxygen helps to cause the rusting of iron; it is present in the green film of verdigris on copper. Some metals, such as gold, silver and platinum, resist the attack of oxygen, and do not corrode by " oxidation " in the air.

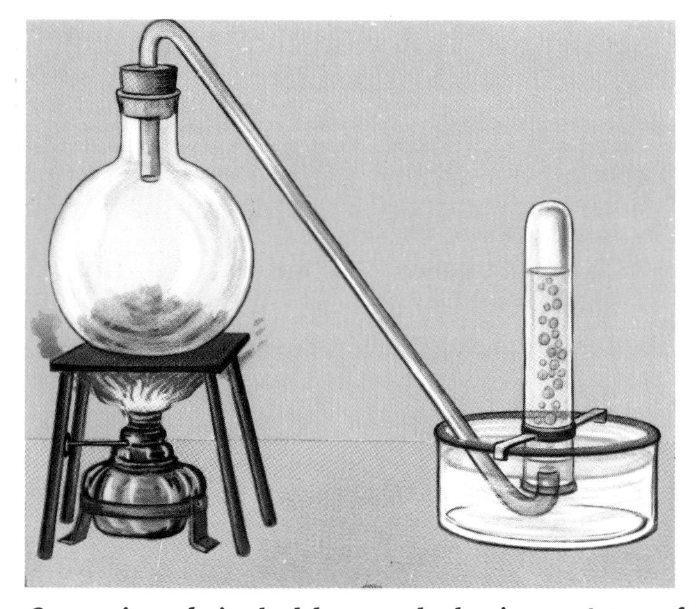

Oxygen is made in the laboratory by heating a mixture of potassium chlorate and black manganese dioxide. The latter substance facilitates the reaction and enables production of oxygen to take place at a temperature lower than that necessary for the decomposition of potassium chlorate.

If we heat red mercuric oxide in a test-tube, decomposition takes place, and the oxygen in the mercuric oxide is thus set free. If a glowing taper is applied to the mouth of the test-tube the taper ignites in the oxygen which has come from the mercuric oxide.

Spontaneous oxidation results in the generation of heat in damp hay, sometimes resulting in fires. Coal dust and slag heaps will often catch fire of their own accord as the oxygen in the air combines with carbon in the coal, producing heat.

Substances which burn in air will burn more fiercely in oxygen itself; the nitrogen dilutes the oxygen of the air, and damps down the oxidation process. Sulphur, carbon, hydrogen and phosphorus will burn with a brilliant flame in pure oxygen. Sulphur produces a beautiful blue flame; phosphorus burns with a white light.

The illustration shows how a steel spring, heated and plunged into a jar containing pure oxygen, will burn brightly.

A piece of glowing coal, immersed in oxygen, will soon burn itself out. Magnesium burns away with a dazzling light.

Oxygen is a colourless, tasteless and odourless gas and is the most abundant of all elements. It is an excellent supporter of combustion, and many metals will burn in it with a brilliant flame. For instance, a hot steel spring (left), *put into a jar containing pure oxygen, will burn brightly and give off sparks. Sulphur, on the other hand, will burn with a pale blue flame* (right).

RESPIRATION

Oxygen takes part in the breathing or respiration which sustains our living processes. When we breathe, oxygen is absorbed into the blood in our lungs. It is carried off to the living cells which form the body tissues. Here it combines with the carbon and hydrogen in the materials of the living cell, transforming them into carbon dioxide and water respectively. The carbon dioxide is carried away by the blood and released in our lungs, from which it is exhaled.

This process of " combustion " inside the body provides energy to keep the body alive, maintaining the living machine just as the energy from burning coal will keep the machinery of a factory running.

If we place a glass jar upside down over a lighted candle the flame will continue to burn as long as there is oxygen available. When all the oxygen has been used up, the flame flickers and goes out.

USES OF OXYGEN

Oxygen is an important industrial chemical, and it is produced on a large scale by the liquefaction of air. When the liquid air is distilled, oxygen, nitrogen and other constituents boil at different temperatures and can be separated.

Oxygen has many uses in various industrial processes. When combined with acetylene gas, oxygen produces an oxy-acetylene flame with a temperature of up to 3,000° C. It can be seen in use in factories and shipbuilding yards, when steel sheets are cut and welded by the powerful, bright blue flame which has become such a familiar sight to-day.

Oxygen is used in heating furnaces for smelting aluminium dust mixed with metal oxides when making synthetic jewels for watches. It is a steriliser for purifying water; it helps to mature wines artificially, and is used for purifying air in enclosed spaces.

Compressed in special bottles or cylinders, oxygen is given to people who have difficulty in breathing as a result of asphyxia or gas poisoning, and to others who are gravely ill. It makes breathing easier at great heights, where the air pressure is low, and the lungs cannot obtain the oxygen they need. Without oxygen, deep-sea divers could not do their work, nor could submarines operate effectively. In the chemical industry it is widely used in the manufacture of sulphuric acid, oxides of lead, zinc oxide, and hydrogen peroxide, which is a powerful antiseptic and bleaching agent.

OZONE

Under normal circumstances, the oxygen atoms forming free oxygen gas are joined together in pairs. But there is another form of oxygen in which the atoms have combined in threes. This is the gas called ozone.

Ozone is formed whenever an electric discharge takes place in air. The familiar smell of ozone can be detected near electric motors and other equipment where sparks are passing through the air.

The ultra-violet rays in sunshine bring about the union of oxygen atoms to form ozone, and there is a region of the atmosphere high above the earth where the concentration of ozone is appreciable.

The three-atom arrangement of ozone is not a stable union, and ozone tends to revert to normal oxygen given the slightest opportunity. In doing so, it produces oxygen in a very active state, and ozone is used as a powerful oxidiser for many applications.

ATOMS AND THEIR USES

Deposits of radio-active minerals are traced by Geiger counters.

Our century will go down in history as the beginning of the Atomic Age. Of all the great scientific developments which we have seen during the last fifty years, none will have such a far-reaching effect as the harnessing of atomic energy. In atomic energy we have tapped an immense reservoir of energy which could bring revolutionary changes in the world's living standards before our century reaches its end.

How is atomic energy generated? In what way and by what means can it be put to use? We have already seen that the atom is a little world in miniature, made up of the *nucleus*, which has a positive charge, and the *electrons*, small particles with a negative charge, which revolve around the nucleus like so many minute planets around the sun. The nucleus in its turn is made up of a number of other particles, *protons* (positively charged), and *neutrons* (which have no charge). This structure is the same for every atom of every substance that exists in the world. The only difference is in the number of particles in the nucleus, and the number of circulating electrons, which varies from one element to another.

SPLITTING THE NUCLEUS

The atoms of certain elements are unstable, and the nuclei of the atoms emit particles like tiny bullets as they gradually disintegrate. These are the " radioactive elements ", such as radium or uranium. If we allow the radiation from one of these radioactive elements to bombard the atoms of another substance, some of the rays will pass straight through the outer layers of electrons, but others may strike the nucleus; when this happens, the nucleus may disintegrate and in its turn produce new radiations. These may then bombard other atoms which again disintegrate and produce further radiations. The multiplication of the radiation caused by this break-up of atomic nuclei is called a " chain reaction ", and this is the process which takes place in a nuclear reactor or in an atomic bomb. In the latter case, the chain reaction proceeds at tremendous speed, the number of nuclei being split at an ever-increasing rate. When atoms undergo this chain-reaction disintegration, part of the matter in the atom is turned into energy, which is released, in the case of an atomic bomb, as an immense burst of heat. If, on the other hand, the chain reaction can be controlled, then the energy so produced can be harnessed for peaceful purposes.

REACTORS

Reactors which can bring about nuclear fission for peaceful purposes are of two types—reactors which generate energy, and research reactors. In the first type the heat energy produced by the atomic reactor is transformed into electrical or mechanical energy by using turbines or similar devices. It is this type, for instance, which was installed in the American atomic submarine *Nautilus*, which achieved fame by finding a passage under the ice-cap of the North Pole. Such reactors can be used to propel ships, and are already widely used in the production of electrical power.

Research reactors, on the other hand, do not produce energy for practical use, but are used for studying the behaviour of substances when they are exposed to the bombardment of atomic radiations.

RADIO-ISOTOPES

Some elements, such as radium or uranium, are naturally radioactive. Other elements, however, can become radioactive when subjected to bombardment by radiation, for example in a nuclear reactor. A radioactive form of an element is known as a radio-isotope. Radio-isotopes of a great variety of elements are now produced commercially, and these substances have found many valuable applications. They behave in exactly the same way as the non-radioactive form of the element, but wherever they go they emit a stream of radiation.

Nautilus, *which sailed under the ice cap of the North Pole.*

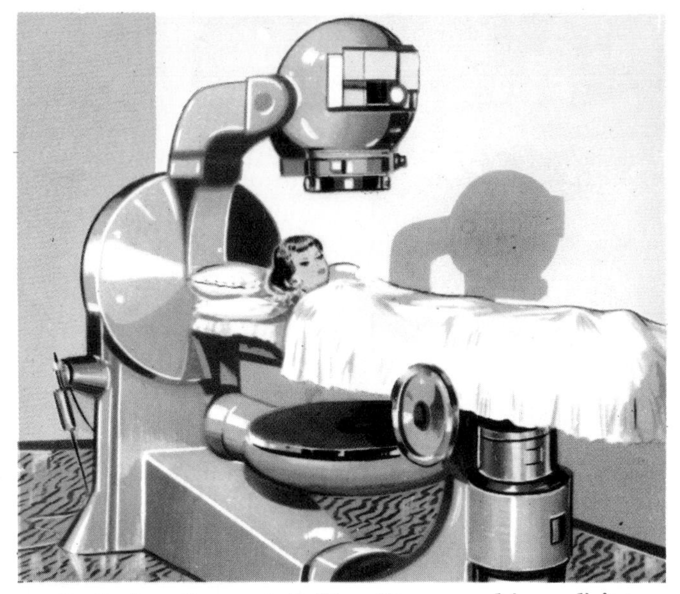

Radiations from cobalt "bomb" are used in medicine.

Nowadays, most forms of cancer are being treated by the cobalt bomb, which is actually an instrument containing a small quantity of radioactive cobalt, whose rays are directed on to the affected part of the patient's body through a tube. Radioactive iodine is used to treat thyroid infections, while radioactive sodium is widely used in research on heart complaints and defects of the circulation. Radio-isotopes inserted into the body are helping physiologists to discover its innermost secrets. By injecting them into cattle it has been discovered how animals turn fodder into flesh and milk. By injecting them into an oak tree, the reproductive system of certain parasitic fungi was revealed.

OUTDOING NATURE

Plant breeders have produced remarkable results by experimenting with the effects of radiation on the seeds of plants, in the hope of breeding new strains, or improving the quality of plants. For example, potatoes which have been treated with radio-isotopes change their physical composition, and their sugar content shows a marked increase. In future we may no longer need to grow sugar-beet to obtain sugar, but will be able to obtain this food from irradiated potatoes. Tomatoes of a new type have been produced, as well as pipless grapes and new, hardy strains of oats and wheat. These were produced by planting the crop in a circular furrow around the radioactive cobalt.

TRANSURANIUM ELEMENTS

Apart from these practical results achieved by nuclear fission, there are others of immense scientific interest. In nature there exist 92 separate elements which, combined together, make up every substance on earth. By bombarding atoms with atomic radiations entirely new elements are formed; that is: elements which did not previously exist in nature. These are the " transuranium " elements, elements heavier than uranium, which is the last and heaviest in the series of elements we know. The transuranium elements are extremely radioactive: by constantly emitting radiation they quickly bring about their own disintegration.

With the help of atomic radiation, it has been possible to reproduce in the laboratory the transformations that occur in interplanetary space, where the powerful cosmic rays disintegrate atoms to produce new particles, including those called mesons. Mesons are now made in the laboratory, by bombarding carbon with the nuclei of helium atoms.

THE POTENTIAL POWER IN WATER

During the last few years, the harnessing of atomic energy has taken another immense step forward. It has been found possible to release vast quantities of energy by bringing about the fusion of small atoms to form larger ones. This process of fusion is the source of the energy that sustains the sun and stars, and it could provide us with unlimited quantities of energy for the peaceful development of the world.

In a nuclear fusion reaction the two lightweight hydrogen isotopes deuterium and tritium are "welded" together to form one heavier nucleus. The resulting fused nucleus, however, is not quite so heavy as the two light ones taken together; some mass is "lost", or converted into energy.

In order to bring about nuclear fusion, temperatures of many millions of degrees must be attained. This has been achieved in uncontrolled fashion in the form of the hydrogen bomb, where a nuclear explosion may produce the temperature necessary to cause fusion of hydrogen atoms. Such a process is called a thermo-nuclear reaction. As yet, it has not been found possible to release energy from nuclear fusion under controlled conditions.

NUCLEAR POWER DANGERS

The development of nuclear energy and its application for practical purposes has faced scientists with immense problems. Most important of all is the provision of adequate protection from the atomic radiation produced by nuclear reactors. This radiation is dangerous to human life, and thick shields of metal and concrete must be placed round a nuclear reactor to absorb the radiation.

There is no doubt, however, that the atom will become a source of energy to be used by man for his ever-increasing needs. In a few years' time, there will be electricity even in the most backward and isolated areas, bringing the benefits of civilisation to everyone; while factories, transport, and all branches of industry from the biggest combine to the humblest workshop, will be able to take advantage of the tremendous power hidden in the innermost heart of matter.

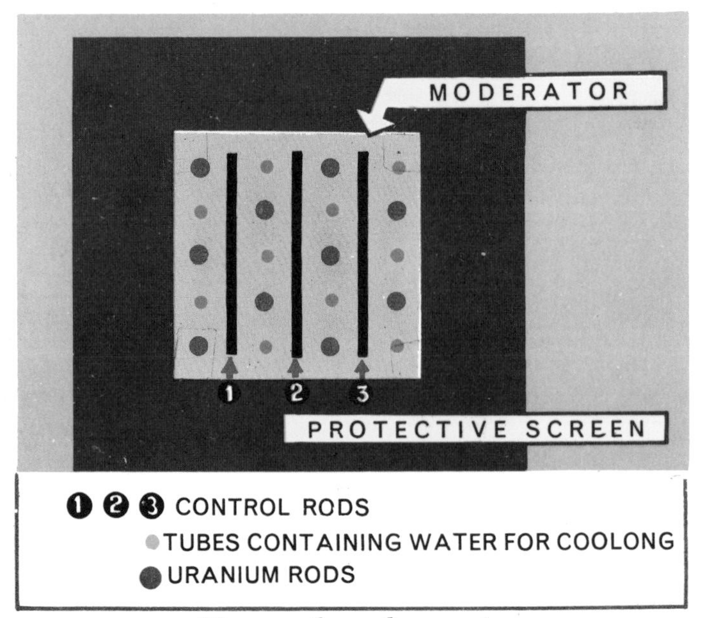

Diagram of a nuclear reactor.

ELECTRIC POWER STATIONS

The modern world runs on electricity. Electricity lights our homes and drives our trains; it cooks our meals and heats our houses; it operates our industrial machines and makes possible our radio and television. Without a sustained and ample supply of electricity, our industrial civilisation would collapse.

The huge quantities of electricity that we need are provided by the electric power stations which are a feature of every industrialised country. Electricity flows in powerful streams along the cables that connect these power stations to the consumers in every home and factory. This electricity is a form of energy, and it is not created from nothing; it is produced from other forms of energy which are in a less convenient form.

The commonest method of producing electricity is to generate it from mechanical energy, the energy of movement. When a copper wire, for example, is moved in a magnetic field, a current of electricity is generated in it. This is the basis on which the electric generator works, and to maintain a steady current of electricity we must provide a steady supply of mechanical energy from which it can be derived.

In many parts of the world, climatic conditions have joined forces with geography to release a copious supply of rainwater high in the hills. This water flows down the valleys towards the sea, and in this flow of moving water there is a potential source of electricity. It is the basis of the hydro-electric power station.

To tap the power of water, the engineer builds a dam across a valley, so that the water collects behind it. This reservoir of water provides a reserve supply, from which a steady, controlled flow can be drawn and used to generate electricity.

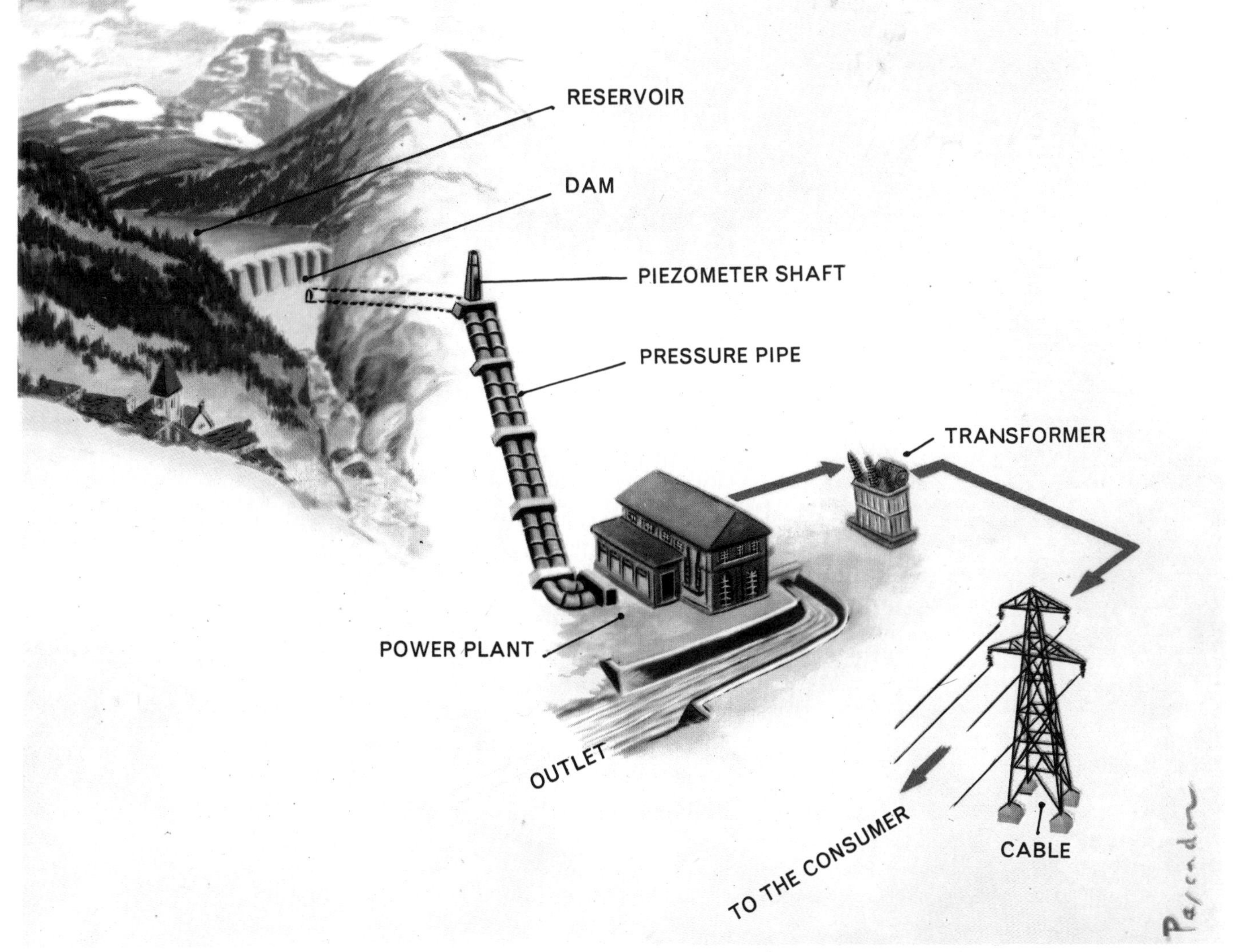

How water is stored and used in a hydro-electric power station. A pipe inside the mountain links the artificial lake to the pressure-pipes. It is the force of the water plunging down the pipes which drives the turbines below. The water-driven turbines transfer mechanical energy to the alternators, where it becomes electricity. Transformers modify the current according to demand; the water then leaves the power station through the escape channel.

The water from the reservoir is brought through pipes to a lower level, where it flows through turbines. These are the modern successors to the water-wheel, in which the flowing water turns a propeller-like wheel by striking against blades set at an appropriate angle. The rotation of the turbine provides the mechanical energy which is turned into electrical energy, or electricity, in the generators.

During the last half-century, water-power has been harnessed in this way all over the world, wherever conditions are suitable. But there is a limit to the amount of water-power available, and in many regions this limit is being reached. Alternative sources of power are therefore needed.

Many countries have only a small amount of potential water power. Others have none at all. The energy needed for transformation into electricity must therefore be provided in other ways, and the commonest method is to make use of fuel such as coal.

Energy is stored away in coal in the form of chemical energy. This can be released as heat when the coal is burned. And the heat can be transformed into mechanical energy by using it to boil water and generate steam; the steam then drives an engine or turbine.

This is the process used in a thermo-electric power station. The turbine, rotating under the pressure of steam, generates electricity as in the case of hydro-electric power. Wherever there is an existing, natural source of heat, however, electricity can be generated in the same way. There are power stations, for example, which draw on the natural steam pouring from fissures in volcanic regions. This steam drives turbines to produce electricity costing nothing for fuel.

The atomic power station, which is now producing electricity in some countries, is novel only in that it is a new source of heat. The heat is turned into electricity in exactly the same way as in the traditional coal-burning power station.

THE ATOMIC POWER STATION

The heat used to raise steam in a nuclear power station comes from the splitting of the nuclei of atoms in the fuel. Part of the matter of the atomic nuclei is converted into energy, which is released as heat.

The British nuclear power programme is based upon nuclear reactors which use natural uranium metal as fuel. 0·7 per cent. of the uranium consists of the isotope uranium 235, which undergoes nuclear fission when bombarded with neutrons. The remainder of the uranium is uranium 238, which is not normally split under these conditions.

The uranium 235 in the core of the nuclear reactor splits when bombarded by stray neutrons. The result of the fission is to provide more neutrons, together with a large amount of energy; the bulk of the nucleus forms two fission fragments which become the nuclei of new atoms.

The neutrons emitted by the splitting uranium 235 bring about fission in other uranium 235 atoms, the process being adjusted and controlled so that a continuous release of heat is sustained.

The basic process which produces heat in a nuclear power station is thus a simple one. But there are immense practical difficulties to be overcome in harnessing this process in practice.

The fuel, in the form of natural uranium, is canned in a material such as magnesium. This contains the radio-active fission products, but it permits the neutrons to escape.

The fuel is held in a core of graphite bricks which is built in the form of a lattice with channels to hold the fuel rods. Neutrons liberated by fission of the uranium 235 in the fuel rods are slowed down by the graphite to speeds in the region of about 2 miles per second. At such speeds, the neutrons are more likely to be captured by other uranium 235 atoms, in which they cause fission and so sustain a chain reaction. The graphite serves in this way as a " moderator ".

The illustration above shows the control room of a modern power station, from which a few technicians can control the working of the plant.

The core of the reactor is surrounded by a layer of graphite two or three feet thick. This is the reflector, which reflects into the core most of the neutrons which would otherwise escape from it.

The heat generated inside this reactor core is removed by a stream of gas (usually carbon dioxide) which flows through the core. As the gas is under pressure, the core is enclosed in a pressure vessel with steel walls some 4 inches thick.

The core of a nuclear power reactor emits dangerous radiations in the form of neutrons and gamma rays, and it is necessary to have a safety shield surrounding the pressure vessel. This safety shield consists of concrete some 9 feet in thickness. It absorbs radiations emitted by the core, reducing the level of radiation to a point at which people can work safely in the neighbourhood of the reactor.

Carbon dioxide gas used for absorbing heat produced in the core has many advantages; it is cheap and readily available, has a low neutron absorption rate and does not raise undue corrosion problems. The gas circulates at high speed through ducts as much as 6 feet in diameter, passing into heat exchangers, where the hot gas heats water and raises steam. This steam then drives the turbo-generators which produce electricity.

The output of heat from the core of a nuclear power reactor of this type is controlled by means of control rods in the core. These are rods of neutron-absorbing materials such as boron, in the form of boron steel, which can be pushed into and drawn out from the core. The rods are suspended above the reactor and can be lowered into channels in the core. The farther they are lowered into the core, the more neutrons they absorb and the slower the nuclear reaction becomes. In an emergency the rods fall into the core under the pull of gravity.

THE CINEMATOGRAPH

We think nothing these days of going to the cinema and losing ourselves for an hour or two in ancient Rome, or joining the crew of a space ship on its way to Mars. The pictures we see on the screen are so absorbing, and the movement is so lifelike, that we can allow ourselves, in imagination, to join the screen characters in their exciting worlds. The cinema is so much a part of our everyday life that we tend to take it for granted. We forget, at times, that it is one of the more wonderful scientific inventions of our modern world, in which all sorts of skills and ideas have been merged to achieve success.

The cinematograph, which throws the moving pictures on to a cinema screen, makes use of a defect in the power of human sight, called persistence of vision. When the human eye sees something, the image of the scene is registered on the sensitive layer, or retina, at the rear of the eyeball. The pattern of light falling on the retina is analysed, and information about it is sent off to the brain via the optic nerve. The brain assesses the electrical message it has received, and registers a " mental picture " of the scene that has formed the pattern of light on the retina.

PERSISTENCE OF VISION

This process takes place very quickly, but is not instantaneous. It takes a fraction of a second for the sequence of events to be completed, and during this time the eye is not able to deal with any change in the scene. It is almost as though it closed down for a short time to enable it to deal with the scene that it had already observed.

This time-lag in the operation of our sense of sight is called persistence of vision. There is nothing new in our knowledge of it; Leonardo da Vinci studied the phenomenon five centuries ago. But it was only with the invention of photography that persistence of vision could become the basis of cinematography.

During the early nineteenth-century, many inventors experimented with devices for creating the illusion of movement by showing a succession of pictures. These all worked on the same principle; every picture carried forward the action of the previous picture by a very small amount. A series of pictures might show, for example, a person with arm outstretched, and each successive picture would show the arm raised a little higher than the previous picture. When the sequence of pictures was shown in rapid succession, the pictures would merge together and give the illusion of the person raising his arm.

This illusion is due to persistence of vision; as each picture is registered by the eye, it merges with the impression of the previous picture which the brain is still " digesting ". Instead of seeing a sequence of individual pictures, therefore, the eye sees a continuously-moving scene in which the changes in the individual pictures merge to create an impression of uninterrupted movement.

EARLY " MOVIES "

In 1824, Peter Roget presented a paper to the Royal Society in England, under the title of " The Persistence of Vision with regard to Moving Objects ". Roget's paper stimulated a great deal of interest among scientists of the day, and many experimental devices were invented for portraying movement by showing a succession of pictures. Sir John Herschell, for example, made a simple toy which embodied the principle that was to make cinematography possible at the end of the century. It consisted of a piece of cardboard on one side of which was painted a bird, and on the other side a cage. The card was held between two silk threads, and when the card

The dark lines of variable length seen on the left represent the sound of the letter "A" recorded on the film. On the right is a sequence of animated cartoon drawings.

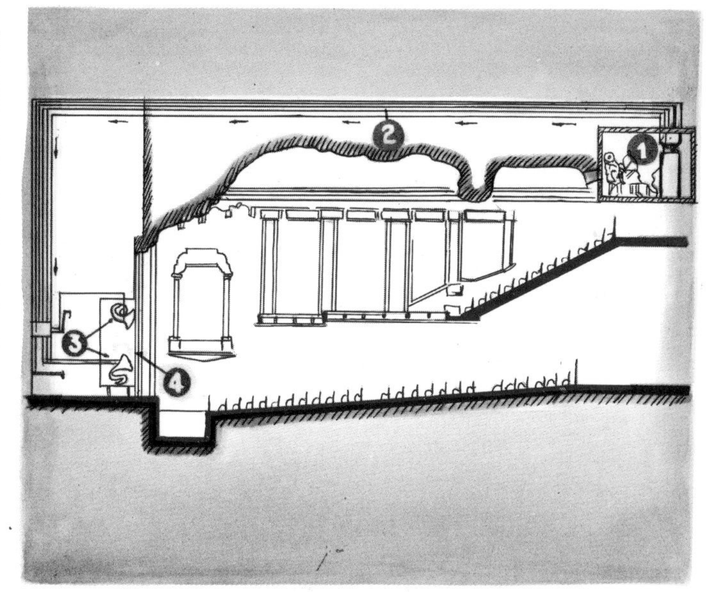

Diagram of the installation necessary for running a sound picture. 1. room with synchronising apparatus; 2. electric circuit for operating loud-speakers; 3. loud-speakers; 4. screen.

was twirled the two pictures merged so that the bird was seen in the cage.

In Vienna, Dr. Simon van Stampfer constructed a device in which a succession of pictures was mounted on the rim of a disc, and seen through slots in a similar disc. In 1853, Franz von Uchatius, an Austrian army officer, carried this a stage further by projecting the pictures through a magic lantern, so that the succession of pictures created an impression of movement on a screen.

The zoetrope, which became a familiar toy of Victorian days, consisted of a cylinder in which a succession of pictures was seen through a slot as the cylinder was rotated.

PICTURE PALACE

Most ambitious of all these early devices was the optical projector operated in a " picture palace " by M. Reynaud in Paris during 1877. This showed moving pictures which were projected on to a screen by a magic lantern. The pictures were painted at regular intervals on a long band of transparent paper, which was passed rapidly through the lantern.

The scope of these devices was limited by the fact that they were all based on the use of drawings. But, in 1881, a British photographer called Eadweard Muybridge brought photography into the moving picture business, and so began the cinematograph industry as we know it to-day.

Muybridge fitted up twenty-four cameras alongside a track on which horses exercised, and fitted each camera with a thread attached to a spring holding the camera shutter. A horse was then ridden along the track, and as it broke the thread of each camera it photographed itself.

GALLOPING HORSE

In this way, Muybridge obtained a series of photographs showing the horse in successive stages of movement. When these were viewed through one of the devices then in use, they gave the impression of a galloping horse.

Muybridge's experiments aroused great excitement and stimulated research and experiment in many countries. The closing years of the nineteenth-century saw cinematography developing rapidly in America and Britain, in France and

A succession of pictures, each one carrying the movement forward a stage, gave the impression of motion.

Pathé Frères made a film of the Dreyfus Case in 1899; *this was one of the first documentary films.*

Germany. It is impossible to credit any one person with the invention of cinematography. Like the motor-car, the modern cinematograph came into being as a result of the work of many people in different parts of the world.

PROJECTION

Once it had been shown that photographs could be used instead of drawings or painted pictures, all sorts of devices were invented for taking photographs of moving scenes in rapid succession, and for projecting these photographs at the same speed when they had been taken. Among the pioneers in these early days were William Friese-Greene of Piccadilly, London, and Marey and Deméney in Paris.

Dr. Marey perfected a camera which could take photographs in one two-thousandth part of a second, and his partner Georges Deméney devised an apparatus for projecting the photographs in rapid succession on to a screen. The effectiveness of Deméney's device, like those invented elsewhere, was limited by the fact that photographs had to be taken on glass plates. Photography was a slow and cumbersome process in those days.

Before cinematography could become a practical proposition, something had to be done to enable photographs to be taken on and projected from an endless band of flexible material, similar to the band used by Reynaud in his picture palace. All sorts of materials were tested, and all sorts of ingenious devices were invented in an attempt to find some way of speeding up the process of cinematography.

CELLULOID FILM

The development of the celluloid film by Eastman, in 1889, was to solve the problem. The flexible celluloid film enabled the photographer to take shots of a moving scene in rapid succession, and to project the shots one after another to create the illusion of movement in the picture.

One of the techniques which contributed greatly to the development of cinematography was the use of intermittent movement of the film. The succession of photographs taken by the cameraman is not passed continuously through the projector. Instead, each individual photograph is projected

The "exterior" scenes in films are often reproduced in the film studio. Sometimes, however, films are shot against actual backgrounds, this is termed "on location." Although stunt men and women are used in filming violent and dangerous scenes, the actors often take risks as great as those originally taken by the people they are portraying.

and shown for an instant. Then a shutter comes across the lens of the projector as the next photograph is moved into position. The shutter is removed and the photograph projected for the appropriate length of time, before the shutter again moves across and the process is repeated. In this way, a succession of still pictures is thrown rapidly on the screen; the movement caused by the removal of one shot and its replacement by the next takes place while the shutter is in front of the projector.

INTERMITTENCY

This principle of intermittency, which has done much to bring cinematography to its present state of efficiency, was established by William Friese-Greene, who described the technique in his patent of 1889.

Once the flexible film had opened the way towards the successful exposure and projection of a succession of photographs, the development of cinematography became largely a matter of technology.

In America, Thomas Edison contributed greatly to the progress of cinematography. He had already devised a machine for showing moving pictures, which he called a kinetoscope. But like others, he had found this of limited value so long as he was restricted to the use of glass photographic plates for the succession of pictures.

In 1889, Edison obtained a supply of the new flexible celluloid photographic film, and exposed a series of photographs on a continuous band of the film. He then passed this band through an improved version of the kinetoscope and obtained moving pictures. This device was to be a prototype from which commercial development of cinematography became possible.

KINETOSCOPE

Edison demonstrated his kinetoscope at the World's Fair in Chicago in 1893. It was a coin-operated device, in which a " nickel " was dropped into a slot in a wooden cabinet. The viewer looked through a peep-hole and saw a moving picture lasting for half a minute, in which children danced and people walked about. The movement was achieved by passing a succession of photographs on a film before the eye of the viewer at the rate of forty pictures a second.

Edison's kinetoscope was adapted by Robert Paul, a scientific instrument maker of Hatton Garden, London, who devised a special lantern called a bioscope, which could throw the moving picture on to a screen. Paul's shouts of joy as he first operated his device successfully brought police running to his home in Hatton Garden at three o'clock one morning in the spring of 1895. The film, forty feet in length, was run through the projector again for the benefit of the constables, who became the first public audience to see moving pictures thrown on to a screen.

PROJECTORS

Meanwhile, in France, the Lumière brothers had been working on the problems of constructing cameras and projectors which could be used for cinématography. They developed mechanisms which controlled the movement of the film by means of claws which engaged in perforations on the side of the film. One of their machines was sent to London about a year after the bioscope had come into use in Hatton Garden. Another machine was sent to the United States, where progress in cinematography had been slow despite the invention of the peep-hole device by Edison.

Once these new cameras and projectors showed what could be done, commercial progress in cinematography was rapid. The production and distribution of silent films became a powerful and flourishing industry during the early years of the present century. The camera developed for commercial use by the film industry takes a succession of twenty-four shots per second on film of 35 mm. width, with four perforations on each side of every photograph or " frame ". In 1923, a smaller film was introduced, 16 mm. wide, and this in turn was followed by 9·5 mm. and 8 mm. films for amateur use.

In 1926, the sound film was brought into commercial use. In recent years, the safety film of cellulose acetate has replaced the highly-inflammable celluloid film, and a number of techniques of colour photography have been adapted for use in the ciné camera.

ALFRED NOBEL

At the beginning of the nineteenth-century, Stockholm was a quiet little city inhabited by well-to-do Swedish and Norwegian merchants who controlled much of the trade between northern Europe and Russia. Behind the town, vast forests stretched far into the interior. Along the waterfront modern industry was beginning to take shape around shipyards engaged in constructing the naval frigates and four-masted vessels of the day.

It was against this background that Alfred Nobel was born on 21st October, 1833. His father, a well-respected engineer of keen intelligence and lively enterprise, was working at the time on the chemical composition of explosives. Before long he was to succeed in making the first underwater mine, a contrivance which at once attracted the attention of foreign powers who wished to add this new weapon to their stock of armaments.

Alfred Nobel was born in Stockholm on the 21*st of October,* 1833, *and died in San Remo, Italy, in* 1896.

AN EXPLOSIVE ENVIRONMENT

Among the many offers that Alfred's father received was one that came from Russia. He accepted it, moved to St. Petersburg, as Leningrad was then called, and went to live in an arsenal for the large-scale production of mines. Alfred, who had been born, as it were, in a powder magazine, now grew up in the midst of explosives of every kind and variety. Thus it was only to be expected that he should devote himself to the study of this subject.

The boy's schooling, which started in Stockholm, was continued in St. Petersburg and finished in America, where he was sent to study mechanical engineering. His aptitude for chemistry and mechanics was soon apparent, and before long, people were talking of him as the young inventor of a new type of gasometer, and a novel device for measuring a volume of water. Meanwhile, those military considerations which had led the Russians to call upon the services of Alfred's father were no longer valid. The revolutions which had tormented Europe for many years after the downfall of Napoleon had run their course, and it was decided to stop making mines at St. Petersburg and close down the establishment. The Nobels had no choice but to return to Sweden and resume work in their own country.

Alfred, son of an engineer, inherited his father's passion for explosives and chemistry.

With his brother and father, Alfred Nobel now set to work on a scheme to make nitro-glycerine on an industrial scale. This substance had been discovered in 1847 by an Italian, Ascanio Sobrero (1812–88), who was later to develop the use of dynamite in agriculture and mining. But no one had succeeded in producing nitro-glycerine on an industrial scale because of the danger inherent in handling such an explosive substance.

Experiments had reached an advanced stage, and it seemed that success was just round the corner, when a disaster occurred which threw the whole family into mourning. The new workshop had hardly been opened before a terriffic explosion blew up the entire building killing several men, among them Alfred's own brother.

THE DISCOVERY OF DYNAMITE

Short of help and lacking sufficient money, Alfred Nobel now faced a crisis which put heavy demands on his courage. If he were to go on with his experiments, he must work in some place where the lives of others would not be endangered. So he hired a boat and transferred his nitro-glycerine aboard a floating laboratory. If it went sky-high there would be no one to answer for it but himself. Fortunately, nothing catastrophic happened. On the contrary, results were so good that Alfred soon opened two factories, one in Germany and the other in Sweden. But the thought that a second explosion might bring operations to a standstill was never far distant. It was with this in mind that the young inventor tried mixing nitro-glycerine with an inert yet absorbent substance.

By modifying the power of nitro-glycerine in this way Alfred Nobel produced a very much safer explosive. This was dynamite, patented on 10th September, 1867, and soon to be used by arms manufacturers all over the world. Its discovery created immense interest. Obviously it was going to solve many difficult problems encountered in road building, mining and the construction of tunnels at a time when railways were spreading across all five continents.

To meet the demands that reached him from all sides Nobel had to build other factories in Europe. Yet he was not carried away by success. He continued with his researches and experimental work, mixing different substances with known explosives and testing the effects. It was in this way that he succeeded in making dynamite gelatine and ballistite. At this point the French authorities refused him the right to new patents in France and in so doing touched off a series of events which deeply affected Alfred Nobel's life.

Just when his discoveries were beginning to bring him rewards which were to make him one of the richest men of his day an anti-Nobel campaign was started in France. Certain politicians and industrialists, backed by the Press, bitterly criticised him for adding to the horrors of war. They overlooked the fact that the materials invented by this Swedish scientist were no less useful for works of peace. Neither the Simplon nor the San Gotthard tunnels, the one twelve and the other nearly ten miles long, could have been constructed beneath the Alps without the help of dynamite. They ignored all this and scoffed at Nobel's reply that the knowledge of these high explosives would remove the danger of future conflicts by making mankind realise how destructive war had become.

Then one morning in Paris, in 1891, Alfred Nobel opened the papers and, to his utter astonishment, read in the headlines the news of his own death. What hurt him most were the bitter comments of the entire French Press in regard to his life's work. One paper called him an " evil genius ", another described him as a " self-educated master of destruction ". They all expressed the utmost relief that " this man who devoted his life to the encouragement of war and to bringing his fellow-beings to the brink of destruction had at last disappeared from the civilised world."

FORCED RETIREMENT

Such violent feeling was too much for him. Rather than suffer the wave of hatred which his presence in France had excited, Nobel decided to leave the country and work in San Remo, then a peaceful little seaside resort on the Italian Riviera. There he made several new discoveries in other branches of chemistry and physics, but he could not escape the odium of the world, even in this retreat. He had given all his time and energy to the development of a particular field of science, and what was the result? A fortune, yes—the money kept pouring in. For the rest, dislike and deliberate misunderstanding from all around him.

THE NOBEL PRIZE

Alfred Nobel knew that he would not live long—he died in fact in 1896—and it was in that last year of his life that he made a great decision. In drawing up his will he set aside money to found the Nobel Trust from which the munificent Nobel Prizes are awarded. Soon afterwards he died, amidst a fresh outbreak of criticism and enmity. His discoveries and inventions were reviled, his life as an industrial scientist was decried. But he was, in truth, a courageous man whose sensitivity had been deeply wounded by the attitude of his contemporaries. It was to ensure that later generations would not see him in this light that he gave his fortune to the founding of the Nobel Prizes.

Five of these prizes are awarded every year regardless of the nationality of the candidate. Three go to those who have made the most important contribution to physics, chemistry and medicine; one, the literary award, to the author whose work shows most distinction in its idealistic qualities; another to whoever has done most to promote the friendship of nations and the abolition of warfare. This last is called the Nobel Peace Prize. The award is made in the form of a symbolic degree accompanied by a cheque for about £15,000, which sum is intended to enable the winner to live the rest of his life without economic worries.

HOW THE AWARD IS MADE

The winners of Nobel Prizes are chosen by specially-appointed institutes and committees. For physics and chemistry, the decision rests with the Swedish Royal Academy of Sciences; the medicine prize is decided by the Stockholm Institute of Medicine and Surgery; the literary award is made by the Swedish Academy and the Peace Prize by a committee composed of five members of the Norwegian Parliament.

Nobel Prizes have always been given to men or women to whom mankind owes a debt of gratitude for work done in various branches of human activity. And since the Prize is more highly esteemed than any other in the field of literature, science and the political arts, some who have won it for work conducted in quiet seclusion have become celebrated almost overnight. When you look through the great names included in the list of Nobel Prize winners, remember that they owe their fame and recognition partly to Alfred Nobel, inventor of dynamite and nitro-glycerine.

The Swedish scientist believed that his discoveries would be used for the benefit of mankind. Instead, they were soon to be applied to weapons of death and destruction, which brought great misery to all.

The harnessing of atomic energy has stimulated a demand for many strange materials. Among them is the precious liquid that we know as "heavy water."

Heavy water is simply what its name implies. It is water that weighs more, pint for pint, than the ordinary water we get from the tap. And this extra weight comes from the atoms of hydrogen in the heavy water, which are twice as heavy as the normal ones.

DEUTERIUM

In ordinary water, the molecules consist of two atoms of hydrogen joined to one of oxygen according to the familiar formula H_20. In heavy water, the two hydrogen atoms each contain an extra sub-atomic particle—a neutron—in the nucleus. This makes them heavier without changing the chemical nature of the element. The heavy hydrogen, or deuterium, unites with oxygen in just the same way, and the heavy water that is formed is just like ordinary water in its chemical behaviour.

Until the early 1930's, nobody realised that heavy water existed. However, scientists, who were beginning to interest themselves in the finer points of atomic structure, found that atoms of hydrogen and oxygen did not always weigh what they should. They suspected that this might be due to a small proportion of double-weight hydrogen atoms mixed with the normal ones in substances such as water.

In December, 1930, chemists in the United States proved that the heavy form of hydrogen, containing an extra particle in the nucleus of its atom, did in fact exist.

By 1932, it had been shown that ordinary water contains a very small proportion of heavy water, in which the molecules consist of atoms of deuterium joined to oxygen. The identical chemical behaviour of the two forms of water made it virtually impossible to separate one from the other by chemical means, but it was found that electricity passed through water would split the ordinary "light" water into its constituent elements—hydrogen and oxygen—faster than it split the heavy water into deuterium and oxygen.

Thousands of gallons of water were split in this way, and by 1933 a tiny drop of pure deuterium oxide had been separated from the mass of lighter water with which it was mixed.

Interest in heavy water at that time was largely academic. It was used as a "tracer" in chemical reactions, doing duty for water yet always detectable by virtue of its extra weight. Using the heavy hydrogen from heavy water, for example, scientists have shown that fat can remain stored in the body tissues even when it is needed for providing energy.

PRODUCTION BOOSTED

This scientific interest in heavy water created a demand for small quantities of it and, in 1935, heavy water was produced for the first time on an industrial scale by Norsk Hydro at Rjuken, Norway. Water power provided the cheap electricity needed for splitting huge volumes of water.

During 1935, Norsk Hydro made about a pint of heavy water a day. By 1939, output had reached one gallon per day; this was the world's only source of heavy water at that time.

To-day, heavy water is being made in large quantities in America and elsewhere. It is used as a "moderator" for slowing down the neutrons liberated as uranium atoms disrupt and release their energy. Either graphite or heavy water can be used for this job. When graphite is used as moderator, 20 tons of uranium need about 650 tons of graphite. But when heavy water is used, a reactor will operate on 3 tons of uranium moderated with only 5 tons of heavy water. By using heavy water we can build smaller, simpler atom plants.

There is now a sustained demand for heavy water, and scientists are trying to find more economical ways of making it. There is only about a pint of heavy water in every 1000 gallons of ordinary water, and separating it electrically is a costly business. In 1954, heavy water was being sold at £70,000 a ton.

HIGH CONCENTRATIONS

The amount of heavy water varies in different parts of the world. Inland seas are richer in heavy water than the open seas; evaporation favours the lighter water, leaving a more concentrated solution of heavy water behind. Water from a Tibetan lake has been found by scientists to contain 10 per cent. more heavy water than there is in ordinary rain water. The Dead Sea is 20 per cent. richer, and it has been reported that water from glacial ice contains three times as much heavy water as there is in the sea.

Often, water of volcanic origin contains an extra ration of heavy water; so, by starting with this type of water as a source, it should be possible to avoid some concentration costs.

TRITIUM

The discovery of heavy water during the 1930's led to speculation regarding the possibility of finding water even heavier than deuterium oxide. A hydrogen atom with two extra neutrons packed into its atomic nucleus was regarded as a possibility, and a search was made for water made from this form of hydrogen which was given the name tritium.

In 1935, Dr. Hugh S. Taylor of Princeton University, believed that he had detected tritium in a sample of heavy water made in his laboratory. But its presence could not be proved with certainty, using the instruments then available. Since then, heavy water has been examined with the help of sensitive modern instruments and the existence of tritium oxide—"super" heavy water—has been proved. It is present in incredibly low concentration in ordinary water.

Unlike its lighter colleagues, tritium is radioactive. The extra particle in the tritium atom packs the nucleus of the atom too tight, and sub-atomic particles are constantly thrown off by the nucleus as it undergoes spontaneous disintegration. In twelve years half of the atoms in any sample of tritium will have decayed in this way.

In the moisture of the air, tritium oxide is present to the extent of 1 part in a million million million parts of ordinary water. The total quantity of tritium water in the atmosphere at any time would just about fill a teacup if it could be separated from the lighter forms of water.

SATELLITES IN THE SKY

SPUTNIK I IN ORBIT

On 4th October, 1957, the world witnessed one of the greatest scientific achievements of all time. On that day Russia successfully launched the world's first artificial satellite.

This tiny man-made moon, circling the earth once every 90 minutes, was undoubtedly the first real step towards the greatest adventure of all time, the exploration of space.

Of course, various earlier technical articles and rocket experiments had, in turn, all been hailed as the " first step ". But the Sputnik, as the Russians called their satellite, was quite different. For years, stories on artificial satellites and space travel had appeared at an ever-increasing rate. As the pattern of development slowly evolved, it became clear that the first step in the technological ladder to the planets would, indeed, be the construction of a man-made artificial satellite.

IMPORTANCE OF SPACE VEHICLE

At the Second International Congress of Astronautics held in London, in 1951, Dr. Shepherd, Technical Director of the British Interplanetary Society, summed the position up thus:

> " The uses to which a satellite vehicle might be put are sufficiently numerous to justify considerable expenditure on their development. Their value as scientific stations would be beyond compare." He continued: " But the real value of the orbital vehicle lies in its importance as an essential springboard in the supreme adventure of interplanetary flight. This without doubt must be regarded as the main reason for our interest in the device, all other purposes being of secondary importance."

News of the Russian satellite filled the radio broadcasts and newspaper headlines of the world. Nearly everybody was surprised at its weight, 184 lb., which was much greater than had generally been considered likely for the very first satellite. Also, with a peak altitude of 588 miles and a low altitude of 142 miles, the satellite's orbit—the path it traced out in space—was very nearly circular, indicating precise and accurate guidance.

Throughout the world public opinion was deeply impressed by the Russian achievement, but many wondered whether the successful launching was due more to luck than to good management.

NO FLUKE

The question was answered dramatically a month later when the Russians launched a second, much bigger, satellite, Sputnik 2. Comprising a huge cone-shaped body 7 feet long by 3 feet 6 inches diameter, this had an astounding weight of 1120 lb. Biggest surprise of all, however, was that in addition to instruments measuring cosmic rays, solar and X-ray radiation, the satellite contained a Husky-type dog named Laika.

Previously, small monkeys, mice and other living things had made brief journeys above the atmosphere in research rockets, but their short up-and-down trips were quite different from the historic journey upon which Laika had embarked.

Now the world was witnessing the first real flight through space. For day after day the satellite radioed back information telling how the dog was standing up to prolonged weightlessness, cosmic radiation and other features of interplanetary space.

Admiration for this second great scientific achievement was mixed with genuine sympathy for the dog. What,

A historic moon trip. On 14*th September,* 1959, *the moon was reached for the first time by Russia's Luna* 2 *moon probe. The* 240,000-*mile journey took* 34 *hours.*

Our first glimpse of the hidden side of the moon was given by Russia's Luna 3. *This took photographs* 40,000 *miles above the the moon's surface and transmitted them to Earth.*

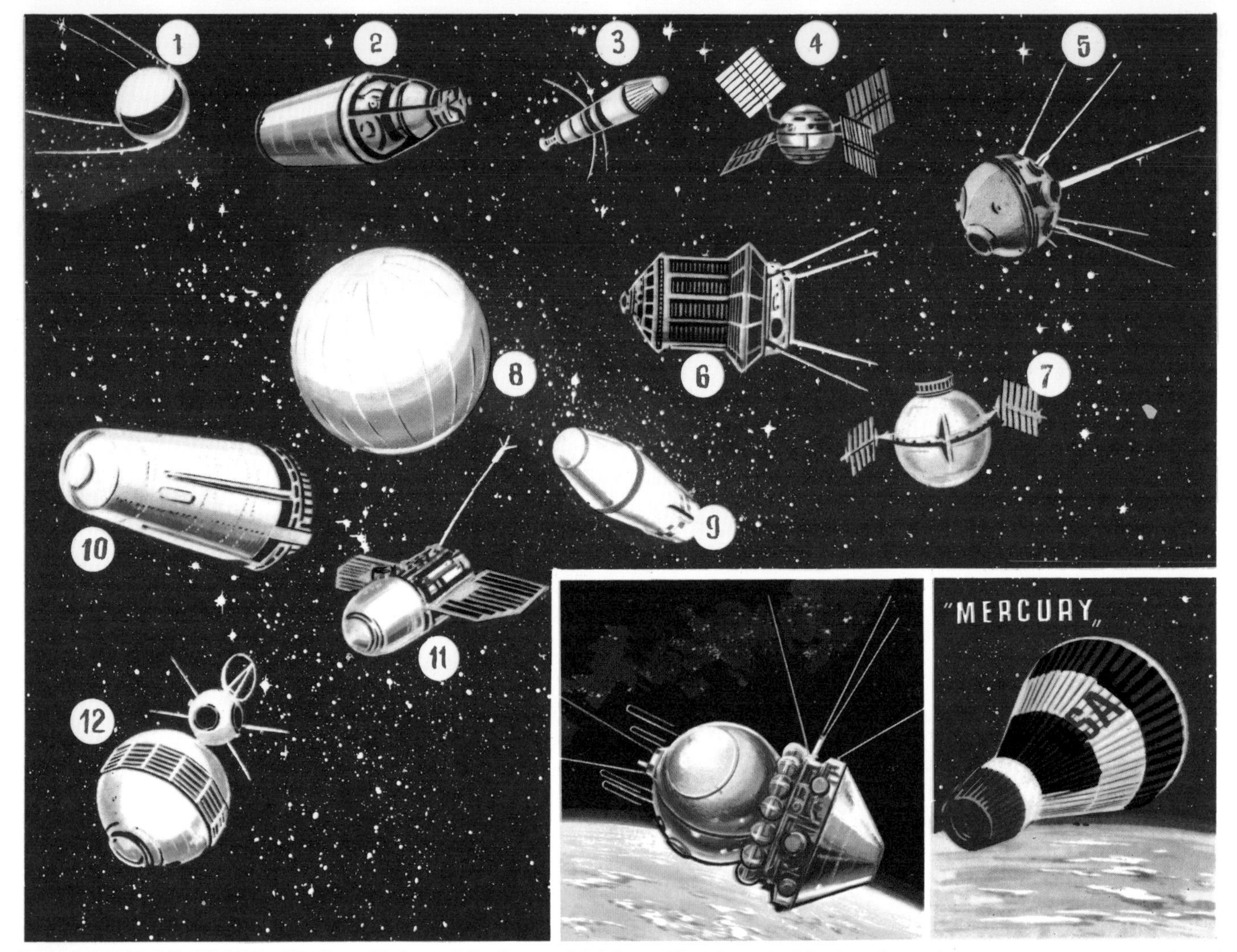

CONQUEST OF SPACE. (1) *Sputnik* 1, *world's first artificial satellite, launched by Russia on* 4*th October*, 1957. (2) *Sputnik* 2, *carried the dog Laika.* (3) *Explorer* 1, *America's first satellite, discovered great radiation belts surrounding the Earth.* (4) *Explorer* 6, *mapped Earth's magnetic field.* (5) *Lunik* 2, *hit moon.* (6) *Lunik* 3, *photographed moon.* (7) *Pioneer* 5, *radioed information from* 22 *million miles.* (8) *Echo* 1, *a* 100-*feet-diameter balloon.* (9) *Discoverer* 14, *brought back from space and caught in mid-air.* (10) *Spacecraft* 2, *landed safely with the dogs Belka and Strelka.* (11) *Venus probe.* (12) *Transit* 3B *and Lofti, two satellites launched together.* Inset: *Vostok, Yuri Gagarin's spaceship. Mercury, the American spaceship in which Glenn made his historic orbits on* 20*th February*, 1962.

people wondered, would happen when the supply of air and food in the little cabin gave out? The answer came in a Moscow broadcast that, after about a week, Laika would die. There is little doubt that the Russians would have liked to have brought Laika safely back, but at that early stage the means to do so had not been developed.

As has often happened in previous scientific developments, an animal was sacrificed in an experiment from which one day man himself would benefit.

On the day before Laika died, the radio of Sputnik 2 ceased transmitting, but the satellite continued on its now silent way for another five months. In the second week of April, 1958, it appeared briefly as a shining, fast-moving " shooting star ". Friction, as the satellite entered the atmosphere, made it first red, then white hot and finally melted it. Thus ended the first journey through space. In these days when much longer voyages are being undertaken by man, we must never forget the little dog Laika who helped to pave the way.

AMERICAN LAUNCHINGS

On the other side of the Atlantic, America was making determined efforts to launch her first satellite, named Vanguard. Unlike the Russians, who adapted a powerful military missile to launch their satellite, the Vanguard rocket was specially designed to launch the 20-inch U.S. satellite weighing about 20 lb. As such it was quite a small rocket in which every part had to perform perfectly if it were to be successful and, not altogether unexpectedly, the first attempt ended in a spectacular failure. To provide for just such a contingency separate plans had been made to launch a " reserve " satellite, using a modified military Redstone missile, and the first attempt with this, on 31st January, 1958, was eminently successful. Named Explorer I, the 30·8 lb. satellite was small by comparison with the Russian satellites, but it will go down in history as having made the first real discovery of the space age; by detecting the now well-known Van Allen radiation belts surrounding the Earth.

Six weeks later the first Vanguard satellite went up. This was a real baby, a tiny sphere only 6·4 in. in diameter and weighing 3¼ lb. However, in spite of its small size, optical observations of its orbit provided information from which the shape of the world was calculated more accurately

Russia's Venus 3 was the first satellite to land on another planet. Launched on 16th November, 1965, it landed on Venus on 1st March, 1966.

than ever before. Other observations enabled the position of several small islands in the Pacific to be accurately located for the first time.

MANY TYPES USED

Since those exciting early days of the Space Age, satellites have been launched in increasing numbers and in a variety of bewildering shapes, until to-day so many exist that few people can name them all.

Russia has launched several hundred satellites under the general name of Cosmos. This term undoubtedly covers a number of reconnaissance satellites and test launches of military rockets, as well as those devoted to research.

Few details of the purpose of individual Cosmos satellites are released, but the purpose of the series is to investigate: the upper layers of the atmosphere and outer space; the energy composition of the Earth's radiation belts, in order to further evaluate the radiation danger in prolonged space flights; radiation from the Sun and other celestial bodies; the effect of meteoric matter on spacecraft materials; and to evaluate different methods of spacecraft construction.

Cosmos satellites have helped to develop the Soviet Union's Meteor system of weather satellites. Cosmos 144 and 184 are moving in orbits with their planes almost at right angles to each other, to enable ground stations to receive information from certain areas twice daily. Cosmos 206 is in the same orbit as Cosmos 144, but 20 minutes behind it, giving forecasters an opportunity to check data received.

Cosmos 186 and 188, launched in October, 1967, were used for an automatic rendezvous and docking experiment. Cosmos 186, the " active " partner, carried out a number of complicated manoeuvres, automatically finding its "passive " partner, Cosmos 188, drawing closer and finally docking with it. Cosmos 212 and 213 were used for a similar experiment; an onboard television camera transmitted pictures of the docking manoeuvre.

Molniya 1, launched in April, 1965, was the first of a series of communications satellites. The craft was placed in a highly elliptical orbit, designed to provide the longest possible communications time between Moscow and Vladivostok. Other satellites in this series form part of the Orbiter network, providing telephone and colour television services for places in the far north of the Soviet Union, Siberia, the Far East and Central Asia.

EXPLORERS AND INTELSATS

America has also launched several hundred satellites. Like Russia's Cosmos, many of these are military reconnaissance craft, but by far the great majority have been research satellites, on which full details have been released. Many have passed beyond the experimental stage and now, fully developed, are contributing to or enhancing older forms of earth systems. Weather and communications satellites come into this category.

Ignoring an early unsuccessful Vanguard experiment, America launched her first weather satellite in April, 1960. Called Tiros, this sent back pictures from a height of 400 miles, and transformed our knowledge of the formation of clouds. Some pictures showed great spiral-shaped formations whose existence was previously unknown. Other pictures showed that some cloud formations thousands of miles apart were, in fact, joined by wisps of cloud and were thus part of the same weather.

From Tiros has developed the ESSA (Environmental Science Services Administration) series of operational meteorological satellites, information from which is being fed into the daily national weather forecasts of countries all over the world. Over 3,000 warnings, based on satellite photographs, have been issued to nations threatened by dangerous storms. In 1968 satellites tracking the hurricane Carla guided the evacuation of over 300,000 people, confining damage to property, not lives. The latest ESSA satellites embody an automatic picture transmission system which enables anyone using relatively simple and cheap equipment to obtain pictures of the weather for several hundred miles around the receiving station.

Another field in which satellites were quickly put to work is that of communications. An early American communications satellite, Courier 1B, launched in 1960, could receive and transmit 68,000 words a minute, or a total of nearly three and a half million words a day.

Still remembered by millions is Telstar, launched in July,

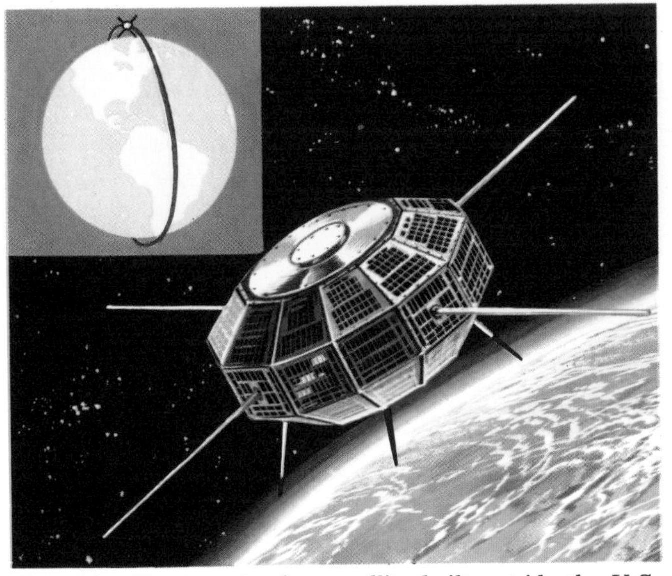

Canada's Alouette, the first satellite built outside the U.S. and U.S.S.R., was successfully launched by a Thor Agena booster on 29th September, 1962. It measured radiation from outer space.

Surveyor 3 *which successfully landed on the Moon on* 19*th April,* 1967, *was examined and partially dismantled by astronauts Conrad and Bean during the U.S. Apollo* 12 *mission to the Moon.*

Orbiting Geophysical Observatory. Among the most advanced satellites yet developed, these carry out up to 26 *different experiments. The experiments usually concern outer space radiation.*

1962, and used for a series of dramatic test television programmes between America and Europe, across the Atlantic.

From these early beginnings have developed the Comsat systems now in daily use. In contrast to the elliptical orbits of Russia's Molniyas, America's Comsats are in synchronous orbits. Placed in an orbit 22,300 miles above the surface, these take exactly one day to complete each orbit and thus keep pace with the rotation of the Earth and so appear to be stationary above the same spot on the map. Intelsat 2B, launched in January, 1967, was successfully manoeuvred into a synchronous orbit above the Pacific. Officially known as Pacific 1, this satellite is popularly known as Lani Bird. Intelsat 2C, launched in March, 1967, was placed in a geostationary orbit over the West Coast of Africa, and is known as Canary Bird.

To study space around the Earth and radiation from the Sun, America has launched a series of Orbiting Solar Observatory (OSO), Orbiting Geophysical Observatory (OGO) and Explorer satellites. OSO craft are used to study the Sun, OGO craft perform up to 26 experiments simultaneously. The Explorer series covers a wide variety of satellites, varying from simple balloons, used to measure upper air density, to complex craft investigating energy and particle phenomena in space.

LUNAS AND MARINERS

The most exciting satellites of all are those which have been sent to explore the Moon, Venus and Mars.

After several unsuccessful attempts Russia was the first to "soft-land" a spacecraft on the Moon and send back clear close-up pictures of the surface. This was the historic Luna 9, which landed in February, 1966. This was followed soon afterwards by America's more refined Surveyor, the TV camera of which sent back over 11,000 photographs of the surface in the Ocean of Storms. These pioneering craft were followed by other Lunas and Surveyors, which scratched and prodded the surface, providing data that contributed to the successful manned landings in 1969.

Both America and Russia have sent probes to the planet Venus. The surface of Venus is perpetually hidden by a thick layer of cloud, and many people held hopes that this covered a world of forests and swamps, like a primeval Earth. This dream was shattered by the faint signals sent back by the probes. Russia's Venus 4 descended through the atmosphere, transmitting details of the pressure and temperature on the way. The signals showed that the surface is probably a vast desolate desert, searingly hot and swept by violent winds of hundreds of miles an hour. The white clouds, so pleasant to look at from the Earth, are in fact choking carbon dioxide gas. Extending up for over 50 miles they probably make the surface quite dark, and exert a pressure ten to twenty times greater than that of Earth. The Venus craft confirmed the earlier readings taken during an American Mariner " Flyby " in December, 1962; later Venus and Mariner probes have indicated that the planet is even more inhospitable.

The news from Venus increased the hopes that Mars, in many respects a twin of the Earth, with great areas changing colour with the seasons, as they do here, would indeed prove to be a second Earth. Unfortunately, dramatic pictures sent back by American Mariners showed a dead world more like the Moon, a world covered with craters and with an atmosphere so tenuous as to be virtually non-existent. The discovery of the Martian craters was one of the biggest achievements—and disappointments—of the space age.

THE GRAND TOUR

Both America and Russia are investigating the possibility of sending deep space probes to the giant planets that orbit the Sun hundreds of millions of miles beyond Mars. Current booster rockets are not powerful enough to launch a craft to these planets direct. However, nature has arranged for Jupiter, Saturn, Uranus and Neptune to be located in rather special positions relative to each other towards the end of the nineteen seventies. This arrangement, which will not occur again for nearly 200 years, will enable a single, unmanned spacecraft to make successive, unpowered swings past each planet. The craft will use the gravitational field of each planet to create a sling-shot effect, thereby giving it enough momentum to hurl it on to another planetary rendezvous. The "Grand Tour" is likely to take 10 years.

STAR CLUSTERS, NEBULAE AND GALAXIES

If you watch the night sky very carefully you will come across several small misty patches which, at first sight, look like tiny whitish clouds. Many of these, when examined through a telescope, are found to be *star-clusters*, or groups of hundreds and even thousands of stars. Other patches, however, cannot be seen as stars even through very large telescopes, and for the very good reason that they are not star-clusters at all but *nebulæ*, or clouds of glowing gas. This gas, consisting largely of hydrogen, has no light on its own account, but is made to shine because of the extremely hot stars embedded in it.

Of all the star-clusters the Pleiades are perhaps the best known. To the naked eye this cluster looks like a little knot of 6 or 7 stars in the back of Taurus, the Bull. A telescope reveals that there are many more stars in the group, and astronomers now consider that it contains over 250 stars. They have found that these stars are all travelling together in the same direction through space—that they form a moving family of suns. This particular cluster looks small because of its great distance of about 450 light-years: we therefore see the Pleiades not as they are at this moment in time, but as they were 450 years ago. The Pleiades are also a good example of an *open star-cluster*, in that the stars appear fairly well-spaced and are not particularly numerous. In some other clusters, called *globular star-clusters*, many thousands of stars form a tightly-knit ball, appearing to swarm like bees about a hidden centre. One of these, known as Messier 13, lies in the constellation of Hercules, and, to the naked eye on a very clear night, looks like a faint hazy star. Yet the distance across it is about 160 light-years. It looks so faint and tiny because it is so far away, about 31,000 light-years.

Our solar system is part of the Milky Way galaxy. The stars which form the Milky Way are so numerous and far away that the galaxy forms a great band of light across the night sky. Seen through a telescope, the Milky Way resolves itself into a myriad tiny points of light, as in this illustration.

MASS OF GLOWING GASES

Of the bright nebulæ the Great Nebula in Orion in Orion's sword is the most conspicuous. Photographs of it taken with large telescopes show that it consists of both gas and dust. The gas is glowing, or rather, *fluorescing* (like the gas in a fluorescent light-tube) and the dust is interwoven with it, cutting off the light of the regions beyond and appearing dark in contrast with the bright gas. This great complex of gas and dust is about 900 light-years away, and it is really just a small part of a much greater cloud of gas and dust which occupies practically the whole of the constellation of Orion.

MILKY WAY

The largest of all the misty patches in the night sky is, of course, the Milky Way. That it consists mainly of stars was first discovered in 1610, when Galileo Galilei turned the newly-invented telescope to the heavens. Nearly two hundred years later the astronomer William Herschel surveyed the sky with large reflecting-type telescopes and concluded that all the stars formed a flattish, disc-like system. We now know that Herschel's conclusion is largely true—the sun, at least, is just one star among many millions which make up our own star city or *the Galaxy*. The Milky Way is an effect produced in part by our position *inside* the Galaxy. It is, in brief, an effect of perspective. When we look in its direction we see not only more stars but also stars out to greater distances than in any other direction.

CARTWHEEL SHAPE

To picture the Galaxy as seen from the *outside*, imagine a swarm of stars which has for its outline the shape of a cartwheel. The swarm, however, must consist of about 100 thousand million stars and the diameter or distance across the " wheel " must be about 100 thousand light-years. In the middle, corresponding to the hub of the wheel, is the *core* or *nucleus*, an immense ball of millions of stars. In the space between the " hub " and the " rim " lie millions more, the greatest number being found in and around the central plane of the " wheel ". Our sun is about half-way out from the centre to the rim, being about 25,000 light-years from the centre. All the stars in the Galaxy move about this centre, but so vast are the distances involved that the sun and neighbouring stars take about 200 million years for one complete journey. The sun is therefore a *moving* star, and in that respect is like all the other stars.

The sun can be imagined as a tiny speck placed on one of the " spokes " of the wheel. As seen from this point, and on looking out in all directions in the plane of the spokes, we see an immense number of stars in the form of a band. This band is, of course, the Milky Way. Why then don't we see a great blaze of starlight when we look towards the central nucleus, for here the stars are most tightly packed? The reason lies in the existence of vast clouds of interstellar dust which lie between us and the nucleus, cutting off its

In addition to the Milky Way, the Universe contains many other great galaxies, all formed of millions of stars. Among these there are spiral nebulae, such as the Andromeda nebula, shown here

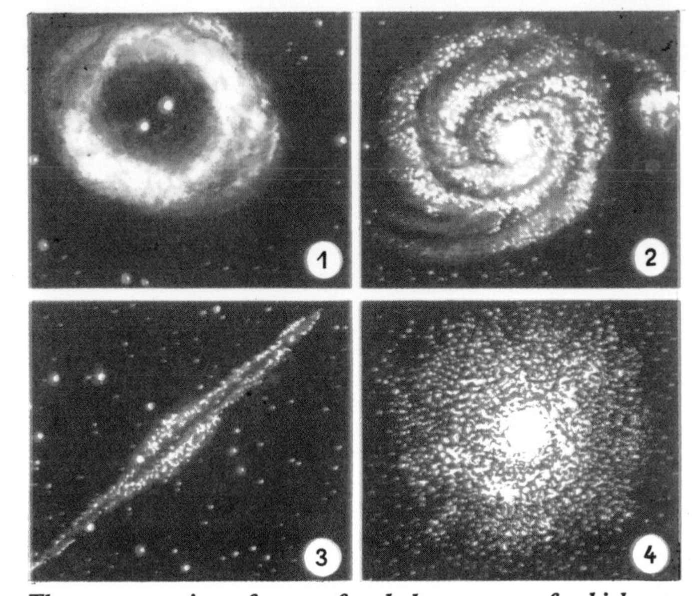

There are various forms of nebulae, some of which are illustrated here. 1. *Ring nebula, a common form of nebula;* 2. *spiral nebula;* 3. *spiral nebula seen from the edge:* 4. *globular cluster, consisting of innumerable stars.*

light and preventing our seeing the starry regions beyond. The Galaxy contains not just stars and clusters of stars but great quantities of dust and gas which fill the immense regions between the stars. Most of this material lies in the direction of the Milky Way, limiting our view and causing the Milky Way to have a broken-up or patchy appearance.

Around the great disc of stars forming the Galaxy is a haze of extremely bright stars and numerous globular star clusters which by themselves form an immense " ball " or spherical system and make the Galaxy an even larger affair than just a star-filled " cartwheel ".

OUR GALAXY ONE OF MANY

Until fairly recently it was thought that all the stars were contained in the Galaxy—that the Galaxy was the Universe. We now know that it is just one of many thousands of millions of separate galaxies, each one of which may contain thousands of millions of stars. One of these other galaxies, a comparatively near one, is thought to be somewhat larger but similar to our own. This is Messier 31, the Great Spiral Galaxy in Andromeda. To the naked eye it looks no more than a misty patch and was once considered to be a bright nebula inside the Galaxy. It looks small despite its immense size because it is nearly 2 million light-years away. And this is one of the nearest galaxies!

The stars in the night sky are, therefore, the stars of our own Galaxy, and all the brighter ones lie in the sun's neighbourhood. Beyond them all lies the stupendous realm of the galaxies, most of them so distant that they appear as faint fuzzy specks on a photographic plate. They form a background to the stars and are found in great numbers in quite small areas of the sky—except in the region of the Milky Way. Clouds of obscuring dust hide them from our view, but there is every reason to believe that they are as numerous there as elsewhere in the sky.

WHERE DOES IT END?

A large number of the other galaxies, like Messier 31, show a spiral or catherine-wheel structure. This is because the stars and dust in them are arranged in curved arms, giving the whole galaxy the appearance of rotation. Recent studies in radio astronomy show that our own Galaxy has a spiral form and that the sun and its neighbours lie in one of the spiral arms. Many galaxies, on the other hand, show no spiral form and appear to be fairly free from interstellar dust.

The best astronomers can do is to estimate the distances of the galaxies, and their estimates get more uncertain as these distances increase. So far the largest telescope in the world, the 200-inch Hale telescope of the Mount Wilson and Palomar Observatories in California, U.S.A., has reached out to an object which appears to be a galaxy at an estimated distance of 6 thousand million light-years. What lies beyond we cannot say—perhaps the galaxies go on and on in infinite space; perhaps they thin out and eventually end altogether.

1. *Section of the cupola of the Mount Palomar observatory.* 2. *The two mirrors (main and secondary) of the reflector telescope can be seen. The main mirror has a diameter of more than 5 yards.*

PETROLEUM

" Underground Fire " was the name the ancients gave to petroleum, which they used not only as a fuel but also for medicinal purposes. Now an essential part of our everyday life, this product was pioneered in modern times by Edward Drake, who sank his first oil well in Pennsylvania, U.S.A., just over a hundred years ago.

Thousands of millions of years ago, the semi-molten mass of our planet wandered through space. It was a silent, lifeless world. Then slowly, the germ of life took root. Tiny, animated cells were born in the warm seas. With the passing of the ages, life took on myriad forms, and the waters teemed with microbes whose lives were as brief as sparks that jump out of the fire.

HOW OIL FIELDS WERE FORMED

The bodies of these minute creatures, together with a mass of decaying vegetation and animal remains were drawn together by marine currents. Huge rubbish dumps were created at different points of the Earth's surface. Slowly, the process of decay and decomposition reduced this once-living, organic matter to the mixture of hydrocarbons which form the petroleum deposits which are so important to us to-day.

As age succeeded age, these deposits were crusted over by drifting silt and sand to form lakes of oil deep beneath the Earth's surface. In some cases they remained more or less exposed, and excited man's curiosity through the centuries. Flames would leap unexpectedly from the Earth, and the red glow of " hell fires " burning low on the horizon must have roused great fear.

BITUMEN IN THE ANCIENT WORLD

Deposits of oil were left in this way in Persia, Iran and around the shores of the Caspian Sea. Bitumen, or pitch, which is rich in inflammable substances like naphtha, petroleum and asphalt, is common to these regions. References to it are made in the Scriptures and old historical works. We are told, for instance, that God ordered Noah to seal the Ark with bitumen and so make it watertight. The Ancient Egyptians mixed it with mortar for the construction of dams. Nebuchadnezzar approved its use for street paving in Babylon.

" Underground fire " was also known to the early Chinese whose extraction technique was so advanced that its principles are still applied to-day. In Roman times bitumen was considered as a valuable material for medical use as well as for building purposes. It was also sought after by Roman ladies who blackened their eye-lashes with it.

Oil, as we know, floats on water and, in the sixteenth-century, the Spaniards observed that the American Indians soaked it up by throwing cloths on to oil-bearing lakes and then squeezing out the liquid into earthen pots.

But many years were still to pass before men realised that petroleum represented a valuable source of motive power. Then the great industrial struggle to control the world's oil-fields started in earnest.

THE THIRST FOR " BLACK GOLD "

During the Middle Ages little interest was shown in the discoveries of earlier times, and the properties of bitumen remained almost unknown. But with the opening up of new lands men began to suspect that petroleum might be valuable. Its possible applications were studied, but these were at first confined to its use as a basis for making lamp-oil.

The ancient Chinese extracted petroleum from wells by sucking it out with immense hand-operated bellows.

About half-way through the nineteenth-century, people began to appreciate that a vast amount of wealth lay hidden in the untapped oil-fields of the world. While looking for gold in Pennsylvania, U.S.A., a prospector named Edward Drake heard rumours that there was oil in the region. He decided to investigate, only to find that it was slow and difficult work penetrating to the deep rock level where the petroleum was believed to be.

EDWARD DRAKE STRIKES A GUSHER

Drake hit on the idea of driving an iron tube through the sand to the rock strata. A shaft with a primitive drill attached was passed down the tube. Work continued steadily until one suffocatingly hot Saturday afternoon in August, 1859, when a black column of liquid petroleum burst up the tube and shot skywards. News of this oil strike spread rapidly and the thirst for petrol was soon to take second place only to the hunger for gold which was sweeping the United States at that time.

Wooden head-frames sprang up in their hundreds. Prospectors descended upon the oil-bearing lands and the farmers and Indian tribesmen who owned them acquired wealth beyond their wildest dreams. Meanwhile, the pioneer work of Edward Drake was forgotten and he died a comparatively poor man in 1880. By that time the oil boom had begun.

Hard on the heels of the prospectors came the financiers

Much has been done to perfect methods of drilling for oil, but occasionally an oil-well still bursts into flames.

whose loans were necessary to put the new industry on its feet. Geologists with special equipment were engaged to examine the local rock and soil formations and to find those underground pockets of sand and clay in which the petroleum was to be found. When technicians were called in to devise large-scale production methods, almost the first thing they did was to replace the old wooden head-frames with stout metal structures called derricks.

Mules and steam engines which, in the early days, had been used to turn the drills were abandoned. The new derricks served as a framework to support high-power percussion drills which thrust their steel heads far into the bowels of the earth. By 1929, some British engineers working at Ploesti in Romania reached a depth of nearly 4,000 feet. Little did those who had actually risked their lives in achieving this feat imagine that within ten years they would see the construction of two-hundred-foot derricks capable of boring a hole three miles deep.

The oil man's work became increasingly urgent, for progress was bringing rapidly-growing demands on petrol production.

In some parts of the world, oil-wells are now drilled in the sea bed by means of floating derricks.

Aeroplanes, ships, and motor cars consume enormous quantities of fuel, and oil deposits do not last for ever. New deposits must be found and tapped and, as the search goes on, bore holes are being driven deeper and deeper into the Earth. Boring is now being carried out on the sea floor. Along the Louisiana and California coasts, for instance, floating derricks may be seen rising high above the water-level. Prospectors have even turned their attention to bituminous formations sometimes found in volcanic areas and have devised methods of extracting oil from oil-bearing rock and shale.

PIPES ACROSS THE DESERT

Meanwhile the oil pipelines, which once extended a mere mile or two from the well-head, have lengthened until to-day they stretch for great distances across barren deserts, spilling their load into tankers which carry thousands of tons of oil at a time to the refineries.

One such pipeline crosses the Great Syrian Desert from Mosul in Iraq to the Mediterranean. Another carries its oil to Sidon by a pipe that reaches back to the oil-fields of Dahran in Sa'udi Arabia. Before the last war, Dahran was a remote halt on the caravan route from Mecca to the Oman. To-day, it teems with American cars and lorries, and for miles the desert landscape is patterned by a rash of steel rigs and derricks.

With Kuwait, not far away from Dahran, churning out something like 80 million tons of oil a year, one would think that there was fuel enough to keep the wheels of industry and transport turning for many centuries to come. That may be so, but just in case the petrol reserves of the world run low, scientists have found a way of making synthetic petrol from other raw materials such as coal or natural gas.

Oil and natural gas-fields have recently been located and put to use in the Sahara, near Hassi Massaoud. This brings hope that the desert may indeed flower.

The most conspicuous features of an oil-field are the rigs and derricks which support the drilling apparatus. Beneath these towers are the feeder tubes which carry the crude product from each well-head to a main pipeline which conveys the oil to a refinery or to its port of shipment. On reaching the refinery the crude petroleum is subjected to what is known as a " cracking " process.

HOW PETROLEUM IS PROCESSED

Crude petroleum is a mixture of many hydrocarbons, and the cracking process is designed to separate the petroleum into its constituents, modifying them in such a way as to provide the products that are needed.

The basis of petroleum cracking is distillation. The crude petroleum is heated, the vapours being drawn off at different temperatures and condensed to form such products as petrol, diesel oil, naphtha, kerosene, lubricating oil and greases.

OUR DEPENDENCE ON PETROL

Throughout the world, fifteen million barrels of petroleum or crude oil are treated daily in this way. The pioneer phase of Edward Drake seems almost as remote as that more distant one of our ancestors who first used bitumen for fuel and light. So dependent on petrol and its allied fuels have we become, that the modern world would collapse without it. Petroleum provides the motive power that drives our aeroplanes, ships and cars, and has become our essential raw material in every type of industry and transport.

For thousands of years, primitive man roamed the Earth as a nomad. He plucked berries and fruits that grew wild around him, and hunted animals for their flesh and skins. When food became scarce, he continued his wanderings and looked for new surroundings in which he could continue to live on nature's bounty.

But as time passed, man found that he could do much to encourage nature to provide him with the food that was the main requirement of his simple life. Instead of eating all the fruit and seeds he had collected, he set aside a certain amount and scattered them deliberately on the soil in order to provide new crops. He herded sheep and goats into enclosures, so that they were near to hand for slaughtering when required.

BECOMING LESS NOMADIC

Gradually, man found himself adopting a more settled way of life. People collected together into villages, tilling the soil around them and growing their food instead of wandering incessantly from place to place. This was a first step towards the development of human civilisation as we know it to-day. And the establishment of community life brought with it a need for new forms of knowledge that would enable people to live an ordered life in harmony with one another. One of these new skills that man had to acquire was the ability to measure and count. He had to learn simple mathematics.

So long as he was a nomad, man had little need for anything more than the most primitive knowledge of arithmetic. His dealings with other human beings would be restricted to simple barter, and he could indicate quantities by holding up the appropriate number of fingers, or by using stones as counters. In this way, for example, he could suggest that four stone axes was a satisfactory bargain in exchange for one animal skin.

MAN MUST MEASURE

Once he adopted his community life, however, man found that he must measure and count in all manner of ways. He had to be able to assess and record the passage of time; he had to be able to count the animals in his flocks and herds, and keep records of his possessions; he had to be able to make the simple measurements that would enable him to erect buildings, and to mark out areas of land. So he began to think in terms of units of length and area, weight and volume.

For thousands of years, these units were of the simplest nature. A man would exchange an armful of corn for an earthenware pot; he would measure land and buildings using the length of part of his body as the unit. These methods of measurement served so long as the needs of man were primitive, but they became inadequate as he became more civilised. He had to learn to standardise his units of measurement, and to assess them by counting and recording.

STANDARDISATION

The realisation of this need for standardisation and assessment developed at an early stage in man's efforts to find ways of marking the passage of time. As long as man lived his nomadic life, time meant little or nothing to him. He experienced the rhythms of night and day, and of the seasons. He would, no doubt, look forward to the coming of spring, knowing by experience that it followed winter. But his sense of time would be of the very simplest. He had no need of anything more refined.

Once he settled in to his community life, he became more conscious of the meaning and importance of time. The agricultural life of a village revolved around seasonal activities; the day-to-day organisation of life depended on being able to specify a certain time of day. So man began to order his life by measuring time, and he looked for units of measurement with which he could do this accurately and effectively. He found these units in the natural rhythms of nature, the most obvious one being the cycle of night and day.

DAY, MONTH AND YEAR

So the day became a basic unit of time. And in order to assess the passage of time in terms of days, it was necessary to record the number of days separating specified events. This was done in the simplest possible way, by making notches in a stick or in the trunk of a tree.

It was a simple step from this recording of time in terms of days to the use of longer units of time. Man would observe, for example, that the periodic changes of the moon took place at intervals of thirty days. During this time, the moon completes its cycle from full moon back to full moon, passing through a stage where its area apparently grows smaller every night until it disappears altogether, after which it reappears and grows in size until it reaches full moon again.

It can be imagined that each cycle of the moon would be recorded for example, by a larger notch, or one of different shape. So another unit of time would become established—a month, consisting of 30 days. Then it was noticed that twelve of these months, amounting to 360 days, almost coincided with the periodic cycle of seasonal change which marks out the year.

This simple calendar, based on the movements of the Earth and other heavenly bodies, was adequate for the needs of man during the early stages of civilisation. But as human life became more sophisticated, it became necessary to measure time with greater accuracy. The 360-day year, for example, resulted in a 5-day error in going from one year to the next, which made for difficulties in an agricultural community that planned its activities on a seasonal basis.

ASTRONOMY AND NUMBERS

The Ancient Egyptians tried to put things right by inventing five feast days that added five days to the 360-day year. This brought the year much nearer to the actual time of about 365 days during which the Earth makes its seasonal cycle of change. But even so, this was not entirely accurate, and it was not until the ancient philosophers were able to base their calendar on the apparent movement of the sun and stars that they could record the passage of time with accuracy.

The Pyramids and other ancient buildings were constructed with the help of simple instruments, including the set square and the plumb line. The Egyptians made right angles by forming a triangle with sides in the proportion 3, 4 *and* 5.

The measurement of time in this way, and the study of astronomy, were inevitably associated with the development of mathematics. The astronomers and philosophers were able to record their measurements only by making marks which would remind them of the number of hours or days or other units of time which had passed. They made their record by carving notches on wood or clay or stone, or by marking on papyrus.

The early development of mathematics was closely allied with simple numerology in this way. About 3,000 B.C., philosophers of the two great Middle-Eastern civilisations of Egypt and Mesopotamia were studying the periodic movements of the Earth and the moon, the sun and the stars. They made numerical records by using simple strokes for small numbers, and different symbols as a form of shorthand to indicate higher numbers.

These skills were inevitably in the hands of the leisured classes of these early civilisations. The priests and wise men used their knowledge of astronomy and mathematics to affirm their special status in society. They were the experts who controlled the calendar; they could predict how the sun and the moon and the stars would behave; moreover, their knowledge of mathematics enabled them to control and influence the lives of other people; they were the measurers and assessors, the arbitrators and accountants.

BABYLON

The earliest of all written accounts in existence to-day have come to us from the ancient civilisation which flourished in the rich lands of the Tigris and Euphrates valleys, thousands of years B.C. These ancient records deal with the accounts of temple estates.

The city of Babylon became a flourishing centre of trade in this early civilisation, reaching a state of immense prosperity by the time of the dynasty of Hammurabi, around 1950 B.C. This establishment of Babylon as a centre of commerce was accompanied by improved skills in the handling of numbers.

Tablets discovered in the ruins of ancient Babylon have shown that there was a decimal system in existence at that time, as well as a sexagesimal system (i.e. in which the base number was 6).

The Babylonians had an elementary understanding of ratios and proportions, and of arithmetical and geometrical series. They knew a little simple geometry; for example, Babylonian Tablets disclose that they knew the circumference of a circle to be about six times the length of the radius.

BARTER INEFFICIENT

The growth of Babylon as a centre of trade resulted in refinements in the measurement of quantities. Simple barter arrangements are adequate in a village community where neighbour negotiates with neighbour. But when goods are carried far afield to be exchanged for the produce of other lands, barter is not necessarily a satisfactory technique. So the merchants began carrying small quantities of precious materials which could be exchanged for goods; metals such as silver or gold were carried in measured quantities, with the weight stamped on them. These were the earliest forms of money.

At the same time, the negotiations involved in trading could be carried out only by having some way of assessing the quantity of goods involved. Merchants could only reach agreement in their bargaining if they had some unit quantity which each side recognised. So, in ancient Mesopotamia, standardised weights and measures were devised.

EGYPT

The civilisation of ancient Egypt flourished along the banks of the River Nile. Every year, the river would flood the valley, leaving behind a layer of fertile soil on which the following season's crops would grow.

This annual flooding of Egyptian farmland maintained the fertility of the valley soil. But it presented the authorities with a considerable problem in the assessment of taxes according to the area of land under cultivation. Every year, the boundaries of the farms were washed away, and the land had to be measured and marked out.

This recurring need for an assessment of land areas did much to stimulate the practical application of simple geometry in Egypt. This branch of mathematics made considerable progress. The priests and philosophers employed their leisure time in the study of mathematics, and made good use of it in astronomy, building, surveying and navigation.

The huge pyramids and temples of Egypt were built with an accuracy that seems incredible in view of the simple tools and techniques available at that time. The builders of the pyramids were able to level the ground and mark it off with great precision; they knew how to trim the huge blocks of stone so that every corner was absolutely square. And they fitted the blocks into place so accurately that the finished pyramid was symmetrical and positioned exactly as planned. All this demanded a knowledge of elementary geometry, including the ability to measure and to mark out right-angles with absolute precision.

The units of length devised by Egyptian builders were based on the lengths of parts of a man's body. The cubit, for example, represented the distance between the elbow and the tips of the fingers. Using standardised units of length, they were able to measure the areas of squares and oblongs by multiplying length and breadth. And they knew that the area of a triangle could be found by multiplying the height by the base and dividing the result by two.

EARLIEST MATHEMATICAL DOCUMENT

The Egyptians used set squares in building, to enable them to measure right angles. They had discovered that three pieces of wood or string of lengths in the proportion 3, 4 and 5 would make a right-angled triangle when joined end to end. They used this knowledge in making their set squares.

In measuring up the land for taxation purposes, the Egyptians used the technique of dividing the area in triangles and assessing the area of each triangle.

The earliest of all mathematical documents is an Egyptian papyrus dating from about the year 1700 B.C. This is the Ahmes papyrus, which appears to have been based on an even older document. It describes how to find the area of plane figures; the area of a circle, for example, is given as about $3\frac{1}{3}$ times the square of the radius. The Ahmes papyrus outlines mathematical problems which require the use of simple equations for their solution.

GREECE

During the sixth-century B.C., the growth of trade between Greece and Egypt brought the Greeks into contact with ancient Egyptian culture. The Greeks were a wealthy people, with ample time for intellectual pursuits. They enjoyed philosophical argument and discussion, and the science of mathematics appealed to the Greek philosophers.

The theoretical development of mathematics, and particularly geometry, made impressive headway in ancient Greece. Thales of Miletus studied the properties of triangles and circles, and he and his pupils Anaximander and Anaximenes put this knowledge to practical use. Pythagoras, who was also a pupil of Thales, developed many of these ideas, and was familiar with the basic principles of proportions.

APPLIED KNOWLEDGE

Although the Greeks were so interested in mathematics as an intellectual pursuit, they applied their knowledge to problems in building and navigation. They knew how to measure the height of a column, for example, by using their knowledge of triangles. They measured the length of the shadow thrown by a vertical stick of known height, and also the shadow thrown by the column at the same time. As the sun's rays forming these shadows were known to be parallel, the triangle formed by stick, shadow and sun's rays was the same shape as that formed by the column, its shadow and the sun's rays. In equiangular triangles, the ratio of the lengths of corresponding sides is the same, so that the height of the column has the same ratio to the length of its shadow as the stick has to its shadow. The only unknown factor, the height of the column, can thus be worked out.

PYTHAGORAS

Using their knowledge of triangles, the Greeks measured distances by indirect methods. Two observers would sight a distant hill from different points, for example, measuring the angles formed between the line of sight and the line joining each other. When these two angles were known, and the distance apart of the two observers was measured, all the information necessary to complete a triangle had been obtained. The distance of the hill could then be calculated.

Pythagoras was greatly interested in proportions, and the relationships between arithmetic and geometry. His name is always associated, for example, with the discovery of the relation between the hypotenuse and the sides of a right-angled triangle.

The abacus has been used for thousands of years for carrying out simple calculations. In its most elementary form, it is a series of parallel grooves containing pebbles. The value of a pebble increases by a certain factor from one groove to the next.

In 331 B.C., Alexander the Great conquered Egypt, and the city of Alexandria became the centre of intellectual thought. Mathematics flourished in Alexandria, and the city produced some of the greatest Greek mathematicians of the time.

FINDING EARTH'S CIRCUMFERENCE

In 240 B.C., Eratosthenes, a librarian in Alexandria, used his knowledge of geometry to measure the circumference of the Earth. He found that the sun at noon on midsummer day could be seen as a reflection in a deep well at Syene in Egypt. This place is almost on the Tropic of Cancer, and the sun at noon on this day is directly overhead. Its rays passed down the well and were directed towards the centre of the Earth.

Eratosthenes measured the angle of the shadow cast by a column in Alexandria at the same time as it was directly over Syene. He found that the sun's rays were striking at an angle of $7\frac{1}{5}$ degrees from the vertical (which is one-fiftieth of the 360 degree circle). He knew also that the distance between Syene and Alexandria was 480 miles, so that the circumference of the Earth must be 50×480 miles $= 24{,}000$ miles.

TO-DAY'S TEXT-BOOKS

Euclid, perhaps the most famous Greek mathematician of all, collected together and compiled all the information that was known about geometry. His books became accepted as text-books on the subject, and served as such until the twentieth-century.

Archimedes of Syracuse (287–212 B.C.) studied a great variety of geometrical figures, and laid the foundations of hydrostatics and mechanics. He applied his reasoning to practical problems, producing devices such as the Archimedes' screw. This is a spiral screw which revolves inside a pipe; it lifts water from the bottom of the pipe to the top and was used for drainage and irrigation.

Apollonius of Perga (260–200 B.C.) wrote many books on geometry, bringing together knowledge of the subject of conic sections into a work consisting of eight books.

The Romans took over Egypt in 30 B.C., and for a time the progress of mathematics was slowed. The Romans were a practical people, and they did not have the intellectual interest in mathematics that had brought such progress under the Greeks.

ABACUS

The development of trade between nations of the old world brought with it the need for methods of carrying out simple calculations. Merchants had to be able to add and subtract, to divide and multiply. And in order to do this they made use of a device called the abacus.

In its simplest form, the abacus was a series of parallel grooves marked in the sand. Pebbles were placed in the grooves to act as counters, the value of the pebbles increasing by a certain factor, e.g. ten, from one groove to the next. The numbers of pebbles in the grooves therefore indicated a certain number just as our written numbers do to-day.

In various forms, the abacus was used throughout the civilised world. The Roman abacus consisted of a bronze plate cut with two sets of grooves, one above the other. The upper grooves held one pebble each, which was the equivalent of five of the pebbles in the corresponding lower groove, each of which held four. The upper and lower grooves together formed a column which would indicate any number from one to nine.

Simple geometrical calculations have been used for measuring distances since the earliest times. The principle of triangulation, illustrated here, is still used in surveying to-day.

The abacus remained in widespread use in Europe until comparatively recent times, and is still used in China and Japan to-day. It was of immense practical value to the philosophers and merchants of the ancient civilisations. The development of mathematical calculation was held up, however, by the use of letter symbols to indicate numbers. The Romans, for example, used simple strokes to represent the numbers one to four, with letter symbols to indicate five, ten, fifty, hundred and thousand. These symbols are still to be seen on modern clock faces.

INDIA'S DECIMAL SYSTEM

In India, the valley of the River Indus supported an ancient civilisation in which mathematics developed much as it did in Egypt and Mesopotamia. By the beginning of the Christian era, Hindu philosophers had begun to use a special system of their own for indicating numbers. They did not use a symbol to represent a particular number in the way the Romans did; instead, they gave a symbol to each of the numbers one to nine, and also to zero, to indicate the number of pebbles in any column of an abacus. That is to say, the symbol was the same for a given number of pebbles, no matter which column of the abacus it represented.

This apparently simple and obvious system had a revolutionary effect on the art of calculation, and mathematics advanced rapidly in India. During the twelfth-century, the Hindu system of numerals found its way into Europe and stimulated rapid development of mathematics. The new techniques were adopted and applied to astronomy and other sciences throughout the Western world.

During the fifteenth-century European mathematicians built up their philosophies on foundations that had been laid by the Moslems, who had combined the teachings of the Greek and Hindu mathematicians. Astronomy made rapid headway, with scientists like Copernicus (*c.* 1520) and Kepler (*c.* 1610) presenting new and revolutionary theories to the world.

The period of the Renaissance was a time of exciting progress in many branches of science, with mathematics playing a vital role just as it does to-day.

MAGNETISM

Magnetism is one of the most mysterious of all scientific phenomena. Although we live in a world controlled by gravitational forces, we do not easily accept the idea of one piece of matter exerting powerful magnetic forces on another piece of matter some distance away. Magnetism requires no material link between the bodies it affects. There are no sparks to be seen when magnetism exerts its influence, nor are our senses affected in any obvious way. Yet the force of magnetism will operate through solids and liquids, through gases and through the voids of space itself.

Though we have little understanding of the basic nature of magnetism, we have made practical use of it in many ways. Magnetism makes possible our dynamos and electric motors, transformers and electromagnets. Without magnetism we should have no radio or television, and indeed the electrical and electronic industries we know to-day would not exist.

A FREAK MINERAL

According to an ancient legend, magnetism was first discovered by a shepherd named Magnete. Looking for a lost sheep among the hills of Asia Minor, Magnete noticed that his boots and stick, both tipped with iron, clung to the mass of blackish stone over which he was walking. This was loadstone, an iron ore we now know as magnetite.

The Greeks and Romans knew about the strange properties of loadstone, but they regarded it as a freak mineral and did not succeed in putting it to any practical use. They did not know that a piece of loadstone, suspended freely, would take up a north and south position with respect to the Earth.

In ancient times all sorts of magical and supernatural virtues were attributed to loadstone. Sailors venturing into unknown seas often feared that their ships might be drawn towards islands with loadstone in their rocks. Superstitious people hung pieces of the mineral round their necks in the belief that loadstone helped to maintain friendship and family affection. The easy acceptance of such ideas checked man's curiosity and slowed down the progress of research on the phenomenon of magnetism.

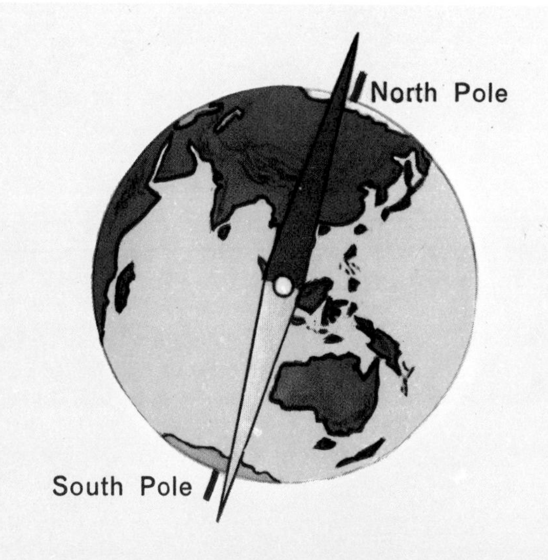

The magnetic needle points to the North Magnetic Pole, forming with the Geographical North Pole an angle called the angle of magnetic declination.

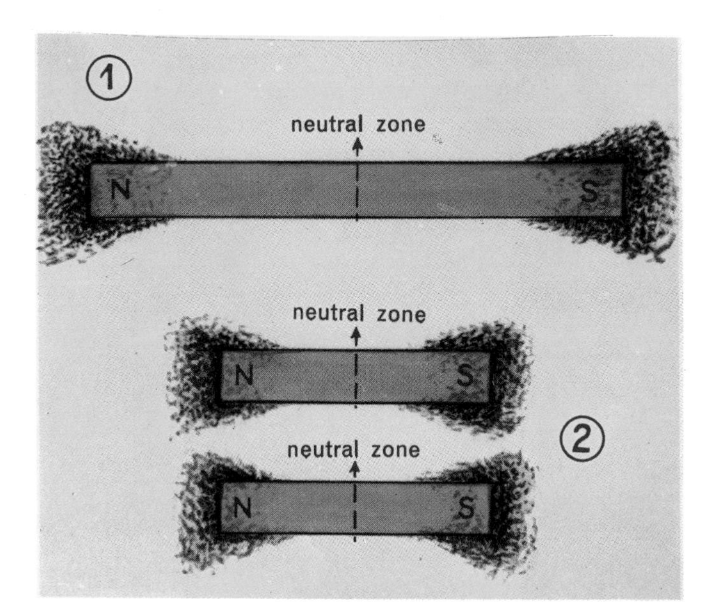

Centres of magnetism are found at the extremities of the bar, that is, at the poles of the magnet. This can be shown by dipping the bar into iron filings. If, however, a magnet is broken in two, it forms two magnets

THE ORIGIN OF THE MAGNETIC NEEDLE

Loadstone is, in fact, nothing more than magnetic oxide of iron, which is composed of countless particles each behaving as a tiny magnet on its own account, with the property of attracting iron, steel, nickel and cobalt. Yet many centuries were to pass before man hit upon the bright idea of using loadstone to make a compass needle.

The magnetic needle was introduced into Europe by the Crusaders, who learned about it from the Arabs. Long before them, the Chinese had sailed as far as India with its aid, and it was probably the Indians who revealed its secret to Arab traders. Early travellers described how magnetic needles were kept in jars half-filled with water resting on the surface with the help of little floats.

Tradition relates that the first real box compass was the invention of an Italian, Flavio Gioia, who lived at Amalfi near Naples. In 1302, he found a way of balancing one of these magnetic needles on a pointed support set in a box or *bossolo*, for which reason the compass is still called *la bussola* in Italy.

Some of the earliest models of the compass bear the lily of the House of Anjou to which the kingdom of Naples was then subject. A subsequent English invention added the windrose, or scale of thirty-two sections, from which compass readings are taken.

Without the compass Christopher Colombus might never have made his great voyage to America in 1492, nor, most probably, would Vasco da Gama have been able to round the Cape of Good Hope six years later. The voyages and discoveries of those days and the resulting growth of commerce could not have come so rapidly had it not been for the part played by magnetism in operating the compass needle.

In due course, the nautical compass was perfected by mounting it on a form of universal joint. This was the work of Gerolamo Cardano, an Italian mathematician and inventor, who lived during the last century. It enabled the compass needle to remain level even during violent storms at sea.

MAGNETIC AND GEOGRAPHICAL POLES

Why it is that a tiny bar of magnetised iron should behave in this extraordinary way? Why should one tip point towards the north and the other towards the south when the needle is suspended so that it is free to find its own direction? The properties of a magnetic needle are difficult to explain and in some ways remain a mystery to this day. We now recognise that the Earth itself behaves as a huge magnet which attracts the compass needle in such a way that it takes up position with respect to the North and South Poles.

On looking at the windrose of a compass we notice a tiny arrow a little to the left of north. This indicates what is known as the declination of the magnetic needle from the true geographic north and south line. So, in order to find the exact direction of north and south, all that is necessary is to move the compass round until the magnetic needle lies directly above the little arrow. This shows that the magnetic pole does not correspond to the geographic north pole but is located at a short distance from it. Thus in Europe a compass needle always points very slightly towards the west.

If we were to draw a line, from wherever we happen to be standing on Earth, which passed through the geographic north pole in one direction and the geographic south pole in the other direction, this line would be called a *terrestrial meridian.*

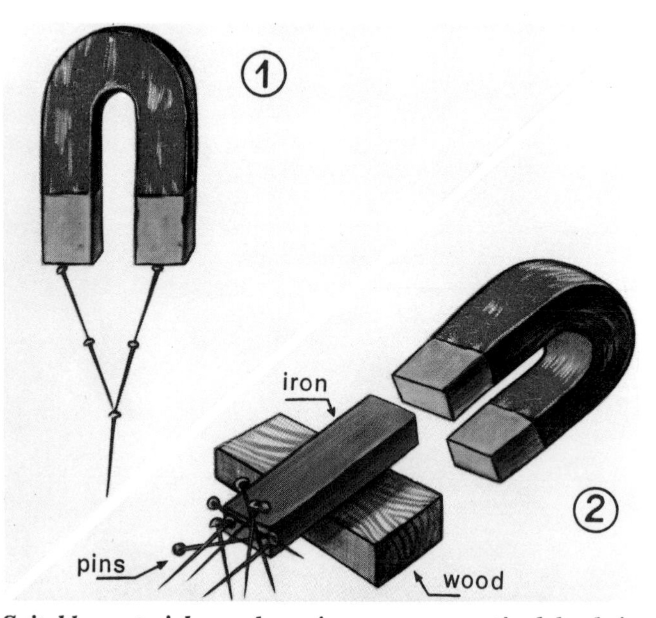

Suitable materials, such as iron, are magnetised by being placed for a time in a coil through which current is passed. Here are two examples of magnetising by induction. A non-magnetised iron or steel bar placed within the field of a magnet is magnetised by induction.

The Earth has a magnetic field in which magnetic variations occur from time to time. The direction of the forces acting in a magnetic field may be seen by letting iron filings drop on to a thin piece of cardboard under which the poles of a magnet are fixed.

We could do the same thing using the Earth's magnetic poles instead of the geographic poles, and in this case the line would be a *magnetic meridian.* The angle formed between the magnetic meridian and the terrestrial meridian is the *angle of declination.* This angle is, in other words, the angle between the direction of the geographic pole and the direction of the magnetic pole at any point on the Earth's surface; it represents the deviation of a compass from true north.

The angle of declination varies from place to place on the Earth's surface. We can join up places of equal declination by imaginary lines, and these are known as *isogones.*

For various reasons, the angle of declination is not always constant at any place on the Earth's surface. The magnetic storms of the aurora borealis or northern lights, atmospheric disturbances produced by the sun and the moon, volcanic eruptions and even thunderbolts may make the sensitive needle deviate.

WHERE ARE THE MAGNETIC POLES?

In 1576, Robert Norman, a London compass-maker, tried setting the needle in an upright position so that it moved vertically between two supporting rods. On pointing it towards the magnetic north he noted that the needle at once swung downwards. The angle that the needle thus forms with a horizontal plane is called the *angle of inclination,* and here again it varies from place to place. Imaginary lines running through all the points of the Earth where the angle of inclination is equal are called *isoclinal lines* (isoclines).

For many centuries it was popularly believed that somewhere near the North Pole there must be a huge mountain of magnetite or loadstone. The actual site of the north magnetic pole was discovered more than a hundred years ago when it was found that the magnetic pole lies at Latitude 70° beneath the Island of Melville to the north of the American Continent. Here the needle takes on an angle of inclination which points directly towards the centre of the Earth. The south magnetic pole is in Victoria Land.

THE THERMIONIC VALVE

In 1883, Thomas Alva Edison came close to making an invention more important than anything we remember him for to-day. He built a simple radio valve ten years or more before it was really needed.

Edison was experimenting with an incandescent lamp he had devised for turning electricity into light. The lamp consisted of a fine filament of carbon sealed inside a thin glass bulb from which all air had been removed. When a current of electricity was passed through the filament the carbon became white-hot and emitted light.

The principle behind this electric bulb is simple enough. The fine carbon filament offers so much resistance to the passage of electricity that its temperature rises; the electrons

These two pendulums are attracted to each other by the action of the electric charges. One has been touched by a positively *charged glass rod, and the other by a* negatively *charged stick of sealing-wax. Opposite charges attract each other.*

struggling to make their way through the fine filament are jostling with each other, so that much of their energy is released as heat.

FILAMENT SEALED OFF

If a filament is heated in this way in the open air the carbon burns away instantaneously, just as it does when a stick burns in a fire. Carbon unites with oxygen, forming carbon dioxide gas. By sealing his filament inside a glass bulb from which air had been removed Edison prevented the filament burning away. There was no oxygen with which it could combine.

Carbon filament lamps, although they had many defects, worked well enough to herald the arrival of the electric light era. Edison found, for example, that the inside of the glass bulb became darkened with use. Carbon from the filament was apparently evaporating and forming a thin layer on the walls of the bulb.

Edison studied this effect, and carried out many experiments

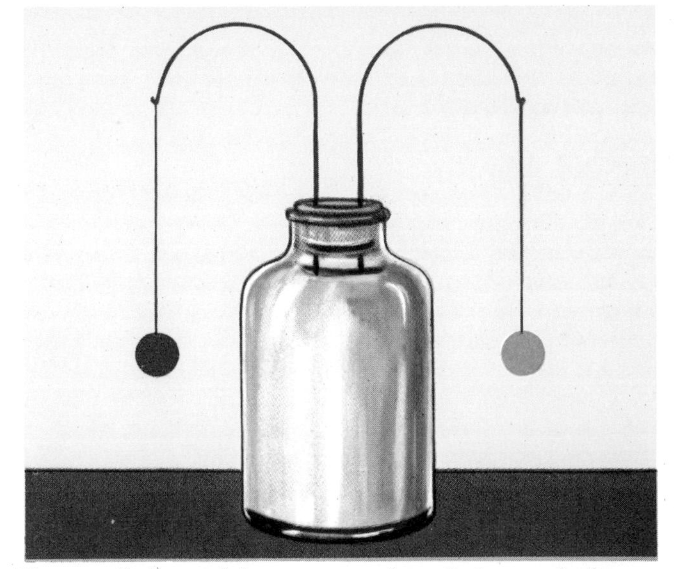

The two little pendulums are used to find out whether an object is electrically neutral, or if it is positively or negatively charged. They can be used to demonstrate the movements of attraction and repulsion.

with special types of bulb. He fitted a metal plate inside a bulb, opposite to the filament. The plate was connected to a wire sealed into the glass wall of the bulb, so that the plate could be charged with electricity from outside.

EDISON'S EXPERIMENT

Edison found that if he gave the plate a charge of positive electricity—that is, persuaded the metal to part with some of its free electrons—a current of electricity would flow continuously into the plate inside the tube. Electrons were apparently "leaking away" from the heated filament of the lamp and flowing across the empty space that separated the filament and plate.

When Edison gave the plate a charge of negative electricity —that is, forced extra electrons into it—there was no flow of current inside the bulb.

In 1884, Edison described his discoveries and exhibited the

Two similarly charged pendulums repel each other. These have both been touched with the positively charged glass or with the negatively charged sealing-wax.

special lamp-bulbs with their extra plates fitted opposite the filament. He showed how current would pass from the filament to the plate only when the latter was carrying a charge of positive electricity.

FLEMING VALVE

This exhibit was seen by a visiting British physicist, Ambrose Fleming who had studied under James Clerk Maxwell in the Cavendish Laboratories, in Cambridge. Fleming returned to England, and subsequently played a leading part in the development of electricity and radio. By the turn of the century he had become one of Britain's most eminent scientists, and for a time was Professor of Electrical Engineering at University College, London. And in 1904, he made use of the Edison effect in the invention for which he will always be remembered: the radio valve.

In 1904, Sir Ambrose Fleming realised that the Edison effect could be used for detecting the oscillating currents in a radio receiver aerial. On 16th November, Fleming took out a patent covering a detecting device which was based on the Edison effect. He called it a " valve ". We now know it as a thermionic valve.

Fleming's valve was a device which allowed electrons to flow in one direction through it, but not in the other direction. In this respect it behaved exactly as its name implied.

Fleming used his valve as a " detector " of radio waves by allowing the feeble oscillations of electrons in the receiver aerial to affect the electron-pressure of the valve plate. When electrons rushed one way in the aerial they crowded into the plate and stopped any electrons flowing between filament and plate; when the oscillating electrons moved the other way they emptied the plate of some of its free electrons, and so encouraged electrons to flow through the valve.

An oscillating current stimulated by electromagnetic waves in an aerial was therefore converted into a succession of pulses of current flowing in one direction only, through the valve. These pulses, following each other in many thousands every second, were in effect almost a continuous current.

DE FOREST AUDION

Fleming's valve brought an entirely new technique to the detection of oscillating currents in radio receivers. It stimulated research in many countries, and was soon followed by new discoveries. In 1906—two years after Fleming applied for his original patent—a modified type of valve was invented by Dr. Lee de Forest in the United States. This valve, which de Forest called the audion, was much more sensitive than Fleming's, and could be used for amplifying the feeble aerial oscillations into currents of enormous strength.

De Forest's valve was, like Fleming's, an essentially simple device. It consisted of the Fleming valve with a grid of metal wire fitted between the filament and the plate. This grid acted as an electrical sluice-gate that controlled the flow of electrons streaming from the filament to the plate.

In de Forest's audion a positively-charged plate attracted electrons from the heated filament. If the grid was electrically neutral it had virtually no effect on the electron stream, which flowed through the holes between the wires forming the grid. If electrons were forced into the grid from outside they repelled the electrons moving from the filament, and so cut down the strength of the stream. If, on the other hand, electrons were drawn from the grid the positive charge left on the grid strengthened the force of attraction drawing the electrons from the filament; the stream was therefore swelled.

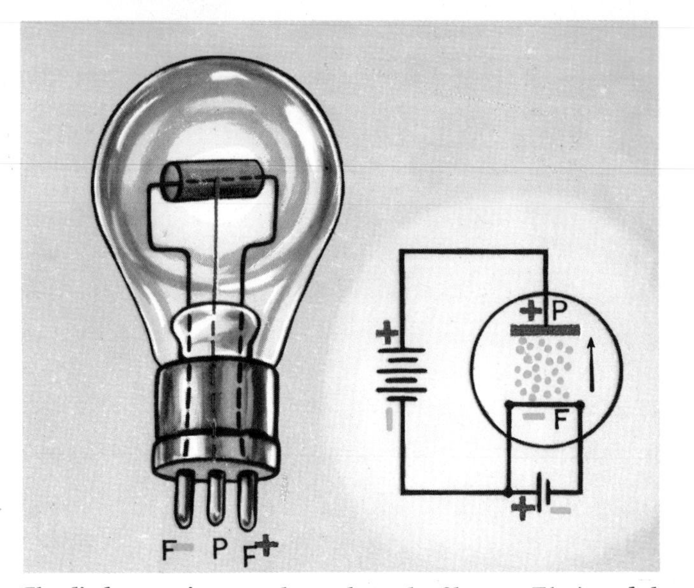

The diode contains two electrodes: the filament F(–) and the metal plate P (+). The movement of the electrons is shown on the right. They can move only in one direction; from the filament to the plate.

DIODE AND TRIODE

As Fleming's valve had only two electrodes, it was called a diode. De Forest's valve, with its grid, had three electrodes and was a triode.

These valves were eventually to become the basis of our modern radio and electronics industry, providing a means of controlling and amplifying the feeble oscillations stimulated by radio waves.

In the last few years, they have been replaced in many of their applications by transistors. These are tiny pieces of germanium or silicon which have unusual electrical properties, and can function in the same way as valves.

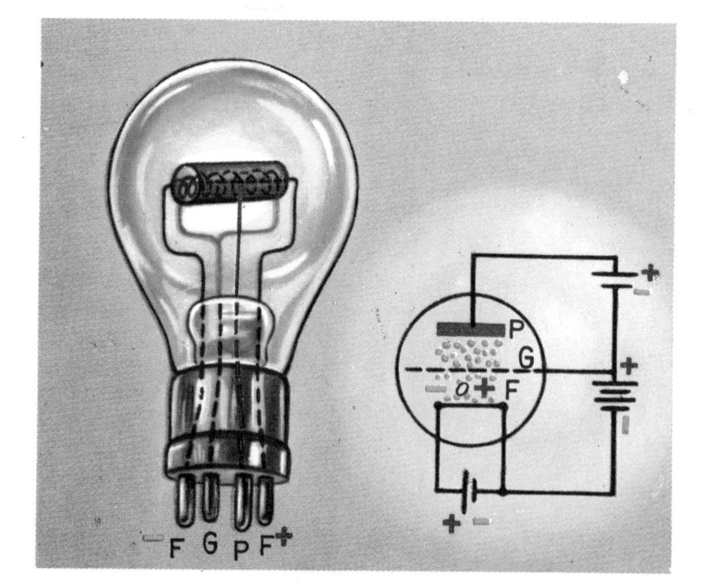

The triode has three elements: the filament F (–), the plate P (+) and the grid G (±). The circuit is shown on the right. The grid regulates the flow of electrons to the plate. It can be negatively or positively charged.

ROBERT KOCH

Robert Koch was born at Klausthal, in Hanover, on 11th December, 1843. At the age of twenty-nine, he was still quite obscure and was earning his living in a routine way as a medical officer at Wollstein in East Prussia. He had originally wanted to be an explorer, so his present way of life must have seemed, even to him, a little tame. He consoled himself for the humdrum nature of his work, however, by spending his spare time gazing down a microscope.

One day he looked at some drops of blood taken from a sheep which had died of anthrax, and he set out on the research which was to make him famous all over the world. Anthrax is a disease which kills sheep and cows. In Koch's time, anthrax was responsible for many animal deaths and for the financial ruin of many farmers. There was no cure for it, and nobody understood what caused it or how it passed from one animal to another. Koch gazed down the microscope at the drop of blood containing many tiny, rod-like objects. Davaine, a French scientist, had noticed them some time before in the blood of animals which had died from anthrax, and he had wondered whether they might be the cause of the disease; but nobody had proved that they were.

EXPERIMENTS WITH MICE

Koch, a young man working alone, right out of touch with the world of science, decided that he would find out for certain. First of all, he invented a way of giving the disease to mice. They would, he thought, be more convenient animals to have in his house than sheep or cows. He had no syringe, but he prepared some sharp slivers of wood, dipped them into blood taken from diseased animals and then inserted them under the skin of his mice. The mice developed anthrax, and in their blood he found the same rod-like bodies which he had seen before in the blood taken from a dead sheep. They were the bacilli of anthrax. Koch, however, still had to prove that these rods were alive, and that they caused the disease.

Koch was a methodical man, who left nothing to chance, often repeating the same experiments time and time again.

It seemed obvious that they *must* be alive, for the bodies of the dead mice were packed with the little rods. It was impossible that they could all have come from one blood-soaked splinter of wood. They must, therefore, have grown and multiplied. This was common sense. Koch, being a very careful and exact scientist, wanted to prove this supposition by an experiment which could not be questioned. So he put a speck of material taken from a mouse which had died from anthrax into some liquid which he had obtained from the eye of an ox. He thought that the rods would be most likely to grow in some natural fluid—fluid taken from a living body. He put the infected drop between two pieces of glass and then placed it in a primitive sort of incubator which he had put together himself. He found that he was right. The little rods multiplied just as he had expected they would, and very soon the drop of liquid was swarming with them.

SOLE SOURCE OF INFECTION

The next thing he wanted to find out was whether the rods alone were the cause of the disease, and to be quite sure of this, he thought he must grow them for several generations right away from any living animal. He would keep transplanting them into a fresh drop of liquid from an ox's eye every day for eight days, and then he would dip a splinter of wood into the newest drop. The infected splinter would then be put under the skin of a mouse which had had no contact with anthrax at all. If the mouse then developed anthrax, it could only be the little rods which had caused it. Again he was proved right. The mouse developed anthrax, and Koch became the first man ever to have proved scientifically that a microbe causes a disease.

DORMANT DISEASE

There was one particularly mysterious thing about anthrax. There were certain fields and regions which seemed to be under a curse, for they could be left unused for a long time, and yet as soon as sheep or cows were put on them, they developed anthrax. Koch knew how easily the delicate rods had died in his laboratory, and he could not understand how it was that they could apparently survive whole winters out of doors. One day he stumbled on the answer. He noticed that some of the rods in one of his infected drops of liquid had become speckled with round dots, and he realised that in certain conditions the rods changed into spores. These spores could lie about out of doors in much the same way as seeds, and be unaffected by cold or heat, until at last they found themselves once more in surroundings suitable for growth. This happened when they found their way into the blood stream of a sheep or cow; then they grew into rods again.

In 1876—four years after he had begun his work on anthrax—Koch was ready to talk of what he had achieved. The shy, unknown young man gave a three-day demonstration to an distinguished scientific audience at Breslau and at once became famous throughout the world. He was given honours and appointments. He was made a Professor at the School of Medicine in Berlin, and later held a Chair in Berlin University. Now he was given every facility for research, instead of having to make do with home-made apparatus, and he set to work to find the germ which causes tuberculosis. This was very difficult, for it is far smaller and more difficult to see than the bacillus of anthrax, but he identified it in the end and proved that it causes the disease. He then made an attempt to discover a cure and called it tuberculin—but this was not a success.

WORK ON CHOLERA

In 1883 an epidemic of cholera broke out in Egypt, and Koch set out with a colleague and an assortment of experimental animals to see if he could find the cause of this disease, too. From France came a rival team—Emile Roux and Thuillier, who were both pupils and followers of Pasteur. There was great rivalry and jealousy between Koch and Pasteur; they argued endlessly on paper and quarrelled in public. There was also patriotic rivalry between France and Germany; they had been at war only a few years before. For a little while the cholera epidemic raged, but neither of the two groups made much progress, and quite soon the cases fell off and there was no more cholera. Thuillier, however, died. He was one of the first of the scientific martyrs, and Koch, forgetting their rivalry, laid a wreath on his coffin.

Koch's work in Egypt had not been quite fruitless, however, for he had seen through his microscope some curious comma-shaped objects which might perhaps be the germ of cholera. Undismayed by Thuillier's death, he set out for India, where cholera could nearly always be found, and managed to demonstrate that the comma-shaped bacilli, which he had seen in Egypt, were indeed the cause of the disease. He was also able to show that the bacillus is harmless until it gets into the digestive tract. This knowledge made it easier to control the disease and prevent it from spreading.

Koch studied other diseases—among them rinderpest and bubonic plague—but it is for his work on anthrax, tuberculosis, and cholera that he will always be remembered. In 1905, he was awarded a Nobel Prize, and he died five years later, in May, 1910, from heart disease.

LIVING LAMPS

In the depths of the sea, weird fishes swim in a world of perpetual night. The daylight is gone, absorbed by the water above. Yet the darkness is lit by strange lights that twinkle and glow, like stars in the sky. These lights come from luminous glands which nature provides for her creatures that live in the stygian gloom.

These living lamps are more efficient than anything that man has yet devised. The light they give is cold; no energy is wasted in the form of heat. And scientists are now studying nature's light-producing process in the hope of being able to put it to practical use.

Some deep-sea fishes pattern their bodies with rows of light patches that shine like the portholes of a ship. These luminous designs are used as recognition signals in the lightless sea.

Many undersea lamps can be switched off and on by their owners. Yet others will light spontaneously, reacting to external stimuli. The "phosphorescent" wake of a ship is lit by the luminous glands of billions of one-celled animals floating on the surface.

Many land animals carry lights too. Fireflies and glow-worms sprinkle the darkness with flashes of light from the transparent windows of their bodies.

We tend to think of living light as a spine-chilling phenomenon; it is the light of goblins and ghosts, and dark, mysterious places. Yet there is nothing extraordinary about the emission of light by living things. Light is a form of energy similar to heat. It is a natural accompaniment to any chemical change, whether it is the burning of coal in a fire or the oxidation of a food-substance in the body.

LUCIFERIN AND LUCIFERASE

The generation of cold, living light is controlled by two substances, which have been extracted from the glands of light-producing animals. One of these, luciferin, is a chemical that burns in oxygen supplied by the animal's respiratory system; light is liberated when this chemical change takes place. The other substance, luciferase, is a supervisory chemical, an enzyme, that controls the process in the living body. Luciferin will "burn" only when luciferase is present.

Mixed with luciferase in a test tube, and provided with a supply of oxygen, luciferin emits light as it does in the animal's gland.

We do not yet know what luciferin or luciferase are, but chemicals have been made synthetically which, like luciferin, emit "cold light" when they are oxidised.

LENS STRUCTURE

Light-glands in the animal body are often quite complicated gadgets. They are backed with a lining of crystal-filled cells, which act as a reflector throwing the light forward. Covering the gland is a window of transparent tissue; often, it is lens-shaped in order to give a better light concentration. Some fishes have their glands equipped with diaphragms and shutters, which control the amount of light emitted. Others have glands that are hinged and swivel inwards, to shut off the light.

Some creatures, instead of using light-glands of their own, are prepared to let bacteria act for them. Fishes carry special sacs near their eyes, in which colonies of luminous bacteria live. In return for a supply of food and oxygen, the bacteria provide their host with light.

Other animals, including shrimps and fleas, are invaded by less welcome luminous bacteria, which bring them a ghostly death.

Experiments have shown that there is nothing unusual about the light emitted from luminous glands. It is ordinary visible light corresponding to definite bands in the spectrum. Some creatures prefer a blue light; others emit yellow, red or green. There are neither ultra-violet nor infra-red rays in the living light.

Though human beings have not, as yet, been able to use the "cold light" process devised by nature, the illumination is not entirely wasted. In India, the weaver bird captures fireflies and uses them to light the inside of its nest.

EARTH'S SATELLITE

As the moon travels round the Earth once a month it goes through a cycle of phases, appearing to grow, or " wax ", from a thin crescent to a full moon, and then to " wane " to a thin crescent again. Long ago it was thought that the moon was actually reborn once every month when it appeared near the sun and that it really did increase and decrease in size. We now know that it is one and the same moon all the time and in reality a dead world, without any light of its own. It just happens that as the moon travels round the Earth we see different amounts of its sunlit side.

At the time of full moon we see all of its sunlit side, for then the sun is on one side of the Earth and the moon is on the other. But sometimes the full moon, instead of being bright when high in the sky, looks dull and copper-coloured. Sometimes it even disappears altogether in an otherwise clear sky. At these times the moon is passing through the Earth's shadow and only a small amount of sunlight, if any, can reach its surface. We then say that the moon is " totally eclipsed ".

LENGTH OF AN ECLIPSE

A total eclipse of the moon occurs only when the sun, Earth and moon, in that order, are directly in line. If at that time you could stand on the near side of the moon the sun would be hidden behind the Earth. The Earth's shadow, therefore, reaches quite easily out to the moon, 238,000 miles away, and actually has a total length of about 860,000 miles. At the moon's distance the width of the shadow is about two and two-thirds times the diameter of the moon, and the moon travels through it in about two hours. Hence for about one-half of that time the moon appears partially eclipsed and we can still see part of its bright face. But during the other half, when all of it is in shadow, it appears totally eclipsed.

The copper-coloured moon sometimes seen during total eclipse means that some sunlight has entered into the shadow area. This is sunlight bent or refracted by the Earth's atmosphere and made dull red by its long passage through that atmosphere. While the red rays get through fairly easily the others, especially the blue rays, are scattered away in all directions. For the same reason the sun often appears orange or red when it is very close to the horizon.

So far we have referred only to the darkest part of the Earth's shadow—the part called the *umbra*. There is, however, a large region of semi-shadow or *penumbra*. When in the penumbra the moon appears slightly dimmed all over and has no part " missing ". Hence a penumbral eclipse is not a very exciting event: only a careful observer would notice that it was taking place.

People often ask why the moon is not eclipsed every time it reaches the full phase. This would happen only if the moon's path or orbit round the Earth was in the same plane as the Earth's orbit round the sun. Instead, the moon's orbit is inclined at an angle of 5° 9′ to the Earth's orbit. It is also a moving orbit, in the sense that it turns round once in nearly nineteen years. For these reasons there can never be more than three eclipses of the moon in a year, while in some years none occur.

GRAVITY AND THE TIDES

Just as the Earth's pull of gravity extends to the moon, so the moon's gravity extends to the Earth. This " pull " of the moon has an important effect on our seas and oceans. The best way of understanding this is to imagine the Earth to be completely surrounded by a layer of water. The moon would distort the shape of this layer or shell of water, stretching it out in one direction and causing it to be compressed in a direction at right angles to this. Meanwhile, the Earth rotates inside this egg-shaped shell of water, and any one place on its surface would have above it different depths of water at different times. In this way the tides occur, for although the Earth has a patchwork of seas and oceans, the effect is the same—the waters are heaped up both in the direction towards the moon and also in that directly opposite.

At the times of new moon, with the moon on the side of the sun and in line with it, the moon's gravity aids that of the sun to produce a maximum tide-raising force. The tides are then most marked in their range from low water to high water and are called " Spring Tides ". But when the moon appears as a half-moon and lies in a direction at right-angles to that of the sun, the range in the tides is least, and we have the " Neap Tides ". You may have noticed, however, that high tide does not always occur when the moon is high in the sky. This is because the Earth, in rotating, drags forward the heaped-up waters, causing the high tide to occur slightly ahead of the moon. In addition, geographical features like the shape of a coastline or the slope of the sea-bed affect the times of the tides, but the main directing force is always that of the moon.

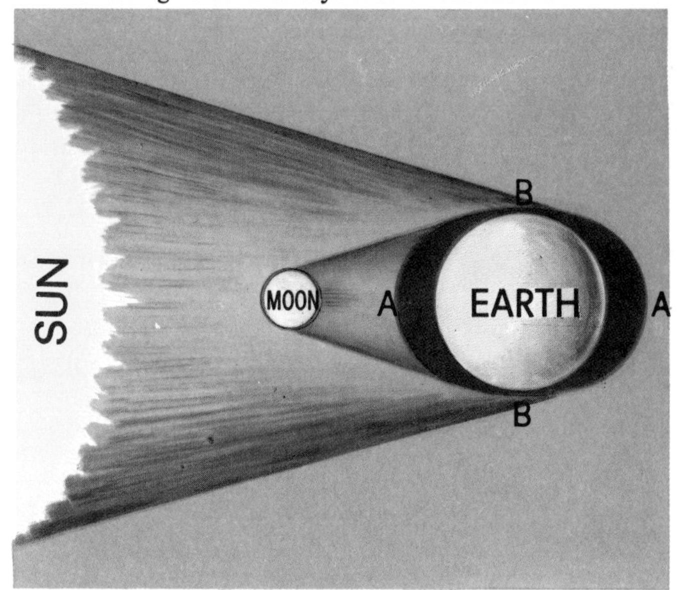

The moon's attraction raises the water level at points A and A, at the same time lowering the level at points B and B.

THE HUNGRY LOCUST

Since Biblical times, the inhabitants of many of the warm countries of the world have been plagued by locusts. Great swarms of these insects still darken the sky, as they did thousands of years ago. Over Africa and the Middle East, over Arabia and India, in Russia and China, South America and Australia, the locust brings a threat of famine and devastation. Where the locusts settle, every blade of grass, every ear of corn, and the leaves of every tree will be eaten. When the swarm departs, the area is devastated and nothing remains but the trash from a crop that was green and flourishing an hour or two before.

RECENT COUNTER-MEASURES

Until comparatively recent times, the locust had things very much its own way. During the 1920's and 1930's, however, scientists began to tackle the locust in earnest for the first time, using all the modern techniques of insect-control and destruction that were available. This scientific counter-attack was forced upon the world by a plague of locusts which began in 1926, and which developed and spread over Africa and other countries during the next fifteen years.

In 1926, small groups of young locusts, or "hoppers," were seen in the region of the flood plains of the Middle Niger. As they grew to maturity, the adult locusts flew off in swarms and, during the next few years, they bred and ranged farther and farther afield. By 1932, billions of the insects had invaded Eastern and Central Africa, bringing ruin and devastation to thousands of acres of staple crops.

In 1933, swarms of these African Migratory Locusts flew high and fast towards the Atlantic and disappeared out to sea. Many flew south into the Union of South Africa, but died in the dry season before they were able to breed. As a result, most of East and Central Africa became clear of the locust during the next two years.

But in West Africa, the plague continued unabated until 1939, when the locusts entered Eritrea, Abyssinia, the Sudan and Somaliland. The following year they were in Kenya and Northern Rhodesia. Once again, however, they had over-reached themselves and found that they had penetrated into territories unsuitable for breeding. So, during 1940, the plague died out.

Africa, however, was not the only region that suffered during these terrible years of the locust plagues. Another species of locust, the Desert Locust, had set out on the rampage at about the same time and, by 1929, was invading a vast area that reached through Persia to the Russian border in the north, east to India and Afghanistan and south into Portuguese East Africa. Countries of the Middle East and the Mediterranean were attacked and, in 1930, the Desert Locust reached Gibraltar. But, like the African Migratory Locust, the Desert Locust had flown too far afield and breeding stopped. By 1935, the plague had died away.

RED LOCUST

Another locust, the Red Locust, was later in starting than its colleagues. The first small swarms were noticed in 1927. By 1933, 900 swarms were reported; two years later there were 6,300 swarms marauding over an area of three million square miles—almost the whole of Africa south of the equator. This was the peak year for the Red Locust. It declined steadily over the next ten years, but left a rearguard of swarms which were still active in 1945 in Southern Africa.

This terrifying plague of locusts brought ruin and starvation to large areas of Africa and other hot countries, but it had the effect of bringing the anti-locust organisations of many countries together. An international locust centre was established in London, where the locust could be studied scientifically and the movements of swarms recorded.

In charge of the work of this centre was a scientist of Russian descent, Dr. B. P. Uvarov, who had studied locusts on the steppes of his native land. In 1941, Dr. Uvarov in Russia and Professor J. C. Faure in South Africa, working independently, had solved one of the mysteries of the locust's origin. They found that the insect lived a double life. On the one hand it could enjoy a solitary existence and was, in effect, a large grasshopper; on the other hand, it could give up this sort of life and begin to live and breed in swarms.

GRASSHOPPER ORIGIN

The extraordinary thing about this double personality of the locust is that the insect changes in appearance as it changes from one life to another. In the outbreak areas, conditions of climate and environment exert some sort of influence on the grasshoppers living their solitary existence. They begin to crowd together, and move about in swarms. They change their colour from green to orange or brown, and the size and proportions of their bodies alter.

In this swarming phase, the locusts continue to breed, the young "hoppers" hatching and growing up as locusts, living a crowd-life from the first. The multiplication rate is rapid, and the progeny from a small swarm of locusts can reach plague proportions in a very short time.

This change from grasshopper to locust has been studied in the laboratory. A young hopper placed among a crowd of locusts in a cage, will change in appearance and habits and become a locust.

To-day, a close watch is kept in countries where locusts are active, and information flows into the Anti-Locust Centre in London. Certain regions have been found to act as outbreak areas, where climatic conditions and the environment encourage grasshoppers to turn into locusts. The African Migratory Locust, for example, develops in a small region of the flood plains of the Middle Niger in the French Sudan. It was from this small area, only 120 miles long and 60 miles wide, that a swarm of overcrowded grasshoppers began a locust plague that invaded ten million square miles of Africa for fourteen years.

When swarms are detected in this and other known outbreak areas, we can now attack them with insecticides. Large areas of ground can be sprayed from the air, destroying the locusts before they are able to get out of hand. Given time and money, the day will yet come when the sky will no longer be darkened by swarms of insects bringing ruin and starvation as they have done since Biblical times.

THOMAS ALVA EDISON

" Our age should be called the Age of Edison. His inventions numbered more than two thousand. There is no great modern invention that is not in some way connected with Edison's genius." (Henry Ford).

Thomas Alva Edison was born in 1847. His boyhood dreams were not the usual ones of distant voyages and impossible conquests. His fantasies were of a scientific kind. He dreamed of chemical substances with incredible reactions and of electrical impulses that worked strange and wonderful machines.

Edison, as a boy, was vague and absent-minded, but against that nature had endowed him with the qualities of greatness. He had plenty of will-power and character; he was enthusiastic and untiring; he knew, too, that ideas have no roots unless nourished by meticulous research. At the same time he was well aware that it was only by hard work that he would be able to afford the scientific books he coveted and to buy the equipment he needed for his experiments.

So, while waiting for his parents to find him a suitable job, he worked first as a greengrocer's boy. Then, plucking up courage, he went round to the railway company and obtained permission to sell newspapers and sandwiches on the train that ran between Port Huron and Detroit. A flourishing little business developed and within a few months, Edison was able to buy magnets, test-tubes and other apparatus, and a number of books. Between trains he went to Detroit Public Library, and carefully copied facts from their reference books into his own exercise books.

HIS FIRST INVENTIONS

Edison decided to learn Morse telegraphy, and while practising he watched with fascination every movement of the transmitter. He studied for a year and then obtained his first post as a telegraphist at Cincinnati. After a short time he transferred to Boston and by the age of twenty-two had moved to the city of New York. Calling one day on an important business agency, he was asked to repair a sudden breakdown in the firm's Morse transmitter. The management saw his worth and immediately took him on as their technical superintendent. Now came his first invention—an electric register for political elections. Alas, like many political enterprises, it did not have the success it promised.

Undeterred, Tom now decided to build a machine that would replace the old-fashioned telegraph used for transmitting quotations of gold prices. This invention turned up trumps and brought him his first substantial earnings: forty thousand dollars. With this money in hand he left his job and opened a laboratory in Newark where he engaged several assistants.

Such was Tom Edison's personality, and so strong the convictions that drove him on to new inventions, that those who worked for him accepted meagre pay with long hours just for the sake of being near him. On the staff was Mary Stillwall, his first secretary. Good, kind and faithful Mary! She accepted his proposal and soon married him, sharing all her husband's hard work, sacrifices and disappointments, and in due time the success which was to crown his career with riches and glory.

During the six years between 1870 and 1876 Thomas Edison registered one hundred and twenty patents for inventions which ranged from a mimeograph for copying letters to an alarm siren for police and fire brigades. Then came his automatic telegraph, the fruit of long and tedious labour. This machine was equipped with a perforated ribbon that took down messages according to the letters used and not from dots and dashes. It was received with tremendous enthusiasm and paved the way for his invention of a transmitter for the simultaneous dispatch of more than one

Edison's first laboratory was the cellar at his home. To prevent anyone from touching his equipment he stuck labels on everything, marking them "poison," or "very dangerous."

At his laboratory and factory at Menlo Park, Edison made many new inventions. Here he is with his mimeograph, a device for making many copies of the same letter.

Another product of his Menlo Park laboratory and factory was the startling invention of a system for duplex telegraphy, afterwards improved into quadruplex and sextuplex transmission. Scientists and businessmen watch Edison demonstrating his multiple telegraph, a machine soon to be in use all over the world.

message on the same line. Meanwhile the inventor had left his Newark laboratories for larger and better equipped premises at West Grange, and it was here that he gained the nickname of " The Magician of Menlo Park ".

For many years now Thomas Edison had been devoting himself to the study of acoustics and it was from these researches that his most original invention was born. The idea of " writing " sounds had occurred to him while working on his automatic telegraph. Strange that it should have been a partially deaf man who gave mankind the first talking machine or phonograph. This was the prototype of the modern disc player. It consisted of a cylinder with a funnel to receive the voice, which in turn passed to a point where the sound vibrations were recorded.

Edison patented over 1300 *inventions amongst which was his discovery that a platinum wire can be heated to incandescence inside an evacuated glass vessel, giving out a useful light.*

THE ELECTRIC LIGHT BULB

Thomas Edison now applied himself to the most difficult task in his life. The world, which was awaiting the fuller developments of electricity, had found Volta's arc lamp to be too strong and not entirely practical. So a group of industrialists and financiers entrusted to Edison the solution of a problem which many others had failed to solve.

Edison believed that an incandescent glass bulb would meet the need, but the path to success was a long and weary one. Aided by his most faithful assistants, he spent over two years experimenting with 6,000 different kinds of filament. In his search for a suitable filament he tested the resistance of every kind of mineral and other material, whether common or rare, raw or manufactured.

The glass bulb, familiar to us all, had itself cost months of work and study. This, at least, was ready. What was missing was a filament which would stand up to white hot incandescence for a long time. Mary, his wife, began to worry about the great man's health, for he was working into the small hours and losing a lot of sleep.

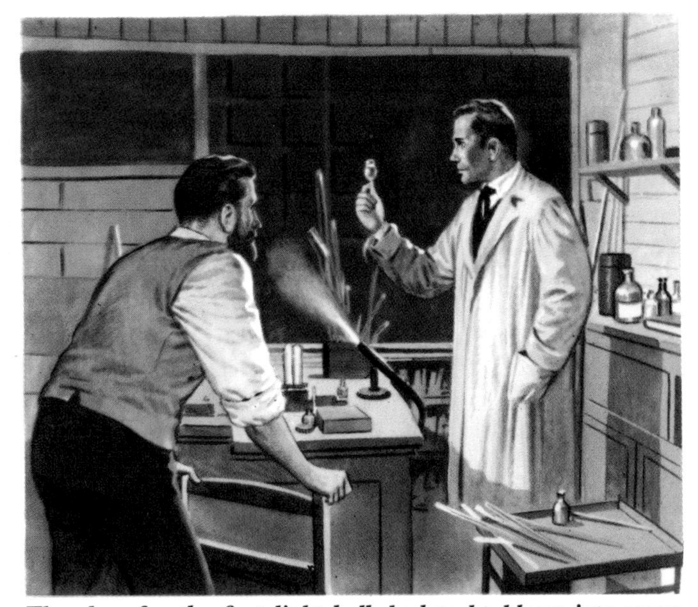

The glass for the first light bulb had to be blown into many different shapes before a satisfactory result was obtained.

Strangely enough, it was while reading in bed by the light of a petrol lamp that the idea came to him that a carbon filament would be capable of glowing without being burned away. The certainty of victory carried him through his subsequent researches and he was eventually successful. The first electric light bulb, the ancestor of those we all use to-day, was tested and passed as satisfactory. Two years later New York turned out to celebrate a great occasion: the inauguration of electric street lighting in 1882.

Now at the height of his glory, Thomas Alva Edison held great riches within his grasp. For one of humble birth he had attained his ambition, some people thought. But he was not a man to pause in midstream. Born in 1847, he was just thirty-five years old, ahead of him another thirty-five years of working life. Besides, the scientific world was expecting other miracles from " the Magician of Menlo Park ".

To his later researches we owe the first practical and effective system for the production and distribution of electrical energy. Edison's " power station " was soon to be taken up throughout the world, rendering possible the industrial developments of this century.

RADIO ASTRONOMY

The space surrounding the Earth is full of a tremendous variety of " rays " of various kinds. These have wavelengths ranging from one twenty-thousand-millionth of an inch to several miles. If we could see all of these rays we should have a wonderful picture of the universe presented to us. Unfortunately, the atmospheric blanket surrounding the Earth prevents all but a tiny proportion from reaching the surface. These are the visible light rays which our eyes can pick up, and without which we could not see.

Ever since Galileo made his primitive telescope over three hundred years ago, almost all our knowledge of the universe has been gained by studying these visible light rays.

" SEEING " INVISIBLE RAYS

Obviously, if we could " see " more of the rays we could learn more about the mysteries of the universe. This is what Radio Astronomy helps us to do. This wonderful " invention " started in 1931, when an American engineer named Jansky discovered that in addition to the light " window " in the atmosphere there is another one which lets through a proportion of the longer waves flashing through space. These waves are called radio waves because they are of the type used in ordinary radio transmissions. We cannot " see " these longer waves with ordinary telescopes, but they can be detected by radio telescopes.

A radio telescope is basically similar to an ordinary optical telescope, except that the familiar mirror, reflecting the visible light waves, is replaced by an aerial collecting the invisible radio waves. Because of this a radio telescope looks quite different. The wave-collecting " dish " on simple radio telescopes is often little more than wire netting spread on a light framework. The signals detected by this machine are fed into a receiver. Finally, there is some device for measuring the signals, such as a pen recorder producing a trace representing the strength of the incoming signals.

This simple type of radio telescope can only investigate that portion of the sky directly overhead. The more complex types, however, have steerable aerials enabling them to point at any part of the sky above the horizon.

The giant radio-telescope at Jodrell Bank, near Manchester.

JODRELL BANK

The biggest steerable radio telescope in the world is the British one at Jodrell Bank, near Manchester. On this, the bowl-shaped aerial is 250 feet in diameter, and it is pivoted at two points so that it can tilt at the push of a button. The towers supporting the bowl move on bogies in a circular railway track 300 feet in diameter. The two movements permit the bowl to be pointed in any desired direction. In addition to long-range astronomical research, this telescope has done much useful work in tracking and receiving information from artificial satellites.

The first experiments with radio telescopes indicated, rather strangely, that there appeared to be no connection between radio signals and the stars and galaxies which could be seen with ordinary telescopes. On the other hand the signals appeared to come from definite *points* in space. And so, an intensive search for the sources of some of the strongest signals was made with the big 200-inch telescope on Mount Palomar, in California, America. Surprising results were achieved. Pictures were obtained of entire galaxies in *collision*, and although each galaxy contains many millions of stars they are so far apart that the individual stars rarely collide. Other photographs indicated that some radio signals came from the remains of stars, called supernova, that exploded with tremendous ferocity millions of years ago.

STUDYING THE MILKY WAY

Radio astronomy is also teaching us new facts about our own galaxy, called the Milky Way. Because of intervening clouds of interstellar " dust " the centre is invisible to ordinary light, but it can be examined with radio telescopes. Measurements of signals confirm the theory that the galaxy is in the shape of a gigantic catherine wheel, with the sun and Earth located in one of the spiral arms, somewhere near the rim.

LOOKING BACK 2,000 MILLION YEARS

In astronomy the distances involved are so great that measurement in terms of miles would be meaningless. So distances are measured in light years, one light year being equal to the distance travelled by light, moving at 186,000 miles a second, in one year. The big telescope on Mount Palomar can detect galaxies 2,000 million light years away. Even travelling at the fantastic speed of 186,000 miles a second, the light takes all that time to reach us.

Now a fascinating thing about this is that we see the galaxy not as it is to-day, but as it was 2,000 million years ago—long, long before life stirred on the Earth.

Radio telescopes may be able to penetrate even greater distances—perhaps up to 7,000 million light years—and thus enable us to look even farther back into the dim and incredibly distant past. This may give us information about the condition of the universe in the remote past and even open the ultimate secret of how the universe started.

THE WONDERS OF COLOUR

Colour is made possible by the phenomenon of light, and nature herself makes the fullest use of light and colour in all manner of ways. She uses camouflage, for example, to enable living things to blend into the colour pattern of their surroundings. Think of the tiger: its black and yellow stripes imitate the colour of the earth and the bush, criss-crossed with patches of sunlight and shade. In the same way, snakes protect themselves by wearing skins which resemble the surroundings in which they live. Flowers attract insects with their colours, thus ensuring that pollination takes place.

REFRACTION OF LIGHT

Each object has its own way of dealing with light rays which strike it—absorbing some and reflecting others—thus creating for itself its own " colour ", which is governed partly by the light and partly by the nature of the substance it is made of.

We know that a sound reaches us by means of a sound wave which travels through the air from the source of the vibration to our ears. Light is also carried to us in the form of a wave motion, and when the vibrations of light waves reach the retina of the eye they stimulate the cells of the retina producing in the brain the sensation of light.

ELECTRONS

The particles of every luminous body are in rapid motion; every atom resembles a small solar system in which the particles move in orbit around a central nucleus like planets around the sun. These particles are called electrons, and it is the movements of these electrons which produce the electromagnetic waves we recognise as light.

The electrons rotate at great speed, completing a fantastic number of revolutions per second. In one second, light travels 186,000 miles—a distance seven and a half times the circumference of the Earth! The light that enters our eyes vibrates at a rate that varies between 370 and 750 billion times per second.

THE SPECTRUM

The colour sensation produced in our eyes by the electromagnetic waves of light depends upon the wave-length of the wave. As the wave-length shortens, the sensation changes from red to orange, yellow, green, blue, indigo, violet.

We can best picture the difference in the wave-lengths that produce these colours by comparing their movements in the air with actual water waves: for instance, red light moves like the long slow waves of the sea, whilst blue light has the rapid oscillation of the fast-flowing ripples of a lake.

We know that white light is not a single colour but a mixture of radiations representing different colours. If a ray of white light is passed through a glass prism, it forms a range of colours when thrown on to a screen. The two outer colours are red and violet, and the band of " rainbow " colours is called a spectrum.

Beyond these visible limits, there are other rays, to which our eyes are insensitive. Beyond red, the waves lengthen to form infra-red rays; these are heat rays, which can be detected by means of a thermometer. Beyond the violet, the wave-lengths get shorter forming ultra-violet rays, which are chemically active. A photographic plate will go black immediately when exposed to ultra-violet rays.

These inyisible rays have a tremendous variety of uses. Infra-red rays can be used for heating, in microscopy, in photography, in telefilming, for certain medical diagnoses, and as an alarm system against burglars. Ultra-violet rays can do duty as " artificial sunshine ".

The rainbow is caused by the refraction of light. The rays of the sun, filtering through raindrops in the air are

Light waves are fundamentally different from sound waves. Sound waves will travel through a solid or a fluid medium, whilst light waves can also pass through a vacuum.

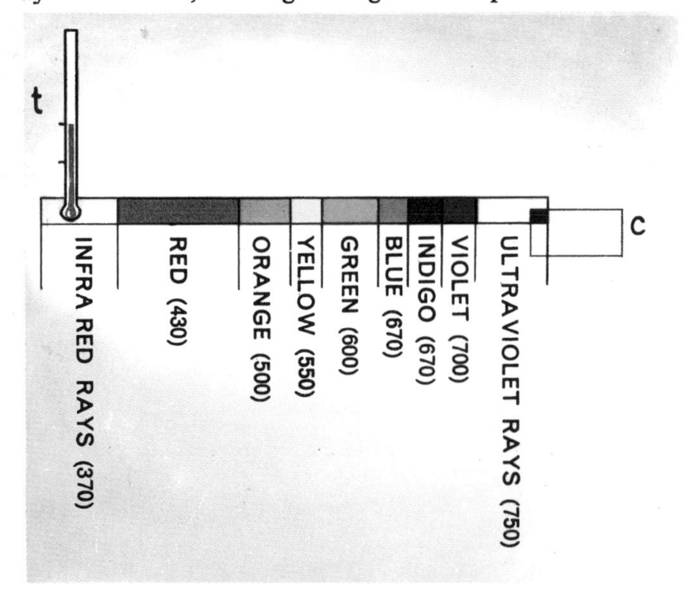

Scale (in billions) of light wave vibrations. A thermometer (t) shows the presence of infra-red rays, and a photographic plate (C) shows the limits of the ultra-violet rays.

bent and scattered, the constituent radiations being separated into coloured bands.

PRIMARY COLOURS

The colours of the spectrum are called the *basic* colours because they cannot be subdivided into others. Coloured glass absorbs the colours of the spectrum that are not related to the colour of the glass. For example, glass made with cobalt has a turquoise tint because it absorbs almost all the yellow, red, orange and green but lets through blue, violet, and a little red (the colours that constitute turquoise).

There are three primary colours, red, yellow and blue. Different mixtures of yellow and red will produce every shade of orange; yellow and blue will make every shade of green; and red and blue will give all the different shades of purple. Black is an absence of colour, which results when an object absorbs all the colours so that no light waves are reflected.

The brightness of a colour depends on the different wave-lengths of the spectrum; there is a broad division of the colours into *warm* ones (i.e. red), and *cold* ones (i.e. blue). An object devoid of colour looks white, because it reflects every colour, and white light is made up of all the colours. There are complementary pairs of colours which combine to form white; green, violet and orange would reproduce white if mixed with the three main colours, red, yellow and blue respectively.

A rainbow is caused by the refraction of sunlight by raindrops in the air.

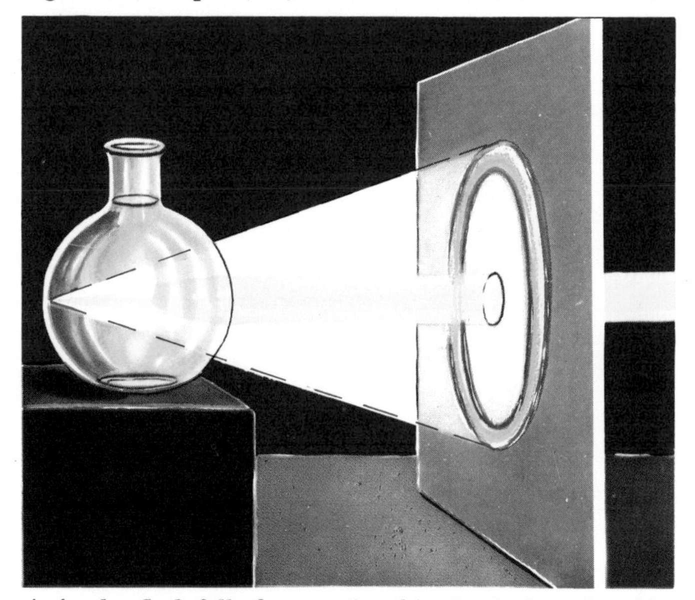

A circular flask full of water placed in the shadow of a white card with a hole bored through the middle, will cast on the card two coloured circles concentric with the hole.

Some substances change colour according to the way you look at them. A very fine sheet of gold leaf will be green if held between the viewer and the light, so that the ray passes straight through it, but yellow if seen from the side, so that the rays of light are reflected from it.

Some people suffer from colour blindness, sometimes called " daltonism ", after the scientist Dalton, who had a particular interest in this complaint because he suffered from it himself. Dalton studied colour blindness and showed that some people cannot distinguish between some colours; most frequently these sufferers confuse red with its complementary colour, green.

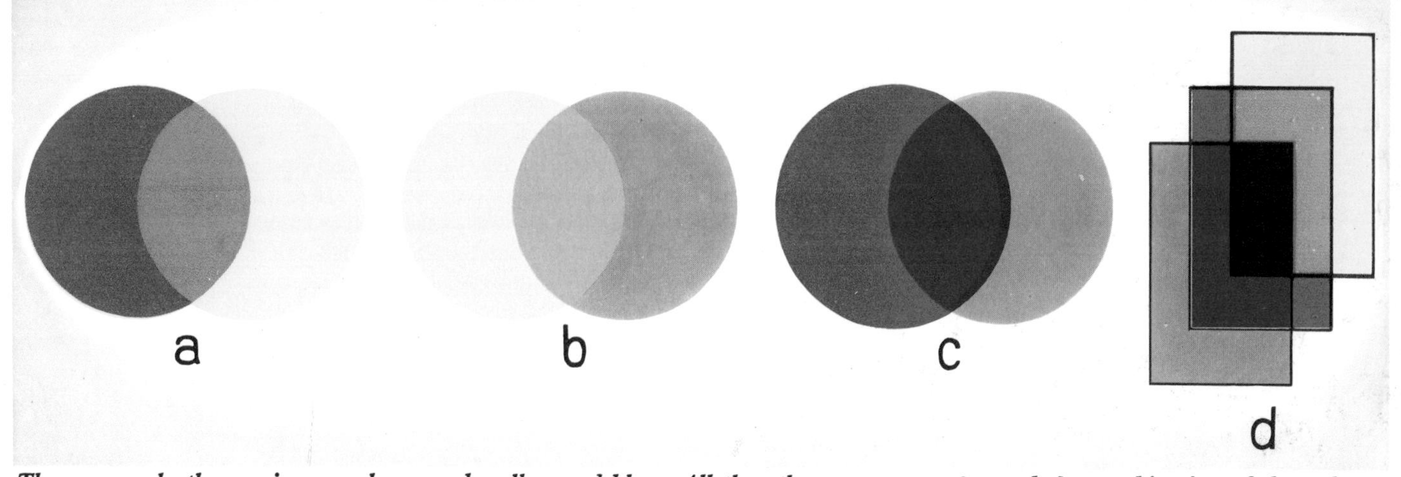

There are only three primary colours, red, yellow and blue. All the other colours can be made by combination of these three. For example: (a) *red and yellow make orange,* (b) *yellow and blue make green,* (c) *red and blue make purple. Black results from combination of all three primary colours. Sunlight is made up of the seven colours of the spectrum. These are divided into warm colours, represented by red* (*longest wave-length*) *and cold ones as typified by blue and violet* (*shortest wave-length*). *The phenomenon of splitting white light into the different colours of the spectrum was first discovered by Newton.*

ASTEROIDS, COMETS AND METEORS

Besides the nine major planets, the solar system contains a large number of minor planets or asteroids. Most of these move in the great gap of 350 million miles between the orbits of Mars and Jupiter, and therefore travel about the sun once in anything from 3 to 6 years. So far, astronomers have determined the orbits of 1,500 of them, but it is highly probable that there are thousands of others which, owing to their extreme faintness, have eluded discovery.

All the asteroids look like faint stars not only because of their great distance from the Earth but also because they are small in themselves. The largest, Ceres, is only 480 miles in diameter, and the great majority found so far are just a mile or so across. The four largest were all discovered in the short span of six years. Ceres was discovered in 1801 by Piazzi, an astronomer at Palermo, Sicily. In 1802, Olbers, a German astronomer, discovered Pallas (diameter 300 miles) and in 1804, Harding, another German astronomer, discovered the third, Juno. Olbers had a further success when he found a fourth, Vesta (diameter 120 miles) in 1807, but the fifth, Astræa (diameter 60 miles) was not found until 1845.

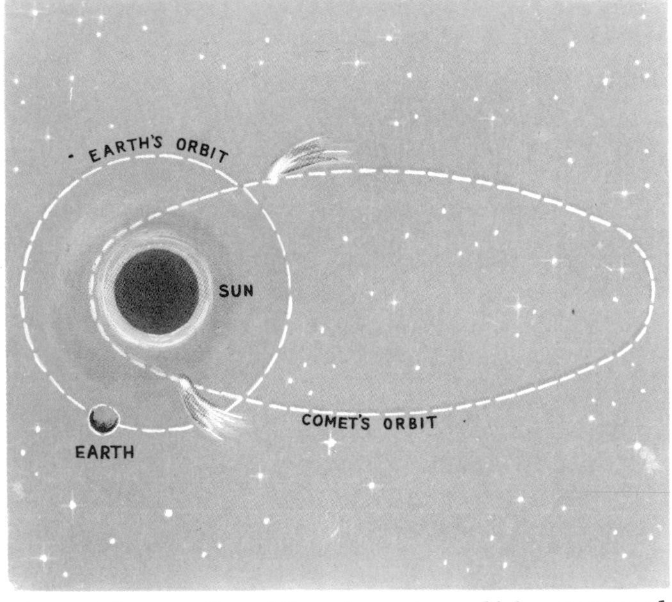

A comet is a member of the solar system, which moves round the sun in an elliptical orbit.

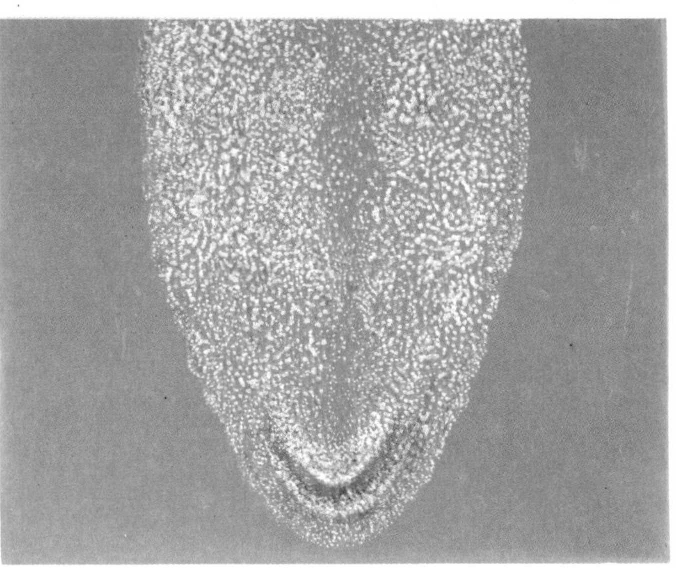

Comets are heavenly bodies of uncertain origin, travelling in orbit round the sun. The material forming the comet is readily disintegrated under the influence of the sun and the large planets.

The Chinese first recorded the appearance of Halley's comet in A.D. *467.*

The other asteroids are much smaller than these five and are probably roughly-shaped chunks of stone and metal. They are all flyweight worlds and airless ones too—none is large enough to hold an atmosphere to its surface.

Other members of the solar system are comets. These are sometimes confused with shooting stars, but they are really quite different. A shooting star or meteor appears as just a thin streak or line of light. It appears and disappears in a few moments and is due to the rapid flight of a small metallic body through the Earth's upper atmosphere. In contrast, comets are enormous affairs which move about the sun in great oval-shaped paths. Like the planets, they are millions of miles from the Earth.

Most comets look like fuzzy stars even when seen through large telescopes: they also give themselves away by their slow movement against the background of far more distant stars. Comparatively few grow tails, but several large comets with splendid tails have visited our skies over the past two centuries. One of these was Halley's comet. It last appeared in 1910, when its tail reached out to nearly 93 million miles. It travels round the sun once in about 76 years and will not be seen again until 1986.

Halley's comet is of particular interest, for its various visits have been recorded over many centuries. Once its

On the 30th of June, 1908, a great meteorite fell in Siberia with explosive force, the shock waves being recorded by barograph in London and Washington. Trees were uprooted and destroyed over a large area, and the sound of the explosion was heard hundreds of miles away. The remains of the meteorite are now deep in the ground.

period, or the time it takes to go once round the sun, is known, it is an easy matter to calculate the times of its past appearances. This was first made possible by Edmund Halley. He noticed that the comets of 1531, 1607 and 1682 had moved in similar paths and suggested that they were one and the same object. He then predicted that this object, since called Halley's comet, would reappear at the end of 1758. Unfortunately he died in 1742, but the comet did return, being first seen on Christmas Day, 1758.

A NORMAL PHENOMENON

In earlier times, before it became possible to predict their returns, comets were usually regarded as warning signs in the sky. They were supposed to forerun famine, disease and the overthrow of kingdoms, for they came suddenly as if from nowhere and appeared to hang in the sky over a particular place. Even in modern times there are people who are frightened when they see a bright comet, forgetting that it is a perfectly natural object—a member of the sun's great family, many million miles away.

Some comets, when moving near the sun, grow immense tails. Yet even the largest comets are quite empty affairs. So thin are the gases in their tails that the faint background of stars can easily be seen through them. Even the " head ", or brightest part of a comet, is comparatively empty, being probably a sponge-like mass of frozen gases and stony lumps of iron. If the Earth collided with a comet's head we should see a magnificent shower of shooting stars: if it passed through a comet's tail we would suffer no ill-effects and have no sign as to what was happening.

CELESTIAL FIREWORKS

From time to time there have been brilliant showers of shooting stars. This does not mean, however, that each time the Earth collided with a comet's head. Instead, these are large quantities of metallic stones, or *meteorites*, which move in interplanetary space, and whenever the Earth meets a swarm of these the stage is set for a fine display of shooting stars. The meteorites which give rise to the " shooting-star " effect are quite small—about the size of a grain of sand and seldom larger than a pea—and are completely vaporised by the heat of their passage through the air. Others, much larger, can penetrate right through the Earth's atmosphere. The really large ones can do a great deal of damage. The one which fell in Siberia in 1908, for example, buried itself deep in the ground and felled a whole forest of trees. The Earth's atmosphere therefore acts as a protective blanket, keeping us safe from all but the largest bodies in this bombardment from outer space. Just how large this bombardment is has been revealed in recent years by radio methods. The use of radar in studying meteors tells us that swarms of these bodies bombard the Earth with unfailing regularity both by day and by night. We also have evidence that several of these swarms are associated with comets, and it may be that they once formed parts of the heads of comets. Hence, while shooting stars and comets look so different in our skies, they may well have had a common origin.

On about the 10th of August every year a small shower of shooting stars, once called "the tears of St. Lawrence", appears in the region of the constellation of Perseus.

MARIE CURIE

Marie Sklodowska was born on 7th November, 1867, in Warsaw. Her father was a schoolteacher who taught physics, and her mother was the principal of a school. They were poor, but intensely patriotic and they greatly resented the fact that their own country, Poland, was ruled by Russia. Like many others of their countrymen, the Sklodowska family tried to keep up the language and traditions of Poland, and this resulted in Marie's father losing his job.

Marie, and an older sister, Bronya, wanted to go to Paris to study at the University there, for women were not allowed to attend a university in Poland; but it seemed as though there would never be enough money. Marie at last hit on a solution. She would become a governess and devote all the money she could save to supporting Bronya in Paris. When Bronya had got her degree, she in her turn would work and support Marie. The plan was carried out and at last, in 1891, when Marie was twenty-four years old, she counted up her money and was just able to pay her journey to Paris.

POVERTY IN PARIS

There Marie lived, in great poverty, in an attic room with scarcely any furniture. It was so cold that sometimes the water in the basin would freeze, and for days she would eat nothing but bread, chocolate and a little fruit. She was not discouraged by these hardships, however, and she graduated in physics in 1893, and in mathematics the following year.

Soon after this she met Pierre Curie, who, at thirty-five, was chief of the laboratory at the School of Physics and Chemistry, but was almost as poor as she was. They fell in love and on 26th July, 1895, they were married. It was a drab wedding, no white dress, no bouquets and bridesmaids, no festive wedding breakfast. Marie wore a sensible blue suit which would do very well later on for work in the laboratory, and the honeymoon was spent touring by bicycle.

But they were happy. They settled down in a tiny flat

Marie was an exceptionally strong-willed and tenacious girl.

At the Sorbonne, Marie took no part in the merry chatter of the students. Determined at all costs to make her mark in scientific research, she studied day and night.

and Marie added cooking to her accomplishments, measuring ingredients with all the painstaking precision of a chemist. Their first child was a daughter, Irene, born in September, 1897. In the same year, Marie had to choose a subject on which to do research for her Doctor's degree. She discussed the problem with her husband and told him that she was greatly attracted by the idea of working on a discovery made by Becquerel the year before.

THESIS WORK ON RADIATION

Becquerel had been studying substances which " fluoresce ". This means that when they are exposed to light, or to invisible radiations such as X-rays, they glow with a bluish-green radiance. Becquerel had wanted to find out whether all substances which fluoresce also throw off X-rays. To do this, he wrapped a double thickness of black paper round a photographic plate, so that ordinary light could not get at it. Then he placed a small piece of silver between the layers of the black paper and put uranium crystals (a substance which fluoresces) on the outside. He exposed the uranium to the sun for a few hours to make it fluoresce, and afterwards he developed the plate. He always found, as he had expected, that the rays from the uranium had penetrated the black paper and marked the photographic plate, showing the outline of the piece of silver where it had interrupted the rays. The thing that *was* unexpected, however, was the discovery that the uranium apparently threw off rays which marked the plates, even when it had not been activated by the sun. This was something quite new. The rays seemed to be producing themselves. In other words, energy seemed to be generated from nothing.

Marie Curie wanted to find out where the energy came from which showed itself in these rays and, above all, what they were. The problem fascinated her. The uranium gave off energy in the form of rays without ever receiving any and so contradicted a universally accepted law of physics. It was impossible; but it happened.

EXAMINING URANIUM

She had nowhere of her own to work, but in the end she was given a little, glassed-in studio, cold and damp and uncomfortable, on the ground floor of the School of Physics. Her first three months were spent in testing the intensity of the rays given off by uranium. She had a gold leaf electroscope, and she would put a charge on the leaves by rubbing them until they stood out at right angles. Then she would put uranium underneath. The rays given off made the air able to conduct electricity, and the charge would escape from the leaves. As it did so, they would slowly sink down.

After three months of this testing, she came upon what seemed a freakish result. She had expected that the more thoroughly she separated uranium from the pitchblende in which it is found, the stronger the radiations would become. She found, on the contrary, that if she put crude pitchblende under the electroscope, the gold leaves lost their charge more, and not less, quickly. Crude pitchblende was throwing off more powerful rays than pure uranium. There was only one conclusion: pitchblende contained some new, unknown element, far more active than uranium.

POLONIUM AND RADIUM

Pierre Curie now collaborated with Marie, and in three months they had discovered a new element, four hundred times more active than uranium, which they christened "Polonium" in honour of Marie's country. Six months later, they found a second new element. "Its activity is nine hundred times greater than uranium," they reported. This was so, even when it was still impure and mixed up with other substances. If only they could isolate it they were certain its activity would be "enormous". "We propose to give this new substance the name of radium," they said.

Next they embarked on the appalling task of trying to isolate the new element in a pure state. They guessed that the uranium ore, which had to be extracted from the crude pitchblende, contained perhaps one per cent. of radium. They were too optimistic. The true figure turned out to be less than one part in a million. But by 1902, after four years labour, one-tenth of a gramme of pure radium had been isolated. It glowed in the darkness of the laboratory.

RECOGNITION AND TRAGEDY

In 1903, the Curies received a Nobel Prize, which they shared with Becquerel. Marie was the first woman ever to have won this great honour.

In 1906, Pierre Curie was killed in a street accident and Marie was almost overwhelmed by grief. She felt that she had now nothing to live for except her two daughters, Irene and Eve, and her scientific work. She devoted herself to carrying on the research into radio-activity, to which she and Pierre had already contributed so much, and she became the first woman ever to hold a Professorship at the Sorbonne. In 1910, she published her classic work "Treatise on Radio-activity", and in the following year, she received a Nobel Prize for the second time. This was given for her work on the chemistry of radium.

Marie Curie died in July, 1934, of leukæmia, a disease which had been caused, ironically enough, by constant exposure to the damaging rays thrown off by the substance she had discovered.

In Pierre Curie, Marie found the ideal companion and collaborator.

Marie Curie dedicated her life to research work.

In the darkness, the two scientists see the luminescence caused by the radio-active substances they have isolated.

MOVEMENT

Our busy world is in a state of constant movement. We ourselves are always on the move. We walk upstairs, or run for a bus; we travel in cars and trains, in aeroplanes and ships.

Movement is part and parcel of our everyday world. We accept the idea of movement without really thinking much about it.

Yet there is much more in this business of movement and rest than we are inclined to realise. A boulder lying on the ground, for example, is commonly regarded as being at rest; it does not move. But when we say that it is at rest, we really mean that it is not moving relative to the Earth on which it is lying. The atoms and molecules of the material forming the boulder are moving; the electrons inside the atoms are whizzing round and round at colossal speed.

Also, the Earth is rotating on its own axis once in every day; if the boulder lies on the equator, therefore, it must travel about 25,000 miles in the course of every day. It is certainly moving in this sense; but, as the Earth on which it lies is moving at the same speed too, we think of the boulder as being at rest relative to the Earth.

Throughout the entire universe, everything is in a state of constant movement with respect to something else. Nothing stands still. There is no rest. Yet scientists accept that there is some point in the cosmos which we can regard as in a state of absolute rest. In the same way, they accept the existence of absolute movement, which is not dependent upon motion with respect to another body in the universe.

This idea of movement as something which relates one body to the position of another body in the universe has intrigued philosophers for thousands of years. But until comparatively recent times, much more attention was paid to the movements of the planets, stars and other celestial bodies than to the movements of objects on the Earth itself.

This preoccupation with the heavenly bodies was understandable. They obviously moved in a rhythmic fashion, revolving about one another in a regular way. These movements could be measured and studied much more easily than the movements of earth-bound objects. The ancient Greek philosophers, carried out a great number of observations on the movements of the sun, moon and planets.

The movement of these heavenly bodies was expressed in terms of circular motion, and was regarded as something special which did not relate to the relative movements of matter on Earth itself.

Until the fifteenth-century A.D., the Earth was commonly regarded as being stationary in the heavens, with the planets and moon, the sun and stars all revolving around it as though part of a vast moving sphere. The irregular motions of the planets did not fit into this simple scheme of things, but this was explained by the theory that planets also revolved in small circular movements of their own; these epicycles were superimposed upon the circular motion of the heavenly sphere.

Copernicus, in the fifteenth- and sixteenth-centuries, took the first step towards our modern conception of the movement of heavenly bodies by suggesting that the sun was, in fact, the centre of the solar system. This is known as the Heliocentric Theory. At the beginning of the seventeenth-century, Kepler put forward his laws of planetary motion, and the movements of the sun and stars, the moon, the planets and the Earth itself were established as being controlled and orderly. The motion and movement of many material objects relative to one another were studied rationally, and the way was paved towards establishing general principles that govern the motion of material things.

Towards the end of the sixteenth-century, the great astronomer and philosopher Galileo studied the movement of objects here on Earth, and realised that these movements conformed to principles and laws which were apparently universal.

At this time, people still accepted the teachings of Aristotle with respect to gravitation and the movement of falling bodies. Aristotle's explanation for the fact that a piece of wood will rise when released under water was that the wood possessed a property of " levity ", whereas the water possessed the property of " gravity ". Galileo decided that this was not a true explanation of the phenomenon, nor did Aristotle's ideas fit in with factual observation relating to the obvious differences in the strength with which materials were attracted towards the Earth.

Galileo proclaimed that the speed of descent of any body in a medium such as water or air depends upon the comparative density of the body and the medium in which it moves. Suppose, said Galileo, we could observe falling bodies in no medium at all? Then, in those circumstances, all matter would descend with equal velocity.

This assertion was contrary to the theories of the day, which were based on Aristotle's teachings. Aristotle had proclaimed that the falling of any body was due to its gravity or heaviness. If this was doubled, then it would fall to Earth twice as fast. This theory had been accepted almost without question for nearly 2,000 years.

Galileo was at that time in Pisa, and it was there that he carried out his historic experiment. One morning, he ascended the famous Leaning Tower, taking with him a ten-pound shot and a one-pound shot. He dropped them together and they reached the ground at the same time.

Robert Brown, botanist, observed that particles of matter are in a state of continuous movement. The diagram shows the paths followed by three particles, seen under the microscope.

It was in Pisa that Galileo made his other classic observation, when he watched a great lamp swinging from the roof of the cathedral nave. Timing the oscillation of this massive pendulum with the beat of his pulse, he found that the swings took identical times, no matter whether they were large or small.

Galileo continued his study of the motions of bodies relative to one another; he found that objects sliding down a smooth slope moved with constant acceleration. As the angle of inclination was diminished, the acceleration was reduced. He studied the trajectories of projectiles, and formulated general theories relating the movements of objects relative to one another. These relationships could be applied universally, controlling the movements of heavenly bodies in exactly the same way as the movements of objects here on Earth.

The great scientist Huygens amplified and extended Galileo's work during the seventeenth-century. Huygens studied the centrifugal force generated by bodies moving in curved paths, and suggested that the variations in the acceleration of falling bodies at different places on the Earth's surface was a result of the Earth's rotation.

LAWS OF MOTION

In 1687, Sir Isaac Newton brought together the theories and observations relating to the motions of bodies and welded them into a general theory of motion, which has formed a basis for the study of motion up to the present day.

Newton established three laws of motion, as follows:

1. Every body remains in a state of rest, or of uniform motion in a straight line, unless it is compelled by impressed forces to change that state.
2. Change of motion is proportional to the impressed force, and takes place in the direction of the straight line in which the force acts.
3. Action and reaction are equal and opposite; or the mutual actions between any two bodies are always equal in magnitude, but oppositely directed.

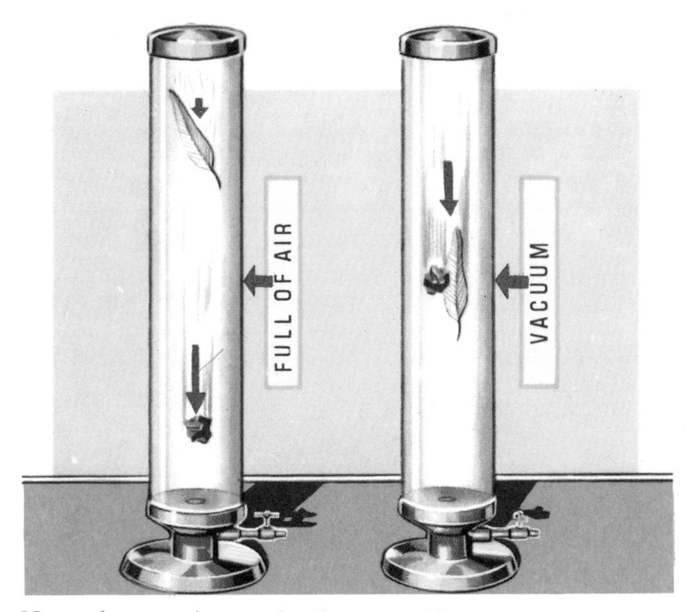

Newton's experiment showing the effect of air on falling bodies. One tube contains air and the other a vacuum. In the air-filled tube, the feather and the stone reach the bottom at different times, but in the other tube they arrive at the bottom simultaneously.

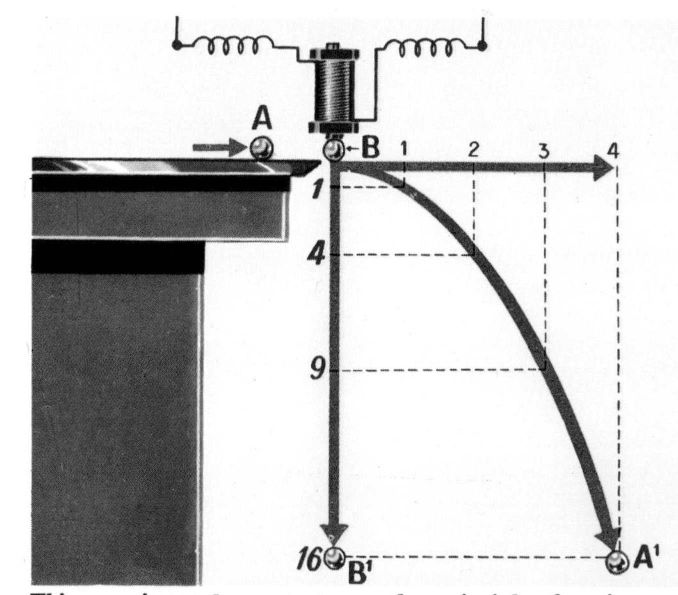

This experiment demonstrates another principle of motion put forward by Galileo. The little ball A, is launched horizontally, and the ball B is allowed to drop vertically by breaking the circuit of an electro-magnet which is holding it. The balls reach the ground simultaneously from equal heights, the former with parabolic motion, the latter with rectilinear motion.

These laws have become the foundation upon which astronomers have studied the movements of celestial bodies in the universe, and upon which physicists have established their researches for nearly three centuries.

The first of Newton's laws is the law of inertia. It means that a body at rest will remain at rest unless acted upon by a force which moves it. And a moving body will continue to move in a straight line at constant speed for ever unless something stops it.

The second law defines how any force will influence any body either at rest or in motion. The fact that the change in motion produced by any force is strictly proportional to the size of that force gives us a principle by which we can measure forces. We can, for example, measure the force of gravity by assessing how many feet a body falls in successive seconds.

COMPLEX FORCES

This second law tells us that the forces acting on any body in the universe are complex, and are rarely if ever a single force. No matter how far we travel away from Earth into space, for example, we shall always be subject to gravitational attraction by the Earth. And we shall be simultaneously attracted by all other bodies in the universe, each one of which produces its result no matter how many other forces may be acting upon us.

The third law of motion is very much in evidence in this age of rockets and space travel. A rocket engine propels a space vehicle by generating a " reaction " force. The burning fuel in the rocket is ejected from the rear at tremendous speed; there is an equal and opposite reaction which propels the body of the rocket in the opposite direction.

There is no need for any air against which the rocket gases can exert a " push ", as people often imagine. A rocket will propel a vehicle in space just as readily as in travelling through the atmosphere. Its " action " generates an equal and opposite reaction in accord with Newton's third law of motion.

MARCONI

Guglielmo Marconi was born on 25th April, 1874, at Bologna in Italy. His father was a country gentleman, and Marconi was educated first in Bologna and then in Florence. After that he went to a technical school in Leghorn where he became particularly interested in the "Hertzian" waves (that is, electromagnetic, or wireless waves). In 1894, he made experiments with these waves on his father's estate near Bologna and was able to send messages a short distance using a crude transmitter and receiver. Later he succeeded in sending signals over a distance of one-and-a-half miles.

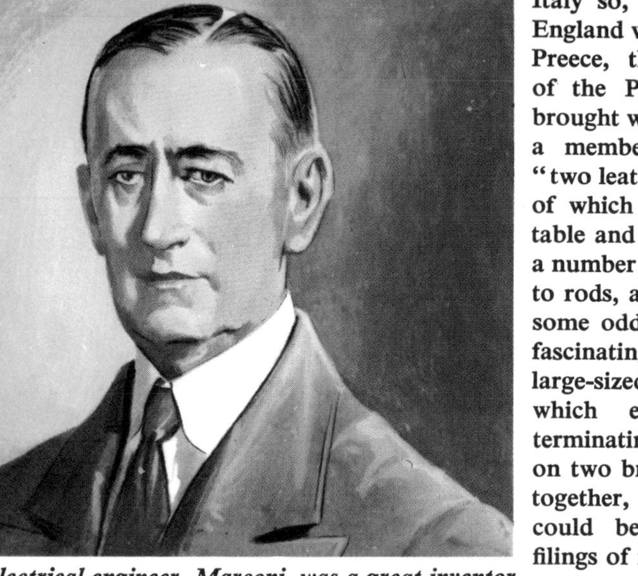

The Italian electrical engineer, Marconi, was a great inventor who had a genius for practical experiments. His inventions were to lead to many of our modern electronic devices, including radio, television and radar. He was awarded the Nobel Prize for Physics in 1909.

The physicist, Ernest Rutherford, who was then a young man, was also making experiments of much the same kind at much the same time, although probably neither knew of the existence of the other. Rutherford succeeded in transmitting a signal from the Cavendish laboratory to his lodgings in Cambridge at just about the same time as Marconi was making his experiments on his father's estate. Rutherford became interested in other things, such as radio-activity, but Marconi worked on radio communication all his life.

MOVE TO ENGLAND

Marconi's work did not receive much encouragement in Italy so, in 1896, he went to England where he visited W. H. Preece, the Engineer-in-Chief of the Post Office. Marconi brought with him, according to a member of Preece's staff, "two leather bags, the contents of which were placed on the table and seemed to consist of a number of brass knobs fitted to rods, a large spark coil and some odd terminals, but most fascinating of all, a rather large-sized tubular bottle from which extruded two rods terminating inside the bottle on two bright discs, very close together, and between which could be seen some bright filings of metal particles."

Marconi proceeded to give a demonstration. He depressed a key in his mysterious apparatus, and immediately a bell placed on a table nearby began to ring.

Preece was impressed and did all that he could to help and encourage Marconi. The first outdoor test of his "telegraphy without wires" was made between the roof of the building in St. Martin's le Grand, now known as the Central Telegraph Office, and a Post Office Savings Bank building in Carter Lane, south of St. Paul's. This was followed by successful tests over a distance of two miles on Salisbury Plain. In the following year, 1897, signals were sent across the Bristol Channel, a distance of nearly nine miles.

Marconi began to dream of sending wireless signals across

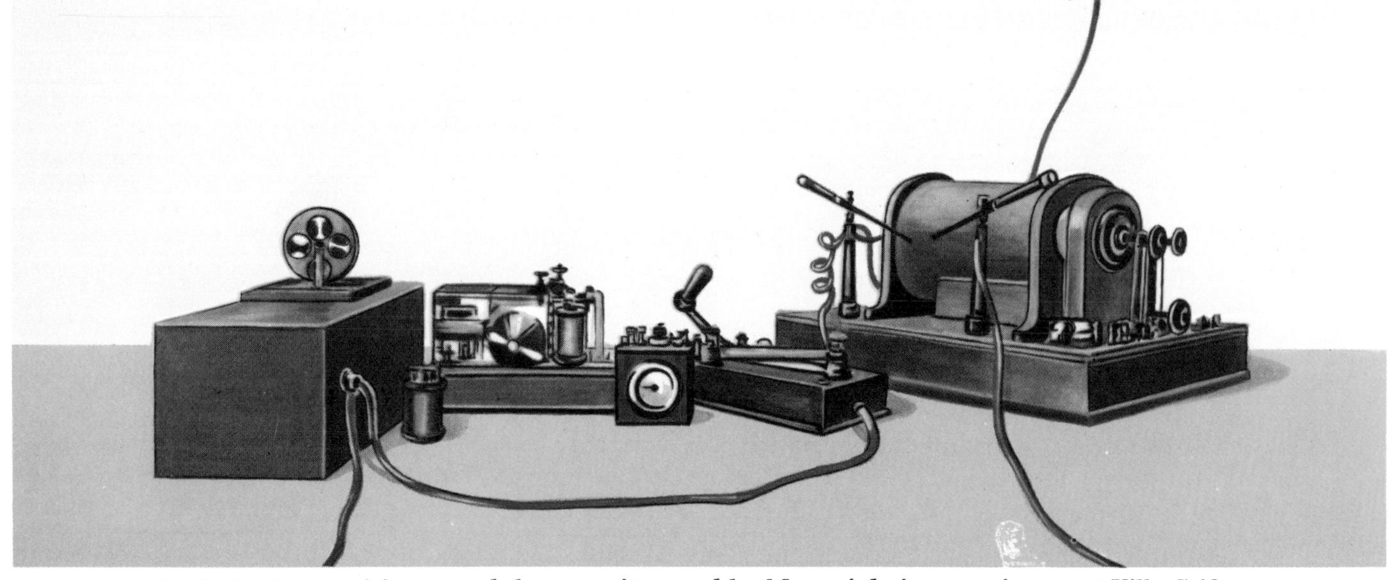

This is the first receiving set and the transmitter used by Marconi during experiments at Villa Grifone.

the Atlantic, but this raised special difficulties. It was not merely a question of building a more powerful transmitter. The real problem lay in the fact that the Earth is curved, and wireless waves travel in straight lines. If you put a pencil on top of a tennis-ball, you do not expect that it will reach half-way round it. In the same way, it was argued, wireless waves could be received as far as the horizon, or perhaps a little beyond, but after that the waves would shoot away from the curved surface of the Earth. Marconi refused to be discouraged. " I *believe* it is possible," he said.

PIONEER TRANSMITTER

In July, 1900, Marconi, accompanied by Major Flood Page, managing director of the recently-formed Marconi Wireless Company, and R. N. Vyvyan, an engineer, went to the barren south-west tip of England and selected Poldhu, near Mullion in Cornwall, as the site of a pioneer transmitter which was to be a hundred times more powerful than any station yet built. A twin station was to be erected at South Wellfleet, Cape Cod, Newfoundland. By the end of August, 1901, the masts were nearly completed, but a cyclone swept the English coast on 17th September, and the big masts were blown down. The work was begun again and this time simpler aerials were used. In two months everything was ready once more, and on 26th November, Marconi sailed for Newfoundland, accompanied by G. S. Kemp and P. W. Paget. They landed at St. John's on Friday, 6th December, and Marconi selected a site overlooking the port. The apparatus was set up and all the preparations were made for the great experiment. " The critical moment had come . . ." said Marconi, " I was about to test the truth of my belief."

SUCCESS AT LAST

The staff in England had been given careful instructions that they were to transmit a certain signal—three dots, (the letter S of the Morse Code). They were to send it out at a fixed time each day, as soon as they had received a cable from Marconi telling them that all the preparations were complete at St. John's.

On 12th December, 1901, Marconi sat waiting with the receiver held to his ear. He could only guess the length of Poldhu's wave and he had to hunt for it. Between St. John's in Newfoundland and Poldhu in Cornwall lay nearly two thousand miles of ocean; but Marconi hoped that the wireless waves might flash across it in one ninety-third of a second.

On 12th December, 1901, Marconi and his assistant heard three short sounds buzzed in the telephone receiver; the letter S had crossed the Atlantic by radio.

For half-an-hour he heard no sound. He checked his instruments, and listened again. At about 12.30, he heard faintly, but unmistakably, three " scant little dots. . . . They sounded several times in my ears," he wrote.

Marconi was delighted that he had been proved right after all and that wireless waves had crossed the Atlantic "serenely ignoring the curvature of the Earth ". It was the starting-point of the vast development in radio communication which has come about since.

RICOCHETING WAVES AROUND THE EARTH

The mystery of how the wireless waves were apparently able to ignore the curvature of the Earth was solved later when it was demonstrated that there are layers in the upper atmosphere from which wireless waves of certain lengths

Marconi, on board the Elettra *at Genoa, sends a radio signal which switches on 2,000 lamps at the Sydney Exhibition in Australia.*

bounce back again to Earth. Wireless waves can therefore travel round the Earth by a series of ricochets between the Earth and these layers of electrified atmosphere.

Marconi devoted himself to the development of long-range broadcasting and, in 1916, he saw the greater possibilities which might result from using shorter electric waves. This led to the development of short-wave wireless communication by which messages could be sent over a far greater distance than had been possible before. In 1924, Marconi secured a contract from the Post Office for the establishment of short-wave communication between England and the British Commonwealth.

NOBEL PRIZE-WINNER

Marconi received many honours. In 1902, he was created a Knight of Italy, and he was awarded half the Nobel Prize for physics. In 1919, he was sent as a delegate to the Peace Conference in Paris, and he was made a Marchese in 1929.

He died in Rome on 20th July, 1937, and was buried in Bologna, the place of his birth.

RADAR

On a summer's day in 1935, British scientists at a secret laboratory on the east coast of England watched a line of light traced out on the base of a cathode ray tube. Slowly, a V-shaped notch moved along the line of light until eventually it reached the edge of the tube and disappeared.

This experiment was a historic one. It marked the beginning of a novel technique for detecting and locating aircraft, which was to play a major role in the Second World War. It became known as radar.

TIMELY INTRODUCTION

The first experimental radar station was built in 1935, and by the time war broke out, in 1939, there were some 40 stations around the south and east coasts of Britain. These were the radar stations which enabled observers to spot and trace the route of enemy aircraft during the Battle of Britain in 1940, even when the planes were flying in the dark or above the clouds. With the help of radar, the Royal Air Force was able to locate the position of approaching bombers and to attack them before they could reach their objectives.

The development of radar began in Britain during the early 1930s. Experiments had been carried out which involved sending radio waves into the upper atmosphere. This was part of an investigation of the reflecting layers of the upper atmosphere from which radio waves were "bounced back" to Earth.

It was noticed that planes flying in the vicinity would often upset these experiments by reflecting radio waves which gave a " false " echo in the receiver. At that time, British military authorities were becoming very concerned about the vulnerability of British cities to air attack in the event of another war, and were seeking ways of getting adequate warning of the approach of enemy planes.

DETECTING AND RANGING

In 1934, a British physicist, Robert Watson-Watt, suggested that the reflection of radio waves by aircraft, noticed during the experiments in atmospheric research, could be developed to provide a technique for detecting and locating aircraft. The speed at which radio waves travel is known and constant, about 186,000 miles a second, so that by measuring the time taken for waves to reach an aircraft and return to the transmitter it would be possible to assess the distance of the plane from the transmitter. And by determining the direction from which the " echo " returned, it would be possible to establish the exact position of the plane in the sky.

Research began immediately in order to find out whether this technique could be made the basis of a practical location system. By the summer of 1935, radar—a word coined from Radio Detection and Ranging—had become an accomplished fact. The V-shaped notch of light which moved across the screen of the cathode ray tube in that early demonstration was caused by the radio waves reflected from a Wallace aircraft heading out to sea. When the plane was 34 miles away, the notch disappeared. But, as the Wallace returned, the notch reappeared when the plane came within 32½ miles. Its course was plotted as it flew towards the coast.

WAR-TIME DEVELOPMENT

By the time the Second World War began, British scientists had developed radar into an efficient radio-location system. The pulses of radio waves transmitted were between 6 and 14 metres in wave-length, and the waves were " broadcast "; they " floodlit " the area around the transmitter.

This type of radar was effective up to a range of about 150 miles, but it was of limited use against low-flying planes. Attempts to improve this early radar centred largely on using waves of smaller and smaller wave-length, and increasing the power of the pulses of waves which were transmitted.

INCREASING ACCURACY WITH SHORT WAVES

As time went on, the use of powerful short-wave radar enabled scientists to focus the radio beams with increasing accuracy. " Searchlight " radar beams were transmitted from rotating aerials which swept the sky on all sides of the transmitter. This type of radar combined with the earlier type of " floodlight " radar to provide the location system which served Britain so well in the early days of the war.

In 1940, a British physicist, Professor J. T. Randall, devised an instrument called a cavity magnetron which made possible the transmission of high-power pulses of radio waves of only a few centimetres wave-length. This and other devices brought revolutionary improvements in radar by increasing its accuracy and range.

By 1943, some hundreds of radar sets carried in planes were using these very short waves; they were invaluable in helping to overcome the U-boat menace.

THE " BOTTLE "

The increasing precision of radar resulted in a technique called P.P.I. (Plan Position Indicator), in which the "blips" on the trace of the cathode ray screen were replaced by an actual map of the district in range of the transmitter.

In a P.P.I. radar set, the line of light traced on the base of the cathode ray tube, known familiarly to pilots as the " bottle ", runs as a radial line from the centre of the tube

Radar (originally called Radiolocation, which accurately describes the process), installed on the turret of a ship.

towards the edge. As the aerial of the transmitter rotates, the line of light on the cathode ray screen is made to rotate at the same speed. Any radio waves returning as an echo are made to increase the brightness of the line at a point depending on the distance of the object causing reflection. The obstacles in any particular direction from the transmitter thus show up as bright spots on the line corresponding to that direction.

ACCURATE RADAR MAP

As the line is rotating in time with the rotating aerial, reflecting obstacles around the transmitter are shown as bright spots on the base of the tube. They remain in view on the tube as a result of the sustained glow of the material forming the cathode ray screen. This continues to emit light for a fraction of a second after the cathode ray line has moved on, and is still glowing when the line returns after completing a revolution of the base of the tube.

P.P.I. radar thus provides what is in effect a radar map of the district in range of the transmitter. The reflecting powers of different materials, such as land and water, differ sufficiently to create echo spots of varying intensities on the radar screen, so that the screen gives, for example, an actual picture of the ground over which an aircraft is flying, or of the ships in a harbour which is shrouded in fog.

The ability of radio waves to penetrate darkness and fog has revolutionised transport control in many ways since the end of the war. Radar enables ships to find their way safely through impenetrable fogs at sea, and guides planes into the airport when visibility is almost nil.

MYSTERY OF THE MERRY DANCERS

A curtain of light flickers over the northern sky. Huge rays stab the darkness as though seeking an intruder from space. The sky glows green and then violet, pink and then blue. The rays converge, forming a cone of light that sets the heavens on fire. The climax has been reached in nature's mammoth midnight spectacle: the aurora borealis, or Northern Lights.

For thousands of years, the aurora borealis has remained a mystery to science. The ancient Greeks believed that the lights were lit by the gods as a portent of evil things to come. To-day, we seek a more rational explanation, and physicists are studying the aurora in the hope of discovering a little more of what goes on in space.

The auroral lights can be seen most often, and with the greatest intensity, on a line that roughly circles the Earth's magnetic pole, passing between the Faroe Islands and Iceland, skirting the south of Greenland and the northern coasts of Europe and Asia. North or south of this line, the frequency of the aurora drops away rapidly.

In the Shetlands, the northern lights dance across the sky almost one night in three; people of the islands call them the Merry Dancers, and accept the lights as casually as they accept the rising sun.

In Scotland, the lights are seen during some twenty nights of the year; in London, there are only about seven auroral displays in an average year. And in southern France they are seen so rarely that they can strike terror into the hearts of people who have never heard of them before.

HYDROGEN SHOWERS

Using modern techniques of light-analysis, scientists have shown that auroral light is coming from atoms of oxygen and nitrogen gases of the air, which are excited by some sort of electrical agitation. Also, atoms of hydrogen gas have been detected in the auroral regions, approaching the Earth in huge showers at speeds estimated at 2000 to 3000 miles a second.

For a long time, scientists have known that the auroral lights come and go in cycles of increasing and decreasing intensity. In peak years, the lights are brilliant and rarely leave the northern sky; they are seen much farther south than they usually are, reaching down towards the Mediterranean.

The rhythm of this auroral cycle brings activity to its height every 11 years. And it has been noticed that this 11-year cycle follows a similar sunspot cycle on the sun.

Dark patches on the sun, which we call sunspots, are believed to be areas of intense activity. Great surges of atomic upheaval boil up from inside the sun. Accompanying these eruptions, huge flares soar out from the sun's surface into space, and associated with these flares are streams of electrically-charged atomic particles that are squirted from the sun like water from a hose.

These huge jets of fast-moving particles are believed to be the cause of our auroras. As they sweep into the upper atmosphere, they bombard the atoms of oxygen and nitrogen, dislodging electrons from the orbits of the atoms. Light is emitted, and we see the aurora.

Experiments with miniature magnetic "Earths" have shown that a stream of fast-moving atomic particles such as electrons will tend to converge over two areas corresponding to the magnetic poles. As the sun's particle-showers approach the Earth, they are caught up as though by a huge magnet, and sweep in towards the north and south magnetic poles.

We now believe that the jets from the sun consist of hydrogen atoms carrying an electric charge. They are not directed specifically at the Earth, but we happen to get in the way of them.

Although a lot of hydrogen must reach our upper atmosphere in this way, little of it penetrates to lower levels. Unlike the mammoth sun, the Earth does not possess the gravitational pull that is needed to capture and hold the fast-moving hydrogen atoms.

Like most theories, this modern theory of the aurora is not a perfect one. It has been widely accepted, but often with misgivings. One difficulty that has arisen, for example, is that the streams of particles from the sun cannot consist entirely of positively-charged hydrogen atoms. A stream of this sort would disperse, as the particles would repel each other.

To overcome this, scientists have suggested that the jet includes a corresponding number of negative electrons, so that the stream as a whole is neutral.

Following a straight-line path between the sun and the Earth, the hydrogen particles would need to travel at 1000 miles a second to get here when they do. But, in fact, the jet will be curved, just as a jet of water is curved when it comes from a moving hose. Also, the magnetism of the Earth will tend to make the particles take a spiral path as they sweep towards the poles. The total distance covered must therefore be a good deal more than the 93 million miles that separates us from the sun.

Estimates have put the speed of the particles at 2000 miles a second or more: over 7 million miles an hour.

Electro-Magnetism

Ever since about 1800, scientists have realised that there is some connection between magnetic and electrical phenomena. They noticed that flashes of lightning and of electric sparks affected the needle of a compass. They observed that when lightning strikes steel objects it turns them into magnets capable of attracting iron particles. And they concluded that if magnets have north and south poles, displaying powers of attraction and repulsion, then positive and negative electrical charges might be expected to have similar properties.

A DANISH SCIENTIST'S DISCOVERY

Soon after Volta invented the electrical battery it was discovered that electricity and magnetism were closely related; under certain conditions each was capable of generating the other. This phenomenon, first revealed by the Danish physicist Christian Oersted, in 1820, is called electromagnetism.

While he was giving a physics lesson at Copenhagen, Oersted connected a platinum wire to the poles of a battery and placed beneath it a magnetic needle lying lengthwise and parallel to the wire. As the electric current flowed through the wire, the needle began to move until it was standing at right angles to the wire. Oersted himself did not fully realise how important his discovery was, but news of it spread to other scientists and curiosity and interest were aroused. Experiments were made with conductor wires of copper, iron and other metals, and it was noted that the needle was invariably affected by the current flowing through the wire.

The French physicist André Marie Ampère was the first to explain this fact properly and to formulate a law of electromagnetism, namely that *an electric current creates a magnetic field around itself.*

Ampère proved that attraction and repulsion took place

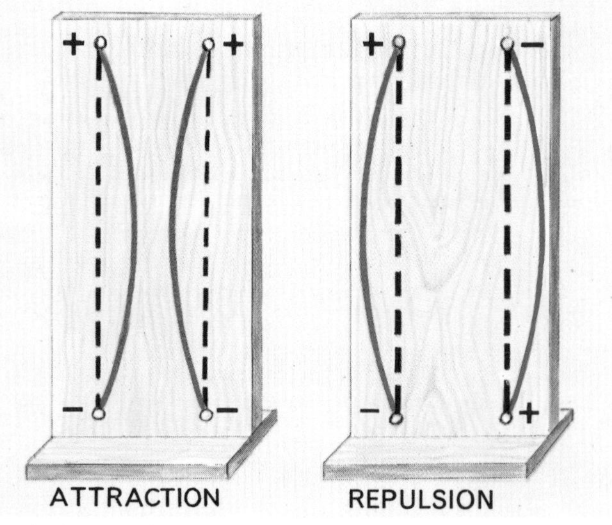

Ampère's experiment showed that two parallel wires carrying electric currents flowing in the same direction are attracted to each other. When the current flows in opposite directions, the wires repel one another.

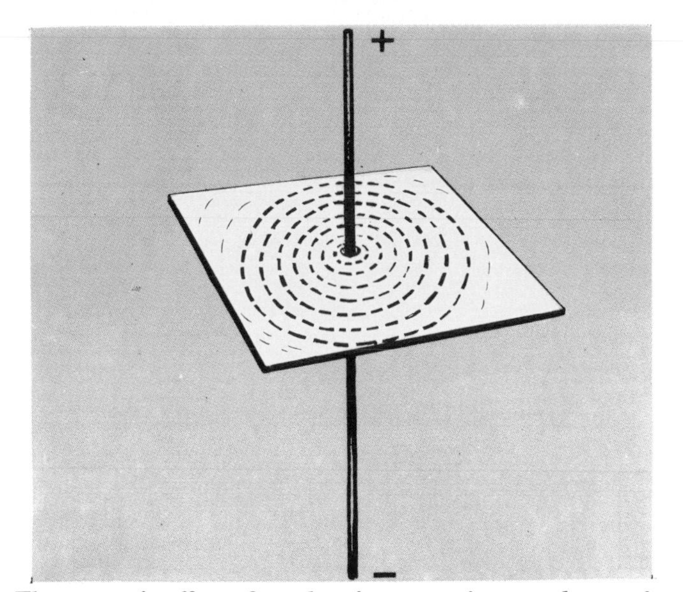

The magnetic effect of an electric current is seen when a wire carrying a current is passed through a sheet of cardboard covered with iron filings.

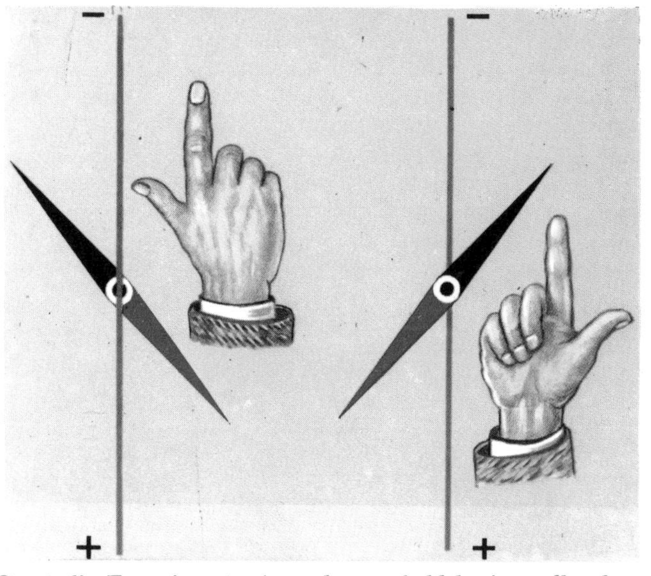

Oersted's Experiment. *A conductor, held horizontally above a compass needle in a direction along the axis of the needle, causes the needle to be deflected to the right or left, depending on the direction of the current. If the needle is placed above, the direction of deflection is reversed.*

when two electrically charged wires were set side by side in a parallel position. He showed that when an electric current passed through them in the same direction the wires attracted each other and tended to draw closer. On the other hand, when the current was passed through them in opposite directions they repelled and drew away from each other. The experiment was carried a stage further by running the wire through a sheet of paper spread with iron filings. It was then seen that the magnetic field set up by the electric current took the form of concentric circles centring on the wire and spreading out at right angles to the direction in which the current was moving.

The direction of the lines of force may be memorised by the Corkscrew Rule, which states that the direction of current and of lines of force correspond to the direction of motion and rotation of a right-hand corkscrew. Another way of remembering it is the Right Hand Rule—if you grasp the wire in the right hand with the thumb pointing along the current, the fingers point round in the direction of the lines of force.

GALVANOMETERS AND GALVANOSCOPES

Meanwhile, Johann Schweigger had invented an ingenious instrument which is now called the *galvanometer* in honour of Galvani who perfected it. Its purpose was to measure the strength of electric currents.

An even simpler instrument is the *galvanoscope* which anyone can build for himself. All that is necessary is to make a circular coil of well-insulated wire about one-tenth of a millimetre in thickness. The centre part, which is left empty —see illustration below—should be large enough to contain a razor blade suspended by a silk thread. The blade, which should first be magnetised, serves as a needle. Directly the wires are attached to the screws at the base the blade will begin to move and change direction, even though the current may be only one-thousandth of one amp.

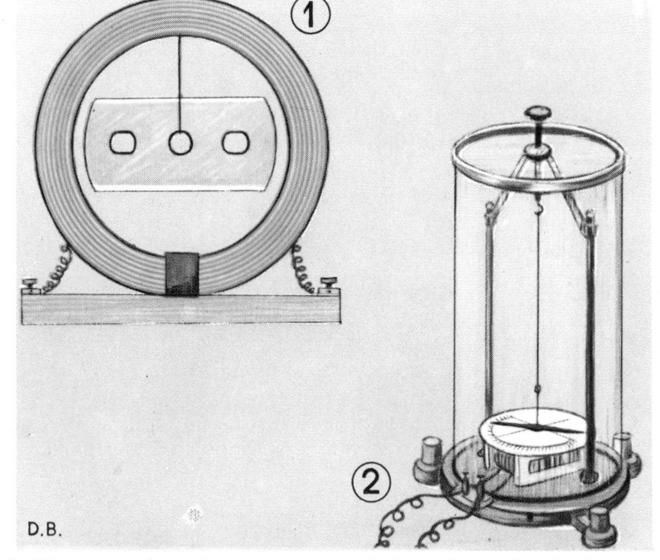

1. *Home-made galvanoscope consisting of a coil of wire, two screw terminals and a razor blade.* 2. *A galvanometer consisting of a magnetic needle set over a coil measures the strength of an electric current.*

A SIMPLE ELECTROMAGNET

The word " amp "—short for ampere, which is a unit of electric current—derives from the name of the A. M. Ampère who now set himself the task of constructing an artificial magnet. With the aid of a simple device, consisting of wire wrapped in spirals round a specially shaped core, he created two magnetic poles, North and South, at either end of the apparatus. The apparatus, which is called a solenoid, functions only when the current is on. It then becomes a simple electromagnet. When the current is switched off it loses it magnetic force.

François Arago, another Frenchman, succeeded in increasing the strength of Ampère's electromagnet by fitting the solenoid with a tiny cylinder of soft iron or of steel. If the cylinder is of steel, the instrument remains permanently magnetised. Meanwhile Michael Faraday, chemist and physicist, had been working on these problems and, in 1832, was to show that magnetism itself could be used for generating electricity.

THE WORK OF MICHAEL FARADAY

Faraday experimented with magnets brought into proximity with a solenoid which had been wired to a galvanometer. On inserting the north pole of a magnet into the solenoid, a current sufficiently strong to swing the galvanometer needle was created; when the south pole was inserted the needle moved in the opposite direction. This phenomenon became known as *electromagnetic induction.*

Electro-magnets like this one are often used for lifting scrap iron. When the current is switched off, the iron falls.

The relationship of magnetism and electricity and the interplay of these two forces have made a great contribution to raising the material level of our civilisation. The saving in manpower which this discovery has effected is immense. We should not therefore forget the names of scientists like Faraday, Ampère and Oersted whose experiments in electromagnetism prepared the way for the more recent application of electrical technology to alternators, dynamos, and telephonic and telegraphic installations.

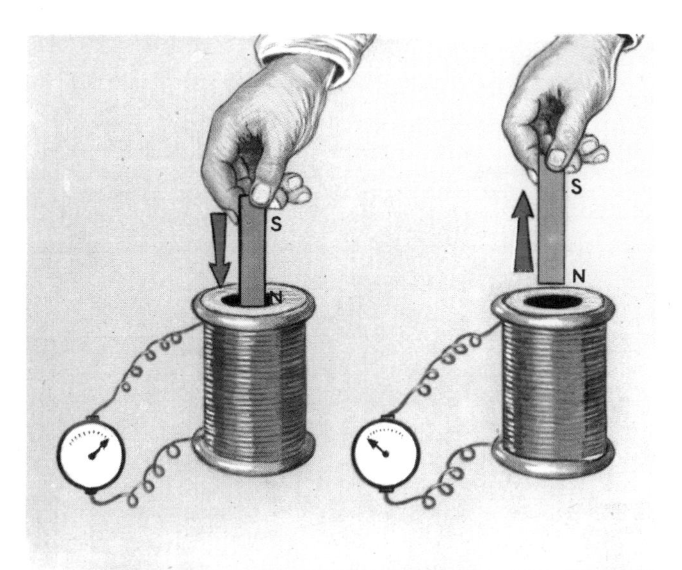

The principle of electro-magnetic induction was proved by Michael Faraday, the renowned experimental physicist, who showed that a magnet pushed into a coil produces an electric current which is detected by the galvanometer (left). *On withdrawing the magnet* (right), *the galvanometer needle swings in the opposite direction. When the South Pole of the magnet is inserted, the needle's movements are reversed.*

OUR SOLAR SYSTEM

From time to time in the night sky a wandering star appears—a star unmarked on any star-map. It looks just like a star but if watched night after night it is seen to move slowly among the stars. If examined through a telescope it is straightway seen to be not just a point of light but a round patch or disc of light. It is a planet, a body much nearer to us than any of the stars and one which shines by reflecting sunlight. Like the Earth, it has no light of its own and moves in a great path round the sun, being held captive by the sun.

The sun controls a family of nine major planets. They are at different distances from the sun but all travel round it in one and the same direction, thereby forming a kind of one-way traffic system. They are also at immensely great distances from the sun and from one another. The Earth, for example, is about 93 million miles from the sun and has Venus and Mars for its nearest planetary neighbours. Yet at its closest Venus is no less than 24,600,000 miles from the Earth, and Mars at its closest is about 35,000,000 miles away. In comparison with these great distances the planets are quite small bodies: the sun's empire is far-flung but extremely empty.

VARYING ORBITS

The planets move around the sun in oval-shaped or *elliptical* orbits and no one planet, therefore, keeps at a constant distance from the sun. The Earth, for example, can be 91,500,000 miles from the sun at its nearest and 94,500,000 miles at its farthest. The figure usually given, 93 million miles, is the mean or average distance. A range in distance of 3 million miles is very large by earthly standards, but in relation to the immense size of the Earth's orbit it is quite small. This means that although that orbit is an ellipse, the ellipse departs very little from a circle.

Between the Earth and the sun move the two planets Mercury and Venus. Mercury lies nearest to the sun, and at an average distance of 36 million miles travels once round the sun in about 88 days. It is certainly the swiftest of all the planets, travelling all the time at a speed between 23 to 35 miles a second. It is also the smallest planet, its diameter of 3,100 miles making it about half as large again as the moon. Being so small, it has probably been unable to prevent any atmosphere it might have had in the past from flying away: if it has an atmosphere, it is doubtless an extremely thin one. Life as we know it could not possibly exist on Mercury. As it travels round the sun it rotates only once on its axis and therefore turns one side or hemisphere always to the sun. On this side the sun beats down without mercy, causing the surface temperature to reach that of the melting point of lead. On the other side, facing always away from the sun, eternal darkness reigns, except, of course, for the light of the stars. On that side the temperature probably almost reaches absolute zero, or −273° C.

BRIGHTEST NEIGHBOUR

Venus moves at an average distance of 67,200,000 miles and therefore gets a smaller share of the sun's light and heat than does Mercury. Unlike Mercury, Venus has an atmosphere, and one so laden with clouds that the planet's surface is entirely hidden from view. Some astronomers think that the surface may have little if any dry land—that beneath the clouds lies one great ocean of water. Yet all attempts to detect oxygen and water vapour in the planet's atmosphere have so far failed, although the presence of the gas carbon-dioxide has been confirmed. Even so, the means at our disposal restrict us to observing the upper levels of the atmosphere: there may be plenty of oxygen and water

THE SUN'S FAMILY OF PLANETS. *Closest to the sun is tiny Mercury; next is Venus, a mystery planet completely covered by dense white cloud, then comes the Earth. Beyond Earth lies the planet Mars, and beyond Mars lies Jupiter, the biggest member of the family, then Saturn with its beautiful rings. Farther out lie Uranus and Neptune, bitterly cold because of their immense distance from the sun, and farther out still is tiny Pluto, lonely and remote.*

MYSTERIOUS MARS. *The most intriguing planet in the solar system is Mars, a "twin" of Earth. It has seasons during which the surface changes colour. Mars has ice caps which extend in winter and melt in summer. Around Mars rotates two tiny moons, Phobos and Deimos, 10 and 5 miles in diameter, respectively. Men may land on these before exploring the surface of Mars.*

vapour nearer the surface. Venus is often referred to as a sister-planet to the Earth, yet it is like the Earth in only two respects—the clouds in its atmosphere and its size, 7,700 miles (only 200 miles less than the polar diameter of the Earth).

As seen from the Earth, both Mercury and Venus keep fairly close to the sun and therefore never appear in our skies in the hours near midnight. Venus is the more brilliant of the two, and when well-removed from the sun becomes, after the sun and moon, the third brightest object in the sky. When watched through a telescope over several weeks, both Mercury and Venus are seen to go through a cycle of phases, but unlike the moon they change considerably in apparent diameter owing to the great range in their distances from us.

" SUPERIOR " PLANETS

Beyond the Earth move the planets Mars, Jupiter, Saturn, Uranus, Neptune and Pluto—in this order. They are called " superior planets ", but are superior only in the sense that their orbits are larger than the Earth's. Of the six, the planet Mars is a comparatively near neighbour of ours. With a diameter of 4,200 miles it is smaller than the Earth, and at its average distance of 142 million miles from the sun it takes nearly 687 days to complete one orbital journey.

Yet in some ways Mars resembles the Earth. It rotates once in 24 hours 37 minutes, its equator is inclined at nearly 24 degrees to the plane of its orbit, and it has an atmosphere clear enough to let us see right down to its surface. This surface appears to be fairly smooth (there are, at least, no ranges of high mountains) and to have an overall reddish colour. This colour is clearly that of the surface rocks and indicates desert-like country. There is evidence of much dust, for sometimes a large area of the planet's surface is hidden from view by a yellowish blanket, thought to be swirling clouds of surface dust.

" LIFE " ON MARS

In addition, there are greyish-green markings which in many places change in colour and shape during the course of the Martian year. These are probably areas of vegetation. The plants in them, however, must be immensely hardy by our standards. They exist in an atmosphere which contains hardly any water vapour and oxygen and which is rarer than the air on the top of Mount Everest. They also have to endure intense cold. At the Martian equator, with the sun high in the sky, the temperature is only slightly above the freezing point of water. At sunset it drops below zero and by midnight is well on the way to 50 degrees of frost. Furthermore, the plants must occasionally be smothered by dust, but this appears to be no great handicap. Any changes in the dark markings are largely changes in detail: the overall pattern is fairly permanent and can be recorded as such on maps and charts.

POLAR CAPS

Mars has two dazzling-white polar caps. These change in size according to the seasons, being large in winter and dwindling down to almost nothing in summer. They are, however, completely different from the polar caps of the Earth. At the most each cap is a layer of snow less than an inch or so thick, but it may be just white frost—a deposit of ice crystals on the frozen ground. So rare is the air above the caps that at the return of spring the snow or frost does not so much melt into water as change directly into the invisible vapour state. As a cap diminishes in size so a " wave of darkening " spreads slowly down towards the planet's equator and beyond. The dark markings, not very clearly defined in winter, become both darker and more sharply defined. This suggests that the moisture, released by the gradual evaporation of the cap, moves towards lower latitudes to help to waken the vegetation from its winter sleep.

THE " CANALS "

Astronomers, looking at Mars through large telescopes,

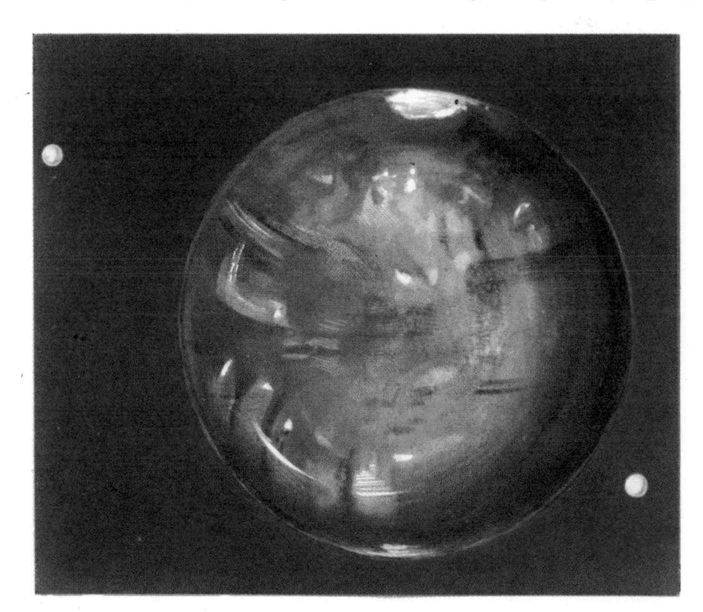

Early astronomers thought the surface of Mars was covered with a pattern of straight lines, and assumed these canals were an immense irrigation system, distributing water over a parched and dying planet. We now know that these lines are not complete, and may be natural clefts or valleys on the surface of the planet, but we will not know until men land and find out.

have sometimes traced narrow dusky streaks across its surface. At times these streaks looked almost like lines and appeared to form a network strongly suggestive of a system of canals. About sixty years ago the American astronomer, P. Lowell, claimed that the lines were natural waterways, built by the Martians to carry water from the polar regions to the arid equatorial deserts. Nowadays the lines are generally regarded as an optical effect—that in reality the astronomer is looking at a comparative jumble of tiny specks and patches and unconsciously joins them to form lines. In other words, if we could get closer to the Martian surface we should see not lines at all but a patchwork of bright and dark patches, perhaps part barren desert and part vegetation.

MARTIAN MOONS

Mars has two tiny moons, Phobos and Deimos. They are so small and so far away that we can only estimate their true sizes. Phobos, thought to have a diameter of only 10 miles, moves round Mars at an average distance of 3,760 miles in 7 hours 39 minutes. It therefore moves faster than a point near the Martian equator and seen from Mars would appear to rise in the west and set in the east. Deimos has a diameter of about 5 miles and is at an average distance of 12,500 miles from the Martian surface. It goes round once in about 30 hours, and if watched from a point near the planet's equator would stay above the horizon for more than 60 hours.

JUPITER

Far beyond Mars, at an average distance of 483 million miles from the sun, moves Jupiter, the largest of all the planets. If we represented the sun by a ball two feet across, Jupiter would be about the size of an orange, while a pea could be used for the Earth. About 1,300 Earths could be packed inside Jupiter. The distance across its equator is 88,700 miles, but that between its poles is 82,800 miles. This gives Jupiter a decidedly flattened or squashed appearance, and it is brought about by the planet's very rapid rotation. At its equator, Jupiter rotates once in only 9 hours 50 minutes, so that objects on the surface are whirled around the distant centre at the remarkable speed of nearly 28,000 miles an hour. If an object had this speed on the Earth it would be flung off, to leave the Earth for ever, but since Jupiter is about 318 times more massive than the Earth it keeps a much tighter hold on the things on its surface. For example, if you weighed 10 stone on the Earth you would weigh over 3 cwt. on Jupiter!

We have no direct way of finding out whether or not Jupiter has a solid surface. All we see when we study the planet through telescopes are the tops of dense layers of clouds. These layers give the planet a banded or belted appearance in small telescopes, but larger ones show that the bands contain a great amount of detail. The detail, however, is the tops of cloud masses: it changes continually, indicating that Jupiter's atmosphere is a highly turbulent one. By studying the positions and movements of particular patches and spots, astronomers have found that Jupiter's speed of rotation is greatest at the equator and gets less towards the poles. They can also make reasonable guesses about conditions lower down and the nature of the forces which operate there.

The clouds on Jupiter are completely different from those on the Earth. They consist largely of crystals of frozen gases like ammonia and methane which float in an atmosphere of hydrogen and helium. All these gases are poisonous to life as we know it.

Jupiter has a family of twelve satellites, the four largest of which were discovered about 1609, just after the telescope was invented. These four are each about the size of the moon and can be seen quite easily through a good pair of binoculars. The others, however, are quite small in comparison, ranging in size from 100 miles down to about 12 miles.

SATURN

Beyond Jupiter moves Saturn, another giant planet, at a distance of 886 million miles from the sun. Saturn is therefore about nine times the Earth's distance from the

The most wonderful sight in the solar system is undoubtedly Saturn with its 9 moons and its incredible system of rings. The rings are probably made up of countless particles of powdered rock and grit of unknown minuteness widely separated, yet close enough to appear as solid matter when viewed from Earth. For all their apparent solidity, the rings are extremely thin, probably 10 miles or less in depth. Saturn, itself, is covered by clouds or vapour.

With a diameter of 86,700 miles, Jupiter is by far the biggest planet in the solar system. It could hold 1,300 Earths, or all the other planets put together. Jupiter is covered with an immensely thick atmosphere of ammonia and marsh-gas, and may have no solid surface such as has the Earth. Future explorers may land on her moons, and not on the planet itself.

sun and takes nearly 29½ years to complete its orbit. Like Jupiter, its globe is flattened; the diameter at the equator is 75,100 miles, that across the poles is 67,200 miles—a difference of nearly 8,000 miles, or the diameter of the Earth.

Saturn is another cloudy planet and its atmosphere appears to contain gases similar to those found on Jupiter. Its cloud belts, however, are less prominent than those on Jupiter, but observations of occasional spots and patches tell us that it rotates once in 10 hours 14 minutes at its equator.

Saturn is unique in being girdled by a system of rings. At first sight the rings look quite solid, but they are really made up of myriads of little moons, or better, ice-like particles. They have an overall width of about 40,000 miles but are so thin (a mere 10 to 20 miles) that when seen edge-on they disappear completely, even when Saturn is observed through a very large telescope.

Saturn has nine satellites. One, named Titan, has a diameter of 3,000 miles (almost the size of Mercury), and is far larger than any of the others. The other eight range in size from 850 miles down to about 150 miles and are therefore very faint objects.

THE FARTHEST PLANETS

Until 1781 it was thought that the sun had only six planets, but in that year William Herschel discovered a seventh, Uranus. With a diameter of 29,300 miles, Uranus is almost in the giant class, but since it moves at an average distance from the sun of 1,783 million miles it appears in our skies as just a faint star. Its atmosphere, like those of Jupiter and Saturn, is probably rich in hydrogen and helium. Clouds of methane and ammonia hide any solid surface from view, although most of the ammonia is probably frozen solid. It has five satellites: they are comparatively small and move in orbits which are all steeply inclined to the planet's own orbit.

NEPTUNE

Neptune and Pluto, the two outermost planets were not discovered until recent times. Irregularities in the motion of Uranus led two astronomers, Adams, of England, and Leverrier, of France, to predict the mass and position of a disturbing planet which, they said was moving beyond Uranus. As a result the new planet, Neptune, was first picked up on 23rd September, 1846, by the German astronomer Galle, who found it very near the predicted position. At a later date, further and smaller irregularities in the motion of Uranus led astronomers to search for yet another planet. As a result, Pluto was discovered in 1930, by Tombaugh, an astronomer at the Lowel Observatory, Flagstaff, Arizona.

PLUTO

Neptune keeps at an average distance from the sun of 2,793 million miles, while Pluto lies far beyond at 3,666 million miles. Pluto's distance from the sun is, therefore, about forty times the Earth's and it takes just over 248 years to go once round the sun. To an observer on Pluto the sun would look just like an intensely bright point of light.

Both planets must be extremely cold; so far as we can tell they are frozen worlds which have never known life and never will. Neptune, with two satellites, has a diameter of 27,700 miles. Pluto appears to have no satellites. Its diameter, still a little uncertain, seems to be nearly 5,000 miles. If this is so, Pluto is smaller than the Earth and only slightly larger than Mars.

EXTREME ISOLATION

By earthly standards the solar system is of immense size. Yet it is surprisingly empty: the planets are extremely small in comparison with the great distances which separate them one from another. It is also a fairly flat system: the orbits of the planets lie almost in one and the same plane. If the solar system out to Saturn could be reduced down to the size of a half-crown, the orbits of the planets would easily fit inside. Yet on this scale the nearest star after the sun would be a quarter of a mile away. The solar system is not only large, empty and flat—it is also extremely isolated in space.

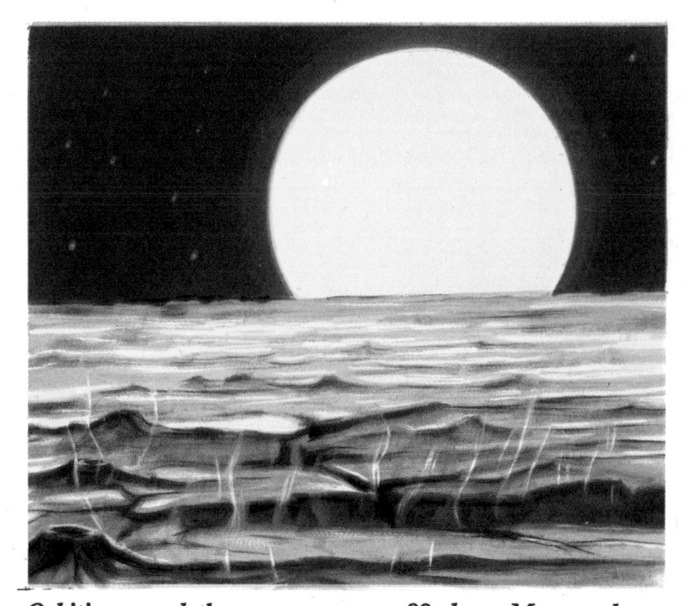

Orbiting round the sun once every 88 days, Mercury keeps one face permanently turned towards the blazing globe only 36 million miles away. This side thus has everlasting daylight and the surface is hot enough to melt lead. The other face, in permanent darkness, is bitterly cold.

COSMIC RAYS

Throughout our entire lives, we are all being bombarded by a storm of flying particles, which penetrate our bodies and reach deep down into the Earth itself. These particles are the cosmic rays.

Scientists have known about these rays for many years, and have studied them intensively. Yet they remain very much of a mystery. We know little of how they are formed, or where they come from. Their very name—cosmic rays—is a confession of our ignorance. They are rays that come from somewhere in the cosmos.

After travelling through space, the cosmic rays that reach the surface of the Earth are not the same as those which first enter the Earth's atmosphere. They are influenced and affected by collision with the particles of gas in the atmosphere as they continue on their way towards the surface of the Earth. The original rays which come from somewhere out in space are called the primary cosmic rays; those which are formed from the primary rays as they speed through the atmosphere are the secondary rays.

TREMENDOUS SPEEDS

Both forms of cosmic ray consist of tiny particles of matter, smaller than atoms, travelling at tremendous speeds; they are sub-atomic bullets generated by atomic disruptions taking place somewhere in the universe.

Man has been living in this atomic hailstorm ever since he appeared on Earth, and it looks as though he will have to go on being bombarded by cosmic rays until the end of time. There is nothing he can do to prevent them arriving in an incessant stream from their mysterious source.

During the early years of the present century, when physicists were beginning to probe into the inner secrets of the atom, they noticed that the air at ground level was able to conduct appreciable amounts of electricity. They suspected that this was due to the influence of some sort of fast-moving particle which was flying through the air. It was known that this is a characteristic of such flying particles; they make gases conduct electricity.

SOURCE IN SPACE

At first, scientists thought that these particles were being thrown out by radioactive substances in the Earth's crust. But the pioneer British atom scientist, C. T. R. Wilson, suspected that the rays came, not from the Earth itself, but from some source out in space. No matter how carefully he insulated his laboratory apparatus, Wilson found that rays were able to penetrate the insulation and cause leakage of electricity through the air inside. The particles responsible seemed to possess amazing power of penetration, far greater than those of the sub-atomic bullets emitted by radioactive substances such as radium.

In 1909, a Swiss scientist, A. Gockel, ascended to a height of 2½ miles in a balloon, carrying detecting equipment with him. He found that the rays were more intense at this height than at ground level. In the following year, an Austrian scientist, Victor Hess, found that the rays were even stronger at a height of 3¼ miles. And in 1913, a German physicist showed that the rays at a height of 6 miles were thirty times as active as at sea-level. It was obvious by this time that Wilson's suggestions were correct; the rays were coming from outside the Earth. Hess gave them the name cosmic rays.

CONTINUOUS BOMBARDMENT

Since those early days, research on cosmic rays has become a part of the world-wide research on atomic physics generally; and much has been discovered about the nature of the rays. We know that the secondary rays reach the Earth in surprising numbers. More than a thousand particles penetrate the human body during every minute of every day.

The secondary rays consist of several types of sub-atomic particle. Some of them are "soft" and are easily absorbed by matter; they have only modest powers of penetration. Others are "hard" rays which are immensely powerful, and can penetrate almost anything that is in their path. These are the rays that upset the experiments of the physicists during the early part of the century.

PENETRATING MESONS

The "hard" cosmic rays will travel through many miles of the atmosphere and continue into the Earth itself. They have been detected at the bottom of the deepest mines, and on the ocean bed, still travelling downwards after penetrating thousands of feet of rock or water.

Shortly before World War II, these supremely powerful cosmic rays were identified as a new form of sub-atomic particle called a meson. Inside the nucleus of the atom, mesons are being constantly created and absorbed. They take part in the complex interplay of forces that hold the nuclei of the atom together, acting as a sort of nuclear glue.

The "soft" rays include electrons, the tiny particles carrying a negative electric charge, which circulate round the atomic nucleus like planets round the sun. These electrons have only slight powers of penetration; they are formed by the atomic disruption of atoms in the atmosphere as a result of bombardment by the primary cosmic rays.

The showers of electrons produced in this way include another small particle, the positron, which is the positive counterpart to the electron. Pairs of electrons and positrons are formed by the disintegration of photons, particles of light.

The primary rays which reach the atmosphere from somewhere out in space are believed to consist largely of protons. These are the comparatively large particles, carrying a positive electric charge, which are present in the nuclei of atoms. Travelling at high speed, these cosmic ray protons disrupt the nuclei of atoms in the gases of the atmosphere. As a result of the atomic explosions, atomic fragments including mesons are formed, together with electrons and positrons which build up into showers as they speed on towards the earth.

TWO MESON TYPES

During World War II, research on atomic physics was

intensified, and many new facts were discovered about cosmic rays, some of which did not fit into this simple scheme of cosmic ray activity. The meson particle, for example, was not behaving as the physicists believed it ought to.

At Bristol University, Professor C. Powell and his colleagues worked out a method of carrying cosmic ray research high into the atmosphere. These Bristol scientists found that photographic plates exposed to cosmic rays could be made to show up the tracks of sub-atomic particles formed by collision between the cosmic rays and atoms inside the photographic emulsion itself. The particles formed by the atomic disintegration took their own photographs as they sped away from the scene of the collision.

Using this technique, scientists were able to study the effects of cosmic ray activity more effectively, and at great heights in the atmosphere. Photographic equipment carried up by huge balloons, for example, could extend cosmic ray research into regions where the primary rays are colliding with atoms of atmospheric gas to form secondary rays.

COLLISIONS PHOTOGRAPHED

When photographic plates were exposed at heights of 10,000 feet in the Andes mountains, tracks formed by mesons were traced out in the plates. But it was found that the track of a meson ended abruptly with the formation of another particle. This new particle was identified as a different meson, slightly lighter than the first one. There were apparently at least two forms of meson, the first one decaying into the second almost as soon as it had been liberated, following the primary ray collision.

This discovery explained some of the anomalies that had been discovered in cosmic ray behaviour. The first-produced meson, which is now called a pi-meson, is some 270 times as heavy as an electron. It survives for only about one-hundred-millionth of a second before turning into the mu-meson which is about 210 times as heavy as an electron.

The mesons travel very fast and cover immense distances. As the mu-meson decays it produces high-speed electrons and another sub-atomic particle called the neutrino.

The primary cosmic ray which forms these mesons is rarely able to reach the ground itself. As it penetrates deeper and deeper into the atmosphere, the odds against it avoiding collision increase rapidly. The atoms of gas in the atmosphere are packed together more and more densely as the height above sea-level diminishes.

MAXIMUM ACTIVITY

At a height of 120,000 feet, the primary rays are still streaming down almost unchecked; at 60,000 feet more than half of them have been absorbed. The atomic fragments produced by collision between the primary rays and atoms of atmospheric gas are, in turn, involved in collisions as they speed onwards to the ground. Gradually, their energies become spent, and the number and vigour of the flying particles diminishes towards sea-level.

At 60,000—75,000 feet, cosmic ray activity reaches a maximum. Here, the primary rays are bombarding atoms of atmospheric gases, forming new sub-atomic particles. These fragments come into collision with the tight-packed atoms in the lower strata of the air. The intensity of cosmic ray activity falls away with increasing height until at 120,000 feet it steadies to nearly 100 times that of sea-level. This represents the activity of the original rays that are arriving from somewhere out in space.

This variation in the nature and intensity of cosmic ray activity at different levels in the atmosphere has carried scientific research into strange places. There are cosmic ray laboratories perched high on mountain tops, such as the Jungfraujoch Laboratory 12,000 feet up in the Swiss Alps. There is also a cosmic ray laboratory deep underground on a platform of Holborn tube station.

QUESTIONS AND ANSWERS

What is Diamond?

Diamond is a form of the element carbon, in which the atoms are arranged in a special geometrical pattern that gives the diamond its characteristic crystalline shape.

There is no chemical difference between diamond and the carbon of charcoal or graphite. They differ only in the way that their atoms are arranged in space.

Ever since it was discovered that diamond is nothing more than carbon, scientists have tried to find ways of making "synthetic" diamonds from other forms of carbon. In 1880, a Scottish chemist, J. Ballantine Hannay, announced to the Royal Society that he had succeeded in doing this by heating bone-oil and paraffin with lithium in wrought-iron tubes. The walls of the tubes were nearly two inches thick, and the materials were sealed into them by welding. The tubes were heated to red heat in special furnaces.

Tremendous pressure was developed in the iron tubes by this treatment, and many of them exploded, wrecking the furnace time and again. But Hannay persevered, and some of his tubes survived. When they were sawn open, a few of them were found to contain a hard black deposit, and embedded in this were small particles of hard glassy material. Hannay tested the particles, and found that they were hard enough to scratch all other natural substances. Moreover, they would burn in air just as diamond does. He concluded that diamonds had formed from the carbon of the bone oil and paraffin under the effects of the immense heat and pressure.

Hannay sent specimens of his diamonds to the Mineral Department of the British Museum. Here, they were examined by Professor N. Story-Maskelyne, one of the world's experts on gems, who confirmed that they were genuine diamonds.

Since then, other scientists have claimed to have made diamonds by subjecting carbon to various heat and pressure treatments, but none of the experiments have been confirmed by other workers. Sir Charles Parsons tried to repeat Hannay's experiments, but was unable to obtain any diamonds, and he concluded that Hannay had been mistaken.

In 1955, scientists of the General Electric Company in the U.S. announced that they had begun making synthetic diamonds by heating carbon under tremendous pressure inside a huge steel press. Squeezed at as much as 400 tons pressure to the square inch, and heated to 2800 deg. C., the carbon atoms were taking up the form we recognise as diamond.

This time, there was no doubt as to the genuineness of the claim. Diamonds are now being produced commercially and sold for use in cutting tools.

SIR ALEXANDER FLEMING

Alexander Fleming was born at Lochfield, near Darvel, in Scotland on 6th August, 1881. He did very well at school and as a medical student, and when he was qualified he joined the staff of St. Mary's Hospital in London. He soon began to do useful work in research and discovered a substance called Lysozyme—an antiseptic substance which is found in the whites of eggs and in human tears. Although his work was always distinguished, and he became a Professor of Bacteriology in London University, it was not until 1928 that he made his big discovery.

He was growing some bacteria called staphylococci on a flat dish of jelly, and one day he noticed that the culture had some mould on it. Instead of throwing the jelly away, he looked more closely and noticed that in the area where the mould was growing there were hardly any bacteria at all. He wondered if there was some substance in the mould which had spread out into the medium and stopped them from growing. He made experiments and found that the mould was very effective, in fact two or three times as effective as pure carbolic, against some kinds of bacteria, but not against others. The mould was identified as Penicillium notatum and Fleming gave the name " Penicillin " to the substance it produced. He made an attempt to isolate and purify this substance, himself, but he failed. He then asked two chemists to work on the problem, but they also failed; so Penicillin remained for a number of years nothing more than a chance discovery of no practical usefulness.

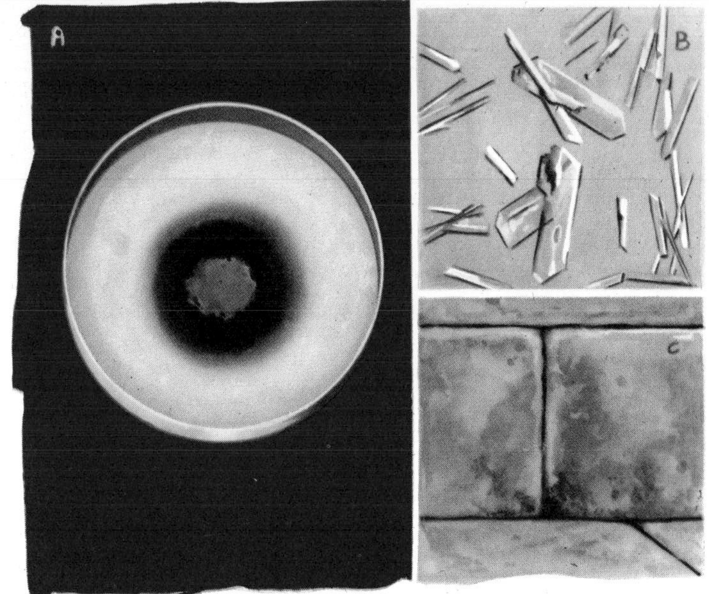

A: *A plate containing a bacterial culture, the development of which has been prevented by penicillin.* B: *Crystals of penicillin.* C: *"Penicillium notatum" is a mould commonly found on damp walls.*

ISOLATING THE ACTIVE PENICILLIN

Then, in 1939, Professor Florey and Dr. Chain decided to work on penicillin. They managed to extract the active substance, in a reasonably pure and stable form, from the mould and they found it proved startlingly effective in treating normally fatal infections in mice. They then decided to try it on human patients, and found that it produced spectacular cures in cases of blood poisoning. Accordingly, it was used in the treatment of wound infections, and there is no doubt that it saved many thousands of lives during the war. It was also used successfully in treating a wide range of diseases, including pneumonia, yaws, gas gangrene, and meningitis. " People have called it a miracle," Sir Alexander is reported to have said. " For once in my life as a scientist, I agree. It is a miracle and it will save lives by thousands." It certainly has.

Fleming was knighted in 1944. The following year he received the Nobel Prize, which he shared with Professor Sir Howard Florey and Dr. Chain. He was a quiet man with a poker-faced sense of humour, and he was often amused by the publicity, sometimes of a rather lurid kind, which he could not escape. He enjoyed outdoor sports, such as swimming and shooting, and he had a gift for painting.

He died on 11th March, 1955.

Fleming sees the "halo of inhibition" which has formed around a colony of mould, grown in one of his plates.

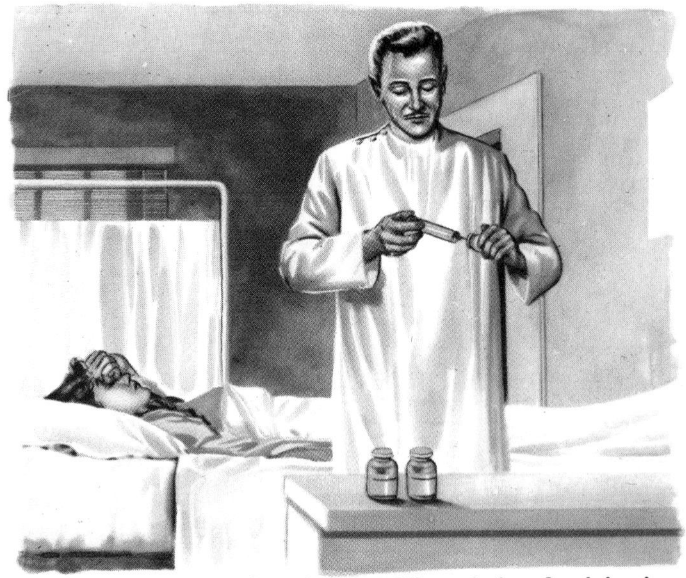

The doctor is preparing the penicillin solution for injection into a patient. Penicillin has already saved innumerable lives.

TELEVISION

The easiest way of understanding the magic of television is to compare it with the human eye, so let us first see how light affects the eye and how the eye passes on what it " sees " to the brain.

THE HUMAN EYE

Light reflected from any object enters the eye through the pupil and is projected by the lens on to the retina; this is a light-sensitive surface at the back of the eyeball. The process is similar to that which takes place in an ordinary camera, where a lens directs the image on to a light-sensitive film. The image recorded on the retina is translated into impulses that travel along the optic nerve to the brain where they are reassembled in the " mind's eye".

The visible light rays which make this sense of vision possible are essentially the same as other electromagnetic radiations such as radio waves, X-rays and infra-red rays. The radiations we call visible light are merely those which happen to be able to stimulate the retina of the human eye. The television camera is a huge electric eye which receives light waves reflected from objects and translates them into electrical impulses, which are radioed over large distances. Just like the human eye, the television camera has a pupil (the shutter of the photographic lenses); a lens (the photographic lenses); a retina (the light-sensitive plate); and an optic nerve (the co-axial cable and the radio waves).

Radio waves transmit the picture from the television camera to the television set or receiver. The picture is transmitted in the form of electric impulses which have to be reassembled in the television set to form the same pattern of light rays which were reflected from the scene in front of the television camera.

Let us look closely at each part of the process and see how it is done.

THE TELEVISION CAMERA

The first stage is the work of the " electric eye "—that is the television camera. The camera has a viewfinder through which the cameraman can check exactly how much of the scene he is shooting and whether his lenses are in focus. For scenes shot in the studio, the camera is usually mounted on a mobile platform but outdoor shots are usually taken with a camera mounted on a tripod.

The television camera not only records the scene, but transforms it, as we have said, into an electrical image which the transmitter sends out in the form of radio waves. The " eye " part of the camera is called an " image orthicon." It can " see " everything that is visible to the human eye. Inside the image orthicon is a plate treated to make it light-sensitive, and it is on this plate that the scene is focused.

In this respect, the plate resembles an ordinary photographic film, which is coated with an emulsion which reacts chemically when light strikes it; but the plate of the image orthicon sets up an electrical reaction when exposed to light. This reaction produces a *voltage* which varies in proportion to the intensity of the light. The camera records electrically the light and shadow contrast of the scene it is taking. Where strong light rays reflected from the scene strike the plate, a very high voltage is produced. A darker part of the scene will produce less voltage and an object that reflects no light will produce no reaction from the plate and therefore no voltage at all.

ELECTRONIC IMAGE

These different voltages form an electronic image on the plate which corresponds to the visual image, formed by light coming from the various points of the scene before the television camera. The moving picture which the television camera transmits is made up of an infinite number of these " electronic images ". Each one has to make way immediately for the next one to take its place on the plate, so it is erased by electrical apparatus which transfers it to a " target " plate.

Each individual image cannot be transmitted in its entirety. It is split up into a number of small sections and each of these is then bombarded with a continuous stream of electrons in the form of a fine beam or " pencil " which is generated in the image orthicon by an " electron gun ". This pencil of electrons scans the target, moving backwards and forwards across it at an incredible speed. For this scanning process

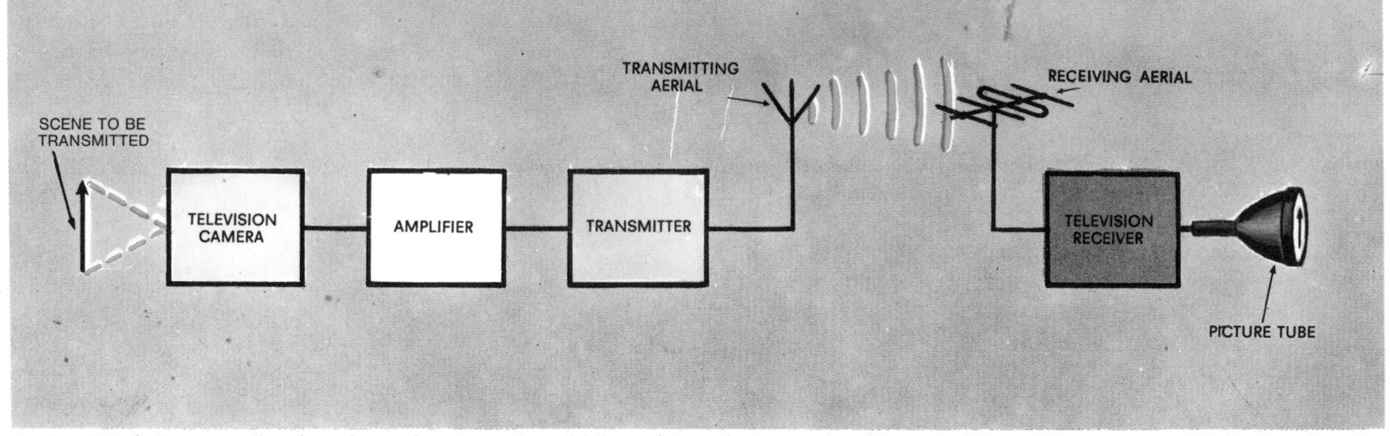

A simplified diagram showing the main stages by which a picture is transmitted by television. The pattern of light forming the image is converted into a series of electrical impulses, which are transmitted by radio.

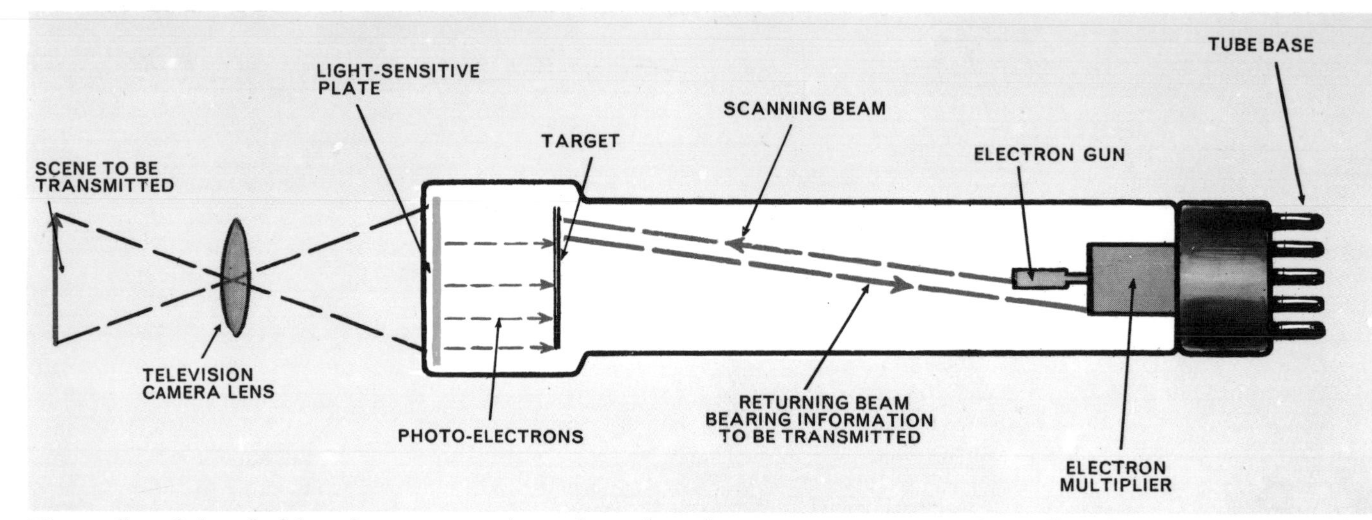

The quality of the television picture you receive at home depends, to a great extent, on the quality of the camera witnessing the events. The most highly developed of the camera tubes is reckoned to be the image orthicon—a remarkable electronic device, with a high degree of sensitivity to light. Above is a plan of the image orthicon tube, which is a cylindrical glass vacuum tube. The dotted lines and arrows indicate the path of the rays.

the target is divided into two groups of lines each called fields. One field is formed of the odd number lines, and the other field is formed of the even numbered lines. The electronic pencil explores the target by gathering the electrical charge of one section at a time. These charges vary according to the brightness of the corresponding section of the scene being shot. Once they are gathered up by the pencil, the electrical charges picked up from the target are passed on to an electrical amplifier, which gives them sufficient power to reach the transmitter. They travel to the transmitter by means of a co-axial cable or repeater station.

THE TELEVISION RECEIVER

The receiver incorporates both sound and vision-receiving equipment. The sound receiver is similar to the familiar radio receiver. The main feature of the vision receiver is the cathode ray tube.

The simplest kind of cathode ray tube—the direct image type that we use to-day—looks very much like a large funnel. At one end is the flat screen, covered with fluorescent material that lights up when bombarded by electrons. The picture tube, like the image orthicon, contains an electron gun in its long glass neck. The action of the electron pencil in the picture tube is perfectly co-ordinated with the action of the same apparatus in the image orthicon. Just as that pencil first stimulates the impulses from the target so this one sends them out as it oscillates behind the screen.

The scanning movement of the electron pencil in the picture tube must be perfectly synchronised with the beam in the image orthicon. This is made possible by electrical impulses called " synchronising impulses ", which are beamed from the transmitter together with the visual image waves. These impulses control the timing of the oscillations of the electron pencil in the picture tube.

The overall brightness of the television screen depends, among other things, on the strength of current of the electric pencil (i.e. the number of electrons contained in the beam of the pencil). But the detailed variations of light that form the picture on the screen depend on the different voltages sent out by each section of the " target " as it was scanned in the image orthicon. The voltage, as we have seen, was decided by the strength of light in each section of the scene as it appeared on the target. These voltages, all transmitted simultaneously, make up the visual image patterns (i.e. the moving pictures) which are picked up, together with the sound waves, by the television aerial. They are fed into the beam of the electron pencil which then gives out light in proportion to each individual voltage strength. Thus it is possible to reproduce on each television screen the same relative intensity of light as was originally picked up by the camera.

The last point to be explained is, of course, the illusion of movement on the screen. This is made possible by the same phenomenon which made the cinema industry possible; persistence of vision. When the reflected light from an image falls on the retina of the eye, the stimulus is immediately transferred to the optic nerve which carries it to the brain. *But* for about one-tenth of a second after the image has disappeared, the optic nerve continues to relay the same message even though the stimulus has ceased to exist.

COLOUR TELEVISION

Colour television has added enormously to the enjoyment of televiewing, particularly when the programmes include fashion shows, sporting events or historical pageants. Basically colour television involves the principles and techniques employed in colour photography wherein three primary colours are used and mixed in varying proportions to obtain other colours and hues.

The primary colours chosen are red, blue and green, and if these are added in the correct proportions yellow (red/green), magenta (red/blue) and cyan (blue/green) are produced. Furthermore if all three colours are mixed in equal proportions white is obtained. This colour additive principle is employed in most colour television systems.

One type of camera used to transmit colour pictures is the three tube (image orthicon). This camera separates a scene into red, blue and green components by means of dichroic mirrors and focuses them on to the tubes via surface-silvered mirrors. The outputs of the three tubes are converted into electrical signals which are proportional to the amount of light falling on them.

Widely used in colour receiving sets is a tricolour or shadow mask tube in which the screen is coated with a large number of red, green and blue phosphors behind which is placed a perforated metal sheet or mask. The electron gun assembly has three separate colour guns arranged in triangular formation in the neck of the tube with a common deflection coil. The positioning of the holes in the mask is such that the colour beams from the guns always fall on their respective dots, that is, red beam falls on red dots, blue beam falls on blue dots and green beam falls on green dots. This relationship persists even when the beams are deflected.

COMPATIBILITY

One of the main aims in the development of colour television was to evolve a system that would be compatible with existing black and white television systems. That is, the system would have to be such that the colour pictures could be received on black and white or monochrome receivers.

It is a known fact that the human eye does not see details of a picture in colour and no advantage is gained therefore in transmitting detail in colour. This factor very considerably influenced colour television philosophy and the National Television Systems Committee of America in 1953 sponsored a colour system in which all the detail of a picture seen by a camera was transmitted in monochrome whilst the colour information was transmitted simultaneously but separately, and added to the monochrome information in the receiver to make up a composite colour picture. The monochrome picture is originated in the three colour camera tube by adding fractions of the three primary colours in the correct proportions to give a white or grey light. Colour information is then added to provide the relative colours and hues.

The scene to be transmitted is broken down into a very large number of elements as in normal transmission and each element is scanned in turn by the three colours. To ensure that the three colours are being received in synchronism with their transmission by the camera there are electronic sequencing switches. These switches are driven together to give the relationship. The monochrome transmission is fed simultaneously to the receiver where it is added to the colour transmission for presentation on the display tube.

DIVERSITY OF SYSTEMS

Three major systems have been developed throughout the world. One is the NTSC system throughout North America and in some areas of Central and Southern America and also in Japan. This is a 525 line scanning system at 60 fields per second. As their are six fields necessary to complete a colour picture this gives a picture rate of 60/6 = 10 pictures per second.

In England and Germany the PAL system and in France and Russia the SECAM system adopts 625 lines at 50 fields per second. While interchange of information between European countries is a relatively simple matter via the Eurovision television link, interchange between the North American continent or Japan is much more difficult because of the different field frequencies. British television engineers have solved this problem by using an electronic converter which can convert 50 fields/second to 60 fields/second and vice versa.

Television transmission is virtually limitless with the placing of communications satellites such as Early Bird and Telstar in Earth orbit. These satellites receive signals from the ground, amplify them and transmit them back to Earth.

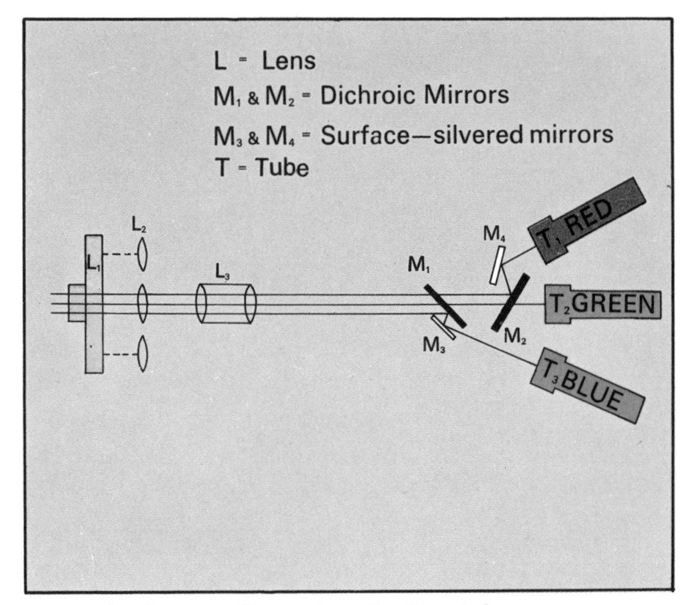

A schematic illustration of a three tube camera.

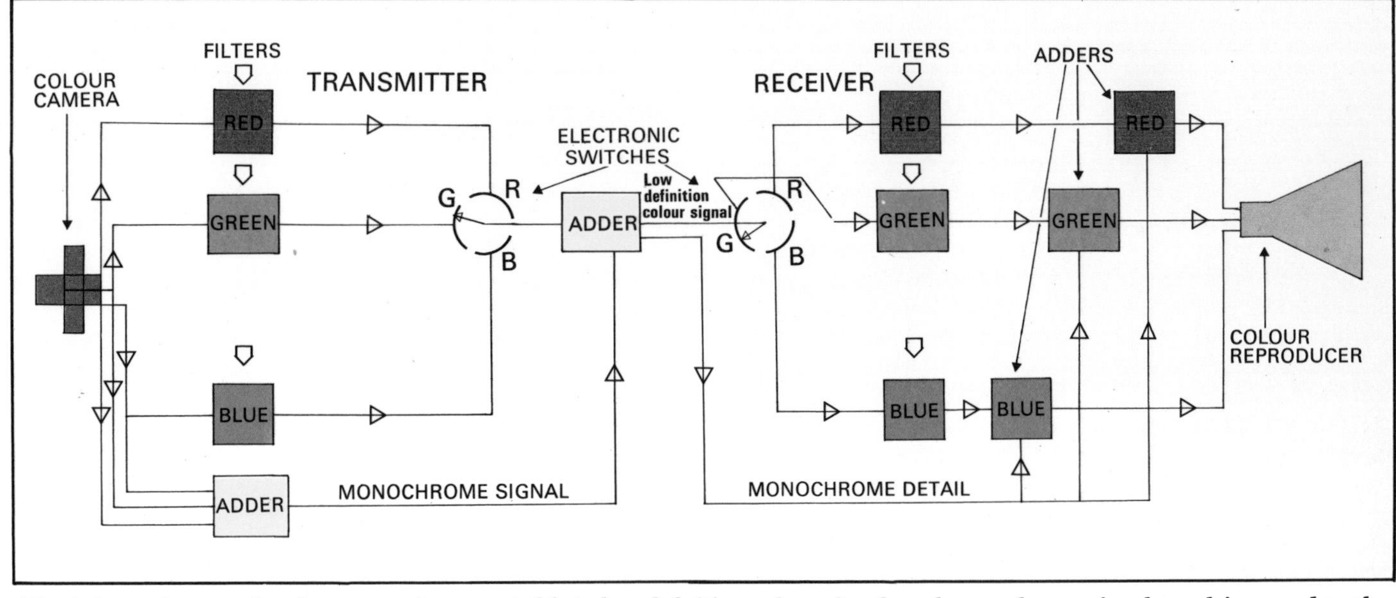

The information seen by the camera is separated into low definition colour signals and monochrome signals, and is passed to the receiver via the electronic switches where an inverse process takes place at the colour reproducer in the receiver.

THE PLANT CALENDAR

In winter, the garden and the countryside are bare and grim. The leaves have gone from most of the trees, and the flowering plants have disappeared. But not for long.

Soon, the first spring flowers have appeared; the primrose and the crocus bring colour back to the earth. They are followed by the daffodils, and then the whole parade of summer flowers.

As summer begins to fade, we find the golden-rod, the Michaelmas-daisies and the chrysanthemums coming into their own. And then, once again, the flowers disappear as winter returns.

Nature, with wonderful precision, organises this programme of flower-blooming. Each season has its own kinds of flowers, which appear as though by magic at the proper time. We take it for granted that we shall see the "spring flowers" in April and May, the "summer flowers" in July and the " autumn flowers " in September.

When the plant produces flowers, it is undergoing a radical change from normal growth. It is no longer simply building up its body structure and growing larger and stronger; something has happened which has made the living processes of the plant take on a new job. Instead of concentrating on the task of building up the tissues of the plant, the multiplying cells begin to produce a new type of structure. They turn their attention to the creation of flowers.

INFLUENCE OF HUMIDITY AND SOIL

This process, as we have seen, takes place at the appropriate time of year, depending on the type of plant. It is almost as if the plant could read the calendar, beginning its flower-production when the proper month had arrived. Yet it is difficult to see how a plant can time its growing-schedules in this way. How does the growing-point in a snapdragon know that summer has arrived, and it is time to produce its flowers? How does a Michaelmas-daisy know that it must wait a few months longer so that its flowers appear in autumn?

Some plants, like tomatoes, do seem to flower when they have reached a certain stage of maturity. All that has to be done to make them flower is to bring the plants to maturity as efficiently as possible.

With many other plants, however, the process is not as simple as this. We can pamper them so that they grow big and strong, but no matter how healthy and "adult" the plant becomes it will not flower until a certain season has arrived.

In 1920, two scientists at the U.S. Department of Agriculture, W. W. Garner and H. A. Allard, found that a certain variety of tobacco flowered later than its usual date when it was grown in Washington, D.C., rather than in its native state of Virginia. Often, this variety, called Maryland Mammoth, did not flower at all in Washington, although it grew well during the summer. The strange thing was that Maryland Mammoth would flower profusely in Washington if it was protected in a greenhouse as the winter came along.

The two scientists were intrigued and puzzled by the behaviour of Maryland Mammoth, and they carried out a series of experiments and they found that the plant was controlling its flowering programme by responding to the relative lengths of night and day. It was following the changing seasons by checking on the length of day.

This amazing discovery was almost more than scientists could believe; yet many experiments carried out all over the world have proved that plants do follow the calendar.

DAY-LENGTH STIMULUS

Maryland Mammoth, the tobacco used in the original experiments, experiences the day-length it needs for flowering early in the season when it is grown in its native soil in Virginia. It flowers in summer and produces its seeds before autumn arrives. But grown farther north in Washington, the days became short enough to bring on flowering only in the autumn, and it was then too late in the season for the flowers and seeds to be produced successfully before winter arrived.

When the Washington-grown plants were protected by a greenhouse during winter, however, they were able to flower and form seeds just as they did in Virginia, once the process had been triggered off by the short days of early autumn.

As more and more people took up the study of this strange behaviour of plants, it became apparent that plants could belong to one of three classes with respect to their reaction to the length of day. The first class, including tomatoes and cucumbers, is indifferent to the length of day, and flowers only when it has reached a certain stage of maturity.

The second class consists of plants which will flower only after the length of day has fallen below a certain number of hours. This group includes the autumn-flowering plants of temperate climates, which wait for the days to shorten to the appropriate length before they flower.

The third class consists of plants which will flower only when the day length exceeds a certain number of hours. This group includes the summer-flowering annual plants.

The discovery that plants control their flowering activities by estimating the length of day has cleared up some of the mysteries of flower production. It explains how the procession of flowers through the seasons is organised, but it also raises many more mysteries than it solves. How does the plant measure the length of day?

It is now known that the leaves of the plant provide it with its "biological clock." When the leaves of a plant are covered up, it will not flower at the proper time, even though other parts of the plant are subjected to the proper routine of daylight and darkness. If all the leaves but one are covered up, the single uncovered leaf will be sufficient to tell the plant that flowering time has come, if it is subjected to the appropriate length of day. In some cases, less than an eighth of a single leaf will control the flowering routines of the plant.

As experiments continued, it became apparent that these flowering routines are organised inside the plant by chemicals. Daylight falling on the leaves of the plant stimulates the production or decomposition of chemicals inside the leaf cells. The balance of chemical production is controlled by the daylight and darkness routine that the leaves experience, and by sending chemicals via the stem to the growing points of the plant, the leaves influence the type of structure that the multiplying cells produce.

MAN INTO SPACE

Although many of the satellites and " deep-space " probes are interesting in their own way, none can compare with those that carry men into space.

It was obvious that as the power of the rocket launching vehicles increased and the accuracy and reliability of the guidance equipment improved, serious attention would be given to the possibility of launching a man into space, and getting him back alive.

That Russia had this aim in mind right from the beginning is indicated by the flight of the second artificial satellite, Sputnik 2, in November, 1957, carrying the dog Laika. Other Russian flights with dogs followed; Spacecraft 4 and Spacecraft 5 both being recovered safely, with their occupants alive and well.

FIRST MAN IN SPACE

It was not, therefore, altogether a surprise when on the 12th of April, 1961, another spacecraft took off from the Russian space centre at Baikonur in the heart of Central Asia; this time carrying a man. The person making this truly historic flight was Yuri Gagarin, a twenty-seven-year-old major in the Soviet Air Force.

It was 9.07 Moscow time when the Vostok, as the spacecraft was called, took off. Forty-five minutes later it was south of Cape Horn. At 10.15 it was over Africa. At 10.25 the retro-rocket fired and the re-entry procedure was initiated. Half an hour later the Vostok was back on the ground with Yuri Gagarin alive and well. In 108 minutes man had taken his first step to the stars.

After the flight Gagarin excitedly described the sights never before seen by man.

" The sunlit side of the Earth," he said, " is very clearly visible and one can easily distinguish the shores of continents, islands, great rivers, large bodies of water and folds in the terrain."

Looking towards the horizon he was able to see the curvature of the Earth. The horizon itself was " most strange and very beautiful."

America's first man in space, U.S. Marine Corps Lieut.-Colonel John Glenn, took off in the Mercury spacecraft Friendship 7 on the 20th of February, 1962. A major difference between this lift-off and that of Gagarin's Vostok, was that the American mission was accompanied by minute-by-minute radio and television broadcasts transmitted to an excited world. After making three orbits, during which the automatic guidance system malfunctioned and Glenn took over manual control, the re-entry procedure was initiated. The astronaut's relieved cry of " that was a real fireball", as he returned through the atmosphere, was heard by countless millions of people all over the world.

Other manned flights followed with increasing frequency. Herman Titov stayed aloft in Vostok 2 to become the first man to spend a whole day in space, and was followed by Scott Carpenter, Walter Schirra and Gordon Cooper in a series of Mercury spacecraft flights.

An important step in the development of space flight techniques was the flight of cosmonauts Leonov and Belyayev in spacecraft Voskhod 2 in March, 1965. While in orbit Leonov donned a spacesuit and then left the comparative safety of the Voskhod's cabin to " walk " in space for several minutes. Three months later the U.S. astronaut Edward White performed a similar feat from the two-man spacecraft Gemini 4. During his " walk " White used a small jet-pistol to manoeuvre himself.

These brave and dangerous acts proved that, suitably protected and equipped, man would be able to work in

Vostok 1 *carried the first man, cosmonaut Yuri Gagarin, into space on* 12*th April,* 1961.

Friendship 7, *the Mercury spacecraft in which the first American, John Glenn, went into space, on* 20*th February,* 1962.

The Eagle on the Moon. As his foot touched the surface, Neil Armstrong exclaimed "That's one small step for a man, one giant leap for mankind." Soon he was followed by his colleague Edwin Aldrin. On the surface the two astronauts unveiled a plaque bearing the words "Here men from the planet Earth first set foot upon the Moon, July 1969 A.D. *We came in peace for all mankind." They also planted an American flag, conducted several scientific experiments and collected a number of rock samples which were brought back to the Earth. A TV camera, pointed at the Eagle, enabled viewers on Earth to witness the thrilling spectacle of men on the Moon.*

space, assembling structures and repairing satellites and spacecraft.

GEMINI PROJECT

It was four years earlier, in May, 1961, that President Kennedy had proposed that the U.S. should set itself the goal of landing men on the Moon by 1970. The two-man Gemini spacecraft helped significantly towards this ambitious aim. With this craft ten highly successful manned missions were accomplished.

The American plan to land men on the Moon involved orbital rendezvous and docking, that is, the close approach and joining up of two spacecraft.

Vital experience was gained with Gemini 6 which, approaching within a few feet of Gemini 7, became the first spacecraft to rendezvous with another craft in orbit. Further experience was gained with Gemini 8, crewed by astronauts Neil Armstrong and David Scott, which achieved the first actual docking in space with an Agena spacecraft, launched as a target. This mission nearly ended in disaster when, docked with the Agena, a thruster began to fire continuously, causing the two craft to spin dangerously. Only Neil Armstrong's skill and iron self-control enabled him to identify the trouble and regain control.

The remaining four Geminis, numbers 9, 10, 11 and 12, were used for futher rendezvous experiments and more space walks.

APOLLO PROJECT

While the Gemini experiments were under way, U.S. scientists were busy designing and testing Apollo spacecraft to be used for the actual landing on the Moon. Weighing some 45 tons, this consists of three sections or modules: the Command Module (CM), the Service Module (SM) and the Lunar Module (LM).

On top is the three-man Command Module, shaped like a spinning top. Under the Command Module is the Service Module housing the navigational and guidance equipment and the rocket motor needed to get the craft into and out of orbit round the Moon. The Lunar Module, fragile and spidery looking, is the portion used for the actual descent to the Moon. For launching the Apollo mooncraft the Americans developed the giant Saturn 5 booster. This is a three-stage rocket, 363 ft. tall and weighing about 3,000 tons when fuelled.

The first manned Apollo, No. 7, carrying Walter Schirra, Walter Cunningham and Don Eisele, was launched in October, 1968, into a low Earth orbit to check the craft and its systems.

So well did it perform that Apollo 8 was launched, just before Christmas 1968, to the Moon, not to land, but to go round it and return. On board were astronauts Frank Borman, James Lovell and William Anders, who became the first man in history to see the hidden, rear face of the Moon.

Apollo 9, launched in March, 1969, was used to test the Lunar Module, and Apollo 10, launched in May, 1969, was the dress rehearsal for the actual landing. Everything went extremely well.

Thus the scene was set for the historic lift-off on 16th July of Apollo 11, carrying Neil Armstrong, Michael Collins and Edwin Aldrin. The quarter-million mile journey to the Moon was accomplished smoothly and safely. Going into orbit round the Moon, Armstrong and Aldrin climbed into the Lunar Module and undocked from the Apollo mother-craft. Thus separated the CM was known as *Columbia* and the LM as *Eagle*.

Then the descent engine was fired and the *Eagle* began to drop towards the surface. During this dramatic period countless millions of listeners all over the world heard the instructions given to the astronauts and their replies. Then came the historic words "Tranquillity base here. The *Eagle* has landed." Man was on the Moon, at 17 minutes past 9 o'clock, on Sunday evening, 20th July, 1969.

INDEX